N-4
DOWN

N-4
DOWN

The Hunt for the
Arctic Airship Italia

MARK PIESING

CUSTOM
HOUSE

FIRST EDITION

Designed by Lucy Albanese
Title page photograph © Sueddeutsche Zeitung Photo/Alamy Stock Photo
Map design by Nick Springer/Springer Cartographics LLC

Library of Congress Cataloging-in-Publication Data has been applied for.

ISBN 978-0-06-285152-9

21 22 23 24 25   LSC   10 9 8 7 6 5 4 3 2 1

To Rebecca, Finn, and Mylo
In memory of Ove Hermansen (1933–2019)

Contents

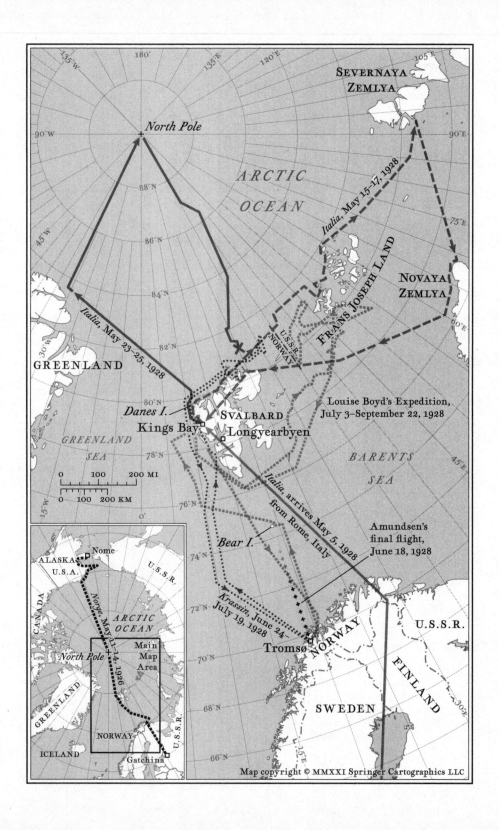

SEVERNAYA
ZEMLYA

ARCTIC
OCEAN

North Pole

Italia, May 15–17, 1928

FRANS JOSEPH LAND

Italia, May 23–25, 1928

NOVAYA
ZEMLYA

GREENLAND

Danes I.

SVALBARD

Kings Bay

Longyearbyen

Louise Boyd's Expedition,
July 3–September 22, 1928

GREENLAND
SEA

BARENTS
SEA

*Italia, arrives May 5, 1928
from Rome, Italy*

0   100   200 MI

0   100   200 KM

Bear I.

Amundsen's
final flight,
June 18, 1928

*Krassin, June 24–
July 19, 1928*

NORWAY

U.S.S.R.

Tromsø

FINLAND

SWEDEN

Nome

ALASKA
U.S.A.

U.S.S.R.

CANADA

Norge, May 11–14, 1926

ARCTIC
OCEAN

North Pole

Main
Map
Area

GREENLAND

NORWAY

U.S.S.R.

ICELAND

Gatchina

Map copyright © MMXXI Springer Cartographics LLC

Introduction

Once upon a Time in the North

THE BOOK SMELLED OLD. It must have been sitting on the shelves of the secondhand bookstore for a long time before I bought it. The title was enigmatic: *With the* Italia *to the North Pole*. What was the *Italia*? And who was going to the North Pole? The author was just as mysterious. Who was Umberto Nobile?

I was looking for a mystery to solve—and now I had found one.

When I opened the stiff pages of the ninety-year-old volume to try to find the answers, I felt a slight draft on my hand. An equally old and irregularly cutout newspaper clipping slipped out of the book and fluttered to the floor.

The faded headline of the story answered some of my questions. It read: "Bound for the North Pole. Italian's Big Adventure. First Day's Thrilling Experiences." The story was bylined London, April 16, 1928.

As I fumbled with the book, an old map unfolded itself from the back cover to offer another clue: "Svalbard," it was titled. Suddenly I could hear the throb of zeppelin engines in my ears.

SVALBARD IS A TINY group of dots in the middle of the Arctic Ocean. In Philip Pullman's His Dark Materials trilogy, Svalbard is described to Lyra, the heroine of the books, as "the farthest, coldest, darkest regions of the wild."[1] It is a land of "slow-crawling glaciers; of the rock and ice floes where the bright-tusked walruses lay in groups of a hundred or more, of the seas teeming with seals . . . of the great grim iron-bound coast, the cliffs a thousand feet and more high where the foul cliff-ghasts perched and swooped, the coal pits and fire mines where the bearsmiths hammered out mighty sheets of iron and riveted them into armor."[2]

It was on Svalbard, I now knew, that I would find answers to my last questions. I caught a Boeing from London via Oslo to Longyearbyen, the "capital" of these remote islands. The two-and-a-half-hour flight time in a modern airliner did make the ends of the earth seem closer. As we dragged our bags across the tarmac to the lonely airport terminal building, the icy wind from the North Pole that cut through our down jackets as if we weren't even wearing them was a healthy reminder of where we actually were. If that didn't make us realize how far north we had traveled, on three sides of the tarmac strip were mountains covered in snow, their glaciers glinting fiendishly in the April sunlight. At the end of the runway lay the cold, gray, and deadly waters of the Arctic Ocean itself.

Jutting out of the mountainside above the airport was the gray rectangular entrance to what appeared to be a nuclear bunker. My guess was not far off. It was the Svalbard Global Seed Vault, a long-term seed storage facility built to stand the test of time—and the challenges of natural or manmade disasters. The seed vault is the world's guarantee of crop diversity in the future; whether any survivors of our civilization would be able to reach it is a question we will hopefully never have to answer.

On the drive into town, it felt like we could slip into Lyra's Svalbard at any time. The mountainsides above the town are covered by the remains of aerial ropeways that once took coal from mines to the harbor; the mine entrances themselves, which are little more than large holes in the side of the mountain; and a handful of forbidding abandoned factories, rumored to host raves. The grim wooden hostels were now bunk rooms for hikers, and the dingy bars they frequented looked as if they'd seen their fair share of fights. The supermarkets warned customers not to bring their guns into the store. I had my picture taken—quickly—by the sign with a polar bear inside a big red triangle on the edge of town. Underneath were the words "Gjelder hele Svalbard," meaning "applies to all of Svalbard."

Down by the quayside, past where the scientists monitoring the melting permafrost park their half-tracks, is a small black wooden shack with a sizable wooden cutout of a polar bear looking straight at you. On the front are the words "North Pole Expedition Museum." Right next to that label is a picture of a zeppelin. Airships had once flown over Svalbard.

Entering the shack is like stepping into a fantasy world. With its faded cuttings, black-and-white pictures, typed notes, and shaky newsreel footage, the museum tells the story of the aeronauts who once upon a time explored the unknown lands of the North Pole by hot-air balloon, airship, and primitive airplane. There is a section about Swedish hero Salomon August Andrée, who decided he would try to fly from Svalbard to the North Pole in a balloon. On July 11, 1897, he and his two crewmen took off for the pole, floated over the horizon, and disappeared. It would be another thirty-three years before their skeletons were found.

Another section of the museum is dedicated to the not-so-derring-do of journalist and all-around chancer Walter Wellman. He attempted three times—in 1906, 1907, and 1909—to fly to the North Pole in a sausage-like airship called the *America*. In 1909, the *America* managed to stay in the air for a couple of hours before it crashed. Despite this further setback, Wellman was determined to return the following year with a larger airship, but he never did. His dream of flying to the North Pole died when he heard of Dr. Frederick Cook's claim to have reached the pole on foot. Instead, the following year he decided to fly across the Atlantic in the *America*, an endeavor that met with as much as success as his polar flights.

In truth, the exhibition is really about one man and one type of machine: Umberto Nobile and airships. Prodigy, dirigible engineer, aeronaut, Arctic explorer, member of the Fascist Party, opponent of Mussolini, maybe even Soviet spy, and always accompanied by his dog, Titina, Nobile twice flew jumbo-jet-size airships—lighter-than-air craft that he designed and built—on the epic journey from Rome to Svalbard to explore the Arctic. The N-4 *Italia* was the second of these flying machines.

In 1926, a dirigible he built and piloted, the *Norge*, became the first aircraft to cross the roof of the world from Norway to Alaska. It may even have been the first aircraft to reach the North Pole. His public falling-out with his famous coleader, Roald Amundsen, over who should take credit for the flight made headlines across the United States—headlines that were perhaps matched only by the news that when Nobile was invited to Washington, Titina, who had flown over the North Pole with him, had relieved herself on the carpet of the White House itself.

In 1928, he ignored all the omens—and all his enemies—to return again to the North Pole in the *Italia*, but he never did become the first man to land at the pole from an airship. The crash of his vessel out there on the pack ice made front-page news around the world. The disappearance of many of his men was a mystery that has never been solved, with rumors of cannibalism never fully disproved. His treatment at the hands of Mussolini when he eventually returned to Rome was compared by his supporters to that of Alfred Dreyfus by the French government at the end of the nineteenth century.

This book, then, is the story of Nobile, his friends and enemies, their expeditions, and the airships and airplanes they flew, of the end of the golden age of polar exploration—that era when the pilot replaced the tough man of Arctic exploration in the public imagination and when the zeppelin and the airplane battled it out in the Arctic skies for the future of aviation, a time when some countries even considered banning aviation altogether because it was so dangerous.[3] It is the story of some of the women, such as millionaire Louise Boyd, who up till now have been written out of the tale. It is a story that incorporates the rise of fascism and the struggle against it. It is also the story of a moment in time when many people thought there was a lost continent hidden at the North Pole behind the ice and fog.

Today, in Bedford, United Kingdom, in Paris, in California, and in Jingmen, China, a new generation of airship engineer, pilot, and dreamer is looking to explore the Arctic skies once more.

In Kings Bay, hundreds of miles to the north of Longyearbyen, a huge metal mooring mast was erected to secure Umberto Nobile's airships. It stands there waiting, still, for the explorers and their airships to return again.

N-4
DOWN

Prologue

The Arctic Ocean, May 25, 1928

"WE ARE HEAVY," the crewman shouted as the giant airship dropped through the fog toward the sea ice below.[1] It was as if Thor himself were hurling the *Italia* out of the sky.

Perhaps the great explorer Roald Amundsen was right, thought General Umberto Nobile, leader of the expedition. The Italians were a "half tropical breed" who did not belong in the Arctic.[2]

It was fifty-four hours since Nobile had left Kings Bay on Svalbard in the Arctic Circle to fly to the North Pole. It was at least seventy-two hours since he had last slept.[3] For two days and nights, Nobile's crew of sixteen men (and his cherished Titina) had battled high winds, fog, snow, and ice in the airship he had designed and built to explore the roof of the world. The lack of sunlight, the howl of the wind, and the tremendous cold turned them into sullen automatons who struggled to keep the dirigible in the air. The heavy woolen clothes they wore lent them little warmth. The N-4 *Italia* had reached the North Pole early on the morning of May 24, 1928, and the high spirits they had enjoyed when they had lifted off from the mining settlement of Kings Bay had briefly returned when the men cried out, "We're there!"[4] For two hours, the suspense built as the dirigible circled the North Pole while it slowly descended through the clouds until the pack ice was visible. There was a moment of disappointment when the crew could not land a party on the ice because the wind was too strong for the "sky anchor" to hold the airship steady. Nevertheless, in "religious silence," the men made ready to complete "the solemn" duty entrusted to them by Pope Pius.[5] At 450 feet, they dropped the Italian flag, the Tricolore, onto the summit of the world, followed by the flag of the city of Milan, and, finally, the cross that the pontiff had presented to them. "And like all crosses," the pope had said with a sad smile at their last audience, "this one will be heavy to carry."[6]

With their jobs done, the gramophone player on the airship belted out the martial notes of the Fascist Party hymn, "Giovinezza," Italy's unofficial national anthem of the time. With their right arms raised in the Fascist salute, the crew sang along heartily under the watchful eyes of a journalist from Mussolini's own newspaper.

The singing rapidly gave way to the cry of "Viva Nobile" and a toast of eggnog. "Few men in the world can say, as we can, that they have twice been to the North Pole," said Finn Malmgren,[7] the ship's weatherman and one of two non-Italians on the crew, to Nobile.*

Now, though, on their return journey, the joy was gone for good, in its stead a growing sense of dread. The ice seemed to be getting closer and closer—and only one man on the ex-

---

* In fact, seven men could say they had been twice to the North Pole. These were the men who, like Nobile, had flown on the *Norge* and then on the *Italia*.

pedition had any experience on how to survive in the frozen wasteland below, the Swede, Malmgren.

Nobile had not appointed a second-in-command because he needed to make swift decisions in an emergency, and he believed that another pilot would slow this process down.[8] Now, exhausted, his brain was stuck in slow motion just when events were speeding up. He was so tired that he was hallucinating. In the picture that hung on the wall of the cabin, his daughter, Maria, now looked as though she were crying. He had to tell himself that it was just the condensation on the inside of the glass.[9]

"All engines full speed," Nobile cried as he became aware of the danger they were in. The sea ice was now very close.

Climb! Climb! Climb! His only hope was that the increased power would pull the giant airship out of its dive.

But it was too late. Looking out of the porthole, he saw that the tail of the great ship was only a few yards from the ice. Five hundred miles from any hope of rescue.

"It's all over," Nobile whispered to himself[10] as he felt his limbs snap.

The great ship smashed tail first onto the ice.

One

"You Are Supposed to Be Dead"

THE GREAT POLAR EXPLORER Roald Amundsen stood by himself on the frozen Arctic shore, staring into the distance. He was fifty-three years old—but looked seventy-five—and bankrupt.

On the ice in front of him, the men of the Amundsen-Ellsworth polar flight had broken open the large, long wooden crates that contained the two flying boats. Now their job was to reassemble the craft, laboring in subzero temperatures with little more than a block and tackle, the coal miners from the Kings Bay Mine ready to provide the muscle power when they needed it. Nearby, a journalist and photographer recorded their every move.

Beautiful white mountains penned Amundsen in on three sides. Their glaciers glinted in the May sunlight. For a moment, the twenty-two houses of the mining village looked more like holiday cottages.

"The Arctic smiles now, but behind the silent hills is death," another journalist would later write,[1] and he would be proved right.

Out in the bay, the sea was filled with great chunks of ice. Beyond stretched the endless, empty ice pack, known as the

Arctic desert, a huge empty hole on the map of the world roughly the size of Canada that had never before been explored. Somewhere on the other side was Alaska.

Men quickly became invisible from the air in this brilliant white landscape. If their primitive flying machines descended and they couldn't get back up, then there was almost no likelihood that they would be found. Even if someone knew where they were, there would be a good chance that they had strayed beyond the range of their would-be rescuers, particularly if they were the crew of a dirigible. These lighter-than-air craft could stay in the air for days at a time and fly much farther than their fixed-wing aircraft rivals.

The sea ice that makes up the ice pack could be many feet thick, and then suddenly only half an inch thick, ready to plunge the unwary—or too hasty—explorer into the frozen water underneath. Nighttime might not bring much relief to the explorer either. The cracking and creaking of the ice could keep many a man from sleeping, no matter how exhausted they were, their bodies braced for the moment when they— and their tent—might suddenly be plunged into the icy water below. Then there was the disorientation. When they woke up, they could be as many as twenty miles from where they had gone to sleep.

To crash out there would in all likelihood mean death, though surprisingly this didn't seem to bother the average adventurer. This was their choice: to be noticed, to be remembered. Glory and fame was what most of them had come there for—and one way or another, they were determined to get it.

Welcome to the Svalbard archipelago.

To locate these mountainous islands on a map, you first have to find Scotland, then trace your finger up past Iceland,

Norway, and Greenland. From the map, it looks as though you could swim—or even march—from the islands to Greenland, Canada, Alaska, or Russia. But of course you can't: the distances are still vast, the passages grim and unwelcoming.

All Amundsen needed, he kept telling himself as he stood out there, was one last big paycheck.

It was 1925: twenty years since the Norwegian had become the first man to successfully navigate his way through the Northwest Passage, the sea route from the Arctic to the Pacific Ocean. Sir John Franklin and his 128 men had disappeared around sixty years previously to this trying to make the same journey in two old warships.* Amundsen had done it slowly with six men over three years in an old fishing boat.

That journey had been surpassed six years later when Amundsen beat the British hero Robert Falcon Scott to the South Pole in 1911. Scott and his four companions died on their way back from the pole. Amundsen had arrived first at the South Pole after claiming to be heading to the Arctic Ocean. He had kept his "coup"[2] secret from most of the crew on the voyage from Norway to Portugal, the politicians fund-

---

* In 2014 and 2016, the wrecks of HMS *Erebus* and *Terror* were finally discovered. While the fate of the survivors is still clouded in mystery, it is now thought that the expedition had managed to explore the unexplored part of the Northwest Passage ("What Happened to HMS *Erebus* and *Terror*?," Royal Museums Greenwich, accessed April 20, 2021, https://www.rmg.co.uk/stories/topics/what-happened-to-erebus-terror-crew-true-story). However, the ships and their ghosts have one more duty to perform to their country: the shipwrecks are helping Canada reinforce its claim to the Arctic in the face of competition from countries like Russia (Simon Worrall, "How the Discovery of Two Lost Ships Solved an Arctic Mystery," *National Geographic*, April 16, 2017, https://www.nationalgeographic.com/adventure/article/franklin-expedition-ship-watson-ice-ghosts).

ing him (whom he detested after they had rejected his plea for more money), the government that owned his ship, and the king of Norway himself.[3] He had even betrayed the trust of his Norwegian mentor, Fridtjof Nansen, who had his eye on the same prize.[4] The fate of others was not much of a concern to Amundsen.

Amundsen's decision to use huskies, which were bred for these conditions, on his race to the South Pole was the difference between his life and Scott's death.[5] The Englishman's choice of ponies and gasoline engine tractors, which were untested in such extreme conditions, had condemned him to second place—and, ultimately, him and his men to their deaths. Yet Amundsen had refused to see Scott when the Brit visited Norway to watch a demonstration of the mechanical tractors prior to his journey to the pole. The Norwegian had kept his doubts to himself.[6] Amundsen didn't get to be a world-famous Arctic explorer by being "nice."

The Norwegian was also savvier than his English rival. Both Frederick Cook's claim to have reached the North Pole on foot in April 1908 and Robert Peary's a year later were swiftly doubted at the time.[7] Despite the rather dubious support of more than fifty psychics,[8] the question mark over Cook's claim was so strong that he was widely seen as a fraud, and his career was ruined.* The scandals that surrounded the

* Years later, the controversy over Cook almost claimed Amundsen's reputation too. His prestigious address to the National Geographical Society in Washington in 1926 was canceled—with the loss of his substantial fee (Stephen R. Brown, *The Last Viking: The Life of Roald Amundsen* [Boston: De Capo Press, 2012], 316.)—when he was misquoted by a journalist as saying he believed that Cook's evidence of reaching the North Pole was as solid as Peary's (Cook, by this time, was in jail for fraud; "Amundsen in Role of Cook's Defender," *New York Times*, January 24, 1926, 2. https://timesmachine.nytimes

"achievements" of these men then threatened to taint the claim of every explorer, and Amundsen was quick to realize this. When he set off for the South Pole, he made sure he would not suffer the same fate as these two men. Amundsen listened to the experts who explained why Cook's and Peary's navigation left their achievements open to doubt. Conversely, Scott ignored their advice. Amundsen then used the latest navigational know-how to make sure accurate records of the route of his expedition were regularly taken and kept as evidence that he had reached the South Pole.[9] Scott used the traditional methods, which were slower, exhausting in such extreme conditions, and less accurate. He paid the price for his decision.

When Amundsen and his men arrived at the South Pole in December 1911, they didn't sing a patriotic anthem, give a speech, or indulge in any other unmanly histrionics. Instead, the Norwegians simply read a passage from the nineteenth-century version of the medieval *Saga of Fridtjof*, a celebration of traditional, heroic masculinity, which had been incredibly popular when it was published but was now fading from memory.

However, the challenges Amundsen faced didn't end when he sailed back home. A life spent at the extremes of the world, in the close company of men, and shifting between the rooms of luxury hotels and the snow and ice of both poles, had not been conducive to any hopes that Amundsen may have had of marriage. Instead, he satisfied himself with affairs with several married women, the wives of powerful men in the towns and cities he passed through.[10] Indeed,

---

.com/timesmachine/1926/01/24/100042962.html?pageNumber=2). In fact, it was another sixty years before anyone could successfully prove that he had reached the North Pole on foot. This was Sir Wally Herbert in April 1969.

Amundsen wasn't alone in this. Many of his fellow explorers also struggled to settle down.[11] In the absence of any children of his own, Amundsen had adopted two Inuit girls a few years earlier, in spite of the gossips who wondered who their real father was, but controversially sent them back to Siberia when he faced bankruptcy.[12]

AMUNDSEN LIKED TO BOAST that he had seen the potential of Arctic exploration by air in the early flights[13] of pioneers such as the Wright brothers in the United States, and the Frenchman Louis Blériot, who flew across the English Channel. (In 1909, Amundsen even had designed for him a less mechanically adept system of man-lifting kites, which he hoped to use for aerial reconnaissance.[*14]) In aviation, the Norwegian could see an end to the long, tedious forced march of the explorer on the starvation rations that had personally aged him so much. Instead, planes and airships that were provided appeared to offer explorers a quick flight into the record books.[15] But he didn't foresee how this new machine age would spell the end of the great explorer himself.

If the Norwegian had any doubts about his view of the future, they must have been banished in 1913. In that year, he stumbled across his first aircraft on a tour of Europe and made his first flight in a plane while he was in San Francisco on one leg of his American lecture tour.[16] Amundsen was so excited about the options powered flight gave to the explorers that he

---

* Amundsen's man-lifting kites actually worked. There is a grainy picture of the great explorer carried twenty feet up in the air by one of these contraptions (Garth James Cameron, *From Pole to Pole: Roald Amundsen's Journey by Flight* [Stroud, UK: Pen & Sword Discover, 2013], 21).

even ordered two flying boats to be used on his next expedition. He later had to cancel them owing to their expense.

Unfortunately, Amundsen missed out on the record for the first Arctic flight. It belongs to the now forgotten Polish aviator named Jan Nagórski. In August and September 1914, the twenty-six-year-old became the first to pilot an airplane successfully in the Arctic.[17]

One year after his own first flight, Amundsen was awarded the first civilian pilot's license* in Norway, on September 18, 1915.[18] By 1916, the cash-strapped explorer was already thinking of flying over the North Pole, a dream he became obsessed with despite the financial risks he was taking. Six years later, he was convinced that the technological advancements brought about by the Great War meant that the time was right. However, the extent to which he understood the workings of the planes and airships he was about to use was open to debate. Amundsen had always concerned himself with the technology needed for success, but this machinery was vastly more complex than sleds and tents. He and his fellow explorers actually had little knowledge of mechanics, and this shortcoming did not bother them. It has been said that "they did not care to understand how things were working for the sake of understanding it. They were satisfied as long as the mechanical machines were working."[19]

Misfortune then dogged his early attempts to use aircraft for exploration. In 1922, Amundsen was given the classic-looking Curtiss Oriole biplane by its designer, Glenn Curtiss, himself. The short-range plane crashed on its second flight

* Umberto Nobile seemed not to know that Amundsen had a pilot's license (interview with Ove Hermansen, curator, friend of Nobile and his representative, June 2018).

during the *Maud* expedition, whose goal was to drift on the ocean current over the Arctic Ocean and, if it was possible, over the North Pole itself.[20] At about the same time, Amundsen acquired two high-tech, all-metal single-engine Junkers JL-6 for his attempt to fly over the pole from Wainwright, Alaska, to Svalbard. The first of these crashed on the journey from New York to Seattle, for the flight to Alaska. The second crashed on landing at Wainwright, when it turned out to be not suitable to land on snow. Amundsen's partner had improvised a set of skis, which buckled on the plane's first landing— and with it, so did the explorer's finances. The flight over the North Pole seemed now impossible.

Amundsen was not alone. Earlier explorers had not had much luck when they attempted the same flight by hot-air balloon or airship. Drinkers in the bars of Longyearbyen still to this day argue about why Salomon August Andrée and his two crewmen died in their attempt to fly a hot-air balloon to the North Pole.

Death or humiliation seemed to be the fate of those who had tried in the past. Amundsen had already been humiliated: that left only death.

AMUNDSEN'S FAMILY HAD MADE their money through farming and shipping on the coast close to the border with Sweden. They lost it because good business acumen wasn't taught in the private schools of Oslo, where his parents had moved for status and prestige.[21] Only one of Amundsen and his three brothers was said to "have a practical understanding of profit and loss,"[22] and it certainly wasn't him. The failure of his attempt to fly over the North Pole[23] left him with disappointed sponsors, plenty of debts, and a Norwegian government fed up with the cost of supporting Amundsen's expeditions. This time, they had paid for two seaplanes to be shipped to the edge of the ice near Svalbard in case he needed rescue. The crash of his plane on its return from a brief test flight over Alaska meant that there would be no new bestseller for Amundsen to write, no magazine articles to syndicate, no sold-out lectures on his latest US tour. The Norwegian was a great public speaker, but the public needed new stories.

What was worse was that this time the crash had made him look careless—and even out of touch. The plane he had bought turned out not to be suitable for use in the Arctic.[24] The fact that he found this out on a test flight rather than during the actual record attempt was small consolation, as his critics thought, with good reason, that he should have understood this beforehand.

Amundsen's situation then grew even worse. He discovered that Haakon H. Hammer, his business agent in America, had enmeshed him in numerous financial commitments that he could not afford. The worst of these was Hammer's purchase on his behalf of three expensive German flying boats for his next attempt to fly over the pole.[25] The discovery of these debts forced his brother Leon to claim back the money Amundsen owed him as well, a betrayal that Amundsen never forgave. The American papers that had once hailed him as the "Son of the Vikings"[26] now reported how he had "quit his polar flight" and described in lurid detail whom he owed money to, beneath such headlines as "Amundsen Is Bankrupt; Explorer Was Unable to Pay for Planes for Polar Flight."[27] The Norwegian papers attacked Amundsen as well. "The same lips that had described my career as the glory of the nation did not scruple to repeat lies of the most transparent fabrication," fumed Amundsen.[28]

Left humiliated, the explorer escaped to his villa, Uranienborg, hidden in the woods outside Oslo, and retreated deep into himself. Uranienborg had been paid for with the profits from his Northwest Passage expedition, so Amundsen's presence there couldn't have entirely helped his state of mind. He couldn't avoid thinking about past glories that he now seemed unlikely ever to repeat, nor could he escape the fear that his career wouldn't end in glory out on the ice but in humiliation on the front page of a newspaper. Amundsen's erratic behavior made the few close friends he still had left worry about his state of mind, not for the first time and certainly not for the last.[29] Amundsen would later describe these years as "the most distressing, the most humiliating and altogether tragic episode of my life."[30]

Yet despite the setback of the failed flight, Amundsen wasn't a man to give up easily. Back in 1905, with his ship trapped in the ice, he had traveled five hundred miles (800 km) by dogsled to the nearest telegraph station to let the world know that he had discovered the Northwest Passage. Once his message had been transmitted, he risked his life by returning straight back to his men. His was a stubbornness that could lead to glory sometimes.

Against common sense, the explorer took a gamble. In the fall of 1924, he decided to head back to America once again to attempt to raise some money by public speaking and writing articles. However, instead of a sold-out lecture tour and well-paid newspaper articles, Amundsen was left dodging his creditors. At the Waldorf Astoria hotel in New York, they pushed final demands under the door to his room while he sat silently inside, his depression rapidly worsening.[31]

When he'd just about reached the end of his tether, the phone rang, and on the other end in the lobby was one Lincoln Ellsworth.[32] The only son of James Ellsworth, a millionaire who had made his money from coal mining, Ellsworth was no ordinary American, and he hero-worshipped such men as big-game hunter and president Theodore Roosevelt, Sheriff Wyatt Earp, renowned for his part in the famous gunfight at the O.K. Corral (who was still alive at this time), and, of course, Roald Amundsen.[33]

Ellsworth had long wanted to leave behind the meaningless life of a wealthy young man in New York to prove his manhood in the Arctic.[34] The problem was that he had to persuade his reluctant father to pay for it. Ellsworth senior was understandably reluctant to see his only heir disappear into the frozen wilderness from which so many men never returned or, if they did return, were never quite the same again. However, it turned out that the seasoned Norwegian explorer was the man to convince the millionaire to open his checkbook. The $85,000 James Ellsworth gave his son to cover the cost of the flying boats was kept well away from the finances of the bankrupt Norwegian in a company set up to deal with the expedition,[35] but Amundsen knew its source.

"Thus, I came to Amundsen a godsend," Lincoln Ellsworth wrote, "bringing not only new blood and enthusiasm to bolster his spirits, but a chance as well to secure financing for some magnificent adventures."[36]

Amundsen was back where he belonged—and Ellsworth was where he wanted to be.

GLORY WASN'T THE ONLY reason Amundsen was on Svalbard. His answer to the question of what the new lands he discovered would be used for was simple: "air stations and bases."[37] Norway had achieved its independence from Sweden only in 1905, and while the Norwegians had been campaigning to be free, the Belgians, Dutch, and British had been busy conquering the world. Now the descendants of the Vikings wanted to make up for lost time with their own Arctic imperialism.[38] It would be a new empire of snow and ice, an empire hacked out of the frozen land by Norwegian men like Amundsen and Nansen, to rival the Atlantic empire that the old Norse had carved out of the rocks of Greenland, Iceland, and the Orkney Islands. The islands of Svalbard and Greenland would be the first territories of this "greater Norway."[*39]

The Norwegians weren't the only nation that coveted Svalbard. The mountainous chain of islands had been "officially" discovered about three hundred years before, in 1596, by Dutch explorer Willem Barents, after whom the Barents Sea was named.[†] Whalers from all over Europe quickly followed in his wake to this new frontier, attracted by the large

---

* This desire for an Arctic empire mirrored the internal "colonization" that occurred when Norwegians were encouraged to settle the Far North of Norway, and the indigenous Sámi were assimilated into Norwegian society (Wilfrid Greaves, "Colonialism, Statehood, and Sámi in Norden and the Norwegian High North," in *Human and Societal Security in the Circumpolar Arctic* [Boston: Brill Nijhoff, 2018], 100–121, https://doi.org/10.1163/9789004363045_006).

† The Norwegian claim to Svalbard was based on a mention in the annals of the Norse from the twelfth century that mentions a land called Svalbarði four days' sailing from Iceland (Andrew McKay, "Svalbard History: The Fascinating Tale of Arctic Wilderness," *Life in Norway*, October 1, 2020, https://www.lifeinnorway.net/svalbard-history/).

whale population in the seas around the islands. Conflict quickly broke out among this ragtag bunch over whose country should claim the islands for itself.[40]

When all the whales had been killed, this "nobody's land," or *terra nullius*, was left to a group of traders and trappers from northern Russia called the Pomors. The regular visits by the Pomors are the source of Russia's historical claim to the islands.[41]

A couple of hundred years later, it was the turn of the hunters, coal miners, tourists, and scientists. Coal had been discovered close to the surface on the archipelago in the sixteenth century. In the 1890s, a Norwegian sea captain opened the first mine, which was soon followed by others. In the early 1900s, British and American mining companies scented an opportunity and purchased the mining claims of the Norwegians. Longyear City, the capital of the archipelago, was established by the Arctic Coal Company and named after Michigan-born John Munro Longyear, one of its founders. The success of these companies proved that large-scale mining was possible in the Arctic—and soon there was a "coal rush."[42] Norwegian, British, Russian, Swedish, and Dutch mining companies all moved in, and not only because of the high price of coal: the big attraction of a *terra nullius* was that they were free to exploit the resources of the land without laws or taxation.[43]

Svalbard's distinctive aerial ropeways soon spread across the mountainsides. These strange contraptions worked on a simple principle: gravity. Gravity propelled buckets of coal down from the mines on cables stretched for miles over the frozen mountainsides, a movement whose opposite effect was to pull the empty buckets back. The wooden pylons and fallen cables of these ropeways still stretch across from mine entrances hacked out of the hillsides to the nearest harbor.

Scientists came from Sweden and elsewhere to explore Svalbard. Norwegian scientists began to visit the archipelago regularly after the young nation was born in 1905, in what could be called scientific imperialism. In 1910, the geologist Adolf Hoel took over the leadership of what would become the prestigious Norwegian Polar Institute.[44] His job was to make Norway's mark on the unclaimed land through scientific discoveries, naming the mountains and bays in Norwegian, and to map the coal seams to boost his country's claim to the archipelago. Svalbard wouldn't stay "nobody's land" for much longer. The newly independent government's demand that Svalbard be incorporated into Norway was unacceptable to the country's former rulers.

Sweden was already jealous of the fame of Norwegian explorers such as Nansen and Amundsen—men who, they feared, threatened to turn the Arctic into Norway's personal property. The Swedish government response was swift. It encouraged its own capitalists to mine coal on the archipelago, reinforcing Sweden's claims to the land, in a chain reaction that turned the coal rush into a coal war.

With its historical claim to the lands in mind, the Russian government encouraged its citizens to mine coal on the island as well. Then the British miners on Svalbard demanded that the islands become part of the British Empire. The Americans, not to be outdone, demanded that they should become part of the United States.[45]

Attracted by the raw beauty of the islands, tourists had followed the scientists and miners. By 1900, the first tourist hotel had opened on Svalbard, a rather ramshackle wooden affair whose skeleton can still be seen today near the settlement of Old Longyearbyen. Plans were made for another hotel even farther north at Kings Bay.

In 1920, the Norwegians surely made their Viking ancestors proud when the Treaty of Svalbard finally gave them control over the islands—although their ancestors doubtless would have preferred a bloodier solution.

The year before, the victors of World War I had met at the Paris Peace Conference to decide the fate of the defeated nations. Britain, France, and the United States had another decision to make as well: to resolve the fate of Svalbard.

It was a case of now or never for Norway. Adolf Hoel's scientific imperialism had played a crucial role in justifying the young nation's claim to the islands.[46] The war had knocked out two of Norway's rivals to the archipelago. The unconditional surrender of Germany in 1918 had removed it from the negotiations, as had, for Russia, the chaos unleashed by the revolutions in 1917 and the subsequent civil war. The falling price of coal did most of the rest. It helped make the islands far less attractive to acquisitive nations like Great Britain and the United States. That just left Sweden.

Sweden continued to oppose the seizure of the islands by Norway, but not for long. The Norwegians simply came out of the war in a better position than the Swedes. The Nordic upstart was able to cash in at the conference a great deal of goodwill it had earned because of its decision to be a "neutral ally" of Britain in World War I. While nominally neutral, Norway had, under pressure from the British, cut trade links with Germany and used its merchant fleet (one of the largest in the world) to aid the Allied war effort.

While Sweden had also maintained its neutrality during

the war, it was widely known that a good number of its citizens believed in "Swedish activism" and, as a result, had
wanted to enter the war on the German side to fight Sweden's
ancient enemy, Russia. There was even a small Swedish bri-
gade that fought with the Kaiser's army on the eastern front
and then in the Finnish civil war.[47]

Despite the advantages that Norway enjoyed in the negotiations in 1919, Sweden's opposition achieved one thing: Norway's
possession of the islands was to be limited. Under the terms of
the treaty ratified six years later, citizens of any of the signatory
countries could live, work, and own businesses there, and there
was nothing the Norwegian authorities could do about it. (In
one of the few lasting achievements of the Versailles peace negotiations, the Norwegians still mine coal near Longyearbyen,
and the Russians still do so at Barentsburg, just on the other side
of the mountains.*) It was also to be forever a largely demilita-
rized zone.

The Russians didn't make the same mistake twice. Like
Svalbard, the Franz Josef Land archipelago 470 miles off the
coast of Siberia and 160 miles east of Svalbard had been re-

---

* Today many Norwegians fear that this settlement may not last for much
longer. The Norwegian government has now decided to wind down the
coal mines on Svalbard in favor of an economy based on scientific research
and tourism, drawing in a workforce from as far away as the Philippines
and Thailand (you can find some excellent Thai food in Longyearbyen). Yet
the mines, and the miners, represent, as they always have done, a powerful
physical reminder of Norwegian sovereignty to those countries like Russia
whose desire for the islands only grows as the polar ice recedes and their
strategic importance increases (Atle Staalesen, "End Comes to 100 Years of
Norwegian Coal Mining at Svalbard," *The Barents Observer*, October 12, 2017,
https://thebarentsobserver.com/en/arctic/2017/10/end-comes-100-years
-norwegian-coal-mining-svalbard).

garded as unoccupied *terra nullius*. In 1926, the Soviet Union annexed the second archipelago, despite Norway's protests. Hunting and scientific expeditions to the islands in 1929 and 1930 by Norway achieved little to reverse this.[48]

Then there was the small matter of Greenland. To this day, if you rummage through the antiques shops of Oslo, you may find a map that has "Erik Raudes Land" (Erik the Red's Land) stamped in capital letters over part of eastern Greenland. The Norwegian claim to Greenland was simple, they argued. In around 1000 CE, the Vikings had settled what they called Erik the Red's Land. Two hundred years later, the settlers recognized the overlordship of the king of Norway and then the North Sea kingdom joined Denmark in a new political union, dominated by the larger partner. When Norway was given to Sweden in the shuffling of cards in 1814 after the defeat of Napoleon, the Danes somehow kept their hands on Norway's Arctic territory, despite the fact that they were on the losing side.

The drawing of a new line on a map didn't stop the Norwegian whalers and hunters who regularly visited uninhabited eastern Greenland. They were later joined by Norwegian scientists who began to explore the coastline to further help reestablish the Norwegian claim, much as they had done in Svalbard and tried to do in Franz Josef Land archipelago. In June 1931, Norway made its next move, when five Norwegian fishermen landed in eastern Greenland. They quickly occupied the whaling, radio, and weather station at Myggbukta that served as the de facto capital of the new territory. From there they transmitted their telegram to Oslo, which read: "The Norwegian flag has been hoisted at Myggbukta. . . . We've called this Erik the Red's Land." Two weeks later, Norway officially proclaimed the annexation of part of eastern Greenland on the basis that the area was *terra nullius*: it had no permanent inhabitants, and its only visitors were Norwegian whalers, trappers, and scientists.[49]

The end came quickly for Norway's ambitions in Greenland. Norway and Denmark agreed to settle their dispute over this barren land at the Permanent Court of International Justice. Two years later, in 1933, the court ruled against Norway. Following the decision, the Norwegians abandoned their claim, although it was briefly revived by Norway's pro-Nazi Quisling government.

In the early 1920s, with at least Svalbard in its hands, Norway's attention turned even farther north. There was a hole in the map of the Arctic of more than one million square miles. Rich coal seams had been found on Svalbard. Might not oil be found in the far north as well?[50]

THE IMAGINATIONS OF STORYTELLERS and hallucinating explorers had long filled this empty space on the map with tales of wondrous lands and terrifying encounters, regularly fueled by real-life mysteries such as the disappearance of the Franklin expedition. The stories told about the Arctic in turn shaped future explorers' own perceptions of this dream-like supernatural landscape in a "magical loop."[51]

Tales of men who had vanished after going ashore and visitations from ghost-like figures were greedily consumed by the public sitting around the fireside at home. Some of the most popular were the stories of explorers who had played checkers with the devil[52] and even survived an encounter with the devil's fleet,[53] come to catch the souls of sailors and explorers. Over one long winter on Svalbard, the men of one expedition were purported to have even laid an extra table setting each night for the devil.[54] Tales of cannibalism were never far behind either.[55] Then there were the tales of ghoulish women and the stories of the ships cursed after they had tried to sail away with Inuit mummies,[56] desirable collectibles for museums back home. Back at home, servant girls reported seeing visions of explorers in trouble, and others organized séances to find out what happened to the missing men.[57] Wilkie Collins and Charles Dickens were inspired to write *The Frozen Deep*, a tale of vengeance and self-sacrifice on a polar expedition, based on a true story. Out of Arthur Conan Doyle's imagination came *The Captain of the Pole-Star*—a ghost story of a sea captain who risks the crew of his ice-bound ship to find the ghost of his dead fiancée.

The ancient Greeks had filled in this hole at the top of the world with stories about the Hyperboreans, a mythical race of giants who lived "beyond the North Wind." A Greek explorer named Pytheas is supposed to have reached Ultima Thule,[58] as this most distant land was called. In the late sixteenth and early seventeenth centuries, maps made by Gerardus Mercator depicted an ice-free polar sea with four great islands and the lodestone mountain. For the German mapmaker, the mountain was the source of the earth's magnetism, its power so great that it could drag a ship and its crew to their doom.[59] Others simply saw the polar area as the realm of Satan. Mary Shelley imagined Dr. Frankenstein's monstrous creation running over the ice of the Arctic Sea. Less alarmingly, in the 1860s, American poet and artist Thomas Nast had placed Santa Claus at the North Pole for the first time.[60]

However, stories about a warm open sea out there on the other side of the ice wouldn't go away.[61] In 1855, the *New York*

Times ran a front-page story about how adventurer and ide-
alist Elisha Kent Kane's expedition had discovered the Great
Northern Sea and the continent of Polynia. Kane was the
first American Arctic explorer of any significance. When his
expedition ship had become trapped in the ice, never to be
freed, two of his men had pushed on by sledge and on foot to
reach the "northern-most land ever trodden by a white man."
What they saw astounded them: "open water stretching to
the northern horizon. The unending shore line was washed
by shining waters without sign of ice." On their return, Kane
believed that his men had made a major scientific discovery.
Now all he had to do was to lead them on a thirteen-hundred-
mile trek to safety, which he successfully did.[62]

Kane's book about his expedition became a bestseller, and
he a national hero, but the explorer never returned to the Arctic to find the Great Northern Sea for himself. Kane died in
Havana two years later, soon after the book was finished, owing to poor heath, claiming, "This book has been my coffin."[63]
A banner where his body lay in state read: "Science Weeps,
Humanity Weeps, the World Weeps." His funeral was "a
grand spectacle of American nationalism," one of the last of
its kind before the division between the North and South of
the United States reached the point of no return.[64]

In fact, no one was able to find the warm open sea again.
The theory was discredited; Kane and his heroic exploits quietly forgotten.

Another story that wouldn't go away was that of the Hollow
Earth. At its simplest, the story, which dates back to the seventeenth century, is the belief that the two poles of the earth are
in reality openings to an inhabited land inside the earth itself.

The story grew in popularity and evolved over the centuries that followed, almost as quickly as scientists debunked it.

In 1906, former fire insurance salesman William Reed helped popularize the Hollow Earth theory with his best-selling book *Phantom of the Poles*. Two years later he went one step further than most other believers. In April 1908, Reed held the first public meeting of the Reed Hollow Earth Exploring Club in the august surroundings of the American Institute of Electrical Engineers in New York. The purpose of the club, or the "Holy Polers," as they were derisively labeled by the press, was to organize and raise funds for expeditions to find the openings to the Hollow Earth. Plans included sending a fleet of three vessels to the Arctic, a purpose-built submarine to explore the sea floor at the North Pole, and an airship to search for the entrance from the sky.[65]

The news that Frederick Cook and Robert Peary had reached the North Pole in 1908 and 1909, respectively, dealt a fatal blow to Reed's plans,[66] if not to the belief in the Hollow Earth. The Hollow Earth Exploring Club had only one documented meeting, with eighty-four people in attendance (many of whom were journalists). By October 1909, it was reported in newspapers as far away as Brisbane, Australia, that the "Holy Polers had disbanded."[67]

In the early twentieth century, there was also Crocker Land. The Arctic explorer Robert Peary reported that he had seen in the distance mountains that belonged to a huge undiscovered continent in the middle of the Arctic Ocean. He placed the land in the Canadian Arctic, west of Greenland and north of Ellesmere Island.[68] It even appears on some maps of the time. Peary named this new continent after his sponsor, a banker who had given him $50,000 toward his expedition. Peary's book *Nearest the Pole* also become a bestseller. Soon Crocker Land was labeled the "last great unknown place in the world."[69]

Seven years after Peary's supposed discoveries, the independent Crocker Land expedition went looking to solve what had been called the world's last geographical problem and claim the land for the United States of America.[70] They came back bitterly disappointed, with the suspicion that Peary had invented the whole thing, as indeed some thought he had done with his claim to have reached the North Pole in 1909.[71]

Still, it actually wasn't until 1938, when a pilot named Isaac Schlossbach flew an airplane over where Crocker Land was supposed to be and found nothing, that the story was definitively discredited.[72] The theory of fraud appears to have been confirmed when Peary's personal papers were examined in the 1980s, long after his death. There was no mention of Crocker Land in his notes or in the first draft of his book.[73]

By 1925, it didn't look like the Arctic would keep its secrets for much longer. As Amundsen had predicted, airships and airplanes could cover in hours what an explorer on the ground would take weeks to traverse. Yet Amundsen was often his own worst enemy. His talk of undiscovered lands grabbed headlines, but it also fired up the politicians. The US State Department and the Norwegian Foreign Ministry each made plans for how their countries would claim any lands that their own heroes discovered.[74]

"The shortest route from England to Japan or California is over the top of the Earth," Amundsen told a reporter. "The shortest route from many other parts of Europe to Asia is over the top of the Earth.

"With the development of dirigibles and airplanes, the north route will be used, and if there is land there, it will be of the greatest importance.

"In case of future wars, air bases in the Arctic would be of great value."[75]

AMUNDSEN MAY HAVE DREAMED of multiple air bases in the Arctic Circle, but in 1925 his was one of the only ones. It consisted of two flying boats, no hangars, and a rough runway made from ice.

For the flight he had a team of six men who would be split between the two planes. Lincoln Ellsworth would be in one, Amundsen in the other. The Norwegian had also brought with him for the first time two journalists and a photographer to record the expedition.

The flying boats that Amundsen transported from Pisa, Italy, weren't just any flying boats. The N-24 and N-25 were state-of-the-art Dornier Do J "whale" flying boats, which went on to pioneer many air routes across the world.[76]

These expensive German-designed machines were cutting edge in 1925. This meant that they were all metal, with a whale-shaped hull and high, raised wings. Two stub wings, known as sponsons, kept the plane stable, while ribs on the hull gave the plane the strength to land on sea or ice. Two chunky Rolls-Royce Eagle propeller engines were arranged back to back: one to pull the plane through the air and the other to push it.[77] The Eagle engines were the first aeroengines that Rolls-Royce ever built.

Alas, the pilots were still housed in an unheated open-air cockpit, obliged to wear woolen underwear, sweaters, two pairs of pants, a sealskin greatcoat as well as a leather jacket, a leather flying helmet, gloves, scarves, and heavy boots to stay warm while flying at high speeds.[78] They each had a parachute (one of the conditions Ellsworth's father made him agree to in exchange for his money), though the terrible battle to survive they would face if their parachutes worked was something it was better not to think about.

The state of aerial navigation wasn't much better. Pilots, who still relied on distinguishing features such as railways, rivers, and castles to help them work out where they were going, were always going to be challenged by the featureless and shifting Arctic landscape. As mariners had done for the last two hundred years, sextants* could be used to determine their aircraft's altitude, position, and ground speed. These sextants were of less use, of course, when visibility was blocked by fog or thick clouds. Then these early pilots could use a magnetic compass, which becomes less reliable the closer to the North Pole the aircraft flies, or a solar compass, which worked like a sundial by using the position of the sun to establish a bearing (particularly useful near the North Pole).

Radio had started to challenge these far older methods of navigation. Radio direction finding allowed a navigator to find the direction to a radio station, or beacon. Then if you could

---

* The sextants used by these early aviators usually came with their own artificial horizon, for use when the actual horizon was impossible to discern. Some were actually designed to be used in an open-air cockpit. The early Boeing 747s had a sextant port for such celestial navigation (Guy Gratton, "Why the Sun Is Setting on the Boeing 747," *The Conversation*, February 1, 2016, https://phys.org/news/2016-02-sun-boeing.html).

pick up the signals of two or more stations, you could work out where you were by simple triangulation. Airplane navigators had to take all these readings in conditions that didn't lend themselves to accuracy, taking measurements and keeping records in what was usually a freezing cold—and sometimes open—cockpit in a noisy and unstable machine.

Unfortunately for the crew of his new expedition, the Amundsen of 1925 was not the Amundsen who beat Scott to the South Pole. It could be said that he had lost his eye for detail.[79]

The planes had been test flown in the Mediterranean before they were shipped by train and boat to Kings Bay. What they hadn't been was properly test flown in the below-freezing conditions of the Arctic.[80] In 1925, no one really understood how these flimsy aircraft and their internal combustion engines would cope with the cold of the Arctic, and Amundsen didn't seem particularly curious about the possible distinction. Then there were the sextants that didn't work and the radio sets that hadn't arrived yet, and which Amundsen decided they couldn't wait for.[81] Finally, Amundsen didn't formulate any emergency procedures in the event that one of the planes had to land. Without the radios, there was no way for the crews to talk to each other midflight if something went wrong. He had compounded this risk by turning down the US Navy's offer of the giant airship USS *Shenandoah* to act as a rescue ship the year before. But he did remember to take a moving-picture camera with them.

Amundsen's haste was due to his worry that a narrow window in the Arctic weather was set to close. There was also the nagging fear that someone else would fly to the North Pole before him.

Finally, on May 21, 1925, after one last leisurely, rather staged cigarette to calm their nerves,[82] and with a final shove of the plane from the miners[83]—who were given the day off for the occasion[84]—the two overloaded planes roared one after the other across the rough-ice runway like toboggans, the crews feeling every bump in the ice through the flying boats' metal hull, then out on to the water and into the air. "It was unreal, mystic, fraught with prophecy," Ellsworth wrote. "Something ahead was hidden, and we were going to find it."[85]

The low-lying fog quickly cleared. The film that the crew shot of the glaciers of Svalbard comprised the first images ever taken from the air of these rivers of ice.

Amundsen's dream of flying over the Arctic Sea was realized. The explorers were covering in hours what would take a week to do with dogs and skis. "I have never seen anything more desolate and deserted," Amundsen remarked. "A bear from time to time I would have thought, which could break the monotony a little. But no—absolutely nothing living."[86]

After eight hours, they should have been near the North Pole, and the plan was to try to land. But one of the engines of Amundsen's plane started to splutter on their descent. It quickly became apparent that they had to land rather sooner than they wanted.[87]

"I have never looked down upon a more terrifying place in which to land an airplane," Ellsworth wrote.[88] For what had looked like smooth ice from high altitude turned out to be cut by ridges, gaps of open water called leads, and icebergs.[89]

Amundsen's plane made it down safely thanks to the skills of his pilot. Ellsworth's was not so lucky. His plane eventually found a stretch of water they too could land on. Unfortunately, distances are deceptive at that height and what had seemed long enough was too short. Ellsworth's plane bounced across the surface of the sea and smashed into an ice floe. Water poured in. That the rivets on the hull had burst due to the rough takeoff only added to their problems.[90]

Soon there was nothing Ellsworth and his men could do to rescue it; the flying boat floated there like a dead whale. Ellsworth's men were cold and wet, and they had been awake for twenty-four hours. They needed rest and food, but there wouldn't be any of either for a while. They had to try their best to protect the plane from being crushed by the ice or sinking while they tried to salvage what they could. Eventually they stopped, exhausted—and the peril Ellsworth and his men were in suddenly hit him. "In the utter silence this seemed to me to be the kingdom of death," he wrote.[91]

The two crews were now separated from each other by many miles. It was twenty-four hours before they spotted each other across the ice pack.

Even when they were in sight of each other, communication across the ice was hampered because no one knew Morse code or semaphore. Instead, the two crews managed to get a rudimentary flag system going between them. It took two to three hours to communicate a simple message. Walking across the ice wasn't an option either. It was simply too dangerous.

They were lucky in the end. The blocks of sea ice floated closer together, making it possible for the crews to be reunited after five interminable days. This still wasn't without risk. Attempts by the men to walk across the ice floes with as much equipment as possible nearly ended in disaster when two of them sank through the slush into the freezing water. One of the men screamed, "I'm gone! I'm gone," as the current tried to pull him under the ice.[92]

Amundsen looked shockingly changed, exhaustion and anxiety cut deep into his face, but he was now back in the world of the ice pack, a world he knew so well. Quickly he took control.[93] He realized that they had to combine the supplies from both planes to give themselves a chance of survival. More important, perhaps, they were able to siphon the fuel out of Ellsworth's plane to give them enough to reach home again with the heavier load of all the men on board. But before they could attempt this, they first needed to carve a runway out of the ice.[94] Of course, they hadn't brought any specialized tools with them, despite having planned to land at the North Pole.[95]

Without radio contact, the world first suspected that something had gone wrong when the planes didn't return to Kings Bay straight away. Even then, some people thought that the aviators could have stayed at the pole for a couple of days or even flown on to Alaska, as Amundsen had long wanted to do. Some remembered conversations where Ellsworth had said it might take a year for them to walk out of the wilderness if their plane crashed.

When nothing was heard from them, newspapers across America started to report that the planes were overdue.[96] There were demands for a rescue effort to be launched. But the lack of ships, planes, airships, and any idea of where Amundsen and his men had crashed presented would-be rescuers with a fearsome challenge. Still, the pressure was there. One headline in the *New York Times* proclaimed, "Coolidge

Favors Amundsen Relief Should He Need It; President Would Approve Naval Plan to Send One of Our Giant Dirigibles to the Arctic."[97]

The US Navy was keen to launch its own expedition to rescue Amundsen. Two years earlier, naval plans to explore the Arctic with one of its huge dirigibles had been canceled owing to the expense. Now they were pushing the president to dispatch the giant USS *Shenandoah* or USS *Los Angeles* airships to search for Amundsen. Either of the two ships could be ready in days for the mission, sources told the *New York Times* journalist.[98] The flight itself to Greenland (a possible base for the mission) would then take a couple of days, depending on the weather and where the ships were based at that time. "Practically, every officer connected with the aeronautical service of the Navy will volunteer in the event that a call for help is made on behalf of Amundsen," the reporter explained.[99]

EVEN THOUGH AMUNDSEN'S MEN didn't know it for sure, they probably could have guessed: their fate was in their own hands. "Men fight for their lives to the last inch," Ellsworth wrote later[100]—and they did.

Working together in the freezing temperatures and sleeping in the remaining flying boat, the six men were able to drag the one aircraft that could still fly out of the sea and onto a flat surface. They checked the engines of Amundsen's plane—and to everyone's relief they still worked despite the cold. They dragged the petrol tank from the ruined plane across the ice.

Then they had to find enough flat space and build the runway. This was exhausting, back-breaking work conducted

on minimal rations, with a single ax and improvised cutting
tools in the form of knives attached to the end of ski poles.[101]
Their shelter was the fuselage of their plane. It may have been
made out of metal and its four walls covered in ice crystals,
but it kept out the damp and fog. The heat from the primus
stove and their bodies was enough to raise the temperature
above freezing.[102] The success of their efforts would determine
whether they lived or died. They recorded their struggle on
celluloid for the newsreels back home.

The men were disoriented by the twenty-four-hour daylight and the ever-shifting ice; they would go to sleep in one
place and wake up in another. With each yank, push, or split
of the surface, their plane risked being crushed by the ice;
their runway was regularly damaged, and they had to start
afresh again and again.

Amundsen appeared to age another ten years during the ordeal, and cracks started to appear in his rock-like persona. On
one occasion, he complained about Ellsworth's snoring. On another, he lost his temper when one of the men dropped some
crumbs of tobacco on the ice floor of their makeshift shelter.

Despite this, he was really in his element. This battle of
life against death, this test of human endurance, was an all-
too-familiar challenge—and one for which his character had
been honed. Somehow, by June 14, the six men had shifted five
hundred tons of ice between them.

Yet no amount of courage could hide the brutal reality
of their predicament. With the food rations all but finished,
survival came down to whether the runway was long enough
and whether the plane could take off with six people on board.
If it wasn't and it couldn't, the men would have to make "the
supreme decision"[103]—whether or not to set off on the four-

hundred-mile walk across the sea ice to Greenland, which they knew they would probably never reach.[104]

By June 15, the men were staring death in the face. They had made five attempts to take off already, but the temperature was rising, melting the ice into clinging slush that prevented the plane reaching takeoff speed, and there was, perhaps, time and fuel for only one more go.[105]

On their sixth attempt, they made it. The flying boat was in the air after a takeoff that lasted only thirty to forty seconds. Within eight hours, they had landed just short of the coast of Spitsbergen, on the far side of the island from Kings Bay. Their fuel was finished.[106]

They were spotted adrift on the sea by seal hunters, who greeted Amundsen with six words: "You are supposed to be dead."[107] No wonder the Norwegians thought their hero was almost immortal.[108]

Two

"There Is No Room for Prima Donnas in the Italian Air Force"

AMUNDSEN HAD FAILED TO reach the North Pole again. This time he was treated like a hero.

As he and his crew of explorers flew over the wide waters of the Oslofjord toward the capital city in their last surviving flying boat, they were met by an honor guard made up of planes from the Norwegian navy. Together, the formation passed the three-hundred-year-old Oscarsborg fortress. Fifteen years later, in 1940, the fierce resistance of its garrison and its elderly guns would hold up the German invasion force long enough for the king and his government to escape to Britain. Its secret underwater torpedo tubes would sink the mighty German warship *Blücher* to the bottom of Oslofjord, where it still lies today.

Closer to Oslo, the flying boat landed on the calm waters of the fjord to taxi the rest of the way. Nearby was the building site of the Viking Ship Museum that upon completion would house the three great Viking ships found in the second half of the nineteenth century and the early years of the twentieth, preserved in burial mounds near the shore of the fjord. Soon the Fram Museum would be built there too, as a permanent memorial to Norwegian polar explorers such as Nansen and Amundsen himself. At its heart would be the *Fram*, the ship with which the two men explored the poles.

The returning explorers found themselves surrounded by what seemed to be all the small boats in Norway, a whole flotilla that followed them all the way to the quayside. In the harbor, the flying boat was dwarfed by a squadron of British warships on a goodwill visit to the capital, whose crews lined the decks and cheered. Their mighty guns fired a salute in honor of Amundsen and his men.

And this was only the start of the welcome that Norway had laid out for them. Fifty thousand people lined the quayside and the boulevard that led up to the Royal Palace to get a glimpse of their heroes. Three horse-drawn carriages carried Amundsen and his crew up from their flying boat to their appointment with the king. The soldiers at the Royal Palace fired a thirteen-gun salute in their honor.[1]

Afterward, Amundsen, his pilot, Hjalmar Riiser-Larsen, and his men would celebrate their "miraculous" return over dinner with their friends, at which emotions ran high. Later in the evening Frederick Ramm, Amundsen's favorite journalist, left rather suddenly. "I went a little suddenly, but I couldn't otherwise," he wrote to Riiser-Larsen the next day in order to explain his abrupt departure. "If I had tried to say goodbye, I wouldn't manage to control myself: I hardly know how I have come through these days since you returned. . . . I have never been happier than when I saw you."[2]

The reaction by the people of Oslo was not surprising. The whole story of the Norwegian's polar expedition, sudden disappearance, and unknown fate was a cliffhanger that had gripped the public's imagination across the world. The journalists and camera crews who had followed Amundsen to the North Pole had kept up a steady flow of stories and newsreel footage to feed their audience's insatiable appetite. Few saw them as failures, despite the fact that the mission came to disaster and hadn't reached the North Pole.

Amid the hullabaloo of his welcome, there were three things that Amundsen knew: he was going to go back to the Arctic; he was going to need an airship; and there was only one man who had an airship for sale.

He needed to send a telegram.

TODAY THE HUGE CIGAR-SHAPED airships of the early twentieth century seem to be artifacts of a lost civilization, the monumental architecture constructed to house them all that remains of the once proud people who designed, built, and promoted them, and the men (and it was usually men)* who piloted them, tragic heroes doomed to fail. It wasn't always thus.

---

* Airship pilots "are rarer than astronauts and, if we're talking about a woman, even rarer still," writes Cynthia Drescher for *The Runway Girl Network*. In Germany, before the outbreak of World War II, women had broken through the glass ceiling to become airplane pilots, and ballooning had become an acceptable activity for a respectable woman, says Guillaume de Syon, author of *Zeppelin!: Germany and the Airship, 1900–1939*. Piloting an airship was a different matter altogether, and only one woman was able to break through to learn to fly an airship, and even then, she only received an honorary pilot's license (Guillaume de Syon, *Zeppelin!: Germany and the Airship, 1900–1939* [Baltimore, MD: Johns Hopkins University Press, 2007], 65). Today things are a little better. There have been at least three women airship pilots over the last twenty years in the United States, including Taylor Deen, who flies one of the Goodyear Blimps (Cynthia Drescher, "Pilot Kristen Arambula on building a career with Goodyear Blimps," *The Runway Girl Network*, November 8, accessed March 20, 2021,

In the collection of the London Transport Museum there is a rare poster designed in 1926 by the artist Montague B. Black for London Underground. Depicting the imagined city of London in the year 2026, the poster shows not a dystopian view of London, but a London a hundred years in the future bathed in golden light with a glamorous skyline rather like New York's. Flying above the cityscape are two craft: planes and airships. The caption at the top of the poster reads "London 2026 A.D.—This Is All in the Air."[3]

When these leviathans of the sky flew like visions of the future over New York, everyone stopped to stare. There is a photograph you can find online of the huge USS *Los Angeles* airship docking with the mast at the top of the Empire State Building in New York. Sadly, this picture is a fake—the giant airship actually flew over the iconic building at night—but there is a real photograph shot from underneath the Goodyear Blimp *Columbia* as it flew low over the airship mast at the top of the iconic building.[4]

In 1929, the owners of the iconic Empire State Building had an airship mast erected at its summit to boost its height by an extra two hundred feet. Airships would, they promised, "swing in the breeze and the passengers [would] go down a gangplank."[5] Seven minutes later, the passengers would be on the sidewalk in Midtown rather than on the airfield at Lakehurst, New Jersey, which the German airship *Graf Zeppelin* used. Airships on four different occasions variously connected to the mast, hovered over it, and lowered newspapers fresh off the press onto the roof. The final attempt to connect to the

___

https://runwaygirlnetwork.com/2016/11/08/pilot-kristen-arambula-on
-building-a-career-with-goodyear-blimps/).

mast failed. Ultimately, passengers preferred to land in New Jersey rather than stepping off their flight from Frankfurt onto "a $2\frac{1}{2}$ ft wide terrace, a quarter of a mile up,"[6] but the romance remained.

There are basically three types of airship. The nonrigid airship, colloquially known as the blimp, like the *Columbia*, offers the most basic and inexpensive design. It usually consists of a large envelope filled with a lifting gas like hydrogen or helium, a cabin attached underneath for a small crew and passengers, an engine of some sort, and a rudder for steering.

The rigid passenger airships promoted by Hugo Eckener in Germany are at the other extreme. They are expensive and labor-intensive craft to build because of their huge size and fragile, complex internal metal skeleton, subject to forces that in the 1920s were barely understood, around which the huge envelope of the airship is stretched, maintaining its shape not through the pressure of the gas, but the metal structure.

The semi-rigid airships favored by Italian Umberto Nobile are somewhere in the middle. They have a stiff keel that usually runs along the full length of the bottom of the ship, which supports the envelope of the airship. The envelope is then left to maintain its shape largely through the pressure of the gas, rather like a blimp, while the keel allows it to lift greater weights. The advantages of this semi-rigid design, Nobile believed, were that they could be cheaper, quicker, and easier to build than the Germans' airships.

In 1925, if Amundsen wanted to buy an airship, there were only two men to whom he would have sent that telegram: one was Colonel Umberto Nobile; the other, a certain Hugo Eckener.

UMBERTO NOBILE WAS BORN in the shadow of Vesuvius and Monte Somma at Marzano di Nola, near Naples in southern Italy, the fifth in a family of seven children. His father was an official in the Ministry of Finance.[7] He didn't like to tell people, but he was a descendant of one of the aristocratic families that used to be close to the Bourbons, the ruling family of southern Italy. His grandfather was Roberto Carlo Ferdinando Nobile delle Piane dei marchesi di Valceronia, chamberlain at the court of King Francesco II,[8] the last of the Bourbon kings who ruled the toe of Italy.[9] It has been said that Nobile first fell in love with flying when he saw one of the earliest planes flying over the congested streets of Rome.

The Bourbons ruled Naples and Sicily for one hundred years before the unification of Italy. In 1860, as part of Italy's long march to becoming a nation-state, Giuseppe Garibaldi led a popular uprising that turned them out. Nobile's family refused to pay homage to the new Italian royal family, the Savoys. Instead, they stayed loyal to the old regime—and they paid the price for it, losing their titles and influence.[10]

The Nobiles weren't alone. The south was filled with many aristocrats who couldn't or wouldn't accept the new order and were stripped of their titles. By the time Umberto Nobile was born, it would appear that all the family had left of their fortune was a little land, the surname that hinted at who they once were, a degree of confidence that came with high birth, and perhaps hints of good breeding in their looks. Worse still, the Nobiles had to watch new families loyal to the new regime come from nowhere to be ennobled.

Umberto Nobile was different from others like him. He was smart—very smart. Today he would be called a prodigy. What's more, he embraced the modern world with open arms. In 1908, he graduated from university with two diplomas: one in mechanical engineering and the other in electrical engineering. He went on to get his hands dirty working on the electrification of the Italian railways.[11]

Three years later, he was one of the first people in Europe to formally study the new science of aeronautics, having won a place on a one-year course at the Central Aeronautical Institute[12] in a competition run by the military. A certain Gaetano Arturo Crocco had helped to found the institute and their fates would quickly become intertwined,[13] and their fates would quickly become intertwined.

In 1912, Umberto Nobile finished the yearlong course at the top of his class. Crocco and his protégé then tested a hydroplane on the shores of Lake Bracciano, north of Rome.[14]

GAETANO ARTURO CROCCO WAS an engineering genius. By 1898, Crocco had started to experiment with balloons tethered to the ground on the shores of Lake Bracciano and then with airships six years later. In 1906, he developed Airship 1 with Ottavio Ricaldoni. Airship 1 featured the revolutionary semi-rigid airship design that Nobile would develop further. On October 31, 1908, Crocco piloted a new design, the N-1, from Vigna di Valle to Rome and back, covering fifty miles (80 km) in one and a half hours at an altitude of 1,640 feet (500 m). The N-1 was the first airship ever to fly over Rome.[15]

Crocco quickly earned himself the epithet "the Airship Man." Soon his airships would go to war.

By the start of the twentieth century, the new Kingdom

of Italy had become jealous of the empires of its European rivals, which often incorporated land they had snapped up while Italy struggled with unification and its aftermath. In 1911, the government, under pressure from nationalists, decided to do something about it. Italy decided to bring what it called civilization to Libya, which was then part of the Ottoman Empire. As with more recent Western invasions, they expected it to be a walkover.[16]

Unfortunately, it didn't go according to script. After landing in Tripoli, the Italian army found itself bogged down by the determined resistance of the Turkish and Arab defenders. Needing every advantage in this fight, airships and early aircraft were drafted to carry out aerial reconnaissance and drop bombs on "some raging lunatics" in the African desert.[17] They had a "wonderful effect on Arab morale."[18]

Three of the rather primitive teardrop-shaped airships designed by Crocco would be among the first aircraft ever used for aerial reconnaissance and the bombing of civilians— and certainly the first airships to be used in this way.[19] They proved to have longer range, flexibility of use, endurance, and greater resilience than the early planes. On more than one occasion, the airships were able to limp home despite heavy damage from rifle fire. Crocco's efforts meant that by the beginning of World War I, Italy had the third-largest fleet of airships in the world, after Germany and France.[*]

Unfortunately, after Nobile had graduated, the engineer

---

[*] Crocco had a restless mind. In the years leading up to the mid-1920s, he tested a hydroplane on Lake Bracciano, played around with the design of a helicopter, designed flying bombs, built wind tunnels, and thought about the problem of navigation in space. By then, Crocco's mind was moving on again, and his attention started to shift to space flight, jet propulsion, and

couldn't work with Crocco immediately, so for a while he worked in northern Italy on the same kind of aerial ropeways that crisscrossed the mountainsides of Svalbard. Then fate intervened.

In 1914, war broke out between the powers of the Triple Entente (Britain, France, and Russia) and the Central powers of Germany and Austria-Hungary (later joined by the Ottoman Empire and Bulgaria). After hesitating on the sidelines for a year, in 1915 the young nation of Italy allied itself with Britain, France, and Russia rather than with Germany and Austria-Hungary, with which she was formally allied.

Like every red-blooded Italian man, Nobile volunteered for the army—but he was turned down on health grounds. In fact, he volunteered again and again, and was rejected each time. When he couldn't get anywhere near the front line this way, Nobile put his aeronautical knowledge at the disposal of the Ministry of War. He was attached to the Stabilimento Militare di Costruzioni Aeronautiche (SCA) in Rome,[20] where he was reunited with Crocco.

By the end of the war, the two men had together built more than thirty airships,[21] which were used for spying on the Austrians, bombing their front lines, and hunting for submarines in the Mediterranean. Nobile also wrote *Elements of Aerodynamics*, which became one of the key textbooks of the new science.[22]

By December 1917, Nobile's star was shining so brightly that he was appointed vice director of the airship factory. In July 1919, he became its director.[23] He would go on to sell four

rocket fuel ("Gaetano Crocco—Italian Aerospace Pioneer," *SciHi Blog*, October 26, 2015, http://scihi.org/gaetano-crocco-italian-aerospace-pioneer/).

airships to Spain (which were used in the conflict known as the Rif War, between the Berbers and the Spanish in Morocco),* two to the United States, two to Argentina, one to Holland, another to Britain,† and finally one to Japan. The Soviet Union wanted to buy one of the ships as well, until a future rival put a stop to that.[24] The young director even had the time to help design the Caproni Ca.73, a light bomber biplane, which was the first aircraft in Italy to be built with an entirely metallic structure.‡

The young prodigy quickly understood how to use the international press to promote his designs and himself. Nobile wrote articles for the international aviation press on subjects such as semi-rigid versus rigid airships, the Goodyear semi-

---

* There is a picture of the Spanish navy's seaplane carrier *Dédalo* sailing to aid the landing of the Spanish army at Al Hoceima in 1925, which marked the beginning of the end of the Rif War in northern Morocco between the Berber tribesmen and the Spanish colonizers. But the *Dédalo* was different from other seaplane carriers. While half the ship was crammed with seaplanes, at the other end there was an airship mast, tied to which was one of the airships Nobile had sold to the Spanish. When it first entered service in 1922, the *Dédalo* actually had a hangar built to accommodate two of Nobile's craft ("Las Sufridas, Heroicas Alas de España," *Blanco y Negro Madrid*, September 20, 1925, 88, https://www.abc.es/archivo/periodicos/blanco-negro -19250920-88.html).

† The British were less enamored of Nobile's design than the Spanish. The British flew their airship back from Rome in October 1918 in what was the first flight of an aircraft of any kind between Italy and Britain, and by September of the following year, it had been dismantled. The British complained that airship engines were unreliable and performed unpredictably. Britain's own designs were naturally considered superior (SR1, Non-British Constructed but Owned Airships, *Airship Heritage Trust*, accessed June 20, 2021, https://www.airshiponline.com/airships/index.html).

‡ Sadly, unlike his former mentor, Crocco, the talented designer didn't pursue his interest in heavier-than-air flight any further at this time.

rigid airship, and his "sky anchor." He would take the opportunity to take potshots at his rivals' designs, which he simply called "the German design."[25]

Thanks to all this activity, it became impossible to work out who was the greater "airship man": Crocco or Nobile.

THE PAIR HAD WORKED on their last airship together. Nobile, Crocco, and two other engineers had built the first of what they hoped would be a new type of huge semi-rigid airship: the T-class.[26]

The T-34 was their zeppelin competitor, an airship designed for war and now repurposed for peace, its innovative rigid keel giving it in theory the strength to be scaled up to compete with far larger German aircraft.[27] Unfortunately, Nobile's and Crocco's different visions for this new class of airship started to push them apart.

The *T* stood for "transatlantic," because the airship, with its distinctive box rudder, had been redesigned to transport up to 100 passengers from Rome to Rio de Janeiro. Unfortunately, plans for this flight were abandoned around the time the British airship R-38 became the first aircraft to fly across the Atlantic and back again. No official reason appears to have ever been given for why the T-34's flight never took place.[28]

Instead, the T-34, now named *Roma*, was sold to the US Navy in 1921 after a visit to Rome by a powerful delegation of military and political leaders. The top brass from America were joined by Umberto Nobile and Gaetano Arturo Crocco on the grass of Ciampino airfield to enjoy a glass of fizzing Italian hospitality, which was carried on during the flight with cold meats, veal, and Chianti. When one of the guests wanted to light his after-dinner cigar, Crocco exclaimed, "No, no! A match lit near the hydrogen is very dangerous. Any spark near it could detonate a large explosion!"[29] Any questions about why the great airship suddenly turned away from Mount Vesuvius rather than fly over it were forgotten by the American guests.[30] Instead of questioning why the ship didn't have enough lift to climb over the volcano, they agreed to buy the ship with its leaky, worn-out envelope—for the knockdown price of $184,000 rather than the $475,000 that the Italians wanted.[31]

The *Roma* would become the largest airship in the service of the US military. It was the largest semi-rigid airship ever built. But rather than fly across the Atlantic, the *Roma* was dismantled and shipped across the ocean.

But on February 21, 1922, life took a darker turn for Nobile.

The headline of the Pathé Gazette newsreel was: "The Wrecked 'Roma': 33 Killed in Terrible American Airship Disaster."[32] In the shaky footage of the crash site in Norfolk, Virginia, shot from the air, the once mighty airship was now a wreck of twisted, blackened girders with plumes of gray smoke rising into the air, blanketing the site like a funeral shroud. Yet the reasons for the disaster were clear. The crew of the *Roma* had been flying too low and too fast, and lost control of the ship. The envelope of the airship was in poor condition, as was the fabric of the gas compartment at the front, and the leakage of hydrogen meant the nose started to droop. Under the strain, the keel that ran the whole length of the ship started to buckle, and the control cables snapped, freezing the rudder at such an angle that the *Roma* was fixed in a terrifying powered descent to its destruction.[33]

Even in these last, desperate moments, there was still a chance that the ship could have landed relatively safely had its engines been switched off. Tragically, they weren't. The mechanics whose job it was to control the engines hadn't received the order to turn them off. Instead, they propelled the airship forward until it hit a line of power cables and burst into flames. Thirty-four* out of forty-five passengers and crew were killed. It was the deadliest crash in US aviation history at that time.

The temptation must have been to blame the Italians for the crash, yet the fault seemed to lie closer to home. The US military had decided to save money by not replacing the worn-out envelope and by using flammable hydrogen in the airship rather than the helium they knew was safer. There were also problems in the way the ship had been reassembled; for example, the Americans replaced the Italian engines with more powerful American-built ones with little thought as to the effects.

In public, Nobile stated clearly the reason for the disaster: "It was an unlucky circumstance that the airship met this high-tension wire. Otherwise, nothing would have destroyed it."[34] In private, Nobile was convinced that the disaster was due to the failure of the *Roma*'s innovative box-like tail, which Crocco had designed and had stopped his rival from replacing[35]—and this conflict turned their existing division over the future of airship design into something permanent.[36] The *Roma* was the last airship they built together. They were now enemies.

Some Americans continued to wonder whether there was a darker reason for all that hospitality in Rome. Had they been sold a dud?

---

* One man had jumped up, far too low for his parachute to work. It is not clear if he died when he hit the ground, or soon after, but he didn't die in the inferno (Nancy E. Sheppard, *The Airship* Roma *Disaster in Hampton Roads* [Charleston, SC: History Press, 2016], chap. 11, Kindle).

However, the Italian designers somehow seemed to escape the blame, and Nobile's stock remained high in the United States. The following year, he even went to work as a consultant for the Goodyear Airship Corporation in Akron, Ohio—home in modern times to the famous Goodyear Blimp—on the construction of another semi-rigid airship. Announcing the collaboration, *Aviation* described Nobile as the "foremost authority on this type of ship in Italy, and consequently in the world,"[37] who would aid the American company in the construction of its first semi-rigid airship.

For whatever reason, Nobile rarely mentioned the *Roma* again, and today the only memorial to the crash is a small, cement stone dedicated to the airship and crew nowhere near the actual site and locked away behind a chain-link fence.

UMBERTO NOBILE MAY HAVE had what's called a good war, but the Italians certainly hadn't, and there was one man ready to take advantage of that: Benito Mussolini.

Yes, Italy won the war against Germany and Austria-Hungary on the Italian front in the end, but at a terrible cost. Out of the 5.6 million men who were conscripted into the army, about 2.2 million became casualties of war (39 percent), of whom 650,000 died (12 percent), another 950,000 were injured (17 percent), and another 600,000 were captured or disappeared (10 percent).[38] More than a million of these casualties of war were the result of eleven offensives launched by the Italian army every bit as futile as those on the western front. In many ways, life for the ordinary soldier was a great deal grimmer than that of his brothers-in-arms in France. Discipline was brutal because the officers didn't trust their peasant soldiers, many of whom had little loyalty to the new Kingdom of Italy. The soldier's rate of pay was considered a joke, as was the compensation paid to their family if they died. An army may march on its stomach, but no one had told the Italian commanders. The rations of the men were cut by a quarter from about four thousand calories a day to three thousand. Leave from the front was also limited, and unlike on the western front, there was little thought given to providing entertainment for the men.

Life as a prisoner of war (POW) wasn't much better. The government was determined to discourage their men from waving the white flag by not providing the same aid for POWs that other countries did. As a result, about one hundred thousand Italian POWs died from hunger and hunger-related causes in the camps, six times the number of French POWs, whose government did provide aid to their men trapped behind enemy lines.[39] Despite this, many preferred to take their chances in the camps rather than fight on. During the Battle of Caporetto in late 1917, at least one officer was shot by his men when he didn't surrender fast enough. The parallels with the Russian Revolution were impossible to miss.

Unfortunately, Britain and France weren't interested in these parallels. They had little sympathy for the suffering of the Italian people because other Allied nations, such as France and Russia, had suffered far more. Three out of four of France's soldiers, sailors, and aviators ended the war as casualties, which was about the same for Russia. The British Empire had lost a similar percentage of men as Italy, but the British weren't complaining and, crucially, weren't surrendering. After Caporetto, at a long-forgotten crunch point in the war, British and French divisions had to be rushed from the western front (where they were desperately needed) to northern Italy to plug the hole left in the front line by the disappearing soldiers. Rather than understand why this had occurred, the leaders of these two countries preferred to fall back on crude racial stereotypes to explain what had happened to the Italian army, even though the advancing German and Austro-Hungarian armies were actually stopped by the Italian army before they reached the British and French divisions.

The peace didn't turn out to be much better. It was soon dubbed the *vittoria mutilata* (mutilated victory) by Italian nationalists. Britain, France, and the United States decided at the Versailles peace talks to give Italy only a fraction of the land it had been promised for entering the war on the Allied side, a decision taken despite all the Italian blood that had been shed for the common cause, almost as if an Italian soldier didn't count as much. Even if the deal Italy eventually received was a little better, the resentment this generated would soon be used by Mussolini to transform the Fascists from a street gang into the new leaders of Italy.[40]

In an event largely unreported in the press,[41] Mussolini, a former soldier and journalist, founded the Fascist movement in March 1919 when he invited all pro-war revolutionary groups (many of whom already called themselves Fascists) to join the League of Combat. The soldiers had come back from the war to find that inflation was rising, pay was stagnating, and their jobs had disappeared as unemployment soared. Egged on by revolutionary socialists, the number of strikes climbed, and so did riots. In the chaos, the nationalists talked about a coup d'état, and foreign ambassadors cabled their governments warning them that Europe would soon have another red revolution on its hands.[42] Mussolini's background as a journalist meant that he knew a thing or two about propaganda, and the story he sold to these soldiers was simple: he wanted to make Italy great again. In tactics that would be copied by Hitler, his paramilitaries, the Blackshirts, terrorized his opponents, amplifying the chaos and allowing Mussolini to represent himself as the strong man who could restore order, even though he was to blame for much of the pandemonium.

Faced with this deteriorating situation, in 1921 Italy's unstable coalition government invited the National Fascist Party to join them—and Mussolini's journey to absolute power had begun. In October of the following year, thirty thousand of Mussolini's black-shirted thugs marched on Rome. Their goal was to intimidate King Victor Emmanuel III into asking Mussolini to form a new government. And it worked. The king balked at declaring a state of emergency, the army let the Fascists into Rome, and Mussolini at the age of thirty-nine became the youngest prime minister of Italy.[43] By the end of the year, the Fascists had seized control of the machinery of government. Over the next three years, Mussolini dismantled the democratic structures of Italy. In October 1926, he felt secure enough to make himself dictator, giving himself the title "Il Duce."[44]

It must have crossed Nobile's mind that his family had lost everything in one regime change. Were they about to lose everything again? The omens didn't look good for him. Yet like many educated people in the 1920s, he would go on to admire Mussolini for his ability to get things done. Indeed, his ambition to explore the North Pole by airship would depend on Mussolini's ability to do precisely that. Nobile was proud of his nation, had private audiences with the pope, and developed a good relationship with the king. Other than that, he never appeared to take much of an interest in politics. The fact that he didn't sup-port the Fascist Party appeared to be less a statement of belief than a sin of omission; however, it would leave him dangerously exposed in the knife-in-the-back politics of Mussolini's Italy.

"IF WE WANT TO trace the origins of the struggle that some years later were moved against me then you need to go back to the years 1919–1922," Nobile wrote years later with the benefit of hindsight.[45] It is hard to tell whether he was referring to his clash with Crocco, or to the rise of the Fascists.

The Italian state had to quickly sell off the "infrastructure of war"—and speculators rushed to buy at ridiculously low prices the workshops and warehouses that were no longer needed for the war effort.[46]

Nobile, however, had started to sell his airships overseas successfully—and to design new models.[47] Such success at-tracted an alliance of hungry industrialists and corrupt air forces who knew an opportunity to make money when they saw one. They offered to reward Nobile very generously for lubricating the transfer of the factory from the state into their grubby hands.[48]

Nobile fought off one attempt to sell off his state-owned factory in 1919, despite being urged by Colonel Giulio Cos-tanzi to "give up the big struggle against private enterprise."[49] Was he going to face another after that? Or did the Fascists have other plans for him and his factory now that they had their hands on the levers of the state? The engineer didn't have to wait too long to find out.

He had to cut short his promising work with Goodyear in the United States when immediately after the Fascists seized power in 1922 he started to receive warning letters from a friend at home. "My dear Umberto, it is with the utmost urgency that I ask you to hasten back to Rome before it is too late. Your enemies are more active than ever" and "My dear Umberto, your life's work is endangered by the ambition of certain fascists."[50]

To Nobile, much of the trouble he now faced could be firmly placed at the door of one man: his former master, now competitor, Gaetano Arturo Crocco, who wanted Nobile's new N-class airship to fail in order to replace it with his own design of airship. Since the crash of the *Roma*, Crocco had morphed, in Nobile's imagination at least, from mentor to backroom villain, who used the bureaucracy of the Fascist state to frustrate his rival's plans. Crocco wanted to build his own superior dirigible—and felt that Italy could only afford one airship man: himself.[51]

Then Italo Balbo arrived.[52]

Balbo had already publicly declared, "There is no room for prima donnas in the Italian Air Force"—a statement that seemed to be aimed at one man: Nobile. Balbo was a different league of villain from the engineer Crocco.[53] A charismatic street-fighting, cigar-chomping Fascist leader brought up amid the faded Renaissance glories of the northern Italian city of Ferrara, by the age of fifteen he had already led his first strike, launched his career as a journalist, and volunteered to liberate Albania from the Turks. Since Mussolini's March on Rome in 1922, this man had had his hands on the levers of power, and his instinct was to eliminate anyone and anything in his path.[54] His goal was nothing less than to restore the status of his family, who used to be aristocrats and generals but who, because of misfortune, were now schoolteachers.[55] And whereas Mussolini was prone to bluster, Balbo was an action man.* Quickly, Balbo harnessed Nobile's "usual adversaries" to support his nefarious plans against the airship designer, such as launching attacks on him. Luckily for Nobile, his allies had enabled him to join the Italian air force in 1923, believing that the ranks of the military offered him some kind of protection.

In 1924, Balbo wanted to rebuild the Italian air force around his ego and with two wings—and Colonel Umberto Nobile and his airships were in his way. On September 28, 1924, Nobile opened the newspaper to discover his airship described in an editorial of a government-controlled newspaper as "so incompetent it could not even cross the Apennines."[56] Attacks in other newspapers and speeches followed. In December of that year, the accusations grew more serious, and they too could be traced back to one man, Balbo. A report to the chief of aeronautics by General Giuseppe Valle, a veteran airship pilot, accused Nobile of being a socialist whose factory was filled with "red laborers" and of refusing government support for his projects because he would be unmasked as a leader of the anti-Fascist resistance.[57]

---

* On June 28, 1940, Balbo would pay the ultimate price for his bravery by being shot down accidentally over the front lines at Tobruk in Libya by his own men (Claudio G. Segrè, *Italo Balbo: A Fascist Life* [Berkeley and Los Angeles: University of California Press, 1987], 399). The reasons for Balbo's death remain suitably mysterious for such a man (Segrè, 403). Few people believed the official explanation that he had crashed during an "enemy bombing action." How could such a highly experienced pilot and war veteran die like this? The British didn't help matters when they announced that he had not been killed in combat. Rumors spread that he had died fleeing to Egypt to set up an alternative government in exile—or that Mussolini had him killed to eliminate an obvious rival.

Forewarned by an insider worried by the increasing illegality of the Fascist Party's actions,[58] Nobile was able to address these charges himself and be cleared of them by January 1925, before they were made public. However, he must have known one thing for certain: Balbo would not fail a second time. Nobile's only protection would be to make sure that whatever he did next would be a triumph for Mussolini.

HUGO ECKENER'S ZEPPELINS WERE conceived on the battlefields of the American Civil War. Count Ferdinand von Zeppelin was the Prussian aristocrat whose name is synonymous with that of the airship. Born in 1838, the count, like many young men with Prussian blue blood running in their veins, became an army officer, keen to learn the skills of modern warfare—and in the 1860s there was only one place to go to do this: the killing fields of the Civil War. In 1863, the young count traveled to the United States in the hope he would be given permission to observe the Union Army at war. Fate was on his side. Zeppelin impressed President Abraham Lincoln when they met, and he quickly found himself attached to the Army of the Potomac in Virginia. Military observers weren't supposed to fight, but he couldn't resist, and more than once Zeppelin got into a scrap with a Confederate from which he was lucky to escape with his life. Wisely taking a break from the war, the count decided to explore the St. Louis River and the Mississippi by steamboat and canoe with Native American guides, and it was on the last leg of the trip that he stopped in St. Paul, Minnesota.[59] St. Paul was the capital of Minnesota and the last place to unload boats coming up the Mississippi River.

Just outside the International Hotel in downtown St. Paul,

the famous itinerant German balloonist, Professor John Steiner, was offering tethered rides in his balloon for $5. Professor John H. Steiner (as he called himself) was one of the most colorful and daring characters in the history of aviation.* He emigrated from Germany when he was seventeen and quickly established himself as a daring aeronaut. During the Civil War, Steiner helped pioneer the military use of aviation: it was from his balloon that he was able to observe Union artillery barrages were falling short of a key Confederate position. Aeronauts in the Balloon Corps were rebellious figures who were civilian employees of the army—and Steiner was no exception. He would regularly clash with army commanders who couldn't see the potential of the new technology, and he left the army at the end of 1862 to tour the length and breadth of the country with his balloon, which is how he ended up in St. Paul.[60]

Unable to resist, the count (who must have heard of Steiner already and enjoyed talking in German) handed over his money and, at the age of twenty-five, made his first flight in a basket between six hundred and seven hundred feet above the ground. It was then, beneath the envelope of Steiner's tethered balloon, that Zeppelin had his vision of the airship that would make his name. "While I was above St. Paul I had my first idea of aerial navigation strongly impressed upon me and it was there that the first idea of my Zeppelins came to me,"

---

* It was Steiner's attempt in 1857 to be the first to fly across Lake Erie to Canada that helped make him famous. Bad weather forced him to abandon his balloon by jumping into the lake, but the wreckage of the balloon was later found in Canada (Chris Bateman, "That Time a Giant Gas Balloon Dazzled Toronto," blogTO, October 19, 2013, https://www.blogto.com /city/2013/10/that_time_a_giant_gas_balloon_dazzled_toronto/).

he later wrote.[61] Eleven years later, he outlined his idea for his very large airships in his diary.

Finally, in 1890, when he retired from the Prussian army at the age of fifty-two, he was ready to begin the design work for his very first airship, the LZ-1. It dwarfed in size the two- or three-man airships that pioneers such as Gaetano Arturo Crocco would build. The first zeppelin took to the air for a twenty-minute flight in 1900. Over the next ten years, Zeppelin built five more airships, funded variously by the state lottery, mortgaging his wife's estates, and even by a public collection. He convinced civil and, more slowly, military authorities to take his ideas seriously. Kaiser Wilhelm II even awarded him the Order of the Black Eagle, the highest award for chivalry in Prussia.*

By 1909, many of the larger German cities, including Frankfurt, Cologne, Munich, and Dresden, were clamoring for the count to build bases for the world's first airline within their boundaries.[62] This airline was known by its initials, DELAG, which stood for Deutsche Luftschiffahrts-Aktiengesellschaft (or German Airship Travel Corporation). Three years later, the first zeppelin lifted off from Airship Harbor Frankfurt, which would in the end eventually become Frankfurt Airport, the busiest airport in Germany.† By the outbreak of World War I

---

* Steiner didn't fare so well after his encounter with the count. His last mention in a newspaper was in 1875, where he was credited with 315 balloon flights. Rather nicely, a 1989 patent by Boeing for an improved method of generating hydrogen referenced one of his patents (Sarah Hopkins, "America's Champion Aeronaut in the Civil War: Daredevil Balloonist John H. Steiner," *Military Images*, Autumn 2015, https://militaryimages.atavist.com /americas-champion-aeronaut-in-the-civil-war-autumn-2015).

† DELAG built Airship Harbor Frankfurt on the old Rebstock estate west of the city. The manor house became the headquarters for the airline

in July 1914, DELAG's zeppelins had transported an astonishing 34,028 passengers on 1,588 flights over 107,208 miles (172,535 km) in 3,176 hours.

Commercial air travel wasn't the only vision that the count had for his airships. A German postcard from 1909 depicts the explorers Cook and Peary fighting over who reached the North Pole first, even though both their "flags" are in the wrong place; high above them a zeppelin hovers, and Count von Zeppelin plunges the German flag into exactly the right spot.[63] In 1909, Zeppelin set up the German Arctic Zeppelin Expedition with the intention of using his rigid airships to explore the Arctic.[64] The count investigated the northwestern coast of Svalbard with two ships (but no airship) for preliminary testing. Alas, despite the German emperor's brother being a member of the expedition,[65] government funds weren't forthcoming, and the plan was shelved.[66]

Like France, Italy, and Britain, the Germans had assembled fleets of dirigibles for reconnaissance, antisubmarine patrols, and aerial bombardment during the war, but the German High Command took aerial warfare to a new level. In January 1915, the era of "total warfare" is said to have begun when German airships unleashed what has been called the first Blitz on England (the bombing of other cities in Europe had actu-

---

("Rebstockpark—History with a Future," *Rebstockpark*, July 2003, https://www.rebstockpark-ffm.de/rebstock_e.htm). The current Frankfurt Airport opened in 1936 to service the boom in commercial aviation, with airships such as the *Graf Zeppelin* and the *Hindenburg* based to the south of the airport. Zeppelin Museum Zeppelinheim is located near where the zeppelins used to take off and land and in the residential estate built for the ground and flight crews ("Information on the Museum," *Zeppelin-Museum in Zeppelinheim*, April 16, 2021, http://www.zeppelin-museum-zeppelinheim.de/html/en_museum.html).

ally already started). No one had ever experienced anything like this before. It must have seemed like "science fiction."[*][67]

The zeppelins in the skies over Britain quickly earned the name "baby killers" for good reason. Three pupils of Trinity School, all from one family, were asleep on the night of October 13, 1915, when a German zeppelin dropped seventeen high-explosive bombs on the county town of Croydon (now a borough of London). Brien, ten, was dead when the rescuers reached him; Roy, fourteen, died on the way to the hospital; and Gordon, fifteen, passed away in hospital. The zeppelin was midway through its circular flight over the Channel to spread terror across the south of England, a population still without effective defenses against this terrifying threat. Six other civilians were killed in their beds in Croydon that night and fifteen wounded.

By the end of the war, there had been more than fifty airship raids responsible for around six hundred dead and fourteen hundred wounded in towns across Britain. That 75 out of the 115 zeppelins that had targeted the United Kingdom were damaged or destroyed would have been little consolation to the bereaved of these attacks.[†]

Count von Zeppelin died in 1917, and Hugo Eckener, a former journalist and economist and now an airship promoter, succeeded him as manager of the Zeppelin Company. Eckener,

---

* In H. G. Wells's novel *The War in the Air* (1908), German airships fly over the Atlantic to launch a surprise attack on New York, destroying landmarks like Union Square and Broadway.

† Ironically, the vulnerability of the zeppelins to ever more advanced British air defenses led Germany to develop a fleet of large long-range bombers that could reach London or Manchester; the British then reciprocated with the development of their own bomber fleet. Large long-range planes would be the airship's deadly rival in the future.

who helped to train the crews of the zeppelins used to bomb Britain, believed that the future of the zeppelin was in commercial air travel.[68] In the years after the end of the war, and before the Allied powers put a stop to it, he was able to build on the count's achievements in airship design. The company's *Bodensee* flew a regular scheduled service between Friedrichshafen and Berlin, which took its well-heeled passengers four to nine hours, compared to eighteen to twenty-four hours by train.[69] In the autumn of 1919, the *Bodensee* flew for 532 hours, on 103 flights, carrying 4,050 passengers over a total distance of 32,300 miles (50,000 km).[70]

Eckener's hopes that the Zeppelin Company would be allowed to return to making airships like this for passenger travel and scientific research rather than war were soon dashed. The *Bodensee* was seized by the Allies and handed over to Umberto Nobile's men in Italy.

Neither was there much hope that the Treaty of Versailles prohibition on the construction of these giant airships in Germany would be lifted. The actions of the German High Command had turned the zeppelin into a symbol of exactly the kind of German nationalism and militarism that was blamed by many for causing World War I. It also meant that few European politicians—especially the British—were keen to see these giant German ships over their cities again. It is easy to understand why.

Despite this hostility, somehow Eckener persuaded the Allied powers to let him build a large intercontinental airship to satisfy Germany's requirement to make further reparations to the United States. Even though the dirigible would be for use by the US Navy, the British would agree to this on one condition, that the new zeppelin would be designed solely for civilian use. This was quite a coup for Eckener because the ZR-3 was a huge zeppelin six times the size of one of Nobile's airships. In October 1924, the former journalist then flew it across the Atlantic in three days to widespread acclaim. US president Calvin Coolidge even called the ZR-3 (USS *Los Angeles*) an "angel of peace," the flight marking a rapprochement between Germany and the United States.

It wasn't just Nobile who had problems with Fascists. Hugo Eckener now needed to persuade the politicians of Germany and its former enemies to let him build his next airship, the *Graf Zeppelin* (named after Count von Zeppelin). The new ship would be even bigger than the ZR-3. It would be designed from the outset to be a transoceanic passenger-carrying aircraft. (The ships after that, he hoped, would be even larger still.)

Peaceful Arctic exploration would be, the airship promoter thought, the perfect pitch to convince the politicians.[71] Unfortunately, when Eckener began his tour around central and eastern Europe to raise money for his airship, the adulation he received really didn't help his airships-for-peace campaign. The German minorities trapped in these countries at the end of the war rallied to the symbol of the zeppelin—as they would soon do to Hitler. In Prague, the public rally in Eckener's honor in May 1925 was so big that the Czech daily *Národní Politika* called it a "nationalist provocation." At the university in Brno, German nationalist students held their own beer-hall rally, singing "Deutschland über Alles." In an awful premonition of the future, at the same time they excluded pro-democracy and Jewish students.[72]

Now Eckener made a desperate bid. He sent his own telegram to ask Amundsen to collaborate on his plan for a polar zeppelin.[73] However, there was only one person Amundsen wanted to hear from in the summer of 1925, and that wasn't Eckener; it was Nobile.*

ECKENER'S WASN'T ALONE IN his vision for transoceanic airships. The British R-34 airship had flown across the Atlantic and back again in 1919, which marked the first transatlantic flight by an airship and the first east–west transatlantic flight by an aircraft of any kind.† Following the success of the R-34, the famous British armaments firm of Vickers proposed a long-distance passenger- and mail-carrying airship called the *Trans-Oceanic* and a similar, medium-range airship, the *Continental*. Croydon Aerodrome, the United Kingdom's first major international airport and one of the world's first civilian airports, built an airship mast ready for the beginning of commercial airship services.[74] On paper, proposed airship passenger routes soon crisscrossed the continent. Unfortunately, this hectic activity achieved very little in practice. It turned out that after

* The story of Eckener's attempt to woo Amundsen is told in the pages of the *New York Times*. First, on June 21, 1925, "Hints at Zeppelin Trip: Eckener Hints at Zeppelin Trip in Co-operation with R. Amundsen." Then on June 23, "Zeppelin Bid for Amundsen: Eckener Asks Explorer to Co-operate with New Expedition." Then, finally on July 12, it seemed that Eckener had gotten his man—"Zeppelin Flight to Pole Assured: Amundsen and Eckener Will Meet This Month to Complete Their Plans." But he hadn't.

† There were many other flights like this. On September 14, 1922, the US Army airship C-2 made the first transcontinental airship flight, from Langley Field, Virginia, to Foss Field, California, under the command of Major H. A. Strauss.

the war there was little real appetite for expensive, revolutionary, and risky new technology—certainly, the postwar recession hadn't helped either—and the Croydon mast was taken down after only one airship had twice used it.

By 1924, the recession was over, and Eckener's flight across the Atlantic later that year in the world's first truly intercontinental airship helped supercharge plans that were actually already in motion. In the United Kingdom, the fires of the state-owned Royal Airship Works[75] at Cardington in Bedfordshire had gone out after the peace in 1918. Now they were lit once more. In its Hangar 1, the huge super-streamlined British airship the R-101 began to take shape, with all the resources of the British Empire behind it. At the desks of Whitehall, civil servants drew up plans for an Imperial Airship Service.[76] Just as some of its dominions were becoming restless and America more of a competitor,[77] a fleet of giant airships bigger than the world had ever seen would be the belt that tied the British Empire together, along "all-red routes," with London at its center. The sleepy Bedfordshire village of Cardington, about fifty miles north of London, was set to become the Heathrow Airport of its day. A huge new mooring mast was built with powerful steam engines capable of holding on to one of these giants without the huge ground crew needed by even relatively small airships like Nobile's N-1. "Small" is of course an understatement—Nobile's airship was nearly half as long again as today's Airbus superjumbo. The mast had a passenger elevator in it to allow travelers to board the airship in comfort.[78]

Meanwhile, 170 miles away to the north in Yorkshire, Vickers built its own streamlined design, the R-100, on a more limited budget, at the former Howden naval airship base. The huge airship hangar (once the largest in the world)[79] had been abandoned, partly demolished after the war when the price of scrap metal meant that it was not worth finishing the job. Barnes Wallis, one of the leading aeronautical engineers of the day (and designer of the bouncing bomb used in the famous "Dambusters" raid in World War II), was to design and build the airship. Wallis would be followed as chief engineer by an Australian by the name of Nevil Shute Norway, who would go on to cofound the famous British aircraft manufacturer Airspeed in a garage in York (and, as Nevil Shute, was the acclaimed writer of novels, including *A Town Like Alice* and *On the Beach*).

The British government had ordered two designs of giant intercontinental airship for the Imperial Airship Service in the mistaken belief that it would get "double the amount of innovation" from the competition between the two teams. Instead, it got double the trouble. The race, soon labeled as the socialist airship versus the capitalist airship, quickly lived up to its branding. The rivalry between the two teams became destructive, fueled by the knowledge that only one of the designs would be chosen, by the perception that Whitehall clearly preferred their own design, the R-101, and by accusations that Wallis's team was building an airship that was a "rehash of German methods" rather than a genuinely innovative, patriotic British design.[80] Shute became convinced that the Cardington team was hiding flaws in its own design.*

---

* Shute wrote about the rivalry between the two airship design teams in his biography, *Slide Rule*. His account has been used to illustrate the reasons why governments shouldn't be involved in projects like this. Recent research has found that there were more contacts between the two teams than previously thought (Peter Davison, "The R.101 Story: A Review Based on Primary

Oblivious to the infighting, across the empire engineers went out to scout locations for airship mooring masts, giant hangars, and all the facilities one would expect to find in a modern airport. Mooring masts were built in Montreal, Alexandria, and Karachi. A giant hangar was constructed in Karachi.[81] Land was purchased in South Africa near Durban and in Mombasa, Kenya, for potential mast sites, and a mast-head was actually manufactured and shipped down to Cape Town.[82]

Despite the rivalry, in 1930 passersby would have been amazed, and politicians delighted, by the sight of the two huge silver airships with R-100 and R-101 in black letters on their sides that filled the sky above the village of Cardington.[83] The amazement may have turned quickly to frustration for locals when they found the country lanes blocked by the day-trippers and journalists who had pulled over to take photographs of the scene.[84] If they were lucky, they may have caught a glimpse of the visiting dignitaries on the coaches that pulled up at the base of the huge mooring mast and disgorged their passengers into the lift that would take them up to the airship docked above.[85] Oxford was even brought to a standstill when the R-100 hovered over the city's dreaming spires while it was on a training flight.[86]

The growth in the size, expense, and ambition of airships meant that they had now become symbols of national pride and prestige, especially as they found themselves caught in the watchful eyes of a more rapid-fire new global media and dependent on capricious politicians for their future. What was

Source Material and First Hand Accounts," *Journal of Aeronautical History*, Paper No. 2015/02, https://www.aerosociety.com/media/4840/the-r101-story-a -review-based-on-primary-source-material.pdf).

forgotten amid all the hullabaloo was how few airships had actually been built compared to the number of planes, and even their trickiness to fly. In reality, the airship had yet to evolve beyond the prototype stage.[*]

Government support often brought with it a hidden danger: secrecy. Whatever the limitations of lighter-than-air flight, the airship industry, divided by national rivalries, became reluctant to share lessons among its members, and this impeded both innovation and safety.[87] "In spite of the number of years' start that the airship had over the aeroplane, little real progress had been made," wrote Lieutenant Colonel W. Lockwood Marsh, renowned airship expert and fellow of the Royal Aeronautical Society, in 1930, "partly, perhaps, because practically all development had been in the hands of Governments, and there had not, therefore, been much opportunity for the exchange of ideas. Even where private firms were involved the same spirit of secrecy prevailed, and, consequently, each type was proceeding on parallel lines by a process of trial and error, so that each was able to learn nothing from the other, and they were all prone to make the same, or similar, initial mistakes."[88]

---

[*] This still holds true of airship projects today. "The most modern airships now are roughly equivalent in evolutionary terms to the wooden biplanes flying at the start of the First World War," says Dr. Giles Camplin, chairman of the Airship Association and editor of the Airship Heritage Trust journal, *Dirigible.* "What few people realize today is how few airships there have actually been since the first attempt to make a balloon 'dirigible' in 1784. Roughly 1,200 have taken to the air . . . compare this surprisingly small number with the hundreds of thousands, if not millions, of fixed-wing aircraft that have flown since the Wright Brothers demonstration at Kitty Hawk in 1903."

HUGO ECKENER'S ZEPPELIN FLIGHT across the Atlantic in the ZR-3 in October 1924 had shown the world that his vision for a commercial transatlantic passenger service by airship, faster than the swiftest Cunard ocean liner and nearly as luxurious, was possible. It also showed how airships like his could revolutionize transportation again, much like the stagecoach, steam engine, and ocean liner had done over the past three hundred years.

Then, in October 1928, the *Graf Zeppelin* made its first transatlantic demonstration flight. It flew from its home base of Friedrichshafen, Germany, to Recife, Brazil, faster than the elderly ships on the route could manage, and offered a more luxurious service to boot.[89] Three years later, commercial services began between Friedrichshafen and Rio de Janeiro, with onward connection to Buenos Aires by conventional passenger plane. At the height of the service, the *Graf Zeppelin* was leaving Germany every other Saturday. The four-day flight meant that the airship would transport freshly cut Christmas trees to the German communities in Brazil and Argentina.[90]

In 1936, the larger and more powerful *Hindenburg* began the world's first scheduled commercial air service between Europe and North America. This time the zeppelin wasn't competing against elderly steamships but state-of-the-art liners, and still it was faster. The two and a half days' service of the *Hindenburg* beat the RMS *Queen Mary*'s four days, and the *Queen Mary* was the fastest liner of the day.[91] While the *Hindenburg*'s 50 to 75 passengers were a tiny number compared to the hundreds aboard an ocean liner, the next generation of airships that were already on the drawing board would take as many as 150 passengers.

Travel by airship was for the few rather than the many, as was the case for nearly all commercial aviation in those days. Flying from Germany to Rio de Janeiro in 1934 cost $590 (roughly equivalent to $11,000 today), so this meant that only minor royalty, A-list celebrities, and business leaders could realistically afford it. The British proposed a similar passenger fare of £150 (nearly $13,000 today) for their Imperial Airship Service route to India. Yet even these sky-high fares weren't enough to cover the running costs of the airship. It was the revenue that the airships earned from freight and airmail that kept them afloat. The *Graf Zeppelin* could deliver South America–bound post much quicker than any ship. On one flight across the Atlantic, the *Graf Zeppelin* carried fifty-two thousand postcards and fifty thousand collectible envelope covers to Brazil, each stamped with the *Graf Zeppelin*'s very own stamp.

The hydrogen-filled envelope of a transcontinental airship may have been massive, but the passenger compartment was tiny. While the passenger accommodation on the *Graf Zeppelin* was in the gondola of the airship, typically on the giant airships like the R-101 or the *Hindenburg* the box-like compartment was sealed off from the explosive hydrogen by a thick hermetic seal and held in place by light crisscross metal girders, similar to the parts found in a children's toy construction set.[92] The passengers would board a German zeppelin via steps that were lowered down to the ground below the compartment, or a British airship via a passageway through the hydrogen envelope that stretched from the passenger compartment to the nose. It was perhaps best not to think what was on the other side of those thin passageway walls. To descend, when passengers reached the nose of the ship they would find that a gangway had been lowered onto the platform of the giant mooring mast. There they would be whizzed down to the ground in a lift that looked as if it belonged in an old Victorian mansion block in London. The steam from the steam engines in the power house obscured the view downward. A bus would be waiting for them at the bottom.[93]

Every new form of transportation takes its first design cues from the last. The railroads initially looked to the stagecoach for the design of their passenger cars (some were little more than stagecoaches on wheels), and the first motor cars were based on the horse-drawn carriages of the gentry. The great passenger airships took their cues from the ocean liners, with a touch of the safari thrown in. In turn, the early commercial airplanes took theirs from the airships.

Inside the passenger compartment of the airship was everything that you would expect to find on an ocean liner: a mixture of lounges, dining rooms—with branded plates, bowls, and cups—and promenades with a view over the ocean. In one design, there was even a dance floor. Passenger cabins with one, two, or four bedrooms might be found on one, two, or sometimes all three floors, depending on the airship.[94]

It was impossible to escape the hierarchical, class-based traditions of the day, even a thousand feet high in the sky. The kitchens, stores of food and drink, linen cupboards, and crew's quarters were found on the lowest deck. The chefs may have come from hotels like the Ritz,[95] but the kitchens looked as though they belonged in a railroad dining car. It was a tight squeeze to fit two chefs into the kitchens of those great airships, let alone the three or four that the menu demanded.

The furniture, of course, had to be extraordinarily lightweight and also fireproof. On the German airships, this meant state-of-the-art aluminum Bauhaus-style furniture—and the world's first aluminum piano, covered in pigskin and weighing 356 pounds. The *Graf Zeppelin* had the world's first all-electric aluminum kitchen.[96] On the British airships, it meant safari-inspired dining chairs and tables, and wicker armchairs that looked like they belonged on the veranda of the Imperial Delhi Gymkhana Club in colonial India.

On board these giant ships, there was little to do other than eat and drink, and the lack of pressurization on these airships meant that passengers could actually taste the food. (It also meant that the airship had to fly so low that the passengers could see the faces of fishermen on the trawlers they flew over.) And there was plenty of food. The *Graf Zeppelin* had a larder stuffed full of "turkeys, live lobsters, gallons of ice-cream, crates of all kinds of fruits, cases of American whiskey, and hundreds of bottles of German beer."[97]

The drinks menu offered fifteen different kinds of wine and sparkling wine, as well as a selection of mixed drinks, divided into such categories as "Sours, Flips, Fizzes, Cobblers, and Cocktails." In addition to classic cocktails, the bar offered "the LZ 129, made with gin and orange juice, and the Maybach 12, the recipe for which has been lost." Despite this abundance, on the first flight of the *Hindenburg* the bar ran dry of gin, a spirit more popular among the American than the German passengers.[98]

The cuisine on the zeppelins, though, was distinctly German. The ships were meant to project Germany to the world, after all. The breakfasts are still recognizable to anyone who has stayed in a German hotel: "German coffee, tea, milk, cocoa, bread, butter, honey, preserves, eggs (boiled or in cup), Frankfurt sausage, ham, salami, cheese, and fruit." The dining menu was dominated by "very, very, German food" like meat and vegetables covered in rich sauces, which American passengers complained about.[99] The British airships would have no doubt offered steak and kidney pudding and fish and chips.

However, these luxuries were not for the crew of a polar airship in 1925. The men would eat tinned pemmican, the high-tech survival rations of its day. Originating among the Native North Americans, pemmican was a highly nutritious dried mixture of meat, fat, and vegetables that few Europeans would choose to eat, but which could mean the difference between life and death.

NOBILE PROBABLY ALLOWED HIMSELF a smile as he reviewed Amundsen's telegram.

On the desk in front of him was the telegram message from the great Norwegian explorer. It requested that the two men meet for an "important and secret conference in Rome."[100] As he read the telegram, at his feet was Titina, the white mongrel dog who went on most flights with him.

Nobile oozed a quiet confidence—even cockiness. The engineer's unravaged good looks and smart military uniform were evidence of years spent with his wife, Carlotta, and daughter, Maria, in southern Italy rather than alone on the polar frontiers. But first and foremost, he was an engineer and airman who lived under Mussolini's regime, which worshipped aviation. Illustrations of large aircraft regularly appeared in Fascist propaganda—flying over the Coliseum, over Africa (uniting Italian East Africa with Italian Libya and the motherland), and later in formation over the Atlantic, linking

Rome, New York, and Chicago—and the men who flew them, like Francesco De Pinedo, were portrayed as supermen.[101] (The Italian aviator caught the attention of the world, and of Mussolini, when he flew from Rome to Tokyo in a seaplane.* Il Duce declared him the "Messaggero d'Italianità" [messenger of Italy] and "a winged envoy to all parts of the world.")

By 1925, Nobile had fully escaped from Crocco's shadow. He was now one of the leading aeronautical engineers in the world in his own right, the director of the SCA in Rome, a position he had ascended to at only thirty-four years of age.[102] The airships he built were exported all over the world.

Today Ciampino is Rome's second airport. Back then, it was at the center of Nobile's sprawling empire of offices and factories. At the heart of the complex was a single German-built hangar, which had been dismantled and shipped to Italy as part of Germany's war reparations. Inside the massive building was Nobile's sleek prototype airship: the N-1, which for now acted as King Victor Emmanuel's personal luxury sky yacht for use in exploring Italy's Mediterranean territories. It even came equipped with its very own throne. And right next to it was the *Bodensee*.

Now Nobile knew that Amundsen's request to meet could mean only one thing: that the Norwegian wanted to buy an airship. And the Italian just happened to have one for sale, for a mere $100,000.[103] What's more, if Amundsen needed an air-

---

* De Pinedo wasn't in a particular rush. The eleven-thousand-mile (18,000 km) flight out took the pioneer aviator four months in 1925. He made forty-eight stops with lengthy layovers in Melbourne and Sydney, where there were populations of Italian immigrants. De Pinedo flew a more direct route back and took only twenty-two days. In so doing, he helped open flight paths across the Middle East and Asia.

ship, then he would also need an airship captain to fly it. Who better than the man who designed and built it?

COLONEL UMBERTO NOBILE WOULDN'T be the first Italian to try to reach the North Pole, but he would be the first to attempt to fly to the pole. Nobile was convinced that by using a modern airship he would avoid the disasters like the one that had befallen the North Star (*Stella Polare*) expedition in 1899–1900.

Like Nobile, Umberto Cagni was an ambitious young man. In 1881, he was commissioned as an officer in the Royal Italian Navy, and he rose up quickly through the ranks to captain; he was close to experienced mountaineer Prince Luigi Amedeo, cousin of the king of Italy. In July 1899, the prince, Cagni, and eighteen other Italian and Norwegian men landed on Franz Josef Land, which had only recently been discovered. Their goal was to establish a winter base on the desolate archipelago and then to reach the North Pole in the spring. Needless to say, events did not turn out as they planned. Their ship, the *Stella Polare* (after which the expedition is sometimes called), was severely damaged by the ice, and the prince was badly injured by frostbite. The expedition doctor had to amputate two of the royal fingers.

With the prince now unable to lead the push to the North Pole, Umberto Cagni was given command of the dogsled party, and in March 1900 they headed north over the sea ice. The four men had three months of supplies with them on the sleds. But misfortune struck again. Going over the ice was much harder than they had bargained for—three men who were sent to support them even died—and Cagni realized that the North Pole was beyond their reach. Instead, when they were sure that they had set a new record for reaching the farthest point north (beating Nansen's 1895 record by twenty nautical miles), they planted the Italian flag and began the long, arduous, and dangerous trip back to base camp. They reached Franz Josef Land in June 1900, twelve days after their supplies were supposed to have run out.* Nobile could hardly do worse than this.

THE ARRIVAL OF THE telegram from Amundsen wouldn't have come as a total surprise to Nobile. The Norwegian had already met with Mussolini the year before to talk about his plans to explore the Arctic by air.[104] Amundsen had taken a test flight on the N-4 as well, during which trip he must have met Nobile. Riiser-Larsen certainly had.[105]†

Nobile, though, could have worked out that Amundsen was desperate even without having met him, simply by reading the daily papers regularly. It was common knowledge that the Norwegian's last two attempts to fly over the North Pole had failed—the first ending in humiliation and bankruptcy, the second in his near death. Years earlier, the celebrity status of Scott of the Antarctic and the resulting newspaper coverage of his plans had meant that Amundsen was able to learn nearly all the details of his rival's intended means to reach the

---

* Today Michele Pontrandolfo follows in the "footsteps" of Cagni and Nobile. The Italian explorer has completed over fifteen polar expeditions, many solo. He reached the geomagnetic pole unaided in 2006.

† Hjalmar Riiser-Larsen, Amundsen's right-hand man and pilot, had even been for a flight with Nobile in his two-man experimental airship, *Mr*, which was known as the smallest airship in the world and looked rather like a bathtub attached to a balloon (Garth James Cameron, *From Pole to Pole: Roald Amundsen's Journey by Flight* [Stroud, UK: Pen & Sword Discover, 2013], 93).

South Pole well before Scott had even set foot in the boat that would take him to the Antarctic, while Amundsen kept his own plans secret.[106]* Ironically, it was now Amundsen's own need for publicity that gave his new rivals the information they required.

The Italian airship designer also knew that there were multiple explorers and engineers keen to beat Amundsen to the North Pole. *Polar Science Monthly* would call the race to be the first to fly from Norway to Alaska "the most sensational sporting event in human history."[107] The *New York Times* described it as a "massed attack on the polar regions."[108]

Despite Amundsen's rebuff, Eckener was talking about a polar expedition with Amundsen's archrival, the great Fridtjof Nansen. The airship Eckener was planning for the mission would be the *Graf Zeppelin*. It would be the biggest dirigible in the world. (The International Association for Exploring the Arctic by Means of Airships [called "Aeroarctic"] was founded in 1924 with Nansen as president to promote such a venture. There were fifty-eight German scientists, fifteen Scandinavians, and a number of scientists from other nations.[109])

There was a rival German bid as well. Wartime airship hero Captain Walter Bruns (and now secretary-general of Aeroarctic) had plans to build his own airship to explore the Arctic. His aircraft was based on the designs of the Schütte-Lanz company, a nearly defunct German competitor to the zeppelin design. However, Eckener had no intention of letting anyone breathe new life into his former rival.

---

* Scott shouldn't be seen as a victim of the newspapers. He used publicity as a way to "clear the field, to cause any potential rivals to back down, to in effect lay claim to the pole, as his and Britain's territory" (Stephen R. Brown, *The Last Viking: The Life of Roald Amundsen* ([Boston: De Capo Press, 2012]).

Eckener wasn't the only one facing a rival bid. General Valle, one of Italy's most experienced airship pilots (and coincidentally the man who led the attack on Nobile in 1924), proposed an all-Italian expedition to the North Pole. The airship, codesigned by Nobile's former mentor, Gaetano Arturo Crocco, would be much larger than Nobile's existing design, which his Italian and German competitors dismissed as too small for the Arctic conditions. They had even enlisted Italy's nationalistic poet-hero Gabriele d'Annunzio to help promote their effort, which he achieved spectacularly by demanding to be left at the North Pole in order to disappear like a legend.[110]

And despite Amundsen's own loss of confidence in airplanes, explorers such as Richard E. Byrd and George Hubert Wilkins were convinced that the rapidly improving reliability of planes meant they could achieve what the Norwegian had failed to.

If Amundsen thought he was only buying an airship and hiring a pilot when he invited Nobile to Norway, then he had another thing coming. Whether the Norwegian liked it or not, Nobile had all the trump cards in his hand—and the Italian rather liked the sound of the Amundsen-Ellsworth-Nobile expedition.

But a careful look reveals something else lurking behind Nobile's apparently confident reaction to Amundsen's telegram. Fear.

It is easy to imagine that on the jotting paper on Nobile's desk, one name was written down and underlined: Italo Balbo.

Three

"Do You Know Where Amundsen Is?"

IT IS EASY TO imagine that Amundsen rolled out the map on the large wooden table in front of the men. That with his finger he traced two dead-straight lines, the first one from Rome to Kings Bay, the second from Kings Bay right over the North Pole to Point Barrow on the north coast of Alaska and one million square miles of unexplored territory.[1] The long, straight lines could mean only one thing: Amundsen was going back to the Arctic. And this time, he was going back in an airship.

It was July 25, 1925. Barely a month after the explorer had escaped the icy jaws of death, Amundsen was making fresh plans to head back to the frozen desert.

He hadn't traveled to Rome for a secret meeting with Nobile. He had made the Italian come to him. In Norway, he had assembled the group of men who, he hoped, would deliver him the final three records of his career: the first aircraft to fly to the North Pole, the first aircraft to fly from one side of the Arctic Ocean to the other, and the first man to have visited both poles.

The men weren't meeting in the ornate surroundings of the Grand Hotel in Oslo—the hotel where Amundsen had held the dinner celebrating his last triumph, the race to the South Pole, and perhaps an appropriate location for the planning of such an ambitious new expedition. Instead, they were meeting in secret, hidden from the prying eyes of rivals, deep in the Norwegian woods at Uranienborg, Amundsen's Norwegian home.

Uranienborg was like a little bit of Switzerland dropped into the forests north of Oslo. Built from the profits of an earlier expedition, the modest Alpine-style villa was named after Uranienborgveien,[2] the district of Oslo where he grew up after his family moved from the coast. At the end of its garden lapped the waters of Bunnesfjord, the inlet that flows into the great Olsofjord, up which Amundsen had flown in triumph just weeks before and down which the great Viking longships may have sailed to discover Greenland and put one foot in the New World.

Amundsen was too obsessed to give up on his dream of a polar flight; too broke to walk away from one last great payday before he retired. His dream of plunging the Norwegian flag into a newly discovered land that he could claim for the Kingdom of Norway must have been so close that he could almost feel the biting cold on his cheek. The Norwegian was even willing to do a deal with a dictator he detested and a regime he hated, to buy the airship he needed.

Amundsen's nickname of "the Governor"[3] was a clue to the kind of leadership style he favored and the personal loyalty he expected—and received—from his men. Norwegian polar explorer Hjalmar Johansen had been driven to suicide by Amundsen's humiliation of him on the expedition to the South Pole after he challenged the Governor in front of the men.[4]

The problem was that this time Amundsen had little choice over who to have on his crew. He had to have Nobile and his men.

Near Amundsen in the room at Uranienborg was Amundsen's loyal lieutenant, Hjalmar Riiser-Larsen. He was a giant of a man, a skilled pilot, a first lieutenant in the Royal Norwegian Navy, and Amundsen's right-hand man, a position that he would for now fiercely protect against any rivals.

Riiser-Larsen had become the hero of Amundsen's failed attempt to fly to the North Pole when, somehow, he had nursed the last flying boat up into the air and back to Svalbard; for a dangerous moment, his fame threatened to eclipse his leader's. Riiser-Larsen was also the only Norwegian who knew anything about flying an airship. There had been a number of proposals for regular passenger airship services from Britain across the North Sea to Norway and the Netherlands, which in the end amounted to little more than scouting aerodromes around Edinburgh, looking for a suitable base.[5] Riiser-Larsen's proposal was the exception. He had actually traveled to Britain to train as a pilot for one such scheme.[6] Now he wanted to fly Amundsen's airship. Unfortunately, Nobile was in the way,[7] and for now at least, he had to settle for second-in-command.[8]

Millionaire Lincoln Ellsworth was next to the giant Norwegian. Ellsworth's dad may have footed the bill for Amundsen's failed attempt to fly to the pole the year before, but he had earned his spurs out there on the ice. He just needed one more expedition to complete his transformation into a true explorer. Ellsworth's father had died while his son was fighting for his life on the ice; now his inheritance would help to buy the airship for Amundsen. The cost that Amundsen had to pay was to have Ellsworth as coleader.

The American was very suspicious of Riiser-Larsen and perhaps even jealous of his relationship with Amundsen. More personally, Ellsworth blamed him for pushing ahead with the publication of the official book about Amundsen's polar flight the year before without allowing him to contribute to it.[9] Ellsworth's grudge would worsen when Riiser-Larsen took the position of navigator on the flight that was his "dream job" despite the millionaire's inexperience.[10]

Next to Ellsworth around the table was Colonel Umberto Nobile, the personal representative of Mussolini at the talks. Like Amundsen, he spoke English, but he didn't speak the first language of the Norwegian half of the crew.

Amundsen and his men were willing to take a gamble on the flight being a success. Their ethos was simply: "One set off—and hoped to come back."[11] If the airship crashed, they were ready to attempt an incredible feat of derring-do to get them out of trouble. These men seemed unworried about the prospect of a crash and then a year spent walking back to civilization over the sea ice. Indeed, they contemplated such an outcome with a degree of macho nonchalance that bordered on glee and recklessness.

But for Nobile, the flight had to be a success. Any outcome that didn't see the airship reach Alaska would be a failure for him, for his family, and for Fascist Italy.[12] The guns would not be fired in salute if he had to trudge on foot to safety across the ice.

There were also three unseen presences at the meeting. If the Italian could feel Italo Balbo's breath on the back of his neck during the meeting, he never admitted it. Also haunting the room was Rolf Thommessen, the editor-in-chief of the nationalistic Norwegian newspaper *Tidens Tegn* and a supporter of Norway's adventures in Greenland; he was also president of the Aero Club of Norway, which sought to promote aviation and train the pilots of the future. Like numerous educated Europeans at the time, Thommessen was an admirer of Mussolini and what he was trying to achieve in Italy.[13] He was also an astute political operator. Unlike Amundsen, Thommessen quickly realized how strong Mussolini's hand was in the airship negotiation.

The final invisible presence was the Fascist leader himself. Mussolini's bombastic style may have been easy to ridicule, but his achievements were not. He was a man who was able to build a movement from the streets up and then use this power base to bully his way into government and establish a totalitarian state. Whatever you thought of Mussolini, he certainly knew how to get what he wanted.

Il Duce had just taken the unusual step of making himself minister of aviation as well as prime minister. In 1919, he had learned to fly.[14] His goal was to revitalize the Italian aviation industry—in which he had had some success already—and further shape the broader perceptions of his Fascist regime. The polar flight had thus become his pet project.

By choosing to buy Nobile's airship, Amundsen had fallen into Mussolini's web. If he hadn't already realized that Il Duce wanted to use his expedition for the glory of Fascist Italy, he soon would.[15]

At the meeting at Uranienborg, Nobile argued that the airship for sale, the N-1, was just a prototype. It was too small, he felt, for such a flight, and too heavy, because it had been built from off-the-shelf components. But the second airship of the new N-class would have the range for the polar record attempt—and this ship was already under construction.[16]

Amundsen made it clear that he wouldn't—and couldn't—wait. The expedition had to leave the following spring if he was going to stand a chance of beating the other teams in the race to fly to the other side of the Arctic Ocean.

Nobile then made an offer that, according to Amundsen, "astonished" him and "which in the light of later events was most significant":[17] the N-1 free of charge for the expedition if it flew the Italian flag.

Amundsen immediately sensed danger in the offer. The explorer may have realized that Mussolini wanted to use the polar flight just as he, Amundsen, had used other people in the past. Or perhaps in Colonel Nobile he sensed a threat to his own leadership of the expedition.

Maybe it was something else. Norway was the nation of the Arctic; the snow and ice were its empire. If the expedition discovered any new land, whose land would it be if the airship was flying the Italian flag? Mussolini's?

Or his reluctance to fly under the Italian flag may have come down to something much darker. In the eyes of many northern Europeans at the time, the Italians were "wops" or "dagos," little better than Africans in the racial hierarchy of the 1920s. How could the brave men of the north be seen in a ship flying the Italian flag?

Then again, Amundsen's wariness might even have stemmed from something more basic: money. The Norwegian didn't want a competitor who would vie for a share of the publicity—and profits—on his last tour before he retired. Amundsen and Ellsworth's exclusive contract with the *New York Times* alone was worth $55,000.[18]

Whatever the reasons, Amundsen's no seemed to do the trick, and Nobile appeared to quickly retreat. In fact, the Norwegian agreed to buy the airship from the Italians for $75,000. It was $25,000 less than Ellsworth had originally anticipated

and less than it cost Nobile to make, a sign of just how important the propaganda value of the mission was to the Italians.
The Aero Club of Norway would control it. They also agreed
to help the Italians build the bases and masts it needed along its
route to Svalbard, as well as buy all the special polar equipment
they needed.[19] The polar flight would be called the Amundsen-
Ellsworth polar expedition. The airship would be reregistered
in Norway. It would fly the Norwegian flag and be named the
Norge. The people of Norway quickly saw it as their ship.

Amundsen would naturally be the expedition leader, Ellsworth the coleader, and Riiser-Larsen second-in-command
and navigator. Nobile would be the captain of the airship,
which in their eyes was little more than a hired hand.[20] But in
the eyes of the world, and in the age of the aeronaut, he would
be the leader of the expedition.

Despite his own reservations, Nobile agreed to convert the
N-1 from a luxury passenger airship designed to fly around
the Mediterranean Sea into an airship capable of flying over
the North Pole. The key, he believed, was to reduce its weight.

The composition of the crew of the airship was an argument that would be finally settled only when the *Norge* lifted
off from Kings Bay in May 1926. Amundsen had said that he
wanted men who could handle themselves in the Arctic. This
meant they could only be Norwegians and other northern Europeans who could ski, handle a gun, and manage a husky
pack. The problem for Amundsen was that there was only a
single Norwegian—Riiser-Larsen—with experience of flying
airships, and while Nobile hadn't led an expedition before, he
knew that he wanted men on board with the technical skills
to fly the airship and carry out scientific research. For Nobile,
huskies and sledges belonged to the past.

The result in August was an apparent compromise.[21] There would be equal numbers of Norwegians and Italians on the crew, and the Norwegians would be trained to fly the airship instead of adding Italian crewmen. That left the two non-Italians on board to play the part of the neutrals. However, the Swedish meteorologist Finn Malmgren and the Russian radio operator Gennady Olonkin had worked with Amundsen before.

Nobile kept pushing Amundsen for more Italians—and Amundsen and Riiser-Larsen pushed back. In doing so, Amundsen broke one of the cardinal rules of Arctic survival that he had always lived by. There was no longer a single leader and a united expedition. Indeed, members of the Amundsen-Ellsworth expedition were divided by their loyalties to two very different leaders in Amundsen and Nobile.[22]

They even disagreed on the nonhuman companions: Nobile's dog, Titina, who went on every trip with him, would end up "a stowaway" on the airship. To Amundsen, a husky was a real dog. He could never understand the Italian's love for this handbag-size creature. Its only use, he mused, would be as something to eat if they crashed in the Arctic.[23]

"DO YOU KNOW WHERE Roald Amundsen is?" demanded chargé d'affaires Ove Vangensten as he stormed into Lise Lindbæk's office in the Royal Norwegian Embassy in Rome.[24]

It was hard not to notice Lise Lindbæk* in Rome in 1925. She was a bright, independent, and charismatic young woman

---

* Lindbæk would go on to become widely acknowledged as Norway's first female war correspondent. Her reputation, established by covering Mussolini's rise to power, was cemented by her coverage of the Reichstag

who the year before, at the age of nineteen, had decided that the best place to study archaeology was on the other side of Europe rather than in Norway. Before she decided to move to Rome, the young Norwegian had first traveled to Naples by herself. While she studied the ancient Roman ruins of the city, she paid her way by working as a freelance journalist recording the rise of fascism in Italy for the newspapers back home in Oslo.

Upon moving to Rome, Lindbæk quickly became good friends with two Swedish men who were in the same guesthouse. The young Norwegian and the two men, a retired foreign correspondent for a Swedish newspaper and a scientific researcher, quickly became inseparable companions. Together, they would eat dinner and argue over Italian literature late into the evening. Lindbæk would describe this period of her life as "euphoric."

Rome, though, was a more expensive city than Naples. A job as a temporary typist in the embassy over the hot summer months was the ideal way to fund her stay, and her lack of skills didn't appear to be a problem.[*]

Now it would appear that her quiet summer job had dramatically changed into something else. As a result of being in the embassy in the middle of Mussolini's capital, she would be on the inside of one of the greatest aeronautical feats of the time.

"You realize that there's a great hubbub in the press;

---

fire in Berlin in 1932 and then the Spanish Civil War. Tragically, she would commit suicide at the age of fifty-six.

[*] "What exactly would it involve?" Lindbæk asked her interviewer. "The only thing we require is that you can type," he replied. "That suits me perfectly," she said. "As I can't type, I'll just have to learn." (Lise Lindbæk, *Brennende Jord* [Oslo: Tiden,1958], translated by Kathryn Pearson, 49.)

they're claiming that Amundsen has come here to Rome undercover!" added Ove Vangensten, now slightly calmer than when he had first entered her office. "Now they're absolutely certain that he's preparing to fly to the pole again, this time in an Italian aircraft. And I know nothing about it!"[25]

The diplomat's departure to search for Amundsen would leave Lindbæk the only member of staff on duty. Realizing that she would be left in the rather unlikely position of being in sole charge of the embassy, he bowed deeply and appointed her the "Official Representative of the Kingdom of Norway for the day."[26]

Soon after he left, a servant came in with a calling card on a silver platter. She instantly recognized the name on it: Hjalmar Riiser-Larsen.[27] It turned out that Vangensten had gone on a "wild goose chase": Amundsen and Riiser-Larsen were staying in secret at a hotel near the station and now needed the help of the embassy to finalize negotiations.

For days after that, the embassy was under siege by journalists who had been tipped off about Amundsen's plans for a new expedition and the fact that it would involve an Italian aircraft. What they didn't guess was that it was one of Colonel Nobile's airships.

While the journalists were waiting outside, Lindbæk was working day and night inside in near-total secrecy to translate the contract for the expedition from Italian to Norwegian. Feeling guilty about the late nights, Vangensten asked her whether there was anything they could do to make up for it.

"I said that I would very much like to meet Amundsen, since I had had so much to do with the whole business," she wrote in her memoirs, "and so Vangensten sent me round to the hotel with the finished contract. 'But be careful!' he warned. 'There are journalists lurking everywhere on the sly and the news mustn't get out yet.'"[28]

Lindbæk held the contract tightly to her chest as she walked to the hotel where Amundsen was staying, hoping that none of the journalists inside would notice the envelope that had the words "Royal Norwegian Embassy in Italy" written in Italian on the front. When she opened the door to the hotel, "the foyer was in uproar, with people buzzing around like flies in a jar."

Riiser-Larsen rushed over to her.

"Have you seen Amundsen?"

"No, I've never even met him," she replied truthfully.

"It's absolutely desperate. Mussolini's waiting, you see," explained Riiser-Larsen. "He wants to grant us an audience. He's sent round two cars, completely out of the blue. But Amundsen's nowhere to be found!"[29]

Over in one corner stood a short dark-haired man who, in contrast to the surrounding chaos, was completely calm. He spotted her, and smiling, introduced himself.

"I see you've come from the Norwegian Embassy. You must be waiting for Amundsen? My name is Colonel Nobile."

"Oh, so you're the gentleman who is going to fly Amundsen to the North Pole," Lindbæk said, fascinated.

"How on earth do you know that? I didn't think the secret was out yet."[30]

At that moment, she wrote, "An elegant-looking Amundsen strode in through the revolving doors in a light summer suit with a carnation in the buttonhole, swinging his cane nonchalantly."

The porter rushed over to Amundsen to explain that Mussolini was waiting.

"Is he indeed?" said Amundsen. "Well, this young lady is waiting for me."

He came straight over to Lindbæk and asked, "May I invite you to take tea in the Palm Garden?"[31]

Amundsen, Nobile, Riiser-Larsen, and Lindbæk went into the Palm Garden, leaving the hotel staff worried about their jobs, as outside the two waiting cars honked their horns impotently. It was half an hour later that Amundsen finally set off for Palazzo Chigi, Mussolini's headquarters in Rome.

"That was the first and last time I met Amundsen in person," Lindbæk wrote. "The next day, Nobile sent me a message."[32]

ON SEPTEMBER 1, 1925, the contract for the expedition was signed in Rome between Benito Mussolini, for the Italian government, and Rolf Thommessen of the Aero Club of Norway.

With the ink still fresh on the paper and a friendly atmosphere between all the men, Nobile took Amundsen and Riiser-Larsen for a drive to the seaside town of Ostia for a swim. Amundsen was in the front and his colleague in the back seat.

Amundsen wasn't used to Italian driving, despite his earlier trips to Rome.[33] Even when he was an elderly Roman in the 1970s, Nobile would think nothing of throwing his car across three lanes of traffic to be able to park outside his apartment in the center of the city.[34]

Now Nobile repeatedly accelerated around the blind bends in the road and braked suddenly when faced with an oncoming vehicle. In the front, Amundsen was terrified. It was the "wildest ride"[35] he had ever taken in any ship, plane, or car. In the back seat, the heroic pilot Riiser-Larsen was muttering to himself, "We shall certainly all be killed."[36] Amundsen turned around in his seat to ask Riiser-Larsen in Norwegian—even though all three of them spoke English—whether he could do something to stop this lunatic killing him.[37]

Some people would have laughed about the drive when they arrived safely back at their hotel in Rome, but not Amundsen. Nobile's performance made Amundsen question his suitability to pilot the expedition. "His whole performance on the round trip was evidence of his extreme nervousness, erratic nature, and lack of balanced judgment," Amundsen reflected.[38] Yet when he asked Riiser-Larsen whether they were wise to trust their lives to Nobile when they were in the air, the Norwegian pilot answered calmly that "some of the steadiest, coolest aviators I know are men who on the ground have exactly this fellow's nervous characteristics. But the moment they take to the air . . . their nervousness disappears, and they are as cool in an emergency as anyone you could imagine."

Amundsen would still come back to the drive to Ostia in the years to come: "Nobile on several occasions during the actual flight across the Arctic revealed exactly the same qualities he had exhibited at the wheel of the motor car, and more than once put us in peril of disaster."[39] For his part, years later Nobile would describe the drive as being to Anzio, not Ostia—and as being perfectly normal.* It has been said that Nobile and Amundsen may have been in the same Fiat, but they were in two different worlds.

---

* Twenty years later, after the fall of fascism, Umberto Nobile still felt he had to defend the way he drove his Fiat that day and would say that the problem was simply that the Norwegians drive very slowly (interview with Ove Hermansen, Copenhagen, June 2018).

After the handover, Ellsworth and Amundsen left for the United States, Ellsworth to settle his affairs after the death of his father, Amundsen to embark on his speaking tour by train. While he was in New York, he took advantage of the opportunity to continue his affair with the beautiful, but married, Bess Magids, whom he had met in Alaska.

Amundsen was a master of spin. With Lincoln Ellsworth as coleader, the Norwegian was planning to head to the States for what he hoped would be a lucrative publicity tour. In every interview or public lecture across the country, Amundsen planned to emphasize the importance of the American's role even though the airship would fly under the Norwegian flag.[40]

Rather than a failed attempt to fly to the North Pole, his unsuccessful polar flight in the flying boats became a reconnaissance mission for the airship expedition that he had always intended to launch.

"Dirigibles are better suited to Arctic travel than airplanes," he told reporters when he arrived in New York, "because experience shows when a plane once descends near the pole it is a great hazard as to whether it will ever rise again.

"It was only a year ago that the German airship flew over to this country," he added. "It is going to be a great means of communication in the north. There will be regular routes over the North Pole. It may take a few years, but it is bound to come."[41]

Later, he would even say, "I'd rather fly over the Arctic Circle in a dirigible than over Ohio. Air conditions are better."[42]

The visit to the United States was possible because unlike the painstaking preparations for his earlier expeditions, this time, a more elderly Amundsen assumed the arrangements would be done for him. All he had to do, he thought, would be to turn up next spring for the flight itself.

Amundsen had made a big mistake.

AMUNDSEN MAY HAVE IMAGINED that with the signing of the contract, the negotiations were over. He was wrong: they hadn't even truly begun.

Personally, Nobile had no intention of playing the part of the hired help; politically, he couldn't afford to do so. But Amundsen couldn't afford to let him play any other part. He needed to be the leader of the expedition to sell his books and tickets for his speaking tour afterward.

Certainly, Nobile was attracted by the fame that would come from a successful flight. He must also have recognized that such a success would bring him one step closer to re-claiming the honor and wealth that his family had lost. And his credibility as an engineer was at stake. Nobile had already come under attack from critics in Germany and his rivals in Italy about the suitability of the N-1 for the harsh conditions it would encounter at the North Pole.

Despite his appointment as commander of the N-1 by royal degree, this concern was amplified by the fact that Nobile's pilot's license only qualified him to fly prototype airships: in other words, he was a test pilot.[43] In Italy, there were more experienced dirigiblists than Nobile, better suited for a flight through the extreme conditions of the North Pole, men who were not shy about sharing their worries about Nobile. Nob-ile also knew that his belief that the airship was better suited to polar exploration than heavier-than-air aircraft challenged Italo Balbo's conviction that the opposite was true.[44]

Then there were his jackbooted masters, who again had made it clear that the reputation of Fascist Italy was at stake. And Mussolini's first act as air minister in 1925 was to sign the agreement for the sale of the N-1.[45]

It was increasingly clear that failure in his mission would make the life of Nobile and his wife and daughter very difficult in Mussolini's Italy. The whispers about Nobile's anti-Fascist sentiments had never gone away.

In fact, there were elements of truth to many of the criticisms. Nobile's urging of Amundsen to wait until the next N-1 had been constructed had been good advice disregarded. His airship was little more than a prototype. It was not powerful enough to stay in the air with the amount of snow and ice that some experts were convinced would accumulate on its envelope during the flight. It could not carry enough fuel for the distances a polar flight would have to traverse. The N-1 had, after all, been designed for a king to float around the Mediterranean in, not as a Viking longship to explore the frozen north. Shouldn't, then, his critics whispered, Gaetano Crocco's plans for an airship six times the size be given the go-ahead instead?[46]

The campaign against Nobile reached a new level of viciousness when his critics warned Mussolini that the safety of the expedition was at risk. The airship, they implied, was not capable of crossing the Apennines and Nobile was an incapable and incompetent navigator. They thought that the Aero Club of Norway should find itself a new pilot. Then Mussolini added to the pressure Nobile was feeling when he quickly appointed General Alberto Bonzani, the assistant secretary of aviation, to investigate and make sure the airship was delivered to the Norwegians on time.[47]

Despite challenges like this, or because of them, Nobile took advantage of Amundsen's absence in America to strike. In January 1926, he traveled to Norway to sign his pilot contract with the Aero Club of Norway. He agreed to be paid 40,000 kroner as the pilot of the airship. The very next day he asked for an extra 15,000 kroner, explaining to the presumably bewildered Norwegians that otherwise he would have to fulfill a lucrative contract with the Japanese that he had already signed. He had, in fact, agreed to go to Japan to the Imperial Navy to teach them how to fly the airship they had purchased—a commitment he obviously knew about before he had signed the Norwegian contract the day before. The implication was clearly that he wouldn't be able to fly the *Norge*. Needing a pilot, Thommessen could only agree to his demand.

Nobile then asked to be allowed to contribute as an author to the book that would be published upon completion of the expedition. He felt that his contribution to the trip would be significant enough to warrant his collaboration with Ellsworth and Amundsen on what would almost certainly be a bestseller. Thommessen agreed that Nobile could contribute a section on technical aspects of the flight. Ellsworth also agreed to this by telegram from New York. He then changed his mind, but his second telegram, he was told, arrived too late. The deal had been done.

For his part, Amundsen was determined to do everything he could to stop Nobile from profiting from the expedition. The sale of the book was a key way that Amundsen intended to make money, and if Nobile contributed to the book, the implication would be that he had played an important role in the expedition and would be entitled to a share in the profits from the book.[48] "We never intended and did not consent to his [Nobile's] sharing of any financial returns from the expedition," Amundsen wrote. "Our money had paid for the expedition, including the payment of a salary to Mr. Nobile. If there were to be any financial returns, as from a book or other writings, certainly we had no reason to share these returns with Nobile."[49]

The president of the Aero Club of Norway, on behalf of Nobile, extracted one further concession from Amundsen and Ellsworth—and perhaps the most important. He persuaded them in last-minute face-to-face negotiations in Rome to agree that the name of the expedition be changed from the Amundsen-Ellsworth polar expedition to the Amundsen-Ellsworth-Nobile expedition.

Amundsen later claimed that he had been promised by Thommessen that Nobile's name would be added to the name of the expedition only because "local pride was running high" in Italy. Thommessen, according to Amundsen, feared that the hosts might not let the airship leave the country if they didn't agree to it. He also claimed that they had been promised that no publicity would be given to Nobile's name once the N-1 was outside Italy–another "promise" that Thommessen would break.[50]

Nobile appeared to have gotten everything that he wanted. But when it came time to set off, the message from Amundsen could not have been clearer. When Nobile boarded the *Norge*, he would find only two velvet-covered safari-style chairs fixed to the floor of the cabin.[51]

Four

"She Would Be There to Inform on Us"

BY THE TIME THE contract to buy the airship was signed in September 1925, Nobile had only six months to prepare the vessel for the Arctic Circle. He was going to need all the help he could get. "Can you stay here and work for us this winter?" Nobile asked Lise Lindbæk when she visited the airship factory at his request. "We're going to need someone who can speak Norwegian!"

"And didn't you say that you're also doing a bit of journalism?" he added. "You will be given priority for Norway for anything to do with the polar expedition."[1] Lindbæk's insider accounts of the preparation for the expedition would appear almost daily in the Norwegian press.

Nobile then made the young Norwegian archaeology student, journalist, typist, translator, researcher, and perhaps even informer,* an offer she couldn't refuse. She could study the Roman Forum and Etruscan memorials with the newly

---

* Tor Bomann-Larsen, *Roald Amundsen*, trans. Ingrid Christophersen (Stroud, UK: History Press, 2011), chap. 41, Kindle, describes how Nobile's wish to have Lindbæk fly on the *Norge* to Svalbard as his interpreter was seen by the Norwegian crew members as probably an attempt to "infiltrate their

founded Swedish Archaeology Institute in the mornings if she spent the afternoons translating at his airship factory. For this, Nobile would offer her a full day's pay.

He clearly needed her—and she was clearly attracted to him. "I liked my boss immensely from the outset and never had any reason to revise my first impression of him," she would later write. "He was forty years old and looked dazzling, almost classically handsome with his pure, noble face and his brown eyes, which sparkled beneath a high, flawless forehead.

"I soon discovered that his employees would gladly go to the ends of the earth for him; no one ever grumbled about unpaid overtime and you never heard a dissatisfied word or querulous remark."[2]

Nobile's giant factory was situated right on the Tiber River in Rome, on whose banks Romulus and Remus, mythical founders of the city, were abandoned as children. The factory employed about four hundred people and covered a huge area. "There were a forge and a carpentry workshop, sewing rooms, large halls for various kinds of metalwork, warehouses, and office space."[3] The complex even had its own landing strip and small hangar. (Nobile would sometimes forgo this, liking to surprise his workers by landing his small experimental airship the *Mr*, "the smallest airship in the world,"[4] which he could fly by himself, right in the middle of the factory.[5])

From the factory, the components for the transformation of the *Norge* would be driven forty-five minutes to the giant hangar at Ciampino, where the airships were assembled. From

_____

ranks" with someone whose job was, according to Riiser-Larsen, to "inform on us."

the factory also, men and materials would flow to northern Germany, Norway, the Soviet Union, and as far as Kings Bay in the Arctic Circle to build the masts and hangar the ship would need.

In the factory, it was noticeable that few employees used the Fascists' "Roman salute" with the right arm outstretched and that Nobile himself never did. There were only one or two pictures of Mussolini up on the walls.[6] It might have been politic to have had a few more, given the allegations that were persistently attached to Nobile's name.

At first, the workers in the factory had difficulty getting used to Lindbæk's independent nature. "For them it was completely unheard of for a young woman to go home alone after nightfall, without a brother or mother to accompany them," she wrote. "Mothers stood looking shocked outside the factory, as they waited for their daughters at the end of the working day.

"But soon my colleagues just shrugged their shoulders and came to the sensible conclusion that all foreigners were just a bit mad, and after that I never had any problems."[7]

Nobile needed to make his airship as light as possible as quickly as possible. Every extra pound he and his workers saved meant that they could carry more fuel to travel farther, vital for the vast polar distances they were aiming to cross. Every pound saved also meant that more of the survival gear that the Norwegians insisted on, including rations, sleds, skis, and even collapsible boats, could be stored on board. Such equipment could mean the difference between life and death if they crashed on the ice.

Out, too, went the luxury fittings suitable for a king and the large gondola embedded under the airship. The gondola had been designed for royal sightseeing as well as the operation of the airship by a crew of four. In came a new, shorter cabin whose walls were more like those of a tent, its light metal tubing and thick fabric covering designed to save weight rather than keep the flight crew warm. (Despite the need to save weight, the king of Italy's throne remained looking out of the window.[8] Perhaps Nobile was dreaming of a triumphant return of the airship to Italy at the end of the expedition.)

When tests showed that the N-1 could lift 1,653 pounds (750 kg) more than was planned, Nobile added two extra fuel tanks. The weight saved by the alterations had one more benefit. It meant that he could install a powerful radio. A radio was vital to receive weather forecasts, or if there was an emergency—and, of course, for sending news reports out. (Ultimately, more than 150 telegrams would be sent on the first leg of the flight from Svalbard to the North Pole.)

"2,000 Mile Range for Norge's Radio," the *New York Times* proclaimed. Nobile Umberto wasn't the only world-leading Italian engineer. Guglielmo Marconi was born in Bologna in 1874. Through his endless experimenting, he developed the first effective system of radio communication. In 1899, he founded the Marconi Telegraph Company, which became the Marconi Company. In 1901, he successfully sent wireless signals across the Atlantic Ocean from Cornwall, England, to a military base in Newfoundland. Eight years later, he shared the 1909 Nobel Prize in Physics. His company went on to dominate the radio industry. He helped set up the British Broadcasting Corporation (BBC), and his technology helped to tie together the British Empire. Marconi married the daughter of a British baron.

Like Nobile, Marconi was an Italian patriot. He served in

the Italian armed forces in World War I, but unlike Nobile, he was attracted by fascism and became an enthusiastic supporter of Benito Mussolini and his regime. In 1923, he became a member of the Fascist Party and, seven years later, a member of the Fascist Grand Council. At Marconi's grand state funeral in Rome in 1937, the largest wreath was sent by Adolf Hitler.

It was therefore natural that the Marconi Company should build a special long-wave radio set for the N-1. The set had to have a range of one thousand to two thousand miles for the distances the airship was expected to traverse. It had to be carefully insulated to work in a wide range of temperatures. The parts were easy to reach and change because it was designed to be repaired by "a man working with half-frozen fingers."[9] There was also an added radio direction finder, which could locate the position of the airship by triangulating the signals of different radio stations.[10]

One of the most visible signs of the change to the original N-1 design were the insect-like antennae that now trailed behind the ship. Rather like the air turbine used as an emergency power source on airliners today, a little propeller was attached to the outside to generate power to charge the radio's batteries when needed.

At the front of the *Norge*, there was another visible change: a cone had to be fitted to allow the airship to be tied up—like a ship—to the forty-five-foot metal mooring masts that Nobile now had to design. The masts were needed to secure the airship on the ground, secure it in bad weather, and reduce the number of people required in the ground crew. They would also be vital to keep the *Norge* in one piece when it was on the ground, even in high winds. The Italians never had to bother with a mast for the N-1 in the comparatively calm Mediter-

ranean weather, so before Nobile could design them for the
Norge, he first had to travel to Britain to study those designed
by engineer Major George Herbert Scott.[11] The major had
commanded the British R-34 rigid airship on its flight across
the Atlantic and back again.

Scott had since spent much of his time designing the im-
posing two-hundred-foot mooring masts for the giant airships
that the British were building. Four of these huge structures
were being built across the British Empire. Each one looked
like a cross between the Eiffel Tower and a lighthouse, each
with its own forty-foot passenger deck, passenger lift, and
three powerful steam engines to haul in the airships. Seven
others were planned.[12]

Distracted by the demands of the expedition, Nobile hadn't
realized that the Norwegians were no longer sharing their decisions with him. When he did, it quickly became Lise Lindbæk's role to find out what going on. That began with taking
out subscriptions to the most important Scandinavian newspapers to translate the latest stories about the expedition.[13]
Nobile was also "very keen," she said, to have stories about
Amundsen's last expeditions translated. In addition, Lindbæk
was instructed to stay in almost daily contact with the Norwegian legation. This information sharing worked both ways.
After one particularly brutal bout of Fascist infighting, editors of Norwegian newspapers, including Rolf Thommessen,
asked Lindbæk to write regular news reports for them to be
sent to Oslo by telegram and post.[14]

In February, with a month to go before the handover of the
airship, the Norwegians arrived in Rome for flight training.
Gustav S. Amundsen, the nephew of the great explorer and
one of the reserve crew, was initially disappointed that the

Norge in its hangar looked smaller than he was expecting, but his spirits lifted when he spied the other dirigible lurking in the hangar shadows, the *Esperia*. He came away energized by having at last seen one of Hugo Eckener's famous zeppelins and other airships. Later Amundsen and the rest of his fellow Norwegians gaped when they saw an even more awesome sight: the *Esperia* flying over the city.

The Italians rolled out the red carpet for their guests from the north. On one of the test flights of the *Norge*, the airship flew so low over the ancient Roman rooftops that the Norwegians could see people staring excitedly up at them. The king himself flew on one of these test flights to demonstrate his confidence in Nobile—and, in private, warn him about the dangers of ice. On another occasion, they saw the silver *Norge* on its first night flight silhouetted against the dark sky, lit up from below by the sea of light from Rome. The Norwegians were even invited to a private audience with the pope. The awkward poses of the Lutheran Norwegians in morning suits were frozen forever in a picture taken at the time.[15]

But no amount of sightseeing could paper over the tensions between the Norwegians and the Italians, which threatened to explode again. Many of the Norwegians who had come expecting excitement and adventure instead found unexplained delays and boredom while they waited to be trained on the airship. The Norwegians must have suspected that the Italians were in no rush to train them while negotiations over Nobile's demands and the composition of the crew were still in progress. Many of them threatened to take the next train home to Oslo.[16]

Instead, Amundsen's right-hand man, Riiser-Larsen, proposed to Amundsen replacing the Italians when the airship reached its stopover at Pulham, Norfolk, on its way to

Svalbard, should they not toe the Norwegian line. The Norwegians could then be complemented by the supposedly more trustworthy Englishmen. If the coup didn't happen in Norfolk, then it could even happen when they arrived at Kings Bay, where there would be plenty of men loyal to Amundsen. The Norwegians could complete the flight to Alaska without the Italians if need be.[17]

A further complication was Nobile's "laughable" plan to have Lise Lindbæk on board for the flight to Svalbard. To the Norwegians, it was worse than merely challenging the natural patriarchal order. It was a ploy by Nobile to infiltrate their ranks. Riiser-Larsen told Thommessen, unwisely, "Omdal [a mechanic Lindbæk had befriended][18] told me he had heard the same thing: she would be there to inform on us."[19] The Norwegian pilot had forgotten—or didn't know—that his fellow countryman had been supporting Nobile in his negotiations with Amundsen and had Lindbæk reporting back to him almost daily.

Of course, Riiser-Larsen did have reason to worry about being "informed on." Yet despite his team's designs for a possible coup against Nobile, it would be Amundsen who would within a year be accusing Nobile of treachery.

At this point, neutral Finn Malmgren, the Swedish scientist on the expedition, gave the chance of the expedition's success as fifty-fifty.[20]

AIRSHIP HANGARS ARE SOME of the largest structures on the planet. Many of them are so large that clouds form at the top. Former airship hangars have found uses today as a film studio and even a tropical island holiday resort.

The hangar at Kings Bay wouldn't disappoint. "It was the probably the largest building in the world of its kind in 1926."[21] Its two huge wooden trestle-like walls dominated the bay, recalling the buttresses of a medieval castle clad in canvas. From certain angles it resembled an alien communications array. To build the hangar at Kings Bays would have been a miracle of engineering at any time. To build it over the Arctic winter of 1925–26 was doubly impressive. (Yet there was no choice: without a hangar, the expedition would have been impossible, because even tied to a mast, the airship would have been smashed to pieces by the powerful Arctic storms.)

The contract for the expedition had been signed only in September 1925. This left less than two months to get men and supplies to Kings Bay before winter set in, and the sea would freeze, cutting master carpenter Ferdinand Arild and his men off from the outside world.[22]

Cement, steel poles, and steel bolts came on the first ship. The second brought twenty-one thousand cubic feet of timber, fifty tons of iron, food and equipment for more than thirty men for three months, and even fifty-one gallons of brandy. If any component was forgotten, or tool broken, then there would be no replacement for another five months. The 108,000 square feet of French sailcloth needed to cover the hangar arrived early in the new year after the ice had started to break up.

To shift all this material from the quayside to the site of the airfield was no simple task. The men had to run a spur to the hangar site from the horse-drawn narrow-gauge railroad that connected the harbor to the mine of the Kings Bay Coal Mining Company. Power cables had to be run from the mine, which had its own generator protected from the weather, to provide the building site with electricity.[23]

Those constructing the facility faced snow so deep that the walls of the hangar would disappear under it, storms so strong that they threatened to tear the walls down, piece by piece, and permafrost so deep that today, builders in the Arctic Circle use jackhammers to open up the earth.

Then there were the low, low temperatures, at which concrete freezes and men lose their hands to frostbite. There was the twenty-four-hour darkness of the Arctic winter, which can drive men insane and make it impossible to work without electric light, at a time when most homes were still lit by gaslight. Making it all the more backbreaking, work on the hangar had to be done mostly by hand; there were only one electric saw and one drill on the site. Yet by laboring ten hours a day, seven days a week, the men had largely completed the wooden framework of the hangar by the middle of February.

"All who have seen the hangar at Kings Bay have been impressed and astonished," Amundsen and Ellsworth wrote. "It is a great work, accomplished under the most difficult conditions that such a building was ever erected under."[24]

ON MARCH 29, 1926, at the culmination of a formal ceremony in the hangar at Ciampino airfield, the Italian flag was lowered and the Norwegian flag raised. The airship now belonged to Norway.

In the audience were all the leading actors in the drama: Roald Amundsen, Hjalmar Riiser-Larsen, Lincoln Ellsworth, Rolf Thommessen, Colonel Umberto Nobile, Johannes Irgen (Norway's ambassador to Rome), and, not least, Benito Mussolini.

Theatrically, Mussolini grasped the Italian flag that had

been flying at the stern of the craft for the past two years, gave it to Nobile, and declared: "This is to be dropped on the ice of the pole."[25]

If anyone doubted the importance of the Amundsen-Ellsworth-Nobile expedition to the Italian Fascists, they just had to look at the pictures that were taken at the event. Mussolini may have worn a suit to the ceremony, but it was impossible to miss all the sharp military uniforms with their dangling medals and knee-high leather boots that were on parade.

On both sides of the airship, the name *Norge* was now painted in large black capital letters in place of *N-1*. Toward the tail of the great ship, *N-1* was painted in the same black letters. This was the new Norwegian registration of the ship, which coincidentally was the same as its Italian name. Amundsen complained that the airship was now flying with both its Norwegian and its Italian names and that the Italians had been allowed to paint the colors of their flag on the airship as well.[26]

In those days, planes were small enough to be shipped to Kings Bay, as Amundsen and Ellsworth had previously done. They were still simple enough to be reassembled by hand when the crates were unloaded. Given that Svalbard was beyond the reach of many aircraft, transport by sea for reassembling was the safest option.

An airship as large as the *Norge* was a different matter altogether, far too large and complicated to be shipped to Svalbard like an airplane. The only option was to actually fly it to the gates of the North Pole.

Rather than travel on the airship to Svalbard, Amundsen and Ellsworth had decided to journey to Svalbard by rail and ship, leaving Nobile in sole charge for the first forty-three-hour zigzag leg of the expedition, from Rome over the over the Tyr-rhenian Sea to the south coast of France, and on to Pulham in England, across the North Sea to Amundsen's hometown of Oslo, and then across the Baltic to Leningrad. The *Norge* would remain in Leningrad until the hangar on Svalbard was ready. Then it had to attempt the crossing of the Norwegian Sea to Kings Bay.

Amundsen would later try to justify their decision to travel separately—rather unconvincingly—on the basis that they were in it "for a trip over the unknown and were not inter-ested in seeing European scenery from the air, or in meeting crowds in England, Germany, and Russia."

But it would turn out that Amundsen had made a terrible blunder in his battle with Nobile. Amundsen felt that Nobile had "grossly mismanaged"[27] the flight by letting three jour-nalists and other guests on the flights to Pulham and Len-ingrad "for the mere notoriety of the experience," but it was a very canny move. At the start of the flight, the reporters who were covering it had no idea who Nobile was. By the end, they did. The tens of thousands of people who saw the airship fly over their hometown or city or on the ground—many of whom were newspaper readers and newsreel watchers—also now knew the name of Umberto Nobile.

"THE TIME IMMEDIATELY BEFORE the launch of the airship was hectic and I had less and less time to devote to archeology," wrote Lise Lindbæk, "as we were often working almost twenty-four-hour days at the airship factory. Couches were made up for several of us in our various offices and we kept having to stay there overnight."[28]

The flight to Svalbard was set to leave on April 3. That morning, even Mussolini turned up to see the airship depart, despite an assassination attempt on him the day before and the pain he was still in from the attack.*

Unfortunately, on the morning of April 3 Nobile had to pluck up his courage to tell Il Duce that the weather was too bad and that the flight needed to be postponed. As Mussolini was due to leave the next day for Tripoli, he embraced Nobile and said, "You will go—and come back victorious."[29] He would not see the launch on April 10, but his brother would be watching.

On board the *Norge*, there were also Major George Herbert Scott, who was there to help with the landing in England, Captain Mercier, a French airship officer who asked to fly with them in case there was a forced landing in his country, and an Italian journalist.[30] (Amundsen would later claim that the two other pilots flew the airship instead of Nobile.)

There was also a stowaway, recalled Nobile. "Besides the persons I have named we had on board, right from the start in Rome, a twenty-second who remained at her post all the way to Teller . . . someone who took up very little room and weighed practically nothing: Titina, ten inches high and twelve pounds in weight—that was all."[31]

Just before takeoff, Nobile made one more decision that enraged Amundsen: he told the Norwegian crewmen that they

---

* A well-to-do fifty-year-old Irish woman named Violet Gibson had shot at Mussolini and missed, injuring only his nose. Somehow the police managed to rescue her from being lynched by the mob, but they could never find a "why." Mussolini simply said, "Fancy! A woman!" She was later released without charge at Mussolini's insistence and deported to Britain. Gibson went on to spend the rest of her days in a mental asylum.

had to leave behind their fleece-lined flight suits that had been especially made for them in Berlin. The reason he gave was simple: they weighed too much. Although Nobile did obsessively monitor the weight of the crowded *Norge* for the whole flight, Amundsen was less concerned. At best he thought it was "a brutal lack of consideration on Nobile's part"[32] that the descendants of the Vikings had to fly in their ordinary clothes to the North Pole, in an airship without any heating and with their "teeth chattering." He noted that the Italians "appeared on the scene clad in magnificent fur coats and equipped with every other comfort of apparel," and to him, represented Nobile's unparalleled "arrogance and egotism."[33]

At 9:30 a.m. on April 10, Nobile gave the order: "Let's go!" With the Italian flag fluttering in the breeze from the cabin, the airship rose.[34] Her job over, Lise Lindbæk was left with a sense of anticlimax after the airship disappeared from sight.[35]

By the afternoon of the next day, the airship had reached what has been described as the "Cape Canaveral" of its day.[36] The great airship base at Pulham, Norfolk, made headlines around the world when the R-34 British airship ended the first-ever return flight across the Atlantic there in 1919—and then again when Colonel Umberto Nobile and the *Norge* stopped at the base.

Today the famous airfield is mostly plowed fields. The concrete foundations of its two huge hangars are nearly all that remains of what, at its height, was a large military base. Pulham had two huge hangars whose doors were so large that they had to be pulled open by an old World War I tank, and one small one. The base also had a sizable factory complete with belching chimney, a branch line from the mainline, its own narrow-gauge railroad, and a workforce of five thousand servicemen and civilians, a usefully large number of people who could be used as ground crew.[37] One of its gigantic hangars was later dismantled and moved to Cardington for the British Imperial Airship Service.

At Pulham, there were British and Norwegian political figures for Nobile and his passengers to meet and British bureaucracy to deal with. Upon landing, the crew had to clear customs and Nobile's dog had to be locked up in a "canine jail." After one of the Italians set her free, Nobile was told by the police, "Kindly keep the dog shut up! If she is found outside, we will be entitled to kill her and there will be a £200 fine." Titina quickly found herself in prison again.[38]

By then, the weather was so clear that Nobile considered flying straight up to Kings Bay. Luckily, before he could set off he was informed by telegram that the base and mooring mast at Vadsø were still not ready. Vadsø is a small town on the coast in the far north of Norway, close to the Russian border.

On Friday, April 13, they flew overnight to Oslo, with two additional journalists on board, including the Norwegian Fredrik Ramm. Planes met the *Norge* as it flew in from across the North Sea. Thousands of people stood in the squares and streets and even on the rooftops to look up at the ship as it passed overhead.

The *Norge* arrived in bright sunshine at the airship mast that had been built on the Ekberg flats on the southern side of Oslo, the foundations of which remain today. The king of Norway met the explorers at the mooring mast to see "our airship," as Nobile later noted.

Nobile then dined at the Grand Hotel with Thommessen— the hotel where Amundsen had his dinner to celebrate his victory over Captain Scott in the race to the South Pole. The

meteorologists Nobile met there warned him to leave immediately for Leningrad because the weather was going to get
worse.

That night, with searchlights illuminating the *Norge*, Nobile ordered, "Unhook!" which left the airship held only by a
thick hemp rope. "Slip the rope!" he then shouted, and the giant slowly rose into the darkness. Finally, "Cut!" and the ship
was quickly lost to sight above the mountains and fjords.[39]

Nobile and his crew, flying the *Norge* in the pitch black and
thick fog, near mountains and without radar (which would
not be developed until the following decade), achieved the remarkable feat of not crashing into one of the peaks that sur-
round the city.

After the airship crossed the Baltic Sea, the fog began to
lift. When it cleared, a snow-covered wooded plain with many
small lakes was revealed—but they had no idea where they
were. It could be Finland, Estonia, or Latvia. The radio goni-
ometer, a primitive method of direction finding by radio, and
the solar observations taken by Riiser-Larsen, the navigator,
were not giving accurate results.

Nobile ordered the airship to go lower. In his account of the
flight, Nobile wrote rather dismissively about Riiser-Larsen's
guess that the color of a mailbox that he could see and the direction of a particular stream meant that they must be in Finland.[40] Instead, Nobile ordered a message to be thrown down to
some astonished peasants that read—in Swedish, Russian, and
German—"What country is this? Finland? If so, raise your arms
in the air!" Despite their amazement at the sight of the aircraft,
the people failed to notice the message, and then confusingly,
the airmen saw a church that looked Russian. In the end, Nobile took the ship even lower so as to read the name of a nearby

railway station. They weren't in Finland. They were at Valga, on the border of Estonia and Lithuania—just a few hours away from Leningrad. Riiser-Larsen had been wrong.[41]

At 8:00 p.m. on April 15, they arrived at their Leningrad base. Less than twelve hours after their successful flight and landing, the *New York Times* headline shouted out: "The Norge Lands Safely at Leningrad Base after Battling Fog." Underneath, in smaller letters, was "Amundsen's Airship Arrives at Its Russian Hangar at 8pm after Long Delays" and, farther below that, "By Wireless to the New York Times On Board the Dirigible Norge of the Amundsen-Ellsworth-Nobile Expedition . . . By Fredrik Ramm."[42] "I was exhausted," Nobile wrote subsequently. "For 60 hours I had been awake, without closing my eyes for a moment. Good training, indeed, for the Polar Flight."[43]

Fredrik Ramm may have been Amundsen's favorite journalist, but now with the "Amundsen-Ellsworth-Nobile Expedition" in print before the eyes of the American people, no matter how small the typeface Nobile had won this round. He was clearly not the hired help.

After landing, Nobile was taken by sleigh to the old imperial palace at Gatchina to sleep. Gatchina was a luxurious spot for a nap. Before the revolution, the grand classical palace around forty miles to the south of Leningrad had been one of the favorite palaces of the Russian royal family, so much so that it had been called "the citadel of autocracy." Since then, it had witnessed the last stand of Kerensky's Provisional Government in 1917 and the defeat of the final advance of the White Army from Estonia in 1919. Today it is open to tourists.

Leningrad itself had been chosen by Nobile because it had a large wooden airship hangar left over from World War I.

Nobile had visited Leningrad four months earlier, in January 1926, and had reported that the structure needed a great many repairs, which were essential because it was the closest hangar to Svalbard that was large enough to house the *Norge*. The Bolshevik government agreed to repair the hangar at its own cost and had achieved the refurbishment on time.

In Leningrad, there was also the world-leading Institute of Northern Studies (now known as the Arctic and Antarctic Research Institute), housed in a former palace. In its ornate rooms Nobile had given lectures to its students, shared research, and cemented a firm friendship with its famous president, Soviet polar explorer Rudolf Samoylovitch, who had made his name on the Russian geological expedition to Svalbard in 1912 to investigate the archipelago's coal reserves. Like many of his colleagues, he would later be arrested and executed in Stalin's Great Terror.[44]

In the days that followed the arrival of the great airship, thousands of soldiers, students, schoolchildren and teachers, and peasants came to see the dirigible in its hangar. The young people asked plenty of questions; some simply wanted to see the Italian flag. But as more than a week passed since their landing, Nobile grew restless. The *Norge* was ready to fly again, but they seemed to be stuck in limbo.

The delay was due to a terrible blizzard that lasted two days and to the fact that the main group of Italian workmen had only arrived at Kings Bay on April 25. Impatient, Nobile sent a telegram ordering them to forget the mooring mast and focus on readying the hangar there.

The scale of the blizzard at Kings Bay on Svalbard made Amundsen wobble because an airship could be destroyed by such a powerful snowstorm. He had already arrived in Svalbard. He telegraphed Nobile to suggest that they postpone the flight until the summer when—"according to him," wrote Nobile disparagingly—"there would be less danger of ice formation on the airship."

"I was completely taken aback by this telegram," said Nobile later. "The opinion . . . was altogether opposed to the conviction of the experts on Arctic weather conditions; and even to his own previous declarations. In fact, if we were to postpone the flight by a month it would, in my opinion, be the equivalent of giving up."[45] The warming temperatures would in fact make it impossible for the ship to carry what it needed in the way of fuel to reach Point Barrow, Alaska.

Amundsen changed his mind again. Finally, Nobile received a telegram that told him the hangar and mast would be ready from May 4. Not wasting any more time, on May 5 the *Norge* set off for Kings Bay—thirteen days after it had arrived at Leningrad.

As the ship rose into the air, there was a great cry of "Viva l'Italia!" from the Russian soldiers. Their band played the Italian national anthem until they could see the great ship no more. In bright sunshine the airship then flew over the Winter Place and down the Nevsky Prospect at 700 feet.

At 6:15 a.m. on the morning of May 7, 1926, the *Norge* reached Kings Bay. Fears of the damp snow pinning the airship to the earth like a lead weight had proved unfounded. The *Norge* was greeted by the sailors of the Norwegian warship *Heimdal* playing Norway's national anthem. The hangar was decked out in the flags of the United States, Italy, and Norway.

Amundsen, Ellsworth, the captain of the *Heimdal*, and the other Italians were there to greet them too. Together with the sailors, they all pulled the ship down to a gentle crunch on a soft carpet of fresh snow.

"An unforgettable moment," Nobile wrote. "At last we had arrived at the gates of the North Pole."[46]

Unfortunately, the Amundsen-Ellsworth-Nobile expedition was not alone in Kings Bay.

Five

"The Most Sensational Sporting Event in Human History"

AT 6:15 A.M. ON May 7, 1926, the *Norge* arrived at Kings Bay. Nobile had never been this far north before. He had never been this cold before.

The wind hurled itself at him across the bay, its gusts like blades piercing his skin no matter how many layers of wool and leather he was wearing.

The mountains with their covering of brilliant white snow towered over him. They were—it was true—beautiful. But they were barren. There were no trees, no shelter, and certainly no other people. No man would last for long trapped out there. Not even a man like Amundsen.

The airship captain had never seen a landscape that was so breathtaking but at the same time so designed to kill. At least, he must have mused, though you might die alone, you would die with a stunning view.

It was almost with relief that he would have turned back toward the dirty black streaks that broke up the pristine snow behind him. Those dark marks were evidence of human industry and even a degree of safety in this brutal landscape; the

crayon-like smears across the landscape marked where coal
was being hewn from the earth and transported by rail down
to the dock, where it was stored in great heaps, not only valuable for export but also handy for photographers and cameramen to hide from their rivals.

Welcome to Kings Bay mining colony. Mussolini, Balbo,
and fascism suddenly seemed both very far away and right
behind him.

Just one thing ruined Nobile's perfect moment: moored in
the harbor was another ship, and it was flying the Stars and
Stripes.

What *Science Monthly* had called "the most sensational
sporting event in human history" had started.[1] Didn't these
Americans know it wasn't a game for him? Their contest had
now placed him in great danger.

Nobile wanted to beat these American interlopers to the
North Pole, but Amundsen wouldn't—or couldn't—act.[2]
The great explorer was paralyzed by the fear of another
defeat or even treachery. He could still remember the
mistakes Scott made when attempting to narrow the lead
Amundsen had built up in their race to the South Pole. He
didn't want to be the victim this time. He also knew that if
the rival expedition made a mistake and crashed, then the
Norge would be called on to rescue the Americans, and his
dream shattered.

"His face was expressionless, and we couldn't read it,"
said one of the crew members about Amundsen when the
American ship arrived. "It was a face carved in a cliff. It was
the face of a Viking. . . . We waited for him to speak, but he
pivoted away on his skis without a word and strode back to his
headquarters."[3]

AMUNDSEN AND NOBILE HAD many good reasons to fear the arrival of the Americans at Kings Bay. The *Chantier* was a surplus World War I transport ship that had been leased to the Josephine Ford Byrd Arctic expedition. Named after Josephine Ford, the daughter of Edsel Ford, president of the Ford Motor Company, the expedition was led by Richard Byrd, an ambitious American explorer and naval aviator. Edsel Ford had backed the flight to the tune of $20,000 even though Byrd hadn't chosen one of his planes, but Ford wasn't the only powerful man funding the expedition. John D. Rockefeller and millionaire philanthropist Vincent Astor had also put their hands in their pockets to help Byrd reach the North Pole.

Richard Byrd's career was very much on an upward trajectory in 1926, partly because he had an instinctive understanding of the "hero business"[4] to rival that of Amundsen's. His flight to the North Pole could transform him from an up-and-coming polar explorer into an international celebrity.

The competition to fly over the North Pole wasn't just about winning a race. It was also about winning the media coverage.

The golden age of Hollywood was just beginning. Byrd had signed an exclusive contract with Pathé News, one of the leading producers of the weekly news features that were shown in cinemas across the United States. Byrd had partnered with the *New York Times*—but not exclusively as the Norwegian had done. More important, Byrd had signed a sponsorship deal with the respected National Geographic Society.[5]

Amundsen merely wanted to conquer the Arctic. The American wanted to conquer it for commerce. Byrd believed that "conquering the Arctic" in multiengine planes would give an impetus to the development of commercial aviation.

"Science has made aircraft safe enough for commercial use," he declared. "The stage is set. Confidence is all that is needed to lift the curtain on an era of rapid development in air commerce."[6]

Despite an earlier expedition that had failed to achieve its goal of exploring remote northern Greenland and the polar sea (and the chance, Byrd had hoped, to fly to the North Pole before Amundsen), Byrd remained convinced that aviation was the future for exploration. "But it will be difficult and hazardous," he predicted. "These things, however, only increase the extraordinary lure of the Polar regions. The world is determined that the North Pole should be reached, and now it will not be content until the secrets of this unexplored area are revealed."[7]

Then there was the "what," the aircraft that Byrd had accompanied to Kings Bay. He wasn't bringing an airship to this remote harbor—although he had been talking to Goodyear about such a move—but rather a powerful, tough Fokker Tri-motor.

The Fokker had three radial engines, a lacquered wooden mono-wing with "Fokker" written along its edge, three windows on either side of the fuselage, and "Josephine Ford Byrd Arctic Expedition" written along each side. Despite its apparent sophistication, the pilots still had to fly the plane in an open-sided cockpit and the freezing cold.[8] The plane could hold just enough fuel in the tanks in its wings and fuselage to make the fifteen-hundred-mile flight to the North Pole and back in one go, but for the pilots it would be taking a big risk. Instead, Byrd and his copilot, Floyd Bennett, decided to take extra fuel in cans stowed in the fuselage, which itself was a risk. The men had now turned their plane into a flying bomb.

The Trimotor had pedigree too. Full-page advertisements in the aviation press proclaimed the design's victory in the Ford Reliability Tour of 1925, a sixteen-hundred-mile schedule of intercity flights across the United States. The same model would go on to set many more world aviation records. By the end of 1926, similar ads would proclaim that the company could no longer make enough planes to meet demand.

The Fokker had the advantage over the flying boats with which Amundsen had tried—and failed—to reach the North Pole in 1925 for one reason: three engines were better than two when you were flying over one of the most extreme environments on earth. Today we are used to commercial airliners flying across the great oceans on just two engines. It used not to be the case. Back in the 1920s, aircraft engines were just as primitive as the planes they powered. Two-engine planes at that time could not fly with one engine owing to their lack of power.[9] Thus, if one engine failed, as it had done on one of Amundsen's twin-engine aircraft, then a crash landing on the sea ice that the crew could walk away from was the best possible outcome. If you had a third engine, you had a chance of staying in the air.

Goodyear had offered to sell Byrd one of its airships, with one eye on the headlines that an airship race to the North Pole would have generated. The company wanted $18,000 for an airship roughly half the size of the Norge—a very good deal.[10] Byrd was still thinking about taking up the Goodyear offer as late as January 1926, when it turned out that he could get his hands on the Fokker for an even better price.[11]

Byrd had another advantage over Amundsen and Nobile. He had brought a second plane with him. It was a more modest conventional wooden biplane compared to the Fokker, called the Curtiss Oriole, available for search-and-rescue if there was a crash landing; and of course, it would film the first part of the record attempt, including the take off.

Amundsen had not been able to afford such a luxury on his previous expedition. Nor would the current crew be bringing such help along this time. The lack of money, together with their machismo, meant the Norwegians and Ellsworth seemed to prefer to get out of a crisis the hard way—across the ice on two feet.

Byrd's wise decision making extended beyond bringing backup. George Hubert Wilkins was an Australian cinematographer, naturalist, pilot, and the third competitor in the "race." He had raised money from the Detroit Aviation Society, the North American Newspaper Alliance, and the *New York Times* to attempt to fly over the pole the "wrong" way, from Point Barrow to Svalbard. Wilkins had offered Byrd a place as his second-in-command on the flight, but Byrd turned him down. The Australian told him that he wasn't interested in flying to the pole, only in exploring unknown lands,[12] when flying to the North Pole and being seen as an expedition leader were the two things Byrd was very much interested in.

Byrd had made the right decision not to accompany him. Wilkins's flight would end in disappointment, a footnote in the history books.

UNFORTUNATELY FOR THE AMERICAN, while he had beaten Nobile to Kings Bay, he hadn't beaten Amundsen. When the *Chantier* arrived in Kings Bay, the Norwegian's ship, a naval gunboat, was tied up to the small ramshackle quayside, and its captain showed no sign of moving it.

Left without any guidance from Amundsen, it was claimed, his men resorted to, at best, being unhelpful and, at worst, dirty tricks to delay the American attempt to fly to the pole. Byrd, however, pinned the blame for the dirty tricks not on the reluctance of the crew but firmly on orders from their leader.[13]

When the *Chantier* was refused permission to dock at the quay, Byrd had to come up with another way to offload his planes—and quickly, as the *Norge* was due to arrive soon.

What Byrd and his crew of volunteers came up with was a daring plan, "which they executed with amazing speed and skill."[14] The American ordered his men to nail planks across five of the ship's lifeboats to transform them into one giant pontoon. The cranes on the ship were used to lower the fuselage of the Fokker, its engines and tail on the now flat surfaces. Just one chunk of ice colliding with the pontoon would send the plane down into the depths of the bay.[15] But it was a risk Byrd had to take. He and his men then punted the plane to safety on dry land. (When the Pathé cameramen had tried to film the unloading of the planes, one of Amundsen's men stopped him. "Great sportsmanship," Byrd wrote in his diary. "They deny us dock, deny movie, make us move out in stream. The Viking valor."[16])

With the Fokker off the ship, the Americans swiftly started to reassemble the plane out on the ice. As Amundsen and Ellsworth had done the year before, they were planning on using the frozen surface as a runway.

Amundsen may have thought that he had a few more days to beat them to the North Pole because the snow on the ground would delay the flight. To his experienced eyes, the Fokker was also clearly too heavy, the wooden skis sure to break under its weight before the plane had taxied very far.

Then one of the oddest moments of Byrd's expedition happened: Lieutenant Bernt Balchen offered to help the inexperienced Americans out.

Balchen was a Norwegian pilot—and a member of Amundsen's expedition. The reasons Balchen seemed to betray Amundsen still aren't clear even today. He might have felt sorry for Byrd when he saw the Americans struggling in the extreme conditions. He may even have felt he had a score to settle with Amundsen when he discovered that he hadn't made the cut for the final flight of the *Norge*.[17] There was even a chance that Amundsen had asked him to help the Americans.

In any case, Balchen made new skis for Byrd's plane out of the wooden oars of the *Chantier*'s lifeboats. He coated these in a special resin to reduce friction on snow and ice. Balchen also gave Byrd's team an insight his own polar experience had taught him: the Americans should take off after dark because the ice would be at its hardest when it was frozen by the cold of the Arctic night.

Later, Amundsen would rage that he was the victim of a conspiracy. "There was a lot of misrepresentation about our attitude to Byrd's expedition which has been foisted on the public mind by unfriendly correspondents. . . . Ignorant critics have tried to make the public believe that I had our expedition purposely hamper Byrd's landing. Their theory is that we were jealous . . . that he would beat us to the pole."[18] The delay at the quay was, he argued, the fault of the Americans, who were unwilling to wait in the bay until his ship was repaired.[19] And perhaps to save face, Amundsen let it be known that he had ordered Balchen to help out the Americans—an act of chivalry that he rarely showed his rivals and a claim that

Byrd did not believe. More likely, Amundsen simply realized that being accused of "dirty tricks" wouldn't go down well in the eyes of the American public on whom he was relying to finance his luxurious lifestyle.[20]

But soon there would be another twist in the story—and, maybe, a hint of guilt and regret. Balchen would go on to become one of the fiercest critics of Byrd's claim to have reached the North Pole.

IT WAS CLEAR FROM the moment Colonel Nobile jumped down from the cabin of the airship that he had wanted to try to race Byrd to the pole. "The *Norge* can be ready in three days," he told Amundsen.[21] But the Norwegian had overruled him, claiming that he simply wasn't interested in the race to the North Pole after Robert Peary had made it there on foot.[22] Few people believed him.

In reality, the reason the *Norge* didn't leave its hangar may have just come down to engineering. The repair, replenishment, and reweighing of an airship that had already taken a battering from the weather was a complex affair that no bravado could alter.

Without warning, just after midnight on May 9, Byrd and Floyd Bennett boarded the Fokker and took off in what appeared to be an unseemly rush. Once airborne, the Trimotor turned north and swiftly disappeared into the eerie Arctic half-light. The pilots, in their open-sided cockpit, were quickly assaulted by brutal temperatures as low as –58°F (–50°C). The roar of the engines and the wind made speech impossible to hear. Instead, the two men had to resort to communicating with hand signals and hastily scrawled notes, which were difficult for the men to decipher in the plane and were nearly impossible for researchers to decipher afterward.

Byrd had been in the air for only a few hours when his nightmare started to unfold. The starboard engine of the Fokker began to spray oil. Surely it would stop soon? The two pilots thought about landing to fix it, but Byrd quickly dismissed the idea. Even if they made it down in one piece, there was every chance they wouldn't be able to take off again. This was the moment of truth for the Trimotor. "Can we get all the way there and back on two motors?" Byrd wrote in his notes, which must have been aimed at Bennett.[23]

Thankfully for the two men, they didn't need to put it to the test: what had doomed Amundsen's flight in 1925 wasn't going to doom theirs. The Fokker's third engine kept running.

At last, at 9:02 on the morning of May 9, 1926, Byrd wrote two words in his notebook: "North Pole." Later, he would write, "The dream of a lifetime had at last been realized."[24]

The Fokker circled around the pole for thirteen minutes while the two pilots took readings and photographs and attempted to film the scene for the newsreels. Then Byrd set course for Kings Bay. During the return, the sextant fell and broke, making it impossible for the men to take any more sightings.

After nearly sixteen hours and fifteen hundred miles, Byrd and Bennett made it back to Kings Bay to a heroes' welcome. They had successfully completed the first flight to the North Pole and back—a flight that Amundsen had dreamed of making for more than ten years, which had eluded him the year before and which was supposed to be one of his career-closing records. While Byrd was drinking champagne, the *Norge* was still safely in its hangar.

And yet . . . Problems with Byrd's story quickly became apparent after he landed. The flight had been expected to take eighteen hours, not sixteen—and it wasn't clear that the Fokker had the speed capacity to fly the distance any faster. Byrd's talk of tailwinds that pushed the plane along didn't convince everyone.[25]

Then there was the decision not to drop any flags to mark their having reached their destination, when everyone dropped flags, and that strange business of the sextant not working on the way back. For Byrd, the only proof that he had reached the North Pole was the navigational calculations that he had made and recorded in his notebook.

It was unfortunate that this notebook was a bit of a mess. Understandably, any calculations that he was going to make in subzero temperatures in a very noisy, shaking, and juddering propeller plane were going to be pretty rough; his messages to Bennett were written in a rush, out of order, and on different pages of the notebook, perhaps because the wind was blowing the pages over. The end result was that the exact order and the time of each note and message were confused.[26]

However, perhaps Byrd's biggest mistake on his flight was that he had been successful. He had beaten Amundsen in Norway's backyard. Kings Bay was a Norwegian settlement full of supporters of their national hero, who were shocked at his defeat—and they weren't going to take it lightly. If there were even the slightest doubts about whether Byrd had really made it to the North Pole, they were sure to be spread.

Byrd now made an error. He didn't go straight back to

New York. Instead, he headed to England and sailed up the Thames on the *Chantier* to spend six days in London. There, a double booking in his diary meant that he had to refuse dinner at the prestigious Royal Geographical Society, of which he was a member. Word soon spread of this effrontery, and the fickle London press switched from treating him like a hero to a villain. The rumors that Byrd hadn't actually made it to the North Pole started by jealous Norwegians and spread by Mussolini's newspapers, which wanted the glory to go to Colonel Nobile and the *Norge*,[27] were now picked up by the press in London and amplified across the British Empire.

Amundsen may have been at home on the ice, and Nobile on his airship, but Byrd was a natural at dealing with the press. In London, he called a press conference to announce that it was normal for people to question whether he made it to the North Pole, and to put an end to the speculation, he would submit his notes to the society (the National Geographic Society, one of his sponsors) on his return to the United States. He had already arranged for an official from the Navy Department to meet his ship and pick up the charts and records for the society to ratify.

Back in the United States, most Americans did not care about the "carping of foreigners."[28] Still, it was important that the US government wait for the National Geographic Society's verdict before it showered Byrd with honors. The society noted the absence of sextant observations on the return trip but concluded that the return flight to Kings Bay demonstrated Byrd's skill in navigating rather than skullduggery.

Byrd's return, the society declared, "is one of the strongest evidences that he was equally successful in his flight northward. The feat of flying a plane 800 miles from land and returning directly to the point aimed for was a remarkable exhibition of skilful navigation and shows beyond a reasonable doubt that [Byrd] knew where he was at all times during the flight."[29]

Off the back of the report, Byrd was hailed a hero. He was given the Medal of Honor, a promotion in the US Navy, and a ticker-tape parade through New York City (the first of three in his life).

Byrd went on to lead four expeditions of ever-increasing size to the South Pole. By the time Byrd died in 1957, he was one of the most decorated American officers in the history of the service. He was buried with other American heroes in Arlington Cemetery in Virginia.

After his death, the challenges to Byrd's accounts by his critics came thick and fast, buoyed by the ambiguities in his notes. His defenders were not idle either. To this day, the arguments rage back and forth between the two sides.

However, this dispute was still in the future. When Byrd and Bennett landed back on the ice on May 9, 1926, Amundsen and Nobile would have had every reason to believe that Byrd had done it: he had made it to the North Pole.

But he hadn't done everything.

TWO DAYS AFTER BYRD'S return, at 9:55 a.m. on May 11, Nobile shouted, "Let's go!" The ground crew let loose the ropes. Free of its ties to the earth, the *Norge* rose quickly up into the sky and turned toward the northwest. Its destination: the North Pole.[30] It was only eight hundred miles away. The headline of the Italian newspaper *Il Piccolo* read the next day: "Under an Italian Flag, in the Spirit of Fascism, the *Norge* Sails in the Polar Sky."[31]

The engineers had labored for days in freezing temperatures to repair the airship after the rough flight from Leningrad. One of the engines had to be replaced because its crankshaft had problems. The surface of the envelope and the structure of the airship were checked for damage. The torn rudder had to be replaced and the lower keel repaired.

The amount of petrol that the airship would carry had to be precisely calculated. Too little and the airship would run out of fuel over the Arctic Sea and become little more than a balloon at the mercy of polar storms. Too much, the *Norge* would struggle to get aloft as the fuel would act as ballast holding it down.

Riiser-Larsen's plan to replace all the Italians on the flight with Englishmen and Norwegians hadn't happened on the flight up from Rome, and it wasn't going to happen at Kings Bay. There were too many Italians, Americans, and journalists from around the world to attempt anything as underhanded as that.

This meant that the thorny issue of the final composition of the crew still had to be resolved. Nobile had agreed with the Aero Club of Norway to have a crew of no more than sixteen for the flight over the North Pole to Alaska. He understandably wanted as many trained and experienced Italian airmen as possible to be among them, while Amundsen wanted a majority of the crew to be Norwegian, or at least men who would owe their loyalty to him.

In the end, the actual crew was only made clear on the day of its departure. It was an "ingenious blend of skilled competence and national allegiance." Nobile had to do without experienced crewmen such as his chief helmsman. Amundsen even had to say goodbye to his nephew, Gustav.

The Norwegian-speaking Russian wireless operator Gennady Olonkin was perhaps the most tragic victim of the power struggle. The Russian had spent seven years freezing on the *Maud* in the Artic for Amundsen and had been the radio operator on the *Norge* for the flight from Rome, but there was one thing that counted against him: he wasn't Norwegian. Olonkin was sacrificed at the last minute for an Amundsen compatriot. The normally impassive Russian was spotted crying after he had been told the news.[32]

Late on the evening of May 10, Nobile had left the hangar to go to his room and pack. He had taken only a couple of steps outside when he was hit by a powerful wind that cut across the front of the structure. It was the kind of wind that would smash the airship against its wooden walls if the ground crew were foolish enough to pull it out, and worse, it was clearly growing in strength. Rather than risk the ship in the high winds, Nobile told Amundsen his decision and sent the men off to their beds.

By 1:00 a.m. on May 11, the wind had abated. It left behind a bitter cold that would have been deadly for anyone trapped on the ice that night, but for Nobile, the chillingly low temperature was exactly what he wanted as it would maximize the lifting power of the hydrogen in the airship's gas bags. With barely any sleep himself, he woke up his mechanics to ready the ship. He sent a message to Amundsen that the Norwegian ground crew could get a couple more hours' sleep as long they were at the hangar at 4:00 a.m. ready for a 5:00 a.m. departure. But 5:00 a.m. came and went—as did 6:00 a.m.—and there was no sign of the Norwegians. The problem for Nobile, now that the sun was up and the mercury rising, was that the hydrogen had started to expand. The Italians then had to start releasing the expanding hydrogen to save the airship ultimately from bursting. Less hydrogen meant less lift, and it also meant that the ship could not carry as much equipment or fuel as Nobile had hoped. Less fuel meant a shorter range, which was dangerous when flying over the huge distances of Arctic wastes. If the ship ran out of fuel, it would remain airborne thanks to the lift from hydrogen in its envelope, but without engines, it would be left at the mercy of the wind.

Finally, at 7:00 a.m., the Norwegian ground crew wandered in, three hours late, and the wind had picked up, threatening to smash the airship against the doors of the hangar. Nobile was by now ready to explode. He had barely slept all night, and when he had it was on the floor of the control cabin, and he was now hungry. When Amundsen, Ellsworth, and Riiser-Larsen strolled in even later, satisfied after their cooked breakfast, he erupted.[33]

Amundsen refused to acknowledge that he had done anything wrong—and later claimed bizarrely that it was not a confrontation at all.[34] Instead, he "contemptuously" dismissed Nobile's anger as "nervous excitement" that had left him "incapable of action."[35] In Amundsen's arrogant eyes, Riiser-Larsen had saved the airship by taking over the job of supervising the ground crew from the hysterical Italian.[36] This was a theme he regularly returned to in his account of the flight.

In fact, the opposite was true. Unlike Amundsen, Riiser-Larsen was an experienced aviator and understood airships better than his leader. He immediately realized that Nobile had been trying to warn the ground crew of just how vulnerable the airship was when it left the hangar. Rather than taking over from Nobile, the huge Norwegian started to transmit Nobile's orders precisely to his fellow countrymen.[37]

After the *Norge* finally took off at 9:55 a.m., the giant craft quickly reached around twelve hundred feet. Even though it was flying at the same height as the Empire State Building, the dirigible was still dwarfed by the surrounding mountains. The smallest peaks were twice the airship's height. One mighty mountain dominated them all: Newtontoppen, or Newton Peak. Named after Isaac Newton, it rose to fifty-six hundred feet.

Staring out of the windows at the sun and the mountains, Nobile quickly forgot his exhaustion and the conflict before takeoff. But when he turned back to his charts, he was rapidly reminded of both. If he needed a further reminder, in the pilot's cabin the two safari-style seats positioned for Amundsen and Ellsworth were screwed to the floor. Draped on their backs was a banner. It still read "The Amundson-Ellsworth Expedition." Amundsen settled himself into his chair and, according to Nobile, barely left it for the duration of the flight. To Nobile, he was little more than an elderly passenger on a cruise, his research and navigational roles forgotten. Instead, the Norwegian gazed out the window looking for new lands. To the rest of the crew, it was clear that he wished to be out on the ice with a husky team and sled rather than trapped in this infernal machine.[38]

Amundsen was focused not only on the view. Nobile had insisted that Titina accompany him on the flight, much to Amundsen's annoyance. Nobile's obsession with the weight of the airship had really irritated him, and to add a dog that wasn't even a husky to the load seemed to go against everything Nobile had been telling them. It reminded Amundsen of the dirty tricks that Nobile had played on them on the flight up, like telling the Norwegians at the last minute to leave their made-to-measure Arctic flight suits behind in Rome to save weight, a discarding that condemned them to fly to Svalbard in their lightweight Mediterranean clothes. What other sleights of hand might the Italian have pulled off?

For her part, Titina wasn't bothered by Amundsen. She quickly found a cozy place on the airship to sleep, oblivious to the potentially record-breaking flight she was on and the hostility of some of her fellow crew. (She probably would have slept less easily if she had known that Amundsen had started to fantasize that her "canine cutlets [would] taste good" if the worst happened and they crashed on the ice.)

The *Norge* soon passed the craggy Danes Island, from where Salomon August Andrée's expedition to the North Pole had set off in a hot-air balloon twenty-nine years ago, never to be seen again. The Swede's mission had been to stop the soon-to-be independent Norway from claiming the Arctic for itself. All that was ever heard of the Andrée expedition after it disappeared over the horizon was a carrier pigeon with the message "All's well on board." Later, two messages in a bottle, like buoys, were found floating in the sea. Although they contained some details of the balloon's route, it would be another four years before the bleached white bones of Andrée and his men, together with the undeveloped film of the last weeks of their lives, were found on a remote island in northeast Svalbard. Seeing the island was a moment for all sixteen of the *Norge*'s crew to contemplate their own mortality amid the hubris and conflict of their expedition.

The belief of Nobile, Eckener, and Nansen that the airship would be the ideal platform for polar exploration was quickly vindicated. Riiser-Larsen used the *Norge*'s relative stability to carefully plot its route. There would be no questioning of his records.

Weighed down as it was with fuel, and needing to avoid the powerful headwind that was blowing at higher altitudes, the *Norge* had to fly so low that it seemed as though the airship was chasing its own shadow across the icy wasteland.[39] The men could even spot Arctic foxes and the telltale paw marks of polar bears. Little streaks of dark blue appeared like cuts across the ice[40]—warning signs to anyone unlucky enough to be on foot that the ice was thin enough to plunge them into a freezing-cold bath.

Norwegian, Italian, Swedish, or American, whatever their nationality, all the men on board could see how rough the surface of the ice was and how dangerous a crash landing would be. Amundsen, Ellsworth, and Riiser-Larsen didn't need reminding—they could even tell their fellow aeronauts how much luck it took to escape it alive. Fortunately, in an airship, if something went wrong with one of the engines they should be able to just "float on" while they repaired it, which was very different from their experiences the previous year.[41]

Then the last vestiges of life disappeared. The adventurers were now above the polar desert.[42] Given its monotony and their lack of rest, it was difficult for many of the crew to stay awake when flying over such a featureless landscape. Crew members even reported seeing squadrons of cavalry out on the ice—mirages that could fool the inexperienced dirigiblists into thinking they had a discovered a new land.

For Nobile, the ordeal was even worse. He had less sleep than most of his men because it was his job to set an example by staying awake. Although we know now how a lack of sleep

muffles brain functioning, resistance to nature was what good
leadership looked like in 1926. It didn't help that Nobile was
also a perfectionist. He thought that no else could fly the airship as well as he could. The cognitive slow-mo moments that
resulted would later lead Amundsen to make his most serious
accusations against him. Three times he accused Nobile of being in some sort of "daze" at the wheel and claimed that each
daze had imperiled the ship until he was shaken out of it by
none other than Riiser-Larsen,[43] of course.

As they proceeded, ice gradually started to form. Ice even
began to form in air bubbles in the fuel, which could cause the
engines to fail.

Then the weather changed. Now it was the turn of snow
and dense fog that wrapped the airship in a shroud, and with
the fog came rapid icing. The metal structure of the airship
was quickly covered in a sheet of ice. It obscured the men's
view of the frozen surface they were flying over in a way that
Nobile thought was rather ironic. Ice even appeared inside the
control room. Nobile ordered the great ship up, to climb above
the fog, which they achieved at about three thousand feet.

Now and again a brave mechanic had to complete a particularly dangerous maneuver. He had to climb out a small
window in the cabin and, in high winds and subzero temperatures, manage to find a ladder that ran up the side of the
airship. After he had climbed to the top of the envelope, he
had to crawl along its spongy surface to make sure the valves
that controlled the release of the hydrogen were not frozen.
Then, somehow, he had to make his way back down and inside again.[44]

Close to 1:00 a.m. on May 12, the sextant finally told Nobile, Ellsworth, and Amundsen that they were nearing the pole.

Nobile ordered the ship down. The crew busied themselves getting the flags ready while the Norge dropped to 1,000 feet, 750 feet, and then 600 feet.

The Norwegian and American flags had been in the cabin since the *Norge* took off. Now they were finally fixed to their staves ready to be dropped. However, the Italians had a little surprise for their rivals. They pulled out a heavy wooden casket that they had hidden on board despite Nobile's protests about the weight of the airship. Inside it was an Italian flag so large that it had to be unfolded before it could be attached to the stave.

Just before 1:30 a.m., the engines of the airship slowed down, their deafening sound replaced by a different kind of roar—that of the wind blowing around the celluloid windows. As their ears grew used to the relative quietness other than the wind, the men could hear the creaking of the airship's frame, as the *Norge* circled tightly over "absolute zero degrees north"[45] at six hundred feet. The circular motion would make anyone sick who hadn't already thrown up from the motion of the dirigible, and a sense of anticlimax was hard to avoid for the members of the crew who were seeing the Arctic for the first time.[46] As Byrd had realized, there was no undiscovered land out here. Instead, all they saw was the ice pack stretching to the horizon.

And then there was the wind, its ferocious gusts making it impossible to use Nobile's "sky anchor" to land men on the ice for the finale of the first half of the flight. Instead, they had to be content with dropping the American, Norwegian, and Italian flags onto the ice. "Ours was the most beautiful," one of the Italian crew recalled. Nobile would write simply: "Planted the Italian flag at the Pole May 12, 1926 1.30am."[47]

Later, Amundsen would bitterly mock the Italians and

their flag. It was too big, he told everyone, a joke. The Italians could barely even organize themselves to throw it out of the cabin window. When they did, the flag was so large it nearly fouled the ship's engines and brought the airship down.[48]

Byrd had reached the North Pole in his plane before them, or so they thought, but no one—not even Amundsen—had flown beyond it.

Shortly after 1:30 a.m., the airship piloted and designed by Colonel Umberto Nobile did precisely that, and its crew flew into the last hole on the map.

FOR SEVERAL HOURS, NOTHING happened. The sea ice they were flying over stretched to the horizon without a break. The sky was gray, the weather quiet. Their decreasing adrenaline levels gave Amundsen, Ellsworth, and Nobile time to fully grasp what they had achieved together.

Amundsen had claimed that he was no longer bothered about reaching the North Pole. Yet it is hard to believe that a moment he had been dreaming of for seventeen years meant nothing to him. Robert Peary and Richard Byrd may have reached the pole before him, but Amundsen was the first man in history to have traveled to both poles.

For Nobile, the flight had to be a success—and it was. The Italian had shown to the world what airships could do. Eckener could no longer say that his semi-rigid airships weren't tough enough for polar exploration. And Balbo had the perfect demonstration of the superiority of lighter-than-air flight over the heavier-than-air alternative. Most of all, Mussolini and the Fascists now had the glory they wanted. Their newspapers were busy discrediting Byrd's claims.

In his sleep-deprived state, Nobile's head started to fill with dreams of giant airships equipped as flying laboratories circling the poles or as freighters supplying a chain of research stations around the edges of the ice caps.

It would take five years before Nobile's dream vision would come anywhere close to being fulfilled. Then he would have only a cameo in someone else's adventure.

SNAPPING OUT OF HIS trance, Nobile noticed for the first time that "the cabin was horribly dirty."[49] Dozens of empty thermos flasks were scattered across the cabin. Tea and coffee were spilled everywhere and there were remains of meals abandoned on their plates. Somewhere underneath this mess, he realized, were the navigation charts and books that he needed to steer the *Norge* to safety.

Right at that moment, with the pole about five hundred miles behind them—and the coast of Alaska a couple of hundred miles ahead—the men heard the first loud bang, followed by another and another. Soon they lost count of the number. Explosions meant only one thing to Nobile's ears: trouble.[50] It was ice again. Ice was forming on the propellers and being flung off as they spun around. These chunks were hitting the airship's metal framework at high speed, making the noise—and causing damage. A number of pieces had already hit the airship fast enough to make a cut in the covering of the envelope itself.

Ice was even forming on the metal components of the ship—the engines, gangways, suspension cables, solar compass—and on the mooring ropes. It was beautiful, it was everywhere, and it was potentially deadly for the airship, weighing it down and pulling it back to earth.

That descent would be accelerated in a horrifying manner if the flying chunks of ice tore a hole in the fabric of one of the hydrogen cells. The loss of the irreplaceable lifting gas could be catastrophic. The sudden loss of buoyancy could be enough to cause the airship to plummet to the ground. Add that to that fact that hydrogen is highly flammable. If the escaping gas was ignited by one of the still-turning engines, then the airship would explode. The resulting fireball would kill most of them, just as it burned to death the crew of Nobile's earlier airship, the *Roma*.

Well, at least they would now die as heroes, Nobile thought, and Mussolini would have martyrs to celebrate as well. If by chance anyone survived the impact and the inferno, rescue this far out over the Arctic desert was no longer merely improbable, it was impossible. It would be better for all the men to die in the explosion, their frozen corpses left for explorers of the future to find.

Somehow neither of these possibilities was put to the test. The airship stayed aloft despite the extra weight of the ice. The sinister bangs grew more intermittent.

At 6:30 p.m. on May 12, the fog lifted enough, and they could see the frozen sea again. But what wasn't there was actually more important than what was.

There was little land between the North Pole and the coast of Alaska. They had solved one mystery of the Arctic.[51] "We could therefore definitely affirm that a sea occupies these regions," Nobile said, "a sea which we were the first men in the world to cross: the Arctic Ocean."

But this discovery offered only a brief respite. The fog returned to swamp the ship—followed by thicker fog and snow mixed together. The explosions started again, this time with ice breaking off the ship and hitting the propeller. The wind had picked up too, whistling through every crack in the airship. At times it must have sounded like the ship was haunted.

Covered in half an inch or more of ice, the *Norge* had started to blend into the landscape. To Nobile's sleep-starved eyes, what he could see of the airship bore a distinct resemblance to a Christmas cake.[52]

Suddenly there was another terrible noise. A chunk of ice flung off one of the propellers had ripped a gash a yard long in the side of the airship. "The Emaillite is almost finished," one of the men warned Nobile.[53]

"Emaillite as tight as a drum!"—so proclaimed the advert for the British Emaillite Co., Ltd., from its offices near Piccadilly Circus in London. Emaillite was "the worldwide premier dope" and "used throughout the world." It was "shipped immediately" worldwide. Aircraft dope, in this case Emaillite, was a plasticized lacquer painted onto the fabric of aircraft by so-called dopers. It was used to tighten and stiffen fabric stretched over airframes to make them smoother, stronger, watertight, and windproof.

Nobile was rightly worried by the news they were running out of Emaillite to repair the airship. Poor doping could cause a plane or an airship to crash.

The next day at 6:45 a.m., they finally heard the cry they had been waiting for: "Land ahead to starboard!"

"It was a moment of joyful excitement," Nobile wrote. Unable to resist, he leaned out of the cabin to take a look. "The keen, cold wind that whipped my face was refreshing. Looking ahead, I saw in the distance . . . a line of pearl-grey hills."[54]

At 8:20 a.m., the crew of the *Norge* saw their first Americans. The distinctive fur-covered figures of the group of Inuit were looking up at them from the ice as the airship motored over. At only six hundred feet above their heads, the Inuit could see every wound in the side of the great whale.

The few figures were replaced by many. The *Norge* was passing over a ramshackle collection of wooden huts on the coast, which they could identify on their charts and from Amundsen's memory as Wainwright, a village of around a hundred Inuit. This was the village where Amundsen had stayed during his first attempt at the pole. Nobile later learned that one Inuit man called the airship the devil, a young boy likened it to "a gigantic flying seal," and wanted to shoot it, and still another, "a large whale."[55]

They flew on. Nobile's notes ended in midsentence. His last words: "Visibility very bad. I slow down again. Soon afterwards . . ."[56]

IN THE PAST SEVENTY-TWO hours, the crew had barely slept at all. Now they were about to face their most terrifying test. "These last hours were the worst of all," wrote Nobile.[57]

First, there was the nightmare of fog. Fog, mountains, and aircraft of any kind are never a good combination. In the 1920s, the mix was often lethal because the main method to find your way in fog was to fly so low that you could follow a feature such as a river or railway line. The downside of this technique was that it left the pilot little time to avoid the mountainside rushing toward them.

But Nobile had a plan. He ordered the speed reduced for safety. He hoped that the airship would now naturally rise and that this would allow the *Norge* to ascend above the fog and over the mountains. He was wrong. The fog kept them a prisoner even above three thousand feet, "the height of full expansion."[58] If they went any higher, Nobile would have to open the valves on the top of the airship, with the subsequent dangerous loss of lifting gas and the fear that they might freeze open.

"We went on flying blindly in the midst of the hills," Nobile recalled. "Our altitude was about 3,500 feet—probably higher than the peaks around, but I could not be sure. . . . Our charts gave us no specific information."[59]

Finally, the fog cleared enough for them to descend through the clouds to about six hundred feet to find out where they were. They saw that the *Norge* was flying over the frozen sea, but where? It could be Asia. There was a chance it was America. They were certainly on the edge of the Pacific.

To find the answer, Nobile took control of the elevator wheel. He had to keep the airship flying east low over the sea toward what he hoped was Alaska and the city of Nome. But flying low exposed the huge craft to the blinding whiteness of the ice and rough air and powerful crosswinds that could suddenly toss the airship up or down 150 feet. If the engines cut out now, and if the airship was where Nobile hoped it was, then they would be driven by the wind out over the ocean to the remote Aleutian Islands or even as far away as Japan.

The radio wasn't much help either. The men on the *Norge* had still been able to pick up weather forecasts from Norway on the morning of May 13. The problem was that inch-thick ice kept forming on the aerial that trailed along behind the ship, making it impossible to send or receive messages. Even when they heaved the aerial back up into the ship to hack the ice away, the ice quickly returned when it was lowered again. In the end, pushed to their limits, two of the aerials (they took three with them) simply snapped in half. In desperation, the men tried to call radio stations twelve hundred miles away in Nome, Fairbanks, and Point Barrow, and even farther away on the Siberian coast, but they never heard anything back. Finally, they had a lucky break. Using a radio compass attached to the envelope of the airship, they were able to take their bearing from a radio station that they hoped was in Nome. A radio compass is a piece of equipment that operates like a magnetic compass. Its needle points toward a station rather than magnetic north, giving a bearing relative to the direction the aircraft is traveling in.

"The worst part of our flight was now beginning," Nobile recalled. "Four hours and a half of torment . . . without a moment of truce. . . . I cannot attempt to give any details of this breathless race under the implacable fog, among the hills, over the ice of what I hoped was Kotzebue Bay, over the frozen lagoons. Who can tell what route we followed, or how we wound in and out through the fog? Even today I can still live through the emotions of this wild flight under the fog . . . but the recollection is confused, as in a nightmare."[60]

At 9:30 p.m. on May 13, Nobile made a fateful decision.[61] Rather than listen to Riiser-Larsen, who wanted to land at an Inuit village they had stumbled across in the fog, Nobile decided that they should fly on—at least while they had fuel left and a good wind behind them. But they first needed to work out where they were. The Italian slowed down the engines to let the giant ship rise out of the fog safely and allow Riiser-Larsen to take their position. But the airship wouldn't stop climbing. The sun was warming the hydrogen, which was expanding quickly, and the pressure in the gas cells was building up.

Sensing that something was very wrong, Nobile ordered valves opened to let out the hydrogen and stop their ascent. But inexplicably this didn't stop the *Norge*, nor the pressure gauge, from climbing.

Time was running out for the *Norge*. It had already climbed to thirty-five hundred feet. If the pressure grew much higher, then the valves would open automatically, and the sudden loss of gas when they descended would send the airship into a potentially fatal plunge toward the ground.

The only way Nobile could now make the craft descend was to use the engines. Unfortunately, the immediate effect was the opposite. With the great airship pointing up, the rate of climb increased. He needed to make the dirigible point downward.

In desperation, Nobile ordered two or three of the Norwegian crew to race to the extreme bow of the ship to tilt it downward. But the Norwegians didn't understand his English. They stood rooted to the spot as catastrophe raced toward the airship and its men.

Nobile shouted, "Subuto a prua," and gesticulated furiously—and at last they understood. The ship was saved and, with it, their lives. All they had to do now was avoid hitting any mountains. The airship descended safely from fifty-four hundred to six hundred feet.[62]

Amundsen would blame this whole incident on Nobile. He accused Nobile of panicking and nearly wrecking the *Norge* because he "lost his head completely" in the crisis.[63] But again, he didn't understand what Nobile was doing. Rather than endangering the airship, the Italian had saved it by getting the Norwegians to act as human ballast in the nose.

And suddenly they were safe: back over Alaska. The crew

identified the Serpentine River and knew that they were now on course for Nome, where there was an airship mast and a welcome party waiting for them.

Nome had made headlines across the world in the winter of 1925, when a diphtheria outbreak was threatening the Alaska Natives in the Nome area. But fierce blizzards across Alaska prevented the delivery of lifesaving serum by airplane from Anchorage. Instead, a relay of twenty dogsled teams safely transported the serum a distance of 674 miles in five and a half days in subzero temperatures, driving snow, and hurricane-force winds. This mercy dash in a one-in-a-hundred storm conditions saved Nome and the surrounding villages from the ravages of a full-blown epidemic.

Radio mania had gripped hold of the United States, and broadcasts turned the dogs into heroes. One particular Siberian husky, the lead dog, Balto, gained particular celebrity. Today a statue of Balto still stands in New York's Central Park.

Unlike the dogs, the *Norge* never made it to Nome. By May 14, Nobile had been in the air for seventy-two hours. They were still ninety-three miles short of their destination. The crew were exhausted and still the ship continued to be buffeted by the strong winds. In front of them, the sky was pitch black, and suddenly the *Norge* lurched alarmingly, throwing everyone off their feet. "To carry on flying in these conditions . . . would have been madness," wrote Nobile. Nobile made the tough decision to land at the settlement of Teller, Alaska.[64]

Airships can land anywhere. The problem is keeping the airship on the ground. Teller was not the ideal landing place for the *Norge* because there was neither a mooring mast nor a landing party ready to help tie the airship down as there was at Nome. About two hundred men were needed to hold down a ship as large as the *Norge*. Instead, Nobile and his men would have to make do with seven or eight men and with another one of Nobile's inventions called the sky anchor, or "landing sack," which hung about a hundred feet below the airship with an anchor at one end. The landing sack had two jobs. The first job was to act like a windbreak to slow the airship down when it came to land. The second was to bring it to a stop. Somehow they managed it.

With nothing to moor the ship to, Nobile had to quickly deflate it by cutting open the emergency rip panels on all the gas cells. The once proud airship was now a heap of metal and canvas on the ground. The ship did not make it back to Italy in one piece by the time the souvenir hunters had finished.

But this didn't detract from what they had achieved.

After Nobile had landed, one of the first things he did was to send a telegram to Rome. He received his reply from Mussolini the next day: "Your triumphant voyage fills the entire Italian nation with emotion and pride. I embrace you and all your intrepid companions."[65]

MUSSOLINI ADDRESSED THE ITALIAN Senate four days after the flyers landed safely in Teller, in his usual grandiose and verbose style. "Gentlemen," he began. "My desire in pointing out what a great share Italy has had in the success of this legendary flight has been to show what powerful and preponderating elements she has contributed, with her men and her material, to the accomplishment of an enterprise which might in truth appear to be a dream; on the contrary it is the result of very careful preparation: moral, professional, and technical, of the cool, well-planned daring, the great energy and tenacity of the fearless commander of the airship and his crew."[66]

When Amundsen heard of Mussolini's address, everything that he had feared about the Italian involvement in the expedition came true. He could see his generous speaker fees, packed auditoriums, syndicated articles, and book sales disappearing in front of him. But it took one particular moment in Seattle to make Amundsen realize how badly he had been outmaneuvered by Mussolini.

When the returning explorers passed through Admiralty Inlet just outside Seattle on June 27 aboard the *Victoria*, they were met by a boat draped in a large Italian flag and cheering men and women. In Seattle, thousands of Americans thronged the quayside desperate to see the adventurers. Standing on the deck, looking out over the crowd, the colonel and his men looked every inch the heroes with their good looks, weather-beaten faces, and military uniforms. The elderly Amundsen less so.

When an American girl carrying a bunch of flowers ran up to the party, there was only one man she was going to give them to. And it wasn't Amundsen.

There seems to have been no going back for Amundsen from this one moment. The Norwegian would rage against Nobile and the Italians about their "resplendent uniforms." He would go so far as to accuse Nobile of "secreting" them on board even as he blocked the Norwegians from taking their own clothes. He even hinted—again—at dark conspiracies at work. "Here in miniature, Nobile had the triumph which his uniform was a part of the planning."[67]

In his rage, Amundsen failed to realize two things. The Italians had worn these uniforms under their sweaters and furs the entire flight. The only thing the men did was get them cleaned when they arrived in Nome. The girl was an Italian-American from Seattle's large Italian community, which Fascist organizations such as the Fascist League of North America had done such a good job mobilizing for the occasion. The crowd was full of Italian-American men taking a break from their work, old peasant women from southern Italy with their rosary beads who shouted, "Blessed be the mothers that bore you!" and young men who embraced the aeronauts.[68] The girl was in all likelihood a setup. She was following a script designed to be played out in front of the cameras of the American media. And, unsurprisingly, the American public did not want to hear from the elderly explorer who had been a passenger on the flight. They wanted to read about the brave Italian airship captain who had flown the craft: the man they were calling the New Columbus.[69]

While Amundsen headed back to Norway in a dark mood, Nobile and his men traveled across America, from Seattle to New York, for about a month in triumph. They were mobbed by crowds of people in San Francisco, Los Angeles, Chicago, Pittsburgh, Philadelphia, and Boston—and dozens of places in between. In fact, wherever they stepped off the train, word soon got around that the heroes were in town.

Nobile would never forget the visit to the White House with Titina. She followed him everywhere and did not like to be left alone in the hotel. They were preparing to leave the little dog in an antechamber in the White House before going in to see President Calvin Coolidge, who had the reputation of being a cold man. Then the usher appeared with the message that the president would like to see the dog, who, after all, was the first dog to fly over the Arctic Ocean. Coolidge even laughed off Titina urinating on the White House carpet.[70]

"Nobile acclaimed on arrival!" declared the *New York Times* after crowds of Italian-Americans cheered Nobile at New York's Grand Central Station. The mood quickly turned darker. "New York City got a dramatic glimpse of Italy's Blackshirts when some 400 Fascists led a crowd of several thousand fellow-countrymen in the demonstration in and outside of Grand Central Station."[71] All the time, Nobile carried a rather bored Titina under his arm.

Amundsen's rage at Nobile for taking credit for the successful expedition spilled out into the newspapers. It was fueled by the realization that the Italians were bound to win any battle between the Norwegian and Italian diasporas and their ability to shape public opinion no matter how many complaints he and Ellsworth made. Yet it was inevitable that the Americans would want to see Nobile. Amundsen and Ellsworth had really just been glorified passengers. The age of the polar explorer was over, and the age of the aeronaut had begun. And it was the real men of the north who had lost.

Six

"Let Him Go, for He Cannot Possibly Come Back to Bother Us Anymore"

"VIVA MUSSOLINI! VIVA NOBILE!"

Two weeks before, Nobile had been mobbed by a thousand Blackshirts at New York's Grand Central Station and by another large crowd when he left for Italy on the state-of-the-art Italian liner *Conte Biancamano* from the pier at the foot of West Fifty-Fifth Street.* (His new friend Rudolph Valentino, Hollywood star and Italian actor, had come to see Nobile off and posed for a picture with the aviator on board the ship.)[1] Now he was standing next to their leader on the balcony of Palazzo Chigi in central Rome[2]—the Renaissance palace that is the official residence of the prime minister of Italy.

The square in front of the palace was filled with cheering Italians desperate to get a glimpse of the two stick figures on the balcony. Towering above them all was the victory column

---

* For a few agonizing moments Nobile had become separated from his dog, Titina, in the crush. The two were soon reunited when the explorer refused to pose for photographs until she was found. ("Nobile Sails Home with Five of Crew," *New York Times*, July 25, 1926, https://timesmachine.nytimes.com /timesmachine/1926/07/25/issue.html)

of Marcus Aurelius, the emperor who to many symbolized the golden age of the Roman Empire—the glories of which Mussolini had promised to restore. Once Nobile would have been intimidated by such a large crowd of people. Now he was used to it.[3]

The ocean liner that had carried General Umberto Nobile and his men across the Atlantic had been met when she had entered the Bay of Naples by what felt like the whole of Italy. In the background loomed the gray brooding shape of Mount Vesuvius. For the moment, it gazed peacefully at the celebrations on the water.

From the deck of the luxurious ship, Nobile had lost count of the number of yachts and flights of planes that had formed the honor guard. Above them, two of his own airships floated majestically in the clear blue sky.[4]

Now it was Mussolini's turn to welcome the heroes. He raised his hand, and the crowd fell silent.

"In the name of the Fascist government, in your name, O Romans!—in the name of all Italians—I tender enthusiastic greetings to the valiant General Nobile and his companions in flight," Mussolini boomed. "The men whom you see at my side today started out in April to attempt a feat that had until now seemed beyond the reach of human daring. They dared to affront the supreme obstacle, that which has neither face nor name: The Unknown. They threw their own souls into the balance, and from the moment they stepped on board their ship renounced all human ties.

"Millions and millions of hearts all over the world followed the flight from Rome—Immortal Rome, whose very name thrills all civilization—straight for the goal. But not one heart beat with more fervent hope than that of the Italian people."[5]

Unbeknown to the thousands of people in the square, Nobile had already made a momentous decision: he was going to return to the pole. In fact, he had made the decision three days after he had jumped out of his rapidly deflating airship in Alaska.[6]

"We had opened the way to the pole," he reflected. "We must go back there to complete the work we had begun. It had to happen. The polar sky had to see an Italian-born airship again."

But even as his feet had landed back on solid ground, time was already running out for him.

Hugo Eckener, savior of the Zeppelin Company, was close to raising the money to build the *Graf Zeppelin*, a German airship seven times the size of the *Norge*. Its stated purpose: the exploration of the North Pole. Its projected first flight: two years away.

And Nobile's fame would protect him for only so long in the cutthroat politics of Fascist Italy. As it faded, so the knives would be out for him. Even his membership in the Fascist Party wouldn't protect him for long. If the general wanted to return to the Arctic in an airship, he would have to move quickly.

UMBERTO NOBILE HAD CLAMBERED off the airship at Teller, Alaska, convinced of three things. First, the age of the land-based explorer was over (it is easy to imagine who he had in mind). Second, he needed to return to the pole with an all-Italian expedition to show Amundsen, and even himself, that, yes, Italy could do it without the Norwegians' help. And third, airships were the best machines for exploring the Arctic.[7]

The *Norge* had reached the North Pole in sixteen hours. By boat and foot, it had taken Nansen one year eight months to reach 84°4'N in 1895, the farthest a white man had ever reached, and he was still hundreds of miles from the pole. The Italian-built airship went on to cover an unexplored area of almost eight hundred square miles in only thirty hours. Nobile wrote for the American Geographical Society's journal:

> Nobody can doubt the superiority of aircraft—airplanes or dirigibles—as a means of exploring the unknown regions of the earth. We can truly say that aviation has produced a revolution in this field. In a few hours, it is possible now to make a journey that in the past required months and years of travel with ships and sledges.
>
> One radical change that has taken place in the matter of polar exploration is this: experts who know how to travel on the ice are no longer needed, and men who know how to navigate in the air will take their place. In addition, it is no longer necessary that the scientists of an expedition be men strong enough to support long journeys on the ice and trained in making them. [Thomas] Edison could be a member of an expedition of this kind and read his own instruments himself. [8]

Later in the same piece he wrote: "It is easy to prophesize that other expeditions with dirigibles will follow our own. We have only started a new era in the history of polar exploration. We have shown the best way to do this successfully, and we have given a practical demonstration."

An editorial in *Aviation* magazine on April 4, 1927, not only praised airships as tools for investigating the far north, but also showed how much of a propaganda victory the trip and the Fascist government's outreach had been:

> The readers of AVIATION may consider themselves highly honored by the distinction conferred on them by His Excellence, Premier Mussolini of Italy. The letter which he has written is so splendid in its cordiality and so complimentary to all phases of American aerial development that it should be regarded as one of those gracious interchanges of good will and kindly sentiments that makes for better feelings between the peoples of the world. . . .
>
> Italian aviation, under the personal direction of the Fascista Premier, has gone forward so rapidly that today it holds a place in world aeronautics that is unsurpassed. The organization and spirit of the Italian Air Force is making it admired by every nation of the world. Its separation from the Army and Navy and its rapid advance due to the stimulus of such a determined and farseeing leader will be an object lesson for all other countries. . . .
>
> In the lighter-than-air field, General Umberto Nobile has given Italy a rightful claim to leadership in the construction of medium sized dirigibles. The *Norge* which flew the Amundsen party over the North Pole blazed a trail through the air from Europe to Alaska that will in the years to come rank with the first Northwest Passage as a historic event.
>
> The Royal Italian Air Force under the able direction of His Excellency Balbo, Undersecretary of State for Aviation, and with the utmost encouragement of Premier Mussolini . . . the new Italy has a defensive air arm that can be regarded as supreme. . . .

AVIATION will not attempt to reply in any way to the magnificent message: it would be presumptuous to do so. . . . All we can do is respond to the greeting to American aviation with the upraised arm and return silently but with a heart filled with appreciation: the Fascista salute.[9]

Like Lincoln Ellsworth and Richard Byrd, Nobile had started to think about exploring the South Pole after he had conquered the North. He had even begun to consider how to explore it by airship. "What is needed is a great base on the coast of the continent and a huge airship able to fly a distance of 15,000 kilometers at a height of 5,000 meters," he said.[10] This was a much longer range than the *Graf Zeppelin* could manage, but it would be within the ranges of its successor, the *Graf Zeppelin II*, the last zeppelin ever built, which had its first flight in September 1938. But in the end, this was just fantasy. Nobile first had to return to the North Pole.

The idea of exploring Antarctica by airship was like science fiction in 1927, whereas Nobile had a very real problem to face. It could be summed up in one word: Lindbergh. The Orteig Prize was a $25,000 reward offered by New York hotel owner Raymond Orteig to the first Allied aviator or aviators to fly nonstop from New York City to Paris or vice versa. In 1926 and 1927, there were six attempts by men to fly across the Atlantic to win the prize, four of which ended in disaster. There had been one serious crash that killed half the crew and one in which all the crew were killed. There had been a flight where the air crew simply disappeared without a trace. Richard Byrd's own first attempt ended in a crash landing that severely injured Floyd Bennett, his copilot from the North Pole flight. Another ended in arguments and lawsuits.

On May 21, 1927, Charles A. Lindbergh won the prize. His was not only the first solo nonstop transatlantic flight in history, but it was also the first nonstop flight between New York and Paris. It made Lindbergh a global celebrity, yet it still didn't match the achievement of the R-34 airship nine years earlier, which was the first aircraft to make an east–west transatlantic flight and the first two-way crossing after the dirigible flew back to the United Kingdom.

Women risked their lives to be the first to fly across the Atlantic as well. In October 1927, actor Ruth Elder nearly came close when her plane ditched three hundred miles short of the Azores. Two months later Frances Wilson Grayson, the niece of President Wilson, disappeared south of Newfoundland. Her plane was never found. In March 1928, actor, aviator, and aristocrat Elsie Mackay tried to fly the other way across the Atlantic. It was reported that five thousand people waited for her to arrive in Long Island. All that was found of her plane was a wheel of its undercarriage washed up on a beach in Ireland. In June of the same year, Amelia Earhart became famous as the first woman passenger to fly across the Atlantic. Four years later, she became the first woman to fly solo across the Atlantic.[11]

If these flights weren't dangerous enough, Mussolini encouraged Francesco De Pinedo in his "Four Continents" flight in 1927. The plan was to demonstrate the ability of a flying boat to fly from Italy to Africa and then to Brazil, the Caribbean, a tour of the United States and Canada, and finally a transatlantic flight back to Rome. While everything on the flight hadn't gone to plan, De Pinedo did land back in the famous Ostia harbor outside Rome, 29,180 miles (46,960 km) and 124 days after he had left. Honors were heaped on the aviator in Italy, the United Kingdom, and the United States.

The opponents of Mussolini's regime had learned from Nobile's visit the year before. For De Pinedo's visit, some two thousand anti-Fascist demonstrators attempted to disrupt his speech in New York. The *New York Times* then reported that "a large part of De Pinedo's audience hurried to the street to give combat and then the patrolmen had to use their clubs on both factions to prevent a battle." When the aviator had finished, the remaining audience went on to the street. The paper reported that ten thousand people were either involved in the riot or watching it.

Nobile quickly realized that after stunts like Lindbergh's and De Pinedo's, it was unlikely the public would remain interested in single flights for much longer. If he really wanted to return to the North Pole, people would want a bigger story of courage and adventure than merely a repeat of the flight of the *Norge*. This time he would have to make several flights over the Arctic in search of undiscovered lands, and this time, wind or no wind, he would have to land a man at the North Pole.

Paradoxically, as Nobile would quickly discover, the more spectacular the stunt he aimed to pull off, the greater the risk to the regime whose support he needed and—if successful— the bigger the threat he would become to rivals in that regime. By 1928, planes could crash almost unnoticed and their pilots be killed without comment. An airship was another matter altogether.

Then there was Hugo Eckener. There was always Eckener. The German was forever just behind him, never giving up, waiting—Nobile must have felt—for him to make a mistake.

Nobile knew that Eckener had been in talks with Fridtjof Nansen, president of Aeroarctic, about using his huge new airship for Arctic exploration (it still wasn't big enough for

Antarctica). And the great American media mogul William Randolph Hearst was interested in financing the zeppelin that was under construction. He wasn't the only one; his representative on the ground in Friedrichshafen boasted that he had closed the deal before "the *Times* man"[12] could get there. In exchange for $175,000, Hearst gained all motion picture and still-image rights, including newsreel rights, for the first flight of the giant.

Hearst wasn't just any media mogul. He had built up his company, Hearst Communications, from nothing to be America's biggest newspaper and magazine group. His life would provide the inspiration for Charles Foster Kane, the media magnate at the heart of Orson Welles's film *Citizen Kane* (1941). The sensationalized reporting of Spanish atrocities by Hearst's papers was widely blamed for leading America into war with Spain in 1898. In the 1930s, Hearst's papers would promote Nazism. They'd run columns by Hitler himself, as well as by Nazi minister Hermann Göring and Mussolini. Now Hearst was going to be backing Eckener.[13]

Hearst's involvement with the *Graf Zeppelin* would climax with plans for the airship to rendezvous at the North Pole with an American submarine renamed the *Nautilus*. If they could pull it off, it would be the first time that a submarine had ever reached the pole. "Why not?" Eckener responded to the proposal. "Provided you make it to the North Pole and really can bore your way up!"[14]

This was no longer exploration for discovery. It was exploration for entertainment. Eckener's crew even had a term for these kinds of missions: "circus flights."[15]

Nobile's more modest initial thoughts about returning to the pole had begun with a series of chats with Riiser-Larsen by the fireside in Teller. The two men had realized that with better weather the *Norge* could have carried on to Seattle and even reached cities farther down the West Coast of America. The Italian and the Norwegian initially discussed repeating the trip, this time flying all the way to Tokyo or San Francisco—and without Amundsen, as the great explorer had decided to retire from the hero business. "My work is fulfilled," he told the *New York Times*. "All the big problems are solved. The work that remains in polar exploration is a matter of detail. Let others handle it."[16]

These fireside exchanges led to the idea of something more ambitious: a new expedition. It would be called the Nobile–Riiser-Larsen expedition, and this time the airship would fly under the Italian flag.[17] Unfortunately, Nobile's deteriorating relationship with Amundsen put an end to this conversation because Riiser-Larsen felt he would be betraying the Governor to side with the Italian, but it didn't stop the whirring of Nobile's brain. "During the month we stayed in Alaska, my mind went on ceaselessly working upon it, sketching out the details bit by bit," he wrote. Riiser-Larsen was left contemplating an expedition to find Crocker Land, which Robert Peary was supposed to have discovered twenty years earlier.

Nobile's plans would come to nothing if he couldn't use the airship base at Kings Bay. Without the hangar and mast, any airship would be smashed to pieces by the Arctic storms. And the use of the base would depend on permission from the Aero Club of Norway, which owned it. Stories swirled around in the Norwegian press that Nobile wanted to buy the hangar and mast.[18] But there was no need for him to do that. Luckily for Nobile, its president, Rolf Thommessen, had become a friend during the negotiations over the fine print of the

Norge expedition. After meeting with Nobile in August when Thommessen was in Italy to receive a medal from Mussolini, Thommessen quickly agreed to let Nobile use the hangar and mast for three years without charge.

All Nobile needed now was an airship—and the permission of his government.

"IT HAS BEEN ONE of my oldest dreams to fly from Rome to Argentina," Colonel Umberto Nobile told the *New York Times* from the luxury of his suite at the Ritz-Carlton in New York before he left for Italy in July 1926. "I have been at work on the aircraft since 1919. I would use a 50,000 cubic meter semi-rigid dirigible, three times as large as the *Norge*, such as the one whose construction will be commenced as soon as I return to Rome. When I get back I will also supervise the building of two more dirigibles of the *Norge* class, one to be completed this year, the other next spring.

"The Rome–Buenos Aires flight would be a matter of 120 hours. The flight from Rome to Teller, Alaska, via Leningrad, Spitzbergen and the Pole was 172 hours. An airship could be made, you know, that would stay in the air a week. If, however, my idea of a continuous flight across the Atlantic was not deemed advisable at first, we could make a stop en route at the Cape Verde islands."[19]

The plans, he emphasized, were only a "possibility" as Mussolini, still air minister, had to approve of them. Nobile didn't tell the journalist they might not even be feasible. The crash of the *Roma* in 1922 had cast doubt in some minds as to whether the semi-rigid type was suitable for such large ships.

But despite such misgivings, the approval for construction

of the airship for the flight from Rome to Buenos Aires or Rio de Janeiro was quickly forthcoming from Il Duce when Nobile returned to Italy. Mussolini was keen to use Nobile's flight to boost the prestige of his regime among the large Italian population in Buenos Aires and Rio de Janeiro as his Arctic flight had done in cities such as Seattle and New York.

Unwisely in a totalitarian state, it is likely that Nobile told friends of his true intentions—that in public he was supporting the flight across the Atlantic but that privately he planned to use the airship for his next Arctic expedition. His enemies were sure to have learned this.

Today there are two monuments in Chicago to a heroic Italian Fascist aviator. One is a street named after him in the city's prestigious Grant Park. The other is a two-thousand-year-old Roman column dedicated to the same man in Burnham Park on the shore of Lake Michigan.[20] And this aviator is not Umberto Nobile.

Nobile hadn't appreciated just how powerful Italo Balbo was becoming.* He may have been too wrapped up in his own plans to fully notice the extent of the threat posed by the former war hero, general commander of the Fascist militia, and

---

* In 1933, Italo Balbo led a group of twenty-five giant flying boats across the North Atlantic to the World's Fair in Chicago and back again. The glamorous Fascist leader was given a ticker-tape parade in New York, received the Distinguished Flying Cross from President Roosevelt, and made it onto the cover of *Time* magazine.

One hundred thousand Chicagoans turned out to see the spectacular flight over their city and the landing of the flying boats on Lake Michigan. There were parades down Michigan Avenue in his honor; a street was named after him; and even a whole day was named after him. A repurposed Roman column was gifted to the Windy City by Mussolini himself in memory of the flight. It is now the only relic of the 1933 World's Fair.

now undersecretary for national economy. Or he may have dismissed Balbo because of the way he looked or even for the humble background of his parents.

Balbo looked more like a Hollywood matinee idol than a Fascist militant. His "chestnut goatee, winning smile, and love of uniforms covered in gold braid and medals" may have made him a bit of a joke to some, but as often is the way, they disguised his ruthlessness and violent behavior.[21] He was able to acquire tremendous power in the Fascist state because he was one of the four men who, along with Mussolini, founded Italian fascism. It was said that even Mussolini was scared of him.

The captain of the *Norge* had done rather well out of the Amundsen-Ellsworth-Nobile expedition. He had been showered with medals in the United States and Italy, met the American president, been promoted to the rank of general, and even been given membership in the party that Balbo had helped to found.[22]

Unfortunately for Nobile, Balbo took a passionate interest in aviation, and his plans didn't have any room for airships or the aristocratic rising star that was now General Umberto Nobile. But Balbo couldn't move against him until attaining

---

On the base of this ancient monument is an inscription in English and Italian: "This column, twenty centuries old, was erected on the beach of Ostia, the port of Imperial Rome, to watch over the fortunes and victories of the Roman triremes. Fascist Italy, with the sponsorship of Benito Mussolini, presents to Chicago a symbol and memorial in honor of the Atlantic Squadron led by Balbo, which with Roman daring, flew across the ocean in the 11th year of the Fascist era" (Christopher Borrelli, "Future of Balbo Monument, a Gift from Mussolini, Uncertain," *Chicago Tribune*, August 18, 2017, http://www.chicagotribune.com/entertainment/ct-ent-balbo-monument-20170817-story.html).

more power. While he waited, he would have to be satisfied with his underlings harassing Nobile's workers with allegations that they were members of the Communist Party and with wrapping Nobile's plans in red tape.

Then Nobile made his fatal mistake. He went to Japan for the winter of 1926–27 with a group of his best men. The general must have thought that he was safe to leave Italy for that long. He was wrong.

The Japanese navy needed help reassembling its *Norge*-class airship, the N-3,[23] which it had bought from Italy, and training a crew to fly the craft. Like the Italians, the Japanese had been given an airship hangar from outside Berlin as war reparations. Now they wanted a fleet of airships to fill it.[24]

The trip to Japan also gave Nobile the chance to enjoy the adulation of thousands again—and he wasn't disappointed. Postcards were printed of the N-3 with fighter planes flying around it. Aeronautical textbooks had his ship on their front covers. Everywhere Nobile went in Japan, he was met by cheering crowds and treated like a hero. He was even given a medal by Admiral Keisuke Okada (who went on to oppose war with America).[25]

Balbo made his power grab within a few weeks of Noble's departure. Out went Nobile's old friend General Alberto Bonzani as undersecretary at the Air Ministry. In came Italo Balbo himself as the new undersecretary,[26] and he would become one of the great—if controversial—leaders of aviation's golden age. His greatest achievements were the building up of the Aeronautica, Italy's air force, and the construction of the huge modernist Air Ministry building in Rome, which was inspired by a visit to the United States. Over the entrance an inscription in marble used to read: "Built while Vittorio Emanuele III Was King, Duce Benito Mussolini, Minister Italo Balbo." Now only Balbo's name survives.[27]

He admired the courage of the "Record Men" and valued the publicity they generated for the development of aviation in general, and the Aeronautica in particular, but hated the individualism of "the prima donna and the diva" that went with these record flights and undermined military discipline, despite being—or perhaps because he was—a prima donna himself. The Record Men whom he saw as a threat to his own position, or to his vision of the future of the air force, quickly found themselves in his gun sights, no matter how famous or skilled they were. The glamorous aviator Francesco De Pinedo clashed with Balbo and ended his career as Italy's air attaché in Argentina. Balbo said of his conflict with one of the best pilots in the world that "there wasn't room for both of us in the same cockpit." Unfortunately for Nobile, he fell into both of Balbo's categories.[28]

The first thing the new minister did was to go on an intensive pilot training course to learn to fly a plane. Then he began building up the Italian Royal Air Force in his own image.

In the spring of 1927, Balbo went on a forty-three-hundred-mile inspection flight around Italian bases in the Mediterranean Sea and Libya. The Italians designed some incredibly beautiful planes before the outbreak of World War II, but the one he flew in looked like it had been invented by Fritz Lang. Largely forgotten outside the forums of aviation enthusiasts, the Savoia-Marchetti S.55 was a large flying boat with two hulls, two shoulder wings, and two huge engines in a push-pull arrangement, which were in turn suspended high in the middle of the plane on a trellis structure. Produced by the hundreds, the plane broke fourteen long-distance, altitude, and payload records during the 1920s.[29]

The route that Balbo took wasn't an accident. It was designed to demonstrate the potential of his concept of air cruises. Like Nobile, he had realized that the time when a single flight by a plane or an airship would automatically grab the world's attention was coming to an end. Instead, Balbo wanted to lead flights of thirty to fifty seaplanes around the Mediterranean and across the Atlantic as a showcase for Italian technology and collectivism as against the individualism of the Record Men and, undoubtedly, for his own leadership skills.[30] Unlike Nobile, Balbo would regularly rely on the advice and leadership of Italy's leading aviators on these cruises.

Soon after Balbo's power grab, Nobile received a telegram from a friend in the Air Ministry—and it contained a warning: "I have been able to discover that an isolating trench is being dug around you," his friend wrote. "The fact is, an atmosphere of diffidence, hostility and coldness is being created towards you. In short the construction of a situation that would render intolerable your presence in the Air Force."[31]

In fact, Balbo's attack on Nobile was about to get a lot more vicious than that. He convinced Mussolini to cancel the construction of Nobile's new airship for the Rome to Buenos Aires attempt, even though it was almost finished. To add insult to injury, Balbo ordered that the whole ship be broken up for scrap.[32] He wanted to make sure that there was no way that Nobile could come back and reverse his decision.

This was a bitter blow to Nobile, who had already spent a year working on the project. "I telegraphed to Rome," Nobile wrote. "But the Italian government had abandoned the construction of the new airship, nor could I induce them to go on with it, although it was well advanced, and, in fact, almost finished.

"I was taken aback by this decision, which I considered a great mistake. But I was more especially disappointed because this destroyed my hope of achieving the Polar expedition with a much larger vessel than before, and so of exploring the Arctic Circle with such important results as would put into the shade the daring flight of the *Norge*."[33]

After Mussolini and Balbo had died, Nobile tried again to explain his fateful decision to leave for Japan. "I would never have thought that in a few months Mussolini, just to please Balbo, would have completely cancelled such a firm undertaking . . . ," he wrote in 1945, for an airship "the construction of which was already well on the way."

Nobile would have to find another airship to take him to the North Pole—and this wasn't the only change. He was accustomed to being received on his own by Mussolini. Now he would have to see his leader together with Balbo. It might have been a good idea for Nobile to immediately call on Balbo on his return from Japan, as military protocol demanded, but his anger wouldn't allow it.[34]

The plan Nobile now pitched to Mussolini at their meeting at which "the Under Secretary for Aviation was also present"[35] was simple. Nobile would complete as many as five voyages from Kings Bay, which would spread out across the Arctic Ocean like a fan. These flights would range from an exploration of the unknown interior of Severnaya Zemlya in the east, another voyage toward Greenland and Canada in the west, and a descent onto the ice itself at the North Pole.[36]

Each of these flights would be longer than the flight of the *Norge*. But with the destruction of the large airship he was building, the only airship that would be available for Nobile to take on this expedition was the same type as the *Norge*. Its code name was N-4, and it would be called the *Italia*.

The *Norge* had barely survived one flight. Now Nobile was going to ask the *Italia* to complete as many as five.

Mussolini listened carefully to Nobile's ambitious new plans. Then he delivered his verdict. "Perhaps it would be better not to tempt Fate a second time," he said. "Still, I recognize the scientific importance of the idea. We will talk about it again next week."[37]

The follow-up conversation with Mussolini never took place. In fact, Nobile would not speak to Mussolini again about the expedition until the eve of departure. "It was clear that Mussolini had abandoned me to my enemies," Nobile wrote.

Nobile later learned that after he had left the meeting Balbo told Mussolini to "let him go, for he cannot possibly come back to bother us anymore."[38]

Nobile was still determined to go ahead despite Il Duce's rather lukewarm support. And at least this time, Nobile would be the undisputed leader of the expedition, or so he thought.

NOBILE COMPARED THE CHALLENGE of organizing the expedition to that of a game of chess. "In short," he wrote, "one had to keep in mind every element of the organizations and coordinate them as a chess-player handles his pieces, foreseeing and anticipating the moves of his adversary: in my case, these were unforeseen difficulties, unexpected hitches, bad weather, and even the possibility of an accident."[39]

Nobile should have added one more item to this list: Italo Balbo.

Over the next twelve months, Nobile would come to firmly believe that his rival was determined to make his prophecy that the aviator wouldn't make it back from the North Pole come true. Balbo's plan seemed to be brutally simple. He would give Nobile enough support to make sure he went on the expedition but not enough to ensure he made it back alive.

Balbo, "who appeared to be warmly supporting my initiative,"[40] restricted to a minimum the financial help the Fascist government would give to Nobile. Instead, the undersecretary of air encouraged Nobile to raise the money that he needed from the Royal Geographical Society and from the City of Milan's Financing Committee.

The plan of his backers was to raise much of the necessary funds through selling the media rights for the expedition to organizations such as the North American Newspaper Alliance,[41] which was willing to pay $20,000 for the exclusive US and Canadian rights and more for worldwide rights.[42] The exclusivity the Americans wanted was in turn dependent on both the expedition's use of the revolutionary short-wave radio technology that Marconi had developed, which could be used to transmit encrypted messages direct to Rome without the need to be relayed and, crucially, on its control of the old shorter-range long-wave radio station operated by the mine at Kings Bay,[43] the only other way to get a sensational story out of the bay to a hungry editor.

The fees would then double if there were "a flight over and stop at the North Pole, the discovery of new lands and sensational episodes, and a disappearance of the expedition for some days and consequent alarm in the world." The additional pressure these financial arrangements placed on Nobile must have been immense.[44]

Balbo agreed to provide the airship and crew for free, but any alterations to the craft had to be paid for by the cash-strapped sponsors of the expedition. With this agreed, the undersecretary of air promptly encouraged the circulation of stories about how unsuitable the N-4 was for such an Arctic expedition.

The Italian navy appeared more willing to help Nobile.[45] Admiral Giuseppe Sirianni, the undersecretary for the navy, was a keen supporter of the expedition. He promised to loan the explorer the *Città di Milano*. To avoid any criticism, it would sail to Svalbard at the navy's expense ostensibly on a training mission.[46] In reality, it would transport equipment for the expedition to the Arctic Circle and provide a base for operations. Its sailors would be handy as the ground crew.

But the *Città di Milano* was a bit of an old tub. It was a former undersea cable-laying ship seized from the Germans in 1918 as part of war reparations. Its captain, Giuseppe Romagna Manoja, appeared at best to be a career naval officer with a startling lack of initiative, which meant every decision had to be approved by Rome. At worst, the captain was a Fascist spy, his job to ensure that Nobile really didn't make it back to Rome. In the months to come, it would be hard for Nobile to see him in any other way.

Finally, Balbo turned down Nobile's request for two or three seaplanes as backup, to help rescue the crew in case of a crash on the ice.[47] Instead, he let the general have a squad of Alpini soldiers from the mountain infantry and a bunch of students from the Italian University Students' Alpine Association to help if the *Italia* crashed. The soldiers were under the command of Captain Gennaro Sora, one of the best ski instructors in the Italian army. Many of the students didn't stay for long in Svalbard. They thought the mission was too dangerous.

The one thing that was on Nobile's side was that the N-4 *Italia*, being the sister ship of the N-1 *Norge*, was a good design. (A version of the *Norge* called the V-6 would join Stalin's airship fleet and in 1937 beat the nonstop-flight record Hugo Eckener set with the *Graf Zeppelin*.)[48]

But the *Italia*'s pedigree couldn't disguise the fact that it was a small ship compared to the other leviathans of the sky.[49] It was another semi-rigid airship whose spine stretched from the bow to the stern. It was lighter than its predecessor, the envelope being made of a thinner material, more than compensating for the slightly bigger gondola. Above it, as on the *Norge*, were the gas cells full of hydrogen that kept the shape of the envelope. Beneath these were the air cells that filled with the amount of air necessary to keep the airship taut when the hydrogen had been released from a vent at the top. (Air was sucked in through a vent in the nose.)

Unlike the *Norge* or the *Graf Zeppelin*, the *Italia* had been built with Arctic exploration somewhat in mind. The *Norge* had its own throne room for the king of Italy. The *Graf Zeppelin*, despite its publicly stated purpose of exploring the Arctic, was built with luxurious bedrooms, dining rooms, and extensive kitchens in which some of the best chefs in the world went about their business. Such fixtures and fittings would be stripped out for any flights to the Arctic and replaced with scientific and survival equipment.

In contrast to all this luxury, the *Italia*'s gondola or control cabin resembled a rather odd tent attached to the bottom of the envelope. Like a tent, it was cold, cramped, noisy, and not immune to wind, made as it was out of steel tubing, three layers of canvas with an air gap for insulation, and a light wooden floor, which was all that there was between you and a three-thousand-foot drop to your death.

Like many airships of the time, the gondola was embedded into the envelope of the airship. Nobile's men could climb up a ladder directly into the keel of the ship. Once inside, the crew could walk down along a fairly flimsy V-shaped corridor stretching the length of the ship, which might bring to the imagination the corridor of an alien spaceship. At one end of which, in the canvas-lined keel, the men could find spare parts, cans of fuel, a hammock to sleep on, and emergency supplies. However, little thought had been given as to how any crew members still in the envelope would escape if there was a crash landing. This oversight would have terrible consequences.

The ship still had three engines, which could provide a modest maximum speed of 75 mph. In some strong Arctic storms, it might even find itself blown backward. Each of the engines was housed in its own protective casing large enough for a mechanic to crawl into and attached to the ship by more steel tubing. Three crewmen had the hair-raising job of crawling out to refuel and repair these engines regardless of current speed, temperature, or height.

Then there was the problem of the ice. Nobile and his fellow crew members on the previous polar mission had seen how sharp fragments of ice flung over from the propellers could rupture the envelope of the airship. After a great many experiments, Nobile's solution was again to add rubberized fabric to vulnerable sections. Three layers of this fabric were stronger than a similar weight of metal nets or hemp.

Ice could also cause the vital gas valves to freeze open so the hydrogen that kept an airship in the sky would pour out, causing the craft to plummet toward the ground. Conversely, ice could cause the valves to freeze shut, making the envelope of the airship burst as it climbed. Nobile decided to use the same protective hoods to go over the valves as he had on the *Norge* and hope they held up again. The keel was strengthened with extra layers of canvas glued to one another.

Yet there was one significant difference between the *Norge* and the *Italia*. The N-4's envelope was lighter, and maybe more vulnerable to tears.

Italy led the world in radio technology, thanks to Marconi. Now an Italian had the opportunity to plunge an Italian radio antenna into the North Pole.[50] For the expedition, the navy installed on the *Italia* and *Città di Milano* high-tech integrated long-wave and short-wave radios that would—via short wave—connect them to a powerful new radio station in San Paolo, Rome, and then on to the Italian colonies in East Africa and the Italian diaspora in the Americas. They could now communicate directly with their political masters in Rome without reliance on the Norwegians.[51] The portable radio that Nobile took on the N-4 would for the first time give a landing party at the North Pole the power to broadcast direct to Rome, and it would give Nobile the chance to bring his dream of establishing a permanent base near the North Pole one step closer to reality.

The radio would also be useful in case there was an emergency in which the airship was forced down onto the ice. The problem was—as ever with new technology—compatibility. If survivors continued to broadcast on short wave rather than long wave, then ships, planes, and nearby settlements would be unable to hear them, as they were likely to be equipped with long-wave radio.[52]

With the airship under construction, Nobile needed to select a crew. The publicity in the Italian press had led to hundreds of men applying—and this time he had the freedom to choose whom he wanted. Ironically, given the nationalistic nature of the trip, two-thirds of the men enthusiastically volunteering for the expedition didn't look particularly Italian. These men with their fair hair and blue eyes were, Nobile mused, perhaps "obeying an instinctive call back to the cold lands of a far-off Nordic origin."[53]

Whatever criticisms Amundsen had about Nobile's conduct on the polar flight were clearly not shared by the Italian engineers. All four of his engineers from the *Norge* signed up at once, despite the greater danger of the multiple flights.[54] For the important role of navigator, Nobile chose two experienced naval officers, Adalberto Mariano and Filippo Zappi, rather than trust his own calculations. Accurate and detailed navigational records were vital if Nobile was to avoid the fate of explorers such as Byrd, whose claim to have flown to the North Pole was questioned.

Nobile felt that Amundsen had largely ignored the potential of the polar flight to gather scientific data, obsessed as he was by claiming the flight as a Norwegian expedition. The Italian was determined to put that right on the *Italia*. Here he broke with the nationalist agenda of the flight. He picked a Czech and a Swede to accompany an Italian scientist on the trip. The two scientists must have felt uncomfortable at times. The men were the only non-Italians on an Italian airship with an otherwise all-Italian crew that had a lot to prove. "Nobile was very conscious of it. They all were," wrote the Czech scientist, Dr. František

Běhounek.[55] During the course of the flight, they managed to communicate in English with a dash of French.

Professor Finn Malmgren had been on the *Norge* expedition. He had impressed Nobile then with his level-headed attitude, open and frank advice, sense of duty, and willingness to take responsibility for risky advice.[56] On the *Italia* expedition, the moody Swedish meteorologist would have the distinction of being the chief weatherman and the only crew member with any actual experience in Arctic survival. Malmgren's forecasts would soon be questioned as relentlessly as Nobile's decisions.

Then there were the men of the press. Both Amundsen and Nobile relied on journalists to write the stories that generated the publicity that funded their adventures—and, in the case of Nobile, kept him safe from his enemies. But beyond that, their attitudes differed. Amundsen liked his reporters on the ground. Nobile (confident, perhaps too much, in his own abilities) wanted them up in the air with him. Nobile should have taken only one reporter on the expedition, but for political expediency he chose two: Francesco Tomaselli, correspondent for the Milan newspaper *Corriere della Sera*, which had the exclusive contract, and Ugo Lago from the Fascist paper *Popolo d'Italia*, to whom Nobile couldn't say no. The paper was founded by Mussolini himself and played a key part in the founding of the Fascist movement in Italy. The reporters would both fly up to Svalbard on the airship and then take it in turns to cover the individual polar flights. At least Tomaselli had the advantage of having been an officer in Italy's Alpine mountain soldiers.

The general also didn't, couldn't, or wouldn't appoint a second-in-command. Balbo may even have denied Nobile the man he wanted. There were certainly men on board who knew about airships: the ambitious Adalberto Mariano had experience of airships, and Filippo Zappi had an airship pilot's license, but none of them would have the authority to question Nobile's decisions in an emergency.[57]

While confident in his own abilities, Nobile did not ignore the question of how his men would cope if the N-4 crashed on the ice. "I stinted neither time nor money on this work," he wrote. Nobile crisscrossed[58] Europe talking to the top Arctic survival experts, including "choosing to ask" the approval of Amundsen's great nemesis, Nansen, on the clothes, tents, guns, and food they should take with them.[59] Following Nansen's advice, Nobile ordered a special kind of pemmican, suited to Italian tastes. The pemmican made for the crew of the *Italia* was 70 percent "pulverized" meat and fat, 5 percent peas, 5 percent oatmeal, 15 percent potatoes, and 5 percent onions, celery, and garlic, in order to reflect Italian tastes.

Nobile was now left with the job of planning the route that the *Italia* would take to Kings Bay. He had already experienced firsthand, in the *Norge*, the challenges of flying from Rome to Svalbard. He knew that they would have to face bad weather more than once on their long flight across the continent, though he couldn't have imagined just how bad it was going to get.[60]

Essential was finding one or two hangars along the way big enough to shelter the N-4 on the thirty-one-hundred-mile flight.[61] Nobile would have preferred to have taken a similar curved approach to the route that he had followed with the *Norge*. But his course was now restricted by the availability of such hangars. The British naval airship base in Norfolk had been shut down. Its giant hangar had been relocated to Cardington, and the British might not want their colonial rivals sniffing around their top-secret airship program. The great wooden airship hangar at Gatchina near Leningrad had been demolished because of wood rot.[62] (Nobile turned down the Soviets' offer to build a mooring mast on the site, fearing that the airship would be too dangerously exposed tied to a mast if they ended up—like last time—stranded in Leningrad because of bad weather.[63])

This left the general only one hangar that he could easily use. The old German zeppelin base at Stolp (now Słupsk) on the Baltic coast had not, in fact, been torn down after the war as required by the terms of the Treaty of Versailles, having escaped that fate because of its commercial location—right where it was thought that the north–south and east–west commercial airship routes would cross.[64] Now at least it could help Nobile.

Nobile then decided to take one of the biggest gambles of his life: he was going to risk his whole expedition by flying directly to Kings Bay in two giant jumps. The first leap would take the *Italia* from Milan over central Europe to Stolp. The second would take it from Stolp over Scandinavia to Kings Bay, with a brief stop at the mooring mast at Vadsø in Norway to refuel.[65] He would have to time the departure of the *Italia* from Milan with the arrival of his two support ships in Kings Bay. These were the *Hobby*, which transported the supplies for the expedition, the ground crew the N-4 needed, and repair materials; and the *Città di Milano*, his official base ship.

As if that weren't risky enough, Nobile then had to gamble again. He could choose to fly across the flat lands of the Karst region on his way to Stolp or to fly over the Alps. The Karst is a high plateau famous for its powerful winds, the strongest of which would be enough to destroy the *Italia*. To fly over the Alps, however, the *Italia* would need to climb to one mile in altitude, which would necessitate a reduction in both crew and payload.

He chose to fly across the Karst. The Zeppelin Company had given Nobile permission to use its hangars at Friedrichshafen on the shore of Lake Constance in case of an emergency.[66] (The only consolation in such a crisis would be that Nobile might get a glimpse of the *Graf Zeppelin*.)

With the route of the flight set, Nobile could now dispatch teams of his men from the factory in Rome to the far corners of Europe. The N-4 could then be flown to Milan, ready for its departure. The wealthy citizens of the city, having funded the expedition, wanted to see the ship for themselves.

OFFICIALLY RETIRED, AMUNDSEN FLUCTUATED between depression at how the last expedition of his career had turned out and fury at how Nobile and Mussolini had stolen the credit for it. Mussolini's welcome speech to Nobile in August 1926 hadn't helped his anger. Neither had his realization that while he had been back home in Norway, Nobile had been traveling around America telling his story of the *Norge*. Attempts by his friends to cheer him up wound the coil further. "Those black gypsies should never have been allowed to join," wrote his friend, the chemist Fritz G. Zapffe, to him, putting the blame on the Italians, [67] but Amundsen likely read such statements as implicit criticism for having allowed Nobile to control the expedition in the first place.

Amundsen's *My Life as an Explorer* was the last book he would write, and it was the kind of book that should never have been written. It was an act of self-destruction. Unfortunately for Nobile, the book was serialized by *World's Work* a month before it was published. The result was fifteen pages of poison directed at him in the August 1927 edition of the now defunct American magazine. No mention of the article was found on the front cover, but there it was on page 389: "Roald Amundsen's 'Inside Story' of the Rows aboard the Norge: The Explorer Complains that Nobile Nearly Wrecked the Airship over the Arctic but Tried to Seize the Honors."[68] The only consolation for Nobile was that their feud was old news. But this was Amundsen's own account of their clash.

The Inside Story of the *Norge*'s flight over the North Pole in the summer of 1926 has never been told.

I should not tell it now were it not that so much misrepresentation has been broadcast about it that simple justice to myself and my companions compels me to reveal all the facts. . . .

But if I should leave the truth about the *Norge*'s flight to be gathered by the public from the mass misrepresentation of the facts given forth by Italian propaganda, I should be permitting a gross injustice to be visited, not only upon my own reputation, but upon the hard-earned laurels of Lincoln Ellsworth and my Norwegian compatriots. . . .

In the light of all these years planning for the flight, how preposterous is the claim now brazenly sought to be established by the Italians, that Colonel Nobile conceived and engineered the *Norge* expedition, or that he had any

other useful function in it than that of pilot of the aircraft.[69]

Amundsen's fury continued unabated:

I was delighted to share the national honors with my
beloved American friend. I did not intend, however, to
share them with the Italians. We owed them nothing but
the opportunity to buy and pay for a second-hand military airship. . . . [T]he expedition was Ellsworth's and
mine. It was our idea. It was financed with our money,
and it would be made in a craft that we had bought and
paid for.[70]

Later in 1927, the final straw for the elderly man came
when he read in the paper that his former loyal lieutenant,
Riiser-Larsen, had now betrayed him as well. He was helping
Nobile prepare for his new expedition.

Yet for all the pressure it heaped on Nobile on the eve of
his new expedition, Amundsen's words revealed his own true
nature to the world, and the world didn't like what it saw.

IN MARCH 1928—AND WITH just one month to go before his expedition was set to leave for Svalbard—General Nobile made a
secret journey to Berlin.[71] This was the Berlin immortalized
in the film *Cabaret*, the city enjoying the Golden Twenties and
reveling in decadence, deviance, and high culture. It was the
era of the Bauhaus movement with its architecture expressing
harmony between function and design; the era of the films of

Fritz Lang, Brecht's *Threepenny Opera*, and the films and music of Marlene Dietrich.

But the party was ending. Goebbels, the Nazis' propaganda mastermind, called Berlin "the reddest city in Europe after Moscow."[72] And in his eyes it was. By the time Goebbels arrived in the city in 1926, the local Nazi Party had collapsed and its sworn enemies, the Social Democratic Party and the Communist Party, together kept winning a majority of votes in elections. Goebbels's solution to this problem was straightforward: the conquest of the streets through a strategy of provoking the opposition. The kind of fighting that had largely disappeared from the sidewalks of Rome or Milan would suddenly explode on the streets of Berlin as Hitler's Brownshirts fought the communists and socialists for control. But the people of Berlin were stubborn. Despite all the violence, the Nazis still achieved only limited success at the ballot box.

Nobile's objective was to meet the great Soviet Arctic pioneer scientist Rudolf Samoylovitch, the new president of the world-renowned Institute of Arctic Studies at Leningrad, who had agreed to meet Nobile there, on neutral ground. His goals were to seek advice from the Russian, who had been on thirteen Arctic expeditions, and, more important, to find out everything the Soviets knew about the relatively unexplored sea and islands off the coast of northern Siberia into which the Italians would be flying, islands that the Norwegians were keen to claim. For Professor Samoylovitch, it seems to have been more straightforward: to get access to the data that Nobile's flight would gather about this large hole in the map.[73]

The risks they both took were immense. If Balbo, who was a fanatical anticommunist, learned about Nobile's trip to Berlin, then he would be lucky even to make it into exile. In the Soviet Union, scientists like Samoylovitch were under pressure to produce the research results the state wanted or risk being denounced as an enemy of the people and given a one-way ticket to Siberia. If Stalin heard about Samoylovitch's sharing with Nobile of intelligence, maps, data, and expedition accounts published only in Russian,[74] he would likely face death in a gulag. For their personal safety, the two men met in the lobby of a busy tourist hotel.

Samoylovitch knew little about airships, but after he heard about Nobile's plans—the Russian reported that Nobile was very guarded about the exact detail—he could easily see how vulnerable Nobile and his men would be in a ship the size of the *Italia*. Even though the *Norge* had survived one flight over the Arctic, the Russian was worried about the danger of ice, the lack of power of its engines, and the cramped conditions in the cabin, which would make worthwhile scientific research difficult.[75] Samoylovitch begged Nobile to abandon his plans to land a party of men on the ice to carry out research. Nobile had intended for the men to be picked up a month or two later when the airship returned—or trudge over the ice floes to find safety at the closest human settlement. Samoylovitch told the Italian that the moment the airship had left the researchers on the ice, it would be almost impossible to find them again. The Arctic landscape had an ability to make people invisible to an aircraft flying overhead. The idea that these men could just walk to safety over the ice was also impractical given the distances involved. The nearest human settlements, Samoylovitch pointed out, belonged to nomads, and it was impossible to guarantee that they would actually be where the map said they were.[76]

Overall, Samoylovitch's verdict was that the expedition was "extraordinarily risky" but that if Nobile succeeded the results would be "very valuable."[77]

JUST LIKE THE CREW of the *Norge*, the last thing the men did before they left Rome was seek an audience with the pope. Despite political infighting, Nobile had continued to have a good relationship with the pontiff on his return from the North Pole. Pope Pius XI had been a keen mountaineer, and in their audiences, according to Nobile, he even had a habit of quoting important details of previous polar expeditions that he had missed. The pontiff seemed more interested in the *Italia* expedition than he had been in the flight of the *Norge*. He wanted to be kept informed of how the preparations were going, and he was keen to help Nobile as well. Nobile later wrote that Pope Pius XI had "personally hunted"[78] for meteorological data collected during an earlier expedition to the Frances Joseph Islands that he had been unable to trace.

At the audience, the pope announced that he was giving the N-4 a special mission. This was to carry "the emblem of Christ to the summit of the world." Inside the hollowed-out oak cross was a parchment, whose words would "consecrate the summit of the world."

His prediction that it would be a heavy cross to carry would turn out to be more prophetic than he likely anticipated.[79]

Seven

"We Are Quite Aware that Our Venture Is Difficult and Dangerous . . . but It Is This Very Difficulty and Danger which Attracts Us"

"WE ARE QUITE AWARE that our venture is difficult and dangerous—even more so than that of 1926—but it is this very difficulty and danger which attracts us," said Nobile in a speech to the wealthy citizens of Milan on the eve of departure. "Had it been safe and easy other people would have already preceded us."[1] His mission: to explore the last big empty space left on the map for any undiscovered land—and to claim it in the name of Fascist Italy.[2]

"But if our enterprise should be wrecked," he added prophetically, "then you will see all these facile critics come forward, leaping for joy, to tell you that they had foreseen it, that things could have been otherwise, that it was only natural that this should happen."[3]

In Norway, feelings were running high against Nobile after the publication of Amundsen's book. Just why did the Italians want to come back? One Swedish commentator summed up the mood as "the Norwegians want the poles to themselves and the Italians should take their explorations towards warmer, more southerly regions."[4] Others thought that Mussolini must think there was oil in the Arctic.[*] One newspaper put it more bluntly. Nobile's venture was part of an "imperialistic colonization policy," it declared. The *Italia* expedition "had the intention of enhancing the prestige of Italian imperialism."[5]

In the early hours of April 15, 1928, the great airship *Italia* was walked out of the hangar in Milan by its ground crew onto the deserted airfield. The time of departure had deliberately been kept secret[6] to avoid attracting the kind of crowds that had been drawn to see the craft since it arrived three weeks ago.

The order was given, and its engines roared to life. With Nobile's cry of "Let's go!" the men dropped their tightening ropes, the roar of the engines grew louder, and the airship for a moment filled the sky over their heads before it joined the other lights in the night sky.[7]

"We shall have some excitement," said the *Italia's* meteorologist, Finn Malmgren[8]—and he was right.

"RIVALS IN THE ARCTIC," shouted the headline of the *New York Times*. Umberto Nobile, the paper claimed, faced a "dangerous rival" in the race to find undiscovered lands near the North

---

* Italy still has a presence in the Arctic today. The Dirigibile Italia Arctic Station is an Italian research station in Kings Bay, Svalbard. The Italian oil company, Eni, produces oil from the Goliat field in the Barents Sea off Norway. In 2017, President Trump gave Eni permission to drill for oil in the Arctic Ocean, off the coast of Alaska.

Pole.[9] It is hard to tell whether the paper was talking about the experienced Arctic aviator George Hubert Wilkins or his state-of-the-art Lockheed Vega.

The *New York Times* asked what kind of man was brave enough to "match the airplane against the dirigible in the Arctic this coming spring."[10] Wilkins was an old hand at Arctic exploration even though he was only thirty-eight. He had gone on three polar expeditions by the age of thirty-four, commanding the Detroit Arctic expeditions in 1926, which Richard Byrd had been invited on, and again in 1927, sponsored by the Detroit Aviation Society and the *Detroit News*. He had learned a great many lessons about Arctic aviation from these abortive exploratory flights off the north coast of Alaska. It is important to remember that engineers in the 1920s understood very little about how planes and their engines would perform in the Arctic; many doubted they could work at all.[11] Now he was back again.

In 1926, Wilkins's flights from Point Barrow over the unexplored Arctic Sea ended in disappointment. Accidents and bad weather limited the flying, and his expedition achieved little in the way of exploration, though a great deal in terms of learning how to fly in the Arctic and the feasibility of flying from Point Barrow to Svalbard.

In 1927, the Australian tried again. For many people, the flight of the *Norge* had ruled out the possibility of any undiscovered land between the Alaskan coast and the North Pole. Wilkins thought otherwise. "The Amundsen-Ellsworth-Nobile flight . . . was popularly believed to have eliminated the possibility of discovering land between Barrow and the pole; but, while these men skillfully flew for a great distance over cloud and reached their destination, the conditions beneath the cloud could not everywhere be observed. Perhaps there was land, perhaps not. But even supposing the trip of the *Norge* had cleared the area north of Point Barrow, there were still great areas to the northwest and northeast to be explored. To investigate these areas was my original plan." [12]

This time, his flight ended in a near disaster. Wilkins crashed on the sea ice around seventy miles from safety. For five days, he and his copilot were imprisoned by a storm in the wreck of their aircraft. After the storm had abated, they discovered that the sea ice they were on had moved two hundred miles from where they had originally landed.

Their only option was to walk out of disaster. Beechy Point on the coast of Alaska was about eighty miles away. Rather than relishing such a challenge as a way to prove his masculinity, for Wilkins it was a terrible ordeal. "Much of the pack ice over which we crossed was so badly broken and so covered with snow that we found it impossible to walk," he wrote later, "and the best means of progress was on our hands and knees." [13] It took the two men thirteen days of "hard traveling" to cover eighty miles.

A year later, Wilkins had upgraded to a much more powerful means of flight.

A mighty aerial engine roared to life in Alaska. "The Hollywood-built" plane, as the newsreels called it, [14] looked every inch the part, with its high wing and streamlined tapered fuselage made of molded plywood with windows for its passengers. The design of its cantilevered wing meant that it didn't need any ugly struts or wires to support it. There was only an advertisement for Richmond "Gasoline of Power" to spoil its good looks.

The Vega was bleeding edge. [15] It was fast, very fast, with a top speed of 138 mph. It had been designed as a four-seater for Lockheed's own airline and would rival the Fokker Trimotor as the aircraft of choice for the next generation of pioneer aviators. (A Vega flown by former barnstormer Wiley Post would break the record for flying around the world held by Hugo Eckener's *Graf Zeppelin*.) While the Vega didn't have the range of Nobile's airship, it certainly had better performance. It could climb fast and fly high to avoid storms, and it could make good time even against the kind of strong headwind that would keep the Italian airship almost stationary in the air.

The Vega's range meant that Wilkins could just about fly directly from Point Barrow in Alaska to Svalbard like an airship could, and cover on his way a region of the Arctic that the *Norge* had just missed. It was also an area where a magnetic compass was unreliable thanks to its proximity to the North Pole. Correcting for its unreliability would add more work to the already busy navigator who was working in temperatures as low as $-49°F$ ($-45°C$).

But Wilkins was always willing to innovate his way out of a problem. The Australian was painfully aware of how engines could freeze in the subzero temperatures of the Arctic. His solution was for the pilot to drain the engine of its oil after the plane had landed and then to pull over the whole engine a large fabric hood attached to a stove, which would protect the engine from the freezing cold of the night. In the morning, the heater would warm up the engine and have it ready for takeoff in about three-quarters of an hour.

NOBILE HAD TO KEEP thoughts of Wilkins out of his head and focus on atmospheric conditions. He needed to reach Svalbard as quickly as possible to take advantage of the good weather window in early spring when the twenty-four-hour darkness started to lighten and before the warmth of the summer sun arrived. As the mercury rose in the thermometer, the more hazardous flying became because the ice started to break up and banks of mist settled over the landscape.

Nobile's airship headed for its first stop in Germany with "a staggering load" for an airship its size.[16] There were twenty men on board, plus Titina, whom Nobile refused to leave behind. Add to that three thousand pounds of equipment, four thousand pounds of ballast, seven hundred pounds of oil, and eighty-six hundred pounds of petrol.

The first test the N-4 faced was to fly over the Karst. Once a lawless frontier land between the Austrian and Ottoman Empires, and then the front line between the Austrian and Italian armies only ten years before, by 1928 the Karst may have technically been at peace,* but it was still ravaged by the bora, a fierce north-northeasterly wind that storms from the mountains down the Adriatic. The name comes from Boreas, the Greek god of the north wind, and among the months it was fierce was April.[17]

Boreas didn't want to let the Italians through.[18] It smacked the airship with a 40 mph wind that shredded the left horizontal fin. The damage was serious. Because the horizontal fin

---

* The peace on the plateau didn't last long. At the start of World War II, the Karst, then part of Yugoslavia, was occupied by the Axis powers of Italy, Germany, and Hungary, and its people were subjected to ethnic cleansing. Later in the war, a brutal conflict broke out between communist partisans and Fascist militia that ended in an orgy of score-settling killing at the end of the war. Today it is known as a center for Far Right activity (Robert Macfarlane, *Underland: A Deep Time Journey* [London: Penguin, 2020], chap. 7, Kindle).

was an important control surface of the ship, the vessel would now be less maneuverable, setting up a potentially fatal situation as they crossed the mountains. But Nobile had no choice but to reduce speed and keep going.

By 8:00 a.m., the great ship was spotted flying over the Hungarian border; by the middle of the afternoon, it was passing over Brno in Czechoslovakia. But there was trouble ahead for the airship. Over Moravia and Silesia were lightning and very high winds, with some gusts almost off the scale.

"Shall we change course, General?" asked First Officer Adalberto Mariano anxiously.[19] Nobile's answer was simply no. They had to keep going.

But the weather didn't look as if it would let them. As the N-4 approached the Sudetes, the mountains that stretch through central Europe like a giant border fence, Nobile realized that the peaks were covered by ominous black clouds. The only daylight that could be seen was up one narrow mountain valley.

Nobile hesitated. In the past, he had turned back rather than risk an airship in such a storm, but he knew this time that such a command would imperil the whole mission. The time needed to fly back to Milan and repair the ship would mean they missed the good weather window in the Arctic and—more important—it would be a gift to Italo Balbo. Nobile might not be allowed to make a second attempt.

That afternoon, Nobile and Malmgren, the meteorologist, made the fateful decision to head straight up the valley. For an hour, the weather was fine, and they started to relax, but the gods were only toying with them. Suddenly the *Italia* was ambushed. Heavy clouds closed in rapidly around the airship. A terrible hailstorm tore at the tent-like fabric of the ship, making so much noise the crew had to cover their ears. Overhead, brilliant flashes of lightning lit up the sky.

"It was a terrible moment," recalled Nobile. "The storm was round us on all sides: flashes followed hard on one another—lightning to right, to left, in front of us, behind us, accompanied by deafening peals of thunder. It seemed as if there was no way out. From one moment to another a thunderbolt might strike the ship and set it on fire."[20]

If they dared to try to escape the storm by flying higher, the electricity from the lightning threatened to turn the hydrogen-filled ship into a burning coffin.

The only option was to go even slower and lower. At four hundred and fifty feet from the ground, Nobile's men would have been able to read the signposts they flew over if the storm allowed them. It was a "wild ride."[21] Intense concentration and faith in their own instincts were necessary if the crew were to see—or even sense—the sheer rock walls of the mountains in their path in enough time to avoid them. The Italia's closest call was avoiding a huge cross on top of a mountain with only feet to spare.

The experience shook Nobile so much that he was determined not to take the same risks again.[22] He was now willing to turn back to Milan despite the dangers of another kind he would face there. The decision hinged on the next weather report. Was there a clear route to Stolp?

"Meteorological conditions permit you to navigate as far as Stolp," the telegram stated.[23] Onward they would go.

At 7:50 a.m. on April 16, the N-4 limped into the old airship base at Stolp and its dilapidated hangar (all its windows had been smashed by boys throwing stones).[24] All that there was to guide her in was a single searchlight that had survived the war and a cross outlined by a hundred or so faint lights. Two hundred soldiers drafted from a local barracks to act as the ground crew were now huddled together for protection from the biting Baltic wind. Some of them had helped the zeppelins land on their return from their raids.

Two-thirds of the *Italia*'s fuel had been consumed by the battle with the storm. Every pound of ballast had gone. The left tail fin that Nobile had strengthened before they left had been "torn to shreds,"[25] and the wooden propellers were so badly damaged by hail that they had to be replaced. Exclaimed the *New York Times*, "Never before had a dirigible been so buffeted by violent winds."[26] And this was only the first stage of the flight.

That wasn't the end of the drama. When Nobile stepped off the airship onto the airfield, he must have sensed the tension in the air. Local right-wing politicians who wanted the return of the kaiser and German military dominance had spread the story that Nobile had been a member of the hated Office of the Inter-Allied Control Commission responsible for the destruction of Germany's airship hangars—such as the one at Stolp—and the factories required to make them, which was a story that the *New York Times* had earlier reported as fact.[27] He was also, they reminded everyone, an Italian, a citizen of a nation that had once been an ally of Germany, but then a betrayer, when it fought with the British and French in 1915. And Nobile was "a bit thick" to want to use the last remaining airship hangar at Stolp to shelter his airship.

The resentment against the Italians had been whipped up to such an extent that locals hurled insults at the Italian crew when they landed (if the Italians didn't speak German, they could certainly understand the body language). The government ordered extra police sent to protect the airship. Titina did her bit by "defeating and routing" the remaining dog on the airfield. She had already sent the other two packing.

Nobile telegraphed Rome for technicians and spare parts. After that, there was nothing he and his men could do other than wait. Nobile took advantage of the time to visit Berlin and seek advice from the leaders of the Society for the Exploration of the Arctic by Airship. He even met President Hindenburg. He would buy warmer clothes for Titina in the city too. The cold was not helping her temper.

It was easy for Nobile to imagine what Balbo was saying to Mussolini about this setback—and he was right. "I think our predictions were right that the expedition will fail, for the airship is already in difficulties just getting to its take-off base," Balbo stated in an official report to Mussolini about the delay of the N-4.[28]

Now Nobile had another problem. Four days later, Wilkins, on behalf of the Detroit Arctic expedition, landed a glamorous California-built Lockheed Vega on Svalbard.

AFTER THREE ABORTED TAKEOFFS, Wilkins made it into the air on the fourth attempt. The Australian was now flying the route he had dreamed of for the last three years. He and his copilot were covering in hours distances that it would have taken explorers months to traverse on foot.

The flight finally answered another question that still obsessed scientists, explorers, and politicians despite the gathering weight of evidence against it. There was no sign of land where, according to Robert Peary, Crocker Land was supposed to be. It was just hundreds of miles of sea ice. In fact, Wilkins was able to confirm that there was no sign of land at all toward the North Pole. The fact that Peary had said otherwise was further evidence that the explorer had never reached the North Pole despite his claim that he had.

Finally, after about twenty hours in the air, Wilkins and his copilot could just make out the mountains of Svalbard. But by then the temperature was −4°F (−20°C) inside the cabin, −45°F (−43°C) outside, and the fog was closing in. The wind had grown so strong that it wildly threw their charts and compasses around the cockpit of the Lockheed Vega.

Unable to find Green Harbor on Svalbard in the severe snowstorm, the two men decided they had no choice but to try to land. Luckily, they didn't have to land on the ice again. This time, the pilots found Deadman's Island, off the north coast of Svalbard, and fortunately it didn't live up to its name: on landing, the powerful wind acted like a brake and stopped the Vega short of the sea. With the plane in one piece, the men had every chance of being able to take off again when the storm abated.

After following Wilkins's procedure of draining the oil and covering the engine, the airmen hunkered down in the cabin of the plane. For four days, the storm howled around the plane, at times threatening to toss the aircraft over on to its back.

On the fifth day, it abated, and a small gap in the bad weather appeared that offered them a chance to escape, which they took. The engine roared back to life just as Wilkins had predicted it would after being warmed up. They were able to get the Lockheed up into the air and quickly saw the radio towers of Green Harbor in the distance. One short hop and they were there.

The newsreels didn't hold back in celebrating Wilkins's

achievement. His flight over the top of the world was a "sensational 2,200 mile trans-Arctic flight from Alaska to Spitsbergen. Scientists and explorers unite in calling it one of the greatest in aerial exploration history."[29]

Amundsen didn't mince his words either. "No flight has been made anywhere, at any time, that compares to it," he declared.[30] King George V gave Wilkins a knighthood, and the Royal Geographical Society gave him a founder's medal.

With his own expedition grounded on the Baltic coast, Nobile was less than enthusiastic about Wilkins's triumph. "I am delighted to hear that his efforts have been crowned with success, and that he has been able to cover in reverse direction, and by other means, the route we traversed in the *Norge* in 1926."[31]

BALBO WASN'T THE ONLY one who didn't think Nobile would make it to the pole. Newspapers such as the *New York Times* were even starting to question whether Nobile would reach Svalbard.[32] "April is the best month for exploring the Arctic with aircraft. General Nobile, detained in Germany due to damage to his dirigible, must doubt whether he can carry out his plans after he arrives at Kings Bay."

Wilkins, no doubt provoked by the Italian's grudging praise of his own flight, encouraged the feeding frenzy when he shared his doubts about Nobile's expedition with an American reporter: "We fear that his misfortune and delay will mean that by the time he is ready to proceed it will be too late in the Summer for productive long distance flying in the Arctic."[33] When Nobile offered him a place on the *Italia*, Wilkins turned it down. He said he needed to write the book of his expedition.

Nobile must have started to think that these doubters were right. Furthermore, even though they were delayed for repairs and then by bad weather, it turned out that they might arrive before their base ship had—the first expedition this would ever have happened to.

The reason for this was that the Italian support ship was still at Tromsø, on the north coast of Norway and known as the gateway to the Arctic. The town is at the end of a fjord towered over by two snowcapped mountains. Today it has a harbor dominated by a statue of Roald Amundsen staring up the bay and out to sea, and there are two or three main roads. Then—as today—it was home to the Institute for Polar Research. Even in 2021, it takes just ten minutes to walk out of the town into the fields behind it.

The *Città*'s captain, Giuseppe Romagna Manoja, had refused to set sail because he had heard that Kings Bay was still locked in by ice. This was despite the fact that Nobile's ship the *Hobby* had already arrived in Kings Bay carrying supplies, materials to repair the hangar, and even Amedeo Nobile, Umberto's brother, and like Byrd, had unloaded them onto the ice.

Romagna's cautious approach to making difficult decisions may have served him well as a certain kind of professional naval officer, but it was now obvious that it was hindering the success of the venture. As the expedition leader, Nobile sent a direct order to the captain to "proceed at once to Kings Bay,"[34] which Romagna obeyed only after he checked with Rome first.[35]

The outspoken Norwegian journalist Lise Lindbæk had no doubt whose side the captain was on. "The Italian rescue ship, *Città di Milano*, under Captain Romagna, tried from the outset to sabotage all efforts to assist, undoubtedly on direct orders from Rome," she wrote in her memoirs. "This was so striking that, during a state visit to Finland, none other than King Haakon [of Norway] himself expressed his utter astonishment to the Italian ambassador in Helsinki."[36]

On April 30, fourteen days after the *Italia* had limped into Stolp, the Geophysical Institute in Tromsø reported good weather over the Scandinavian peninsula but winds of up to 25 mph over the Barents Sea toward Svalbard. This was going to be as good as the weather got at this time of year. Nobile had to decide whether to go now or wait and risk the weather's worsening. "There are uncertainties and risks, but these are inevitable," the weather report ended on an unhelpfully philosophical note. [37]

Nobile decided to take off, but a strong wind started to blow across the airfield. The wind was so powerful that the ground crew could not even pull the airship out of the hangar. Nobile's wife, Carlotta, and daughter, Maria, who had arrived from Italy, rushed to pray at the church on the airfield.[38]

On the evening of May 2, the wind finally abated—and, after a last consultation with Finn Malmgren, Nobile decided once again it was time to leave. The going would be tricky over the Baltic Sea, but the weather would improve over Scandinavia. Rainstorms and snowstorms were likely at any time. If the airship was struggling with this weather, Nobile must have known it would surely get worse over the Arctic. "Perhaps it would be better not to tempt Fate a second time," Mussolini had told him. It looked like he was right. Now the lives of the crew, the survival of the airship, and indeed the future of his airship program were at stake. It was equally true that all the men on the expedition were volunteers and they knew what they were getting themselves into. He then told Carlotta of his decision to continue, and she refused to leave his side until he left to board the airship.[39]

At 3:28 a.m. on May 3, the *Italia* set off for Svalbard with a crew who, after the delays, must have been glad to get into the air. The eighteen men may now have been on their way to Svalbard, but it became immediately clear that it wouldn't be so much a flight as a fight to get there. The strong headwinds over the Baltic Sea reduced their speed to just 30 mph. It was an ominous sign of what was to come.

The N-4 reached the Swedish capital of Stockholm after eight hours and was met by an escort of seaplanes from the Swedish navy. The airship descended to circle over Malmgren's home and dropped a letter wrapped in a flag for his mother, who he had hoped would be there. It turned out that she had gone into central Stockholm to see the airship fly by. When she returned, she read out the (rather mundane) message in front of the media scrum. She didn't know it then, but Mrs. Malmgren had missed her chance to see her son one last time.

Some Swedes who were children at the time remember to this day how they saw the *Italia* fly over the city. It was beautiful, sunny weather, and it felt like every single citizen had turned out. First, three planes with photographers, reporters, and artists on board flew low over downtown Stockholm to observe the airship close-up. More airplanes turned up to escort it, and still others carried even more photographers to take pictures from all angles—including from above—for use in the newspapers and on postcards. Some of the planes that escorted Nobile and his crew had floats on them and were seaplanes from the Royal Swedish

Navy. Their pilots couldn't have known that the next time they would see General Nobile would be under very different conditions.[40]

Nobile had by now had enough of the show business and just wanted to fly directly to their Arctic base. The trip to Kings Bay had already taken eighteen days—and his critics at home were sharpening their pens. But a powerful wind combined with fog made their journey directly north impossible. Instead, they had to take a circular route over the Gulf of Finland and Finland itself.

The latest weather report had made it clear that the explorers were in a race against time.[41] "Advisable to increase the speed of the ship to utilize the present favorable landing conditions."[42] Nobile ordered full power on all engines.

By 6:00 a.m. on May 4, the visibility was so bad that the crew could no longer work out where they were. After three hours flying using only their primitive instruments, Nobile ordered the airship to descend below the clouds to see if they could spot any landmarks. Down the airship flew until it broke through the clouds only a few hundred feet above the sea. Incredibly, there in the distance was Vadsø, their next destination.

It was low tide when they arrived. While the *Italia* was being tied up to the mast, it found itself next to several old sailing ships left "high and dry" on the mud flats. A gang of small boys looked on.[43] Finn Malmgren was lifted high by two Norwegian naval officers who were overcome with relief that the *Italia* had made it.

Nobile had planned to stay at Vadsø for only a few hours to refuel and replenish the gas cells. But again, the weather had other ideas. A gust of wind rammed the N-4 against the mooring mast. Another storm blew in from the north; the blizzard was so strong that it regularly blew the airship 360 degrees around on the revolving masthead. Nobile had decided to sleep on board the ship in order to be on hand if the situation worsened. He was now woken up by his men. "The situation appeared dangerous," he wrote. The next blast could rip them from the masthead. He ordered his mechanics to start two of the engines just in case this happened. Those on board could hear the ship's framework creaking after each blast of the wind. It felt like it could break at any time.

Then the blizzard appeared to ease, before it grew worse again, with gusts of 40 mph, and then it started to snow—a deadly threat. The *Italia* was longer and taller than a modern Airbus A380. Left out in the open, a large amount of snow could easily amass on the top, weighing it down and preventing the airship from leaving.

Nobile ordered one of his men to climb up to the top of the ship to see what was happening, and for once he had some good luck. The mechanic reported that the wind was blowing the snow off.[44]

The general had just ordered the men who were not on duty to evacuate when there was a loud crack. One of the metal struts of the vertebrae of the ship had snapped.[45] For a moment, Nobile's heart must have stopped. He must have thought it was all over. Perhaps for a second there was even a strange sense of relief.

Before much could be done, the snow turned into a heavy rain that was so intense that it drenched everyone. The water poured down the sides of the airship and through every little gap it could find. Soon everything in the cabin was also soaked. But the change in the weather gave them a chance to leave, even with the broken strut. At 8:34 p.m. on May 5, the *Italia* left for the last leg of its trip to Kings Bay despite the warning of a storm ahead.

The weather report turned out to be right, and the winds were gentle. But of course, Nobile was just being toyed with. Before long, the N-4 and the nineteen souls now on board were met by a violent storm system with wind speeds of up to 50 mph—cruelly, just as they reached the treacherous if majestic mountains of Svalbard. "The situation is rather dangerous, the atmosphere is full of energy," warned Malmgren. For Nobile the sight of "the whole atmosphere in tumult" was "magnificent."[46]

For a second, the wind tempted Nobile to take the airship directly out on what by default would be its first exploratory flight, way beyond Svalbard into the Arctic Ocean. With the wind behind it, the *Italia* had fuel enough to cruise on for three days more, and there would be no mountains to worry about over the sea.[47] The alternative was to fight the weather to land at Kings Bay. He had received a message over the radio that the wind speed was picking up at the airship base, making the landing treacherous and the possibility of getting the *Italia* safely into its narrow hangar ever more remote.

But the *Italia*'s situation grew even worse. One of the engines developed a fault and had to be shut down even as the storm raged. Now it was doubtful that the airship could reach safety at all, and the crew would perhaps be obliged to ride the storm until it abated. Any thought of an expeditionary flight was over. On the plus side, as Nobile and his men inched closer to Kings Bay, they could use the radio station as a fix for navigation.[48]

Suddenly the pilot who was at the controls sighted Kings Bay—and the *Città di Milano*, which had just arrived.

As the *Italia* hung over Kings Bay with the stormy clouds overhead, the homes of the miners looking like toy houses and the men like toy soldiers,[49] Nobile radioed Romagna for fifty of his crewmen to supplement his own tiny ground crew. Instead, he was told they "could not be spared from their duties."[50] When Nobile protested, he was told he would have to wait for the captain to get orders from Rome, which could take hours. Nobile was warned that Romagna considered his primary duty to be making weather observations and collecting meteorological data rather than helping his expedition. But Nobile didn't have hours to wait. He had to bring the N-4 down now.

It may have occurred to Nobile that perhaps it wasn't just the gods who didn't want him to complete this expedition. Someone in Rome didn't either.

For a moment, the general hesitated, and then he picked up the megaphone and called to his men on the ground below. "Get me the miners!"[51]

The ground crew, thus bolstered, made sure that the *Italia* was secured.

"Now we are in the fighting line we can even afford to fall as men die in Battle," Nobile wrote in his diary after the successful landing. "But it would have been a bitter blow to fall out during the approach march. . . . Two years before, I had steered up here a ship with a foreign name: and so, at all costs, I must now bring the ship which bore the banner and name of Italy. There could be no failure. And there has been none!"[52]

Yet.

Eight

"God Save Us!"

WITH SO MUCH TIME having been lost on the flight to Svalbard, Nobile was keen to begin his assault on the Arctic before the weather worsened. However, the damage to the N-4 had been substantial. One engine needed to be replaced, the prow and structural beams had been weakened, and the envelope had taken a heavy pounding.[1]

One of the five planned flights of the *Italia* would be along the coast of Greenland. The goal of another one was to reach the North Pole. Nobile's daring plan to try again to land a party of scientists on the ice would more than make up for the fact that this was the shortest flight of all. The most demanding trip would be far to the east to the unexplored Severnaya Zemlya.[2] This would be a far longer flight than that of the *Norge* two years before.

The lost time meant the N-4 and her crew would have to face flight after flight, with little time for man or machine to rest in between—a demanding campaign on top of the already exhausting journey from Germany. The actual order of the flights and the size and composition of the crew would be determined by the weather reports they received on the day.

Despite the freezing temperatures of the Arctic Circle, the comprehensive set of parts that Nobile had shipped to Kings Bay meant that his men had the ship repaired and ready to fly again in four days.[3]

Had his men had the time to do the repairs properly? Nobile would soon find out that they hadn't.

ON MAY 10, THE TROMSØ INSTITUTE telegraphed Nobile that the weather conditions were good for a flight to Severnaya Zemlya.[4] The temperature had risen from $-10°F$ to $0°F$. Unfortunately, this meant that the airship had less lift, and Nobile had to reduce its weight. He had hard choices to make in terms of the equipment, the crew, and the amount of fuel to carry, and he decided on a balancing act: he would leave both some of his crew and some fuel behind.

Almost as soon as the *Italia* took to the sky again on May 11 for the long flight to Severnaya Zemlya, the crew made a terrifying discovery: the wire cable that ran from the control room to the ship's rudder was badly frayed and in danger of breaking.[5] If it did, it could mean that the ship would be uncontrollable in the middle of the storm that was on its way. The mechanics on board had to strengthen the cable with an emergency splice that they could only hope would get them through the flight. For Nobile, this incident was particularly troubling because he had given explicit orders to his crew to overhaul every rope controlling the rudder and the elevator.[6]

The storm Nobile worried about soon arrived and engulfed the *Italia*. By the time they reached Cape North, ice had begun to form on the envelope and on the canvas outer walls of the cabin. Snow began to stick to the envelope. The

Norwegian Arctic explorer Roald Amundsen, 1909, had an instinctive understanding of the "hero business." Amundsen discovered the South Pole on December 15, 1911—about four weeks before Robert F. Scott.

Sueddeutsche Zeitung Photo/ Alamy Stock Photo

Aeronaut Umberto Nobile, 1926, with his dog, Titina: a very different kind of polar explorer from Amundsen.

MARKA/Alamy Stock Photo

ABOVE: Fighting to save the zeppelin: Dr. Hugo Eckener arrives back in Bremerhaven after the successful transatlantic flight of the ZR-3 in 1924. Former journalist Eckener, who was the pilot of the giant airship, was cheered by the crowd.
Sueddeutsche Zeitung Photo/ Alamy Stock Photo

LEFT: Italo Balbo as he saw himself: heroic aviator and Hollywood idol. It is said that Mussolini was scared of Balbo. Nobile should have been.
FAY 2018/Alamy Stock Photo

ABOVE: The true nature of the men that Umberto Nobile had to deal with: Benito Mussolini, during the March on Rome on October 28, 1922, with three of the four principal Fascist leaders, or Quadrumvirs, who helped his rise to power. Italo Balbo is standing to Mussolini's left.
Niday Picture Library/Alamy Stock Photo

RIGHT: Lincoln Ellsworth and Roald Amundsen, July 3, 1926, holding an American flag after the successful flight of the *Norge* over the North Pole. The fifteen years since Amundsen won the race to the South Pole had taken their toll on him.
Sueddeutsche Zeitung Photo/ Alamy Stock Photo

In 1926, millionaire Louise Boyd become the first woman to organize, pay for, and lead an Arctic expedition. Two years later (pictured) she was back in Tromsø to search for Roald Amundsen. The *New York Times* headline was simply "Woman Joins Arctic Search."

Historic Collection/ Alamy Stock Photo

The Norwegian explorers were outraged when Nobile wanted a woman to accompany him on the flight to Svalbard in 1926. It appears that many writers feel the same. War correspondent Lise Lindbæk (pictured, 1951) is rarely named in accounts of Nobile's flights.

Dagbladet/Norsk Folkemuseum

The official description of this picture has left someone out: "Airship *Norge* in its hangar before the Amundsen-Ellsworth Transpolar Flight."

Everett Collection, Inc./Alamy Stock Photo

The *Norge* airship in flight (1926).

914 collection/Alamy Stock Photo

The industrial nature of Kings Bay is evident in this postcard (no date given), as is the ingenious design of the airship hangar, which was "probably the largest building in the world of its kind in 1926."
© *Svalbard Museum*

It was a tight squeeze fitting the *Norge* (Kings Bay, 1926) into the hangar.
ARCHIVIO GBB/Alamy Stock Photo

RIGHT: The conflicting
narratives of the flight of the
Norge were played out in the
media. The Italian weekly
newspaper supplement
Illustrazione del Popolo knew
its patriotic duty: the flight
of the *Norge* was a heroic
achievement by an Italian
aircrew.

*Pictorial Press Ltd/Alamy Stock
Photo*

BELOW: Nobile thought he
could challenge Balbo,
but this picture shows an
almost bashful Mussolini
personally giving Italo
Balbo his pilot's license on
June 23, 1927.

*World History Archive/Alamy
Stock Photo*

L'eroica impresa del «Norge». — Mentre la bella aeronave si abbassa sopra la ghiacciata solitudine del Polo, vengono lanciate tra la più viva commozione dell'equipaggio le bandiere della Norvegia, degli Stati Uniti e dell'Italia come segno di questo meraviglioso successo della navigazione aerea

A mezzogiorno del 6 maggio, marinai e alpini italiani, a bordo della "Città di Milano" bloccata dai ghiacci dello Spitsbergen avvistano entusiasti il dirigibile "Italia" col gen. Nobile, che giunge alla King's bay, penultima tappa verso il Polo

LEFT: The flight of the *Italia* captured the public imagination: this front cover of the Italian newspaper supplement *Il Mattino Illustrato* re-creates the moment Nobile's airship flies over a ship near Svalbard in 1928.
Chronicle/Alamy Stock Photo

BELOW: Pictures like this make it is easy to imagine that Umberto Nobile's flights may have inspired elements of Philip Pullman's His Dark Materials trilogy: the airship *Italia*, designed, built, and flown by Umberto Nobile, before the coast of Spitsbergen, 1928.
Sueddeutsche Zeitung Photo/Alamy Stock Photo

This is apparently the last picture taken of Umberto Nobile before his expedition left for the North Pole. He would soon be fighting for his life on the ice floes.

Topical Press Agency/Hulton Archive/Getty Images

Largely forgotten today, the flight of the *Italia*, its crash, and the desperate search for survivors captured the imagination of the American public, as did the mysterious disappearance of the famous explorer Roald Amundsen on a heroic mission to save his former rival.

RareNewspapers.com

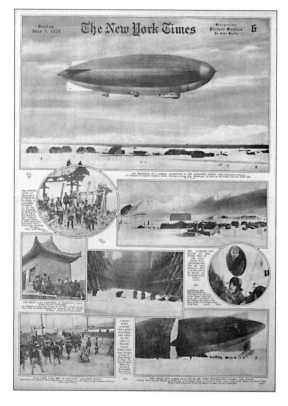

DOMENICA DEL CORRIERE

Anno 63 - N. 3 - L. 40   *Settimanale del* **CORRIERE DELLA SERA**   15 gennaio 1961

La catastrofe della spedizione Nobile. Al ritorno dalla tra- svolata polare l'aeronave precipita sulla banchisa. Così il pittore Walter Molino ricostruisce la drammatica scena.

Continuano le rivelazioni di Cesco Tomaselli sulla tragedia del diri- gibile "Italia,, (alle pagg. 14, 15 e 16).

Without any pictures of the crash, the public has always had to rely on illustrations like this one, which appeared on the front of the Italian weekly newspaper *Domenica del Corriere* in 1961.

Image copyright © Archivio storico Fondazione Corriere della Sera, published with permission

The Lost Zeppelin (1929) is clearly Hollywood's attempt to re-imagine the crash of the *Italia*—this time at the South Pole rather than the North Pole, and with a hero who is a thinly disguised Richard Byrd taking the place of Umberto Nobile.

Everett Collection, Inc./Alamy Stock Photo

The bravery of the pilots who searched for the crew of the *Italia* and their primitive aircraft were caught in this cigarette card illustration of two Heinkel seaplanes flown by the Swedes. It is from *Die Eroberung der Luft* (*The Conquest of the Air*), a cigarette card album produced by the Garbáty Cigarette Factory, 1932.

The Print Collector/Alamy Stock Photo

This is how the illustrators of the Italian newsmagazine *Illustrazione del Popolo* imagined the moment when the survivors of the crash made contact with their rescuers.

Chronicle/Alamy Stock Photo

This appears to be the world's first glimpse of the survivors of the *Italia* and the Red Tent, a still from film shot on June 22 from the tail of one of the rescue aircraft.

Sueddeutsche Zeitung Photo/Alamy Stock Photo

The photograph that helped sow the seeds of distrust in Lundborg's intentions: General Umberto Nobile, with his dog, Titina, and his rescuer, Lieutenant Lundborg. Shortly afterward, Lundborg would pressure Nobile to be the first survivor to be flown off the ice. Nobile's decision to leave his men on the ice would be used by his enemies to destroy his reputation.

Haynes Archive/Popperfoto via Getty Images/Getty Images

This picture captures the moment when General Umberto Nobile, having been rescued by the Swedish flyer Lieutenant Lundborg, is transferred to the Italian base ship *Città di Milano*. Within days, Nobile realized that he was a prisoner on board the ship, and that his enemies had no intention of letting him play the role that might redeem him: leading the rescue effort to save his men.

Haynes Archive/Popperfoto via Getty Images/Getty Images

On July 12, 1928, the *Krassin* managed what all the high-tech air power had failed to do. It reached the survivors of the *Italia* despite the damage to the ship. In fact, the *Krassin* achieved the remarkable feat of sailing to within a hundred yards of the Red Tent.

© *Norsk Polarinstitutt*

A haunting image that shows the extreme environment that the survivors faced and reinforces journalist Davide Giudici's point: that the ice runway near the Red Tent was actually in the same condition as that of the polar aerodrome the crew of the *Krassin* had built for their Junkers. The Swedish or Finnish trimotors could have landed and taken the crew off the ice weeks before the *Krassin* arrived.

© *Norsk Polarinstitutt*

The Soviet icebreaker *Malygin* rendezvoused with the German airship *Graf Zeppelin* at Tikhaya Bay in 1931. On board were two of Nobile's former rivals: Hugo Eckener, who piloted the giant dirigible, and Lincoln Ellsworth. Eckener had declined to have Nobile on board as a "polar expert" because he didn't want to crash on the ice. Instead, Nobile had been invited onto the *Malygin* by the Soviets, and was in the rowboat (pictured, foreground) that went out to the dirigible. Ellsworth shook Nobile's hand through the portal of the airship. The disaster, he thought, had aged him. Then the wind blew, and the *Graf Zeppelin* was gone. They don't seem to have ever met again.

© Norsk Polarinstitutt

A 2010 photo of the 1926 mooring mast built for the *Norge* in Kings Bay that waits still for the explorers and their airships to return.

deadlyphoto.com/Alamy Stock Photo

combined weight threatened to pull the ship down onto the ice below.

The weather had now worsened along their entire route and in every other direction they attempted to go. When Malmgren told Nobile they had to head back, Nobile had no choice but to turn the ship around.

The omens for the rest of the flights weren't good either. In May, Kings Bay should be bathed in daylight for twenty hours a day. Yet that afternoon, the sky over the mining settlement turned black as night.[7]

The *Italia* barely made it into the safety of the roofless hangar before the blizzard descended on them. The flight had lasted a scant eight hours. It wouldn't be the last time they encountered exceptional weather that May.

ONCE BACK IN KINGS BAY, General Nobile had to face another problem: the foreign press.[8] He was contractually obliged by his media sponsors to say little about the flights to journalists from rival news organizations, and his own experience suggested that was wise advice. He had been misquoted by reporters after the flight of the *Norge* in 1926—and these misquotes, he believed, had helped trigger the open warfare between Amundsen and himself.

Now Nobile was back in the Arctic Circle. This time he was facing a press pack who were under pressure from their editors for stories. Nobile had already accused one of the journalists of selling a fictitious interview with him to the American papers. The news that the *Italia* had returned early was not going to please their editors.

"Why does the *Italia* not start?" demanded a telegram sent

by an editor to one of the bored reporters. The reporter's reply
was simple: "It really isn't my fault."[9]

A good number of the journalists were Norwegian, men
of the north who tended to see almost anything the Italians
got up to in a negative light. Through this prism, if Nobile or
Malmgren chatted to them in English, it was an insult.[10] If the
crew asked for bearings to be taken by the ship's radio signal,
they were chastised for being lost rather than praised for navigating using cutting-edge technology.[11] And if Nobile didn't
wish to talk about an incident, then it was assumed he didn't
know anything about it.[12] When Nobile responded by asking
to see their copy to verify factual accuracy, the reporters complained he was overbearing and treating them like children.[13]

The favorite sport of the Norwegian journalists was to
laugh at the Italians' struggle to cope with the snow and ice.
Romagna's attempts to bring the *Città di Milano* alongside the
quay in order to unload its stores for the N-4 were particularly amusing to them. A job that would take just two Norwegians involved forty Italian sailors and their officers shouting
through a megaphone: *"Forza-forza-piano-forza!"*[14]

Journalist Odd Arnesen's verdict on the Italians' preparation for the Arctic was damning. The Italians were "poor
ice-men" from a "soft, smiling and sunny country" who were
"found manifestly wanting."[15]

THE NEXT DAY the reporters got what they wanted: a story. Heavy
wet snow started to fall, turning an evening in front of the
warmth of a coal fire into a "night of horror" for the Italians.[16]

The design of the Kings Bay hangar was innovative, but
the huge wooden and canvas structure had been built quickly

and cheaply. To save money, one feature that was left off was the roof. Today this decision may sound ridiculous, but the *Norge* had been expected to stay only two or three nights in the hangar, if that. The hangar itself was not expected to remain standing for much longer than that. (Master carpenter Ferdinand Arild, who led the building work, was astonished that it was still in good shape two years after the flight of the *Norge*.)

The clear skies Amundsen and Nobile had previously enjoyed meant that it really didn't matter that the hangar had no roof. Unfortunately, the Italians weren't so lucky with the weather and would quickly find out the downside of a giant windbreak.

The blizzard that hit them was so powerful that it quickly became a challenge to leave the protection of their lodgings—and even to find the massive structure of the hangar in the first place. When they were able to inspect the airship, they realized that the snow was quickly piling up on the topside of the N-4's huge envelope. "One centimeter, two centimeters and then ten centimeters,"[17] Nobile wrote. Soon there was so much snow that the envelope began to crush the cabin and stern engine underneath into the concrete floor of the hangar. The metal struts that gave the *Italia* some of its shape looked as though they might buckle at any moment.[18]

The structure that supported the huge lateral fins bowed under the weight of the snow as well. Creases in the outer covering were clear evidence that the metal itself was buckling underneath.

Nobile could have been forgiven for feeling sorry for himself. "It was fated that this time we should be spared no trial," he wrote. "During the two days and nights, which seemed like an interminable nightmare, the very existence of our ship seemed to be threatened. Such a heavy and prolonged snowfall was quite exceptional for Kings Bay at that time of year."[19]

The only solution—and a desperate one at that—was to employ every man they could find to clear the estimated "ten tons of accumulated snow" off the surface of the envelope. Yet this wasn't without its own risks. While the men sung fascist anthems to bolster their spirits, the thin surface of the airship's envelope shook with every sweep of their brooms, and there was the constant fear of a tear or a gash in the fabric.[20]

Yet despite the anxiety Nobile felt that the envelope wasn't designed to be stomped on by big men in heavy boots, the only damage was a few minor tears and a bit of wear in areas of the heaviest snowfall and greatest broom action. Nobile sent men back up in these places to strengthen the damaged areas with thick rubberized fabric.[21]

THREE DAYS AFTER THE BLIZZARD, by some miracle Nobile had the *Italia* ready to fly again. The intention now was to explore the two gaps in the map between Svalbard and Franz Josef Land, and between Franz Josef Land and Severnaya Zemlya, of which only a thin strip of the east coast had ever been visited by a non-Native before.[22]

The weather forecast was excellent, but the twenty-two-hundred-mile flight would be demanding. It was almost as long as the flight of the *Norge* itself, but unlike that one-way trip with Amundsen, the *Italia* would be flying to its destination and back again.[23] For Nobile, this made the flight to Severnaya Zemlya trickier than the flight to Alaska because the *Italia* had to get back to one specific spot. Two years ago, Nobile, Amundsen, and Ellsworth could more or less choose where to land when once they reached Alaska.

And then there was the wind. If it was behind the N-4 when they left Kings Bay, the return trip would be dicey at best. To cope with this danger and the more than eighty hours of flying at a normal speed of 50 mph (85 kph) that would be required, Nobile had to turn his airship into a flying petrol bomb by loading 15,430 pounds (7,000 kilos) of fuel and leaving behind almost all the ballast.[24]

The amount of fuel aboard the ship and the need to carry survival equipment meant that he had to reduce the number of men on the flight to sixteen.

With these decisions made, the *Italia* was finally ready to depart on her epic flight in the early morning of May 15.

The sky was blue. The sun was hot. The two hundred men needed to handle the ship on the ground walked it carefully out of the hangar to the mooring mast. The pope's representative, who had traveled up there by ship, Father Gian Franceschi, said a prayer, and a bottle of Italian sparkling wine was smashed on the front of the control cabin for good luck.[25]

The men slowly let go of their ropes. To their cheers, the *Italia* rose to three hundred feet. Then it turned to head out over Kings Bay to meet its fate over Severnaya Zemlya.

From behind a coal tip, a German newsreel cameraman filmed the whole event in secret—hiding because his company wouldn't pay the large sum demanded by Nobile's backers for the rights to the film.

The ship flew again toward Severnaya Zemlya, and this time they were able to explore 205 miles (330 kms) of unknown seas, photographing much of it for the mapmakers of the future. There was no trace of Gillis Land that supposedly had been seen by a Dutch captain two hundred years earlier.[26]

"I looked out of the porthole to see the pack," noted the general, "and once more I was struck by the glorious harmony between the pure white of the snow and the delicate cloudy white of the ice, and the delicate cloudy pearly-grey of the freshly frozen pools, bordered with blue ice."[27] He would later use the valuable information that was gained by observing the ice and measuring the magnetic fields and atmospheric radio-activity to defend the value of his flights.

Fog started to descend, which caused "baffle and worry" among the men just when the airship reached the area they wanted to explore. Ice, too, started to form—this time every-where, particularly on the canvas covering of the cabin, on the keel, and on the envelope. Alarmingly, the quantity building up was much greater than on previous flights. These "disqui-eting phenomena" stopped when they flew below the fog.[28]

When the *Italia* had reached the northernmost point of its flight at the northeastern point of Franz Josef Land, Nobile sent a telegram to Mussolini, which was seen by all the jour-nalists waiting for news at Kings Bay.

"My promise to guide the *Italia* across unexplored polar territories is now being fulfilled," he cabled. "I send Your Excellency respectful greetings from myself and my whole crew. . . . The ocean is ice-free here. Perfect visibility increases my hope of landing on Severnaya Zemlya during the course of the day."[29]

No one knew what was out there on Severnaya Zemlya. It had been found by the Russian explorer Boris Andreyevich Vilkitsky only fifteen years before, and most maps still didn't show it. Unfortunately, things were going to stay that way.

It was now close to midnight on May 16. The ship had been airborne for thirty-four hours and still Severnaya Zemlya was not in sight. But the crew of the N-4 did think they saw new land of some sort ahead.

"At 11.15 a strange optical illusion attracted my attention: in the sky on the horizon there appeared a vague outline, like some fantastic city of white and blue crystal rising from the ice," noted Nobile.[30]

The side wind that had been blowing from the north started to grow stronger. The job of the helmsman to steer the ship manually had become impossible. It was clear that a landing on the ice was no longer possible. Furthermore, the side wind had reduced the speed of the *Italia* to a crawl, and the ship had already used up almost half of its fuel. Everyone on board realized that the danger to the ship and its men was growing.

Back at Kings Bay, the growing anxiety of the crew of the *Città di Milano* was evident for the journalists to see and hear. Their tone of voice had changed, and they were now peering over maps and compasses.[31]

The side wind was pushing the *Italia* south. Nobile requested that regular radio bearings be taken at Kings Bay and transmitted to him. While these bearings wouldn't show how far the *Italia* was from safety—at least two receivers were needed to do that—they would tell the crew the direction they had to fly in.

If the N-4 couldn't make it back to Kings Bay, then the nearest airship mast was at Vadsø, where they had stopped on the flight up. Failing that, it would have to crash-land somewhere in Europe—a "humiliating end" to Nobile's expedition.

Unable to fly directly against the wind back to Kings Bay,

Nobile decided to "catch the wind, like a sailing ship," to the south on what was the most fuel-efficient route. Though unable to explore Severnaya Zemlya, the *Italia* was able to complete four hundred miles of pure exploration over the interior of the partially explored Novaya Zemlya. It is an archipelago in the Arctic Ocean to the south of Severnaya Zemlya, which proved to be covered in rocks and a thin layer of ice rather than the glaciers that were shown on many maps. The *Italia* then flew over the Svalbard archipelago at "a great height" of ninety-two hundred feet (2,800 m). Below them, the mountains looked like models, covered in snow and ice that glinted in the sun.[32]

Nobile had made the right decision, and he and his men were in a good mood as they approached Kings Bay. Sixty-nine hours after setting off, the *Italia* limped back and moored to the mast under clear blue skies, against the backdrop of the mountains behind. It had covered an incredible twenty-five hundred miles (4,000 km), and flown over eighteen and a half thousand square miles (48,000 square km) of unexplored land.[33] The men were confident that the forthcoming flight to the North Pole would be a historic event.

Nobile was the first man down the steps from the control cabin, greeted by a blaze of flashbulbs. The nervous Titina at his heels, he posed for cameras before boarding the *Città di Milano* and was reported by the newspapers the next day to be "tired and worn."

Nobile and Malmgren, unable to talk to the journalists because of their contracts, could say little of interest to satiate the waiting press pack—and they weren't trained in the modern art of saying something that sounds interesting but doesn't give anything away.

"You threw down a flag on Franz Josef Land, didn't you?" asked a reporter, hoping to catch the men off guard.

"I don't know, I was asleep at the time."

"We know you threw down a flag there," he probed again.

"Then why are you asking me?"[34]

What the journalists overlooked—because the Norwegians took it as a sign of the Italians asking for help—was that the N-4 had successfully navigated a large part of its complex route by radio for the first time, a pathbreaking achievement over a featureless landscape.[35] What they did pick up on was the significance of the flight for Nobile. Arnesen wrote that Nobile had successfully completed a flight that in length matched that of the flight of the *Norge*, and its challenge was far greater, being undertaken entirely "on his own responsibility," which every Norwegian knew meant without the advice of Amundsen, Riiser-Larsen, or any other well-known polar explorer, something "disgraceful" to a Norwegian.[36]

The world was now waiting for only one thing: the flight to the North Pole. The time had come.

THE HIGH POINT OF the *Italia*'s flight to the North Pole was intended to be the landing of a man or party of men briefly on the ice or on the sea. Nobile had promised this in 1926, but the wind had prevented it. Now he was determined to try again.

Nobile argued that this had some kind of scientific purpose, but no one was fooled. This was one of those "circus flights" in Eckener's crew's lingo. General Nobile would be the first man to land on the North Pole.[37] As a piece of theater for hungry front pages and newsreels across the world, it couldn't be beaten, but it was a risk. Nobile had never tried the maneuver before and didn't know if it would work, and it depended on good weather—something they hadn't been blessed with on the expedition so far.

To achieve this feat, the huge airship would have to descend to 330 feet (100 m) above the ice in the first instance, then descend again to 160 feet (50 m) above the ice to drop Nobile's patented sky anchor. Nobile, clutching the Italian flag, would then be lowered onto the ice in a pneumatic basket that could act as a raft as well. If this was a success, three scientists would be sent down to take sea temperature measurements.[38]

The danger was clear. If a wind blew up, the men could be left stranded on the ice or sea for days—even weeks, if the *Italia* had to return to Kings Bay to refuel and if the bad weather settled in.

Nobile, in his methodical way, had prepared for this eventuality. He had filled large canvas bags with everything they would need to survive a prolonged stay on the ice, including tents, wind-tight suits, chemicals to make smoke signals, a stove, food, and guns.[39]

He made sure that each member of the crew was equipped with the thick layers of clothing necessary to survive temperatures as low as −4°F (−20°C). This included woolen underwear, a mountaineer's cap, long woolen hose, heavy gloves, leather gauntlets, leather shoes, and a thick woolen sports suit, over which would be a lambskin suit of trousers, tunic, and hood.[40]

Mid-May meant that again Nobile was facing rising temperatures, which could compromise the airship's lifting power because of the expanding hydrogen. In addition, the summer fogs made flying especially hazardous.

Nobile had been desperate to avoid these conditions, but the flight across Europe had changed everything. He now started to think the unthinkable—of postponing the flights to autumn, when the temperature would drop again.

However, the weather changed on May 22. A high-pressure system covered Greenland with colder-than-expected air, a blessing since their planned route to the North Pole would take the airship over the massive island. But there was—of course—a caveat. The Tromsø Institute warned that the "favorable situation [was] not likely to last much longer, because the warm currents [would] give rise to the formation of fog."[41]

Nobile had to pick a crew of sixteen for the flight. In the end, they mostly picked themselves.

One thing was certain, the journalist Ugo Lago from Mussolini's newspaper *Popolo d'Italia* had to be on board. Giuseppe Biagi, one of the two radio operators, would go because he was physically fitter than his rival and better able to cope with the stress and confinement of the long flights. The two senior naval officers, the reliable Adalberto Mariano and the fashionable Filippo Zappi, would be the navigators.

Scientific research should take priority. This meant Finn Malmgren and Professor František Běhounek, the only two non-Italians.[42] Běhounek had missed out on previous flights because of his weight. Malmgren was one of Nobile's most trusted advisers.

Malmgren was due to get married on his return to Sweden, but he agreed to take part because he thought too highly of Nobile and the *Italia* to abandon them. The Swede had been warned by someone—Amundsen was the likely suspect—that the Italians weren't as well prepared as they should be for the Arctic, but Nobile needed him. No one knew the ice better than Malmgren did.

As the ship was made ready, Nobile bustled about making

the last checks on the new engine and obsessively calculating the weight of the airship. He picked up a box of chocolates and placed a couple of the bars in the cabin and left the rest behind, along with half the life belts.

The third naval officer, the young Alfredo Viglieri, was crestfallen not to have been picked by Nobile because of the need to save weight, even though his kit was already on the ship. After the airship had been pushed out onto the field, Nobile suddenly changed his mind and told Viglieri to hurry up and get on board.[43]

It was now 4:30 a.m. on May 23, and more than 150 men were now holding the *Italia* with the engines ticking over and the airship floating just above them. The chaplain, Father Franceschi, offered one last prayer. Nobile shouted, "Let's go!" The ground crew let go of their ropes with a chorused "Hurrah!" The engines roared to life, and the N-4 *Italia* lifted off, disturbing a flock of gulls that rose screaming into the sky.[44]

The sun was glinting off the envelope as the airship rose majestically over the mountain and headed north. To many of the men, it was a vision of the future of Arctic exploration.

"A shimmering silver shape, glinting far above the ice hummocks and dimly seen from below," one journalist wrote. "How different from those labored tours of old, when sledge parties left their floe-hemmed craft to toil among the ridges in the white glare of the Arctic."[45]

The weather report had been as good as it was going to get—but how many times since they had left Milan had the men on the *Italia* heard that? By the afternoon, the thin layer of dense fog that had accompanied them from Kings Bay out toward Greenland started to turn into something more worrying—a wall of fog. The unbroken whiteout wrapped the airship, preventing the navigators from taking their bearings in this featureless landscape.

Finally, at 5:30 p.m., the fog cleared enough that they were able to identify Cape Bridgman on the north coast of Greenland, the point at which they would turn and head straight for the North Pole. Fortuitously, a strong wind suddenly picked up and blew them in the direction of the pole.

The *Italia* was again crossing a hole in the map. Peary's route to the pole in 1909 was to the west of the *Italia*. Its sister airship had taken in 1926 a route to the east to the pole. Now Nobile and his men crossed the icescape below in clear skies that let them see for sixty miles (100 km) in every direction. If there had been land out here, they would have glimpsed it— and they saw nothing.[46]

If the wind kept up, Nobile realized, it would be impossible to land a party or even a single man on the North Pole— and the press would go away hungry, which was never a good thing. Moreover, the wind meant that even if the flight to the pole took a very fast twenty hours because of the assist, the N-4 would be fighting every inch of the way against a strong headwind on its return flight. This taxing battle, Nobile calculated, could consume forty hours and perhaps every drop of fuel they had, because the irregular zigzag pattern they would have to fly would cover many more miles than the straight-line distance back to Kings Bay, as well as exhausting the helmsman who had to manually steer the ship.[47]

Nobile spread the maps out on the table in the cramped cabin. He had another plan: to just keep cruising beyond the pole, bearing east to land at Mackenzie Bay in northwestern Canada— a route that he knew well, having flown it successfully in the

Norge. He had even made sure that the charts for that eventuality had been stowed on board.

Nobile asked Malmgren for his advice. "Better to return to Kings Bay," he responded. "Then we can complete our research program."[48]

Nobile also wanted to return to Kings Bay. They hadn't actually made it to Severnaya Zemlya, and they would still have the chance to use his sky anchor to land scientists on the ice. If they headed for Canada, it would all be over because it would be a one-way flight. Without an airship mast or a hangar big enough, the *Italia* would suffer the same fate as the *Norge.* It would have to be deflated the moment it landed.

But still he hesitated.[49] He didn't want to put his men and ship through another exhausting battle against headwinds like they had experienced on the previous flight. Maybe they could fly the long way home, back over Severnaya Zemlya. "This was truly a venturesome and attractive plan," he wrote. But Malmgren was "adamant" that the direct flight home was the best option.[50]

Malmgren finally got his way after he convinced Nobile that the winds would die down. "This wind won't last," he said confidently. "It'll drop a few hours after we have left the pole, and then it'll be succeeded by more favorable winds, from the northwest."[51]

There was only one problem. Malmgren was wrong.

AT 10:00 P.M., ALONG the horizon lay a wall of cloud thirty-three hundred feet (1,000 m) high, as if the "walls of some gigantic fortress,"[52] Nobile imagined, had formed to defend the North Pole against the aviators. Somehow they broke through it.

At 12:24 a.m. on May 24, the cry went up: "We are here!"[53]

Nobile ordered the engines slowed and the helmsman to circle the pole.

They were now directly over geographical zero. He had done it. He had proved Amundsen and Riiser-Larsen wrong. The Italians could conquer the Arctic.

Slowly the huge airship circled lower and lower, until they could see the tortured, fractured, and jumbled surface of the ice pack below them.

Nobile had been here before—but this time it felt very different. It felt, in a way, almost as if it were the first time. At a height of four hundred and ninety feet, they dropped first the Italian Tricolore and then the flag of the City of Milan. Finally, it was the turn of cross that the pope had given them to be dropped onto the summit of the world. With their jobs done, one of the crew put a record on the gramophone player and the martial notes of the Fascist Party hymn filled the ship.

Back on the *Città di Milano*, the journalists paced up and down on the deck despite the cold. At 8:00 p.m., the *Italia* sent a coded message to Rome that the crew could hear but not decode—and this aroused suspicions that perhaps something was going wrong on the flight. Around midnight, Captain Romagna rushed out of his cabin in his slippers and smoking jacket and into the wireless cabin. Again, the journalists wondered if the fuss was because there had been a landing at the pole, particularly when Romagna complained that their radio messages were interfering with those from the *Italia*.

Finally, they were told that at twenty minutes past midnight the *Italia* had reached the North Pole. The Italian crewmen were smiling and celebrating. One man tried to get the

Norwegian journalists to sing with them. Inside the *Città*, the Italian officers were bargaining with local hunters for the skins of white foxes and polar bears, the perfect souvenirs for their families at home.[54]

But suddenly the atmosphere changed. Those strong headwinds that Malmgren said would die away hadn't—and the N-4 was in trouble.

AT 2:20 A.M. ON May 24, the *Italia* left the North Pole flying directly to Kings Bay in the face of very strong winds that Malmgren had convinced Nobile would clear.

Five hours after leaving the North Pole, the ship was in a battle for its life. The fog was thick and gray. There was no sunlight. The wind whistled through every crack in the canvas-walled cabin. The metal structure of the ship creaked as if in pain. Its engines were roaring just to keep it inching forward. What sounded like bullet shots from the ice breaking off the propellers made the exhausted men hold their breaths, the cold cutting through their heavy lambswool clothing. (Nobile was still in his uniform and woolen sweater that he wore because it left him free to move quickly. He would soon regret that.)

"Each man went about his work in silence," wrote Nobile. "The vivacity and cheerfulness that had accompanied our outward journey had now disappeared."[55] Everyone knew that the fuel was running out.[56]

The ship suddenly felt very small. If the men wanted a chance to get any sleep, they had to bed down in the gangway in the keel. There had been too little rest between the long, demanding Arctic flights.[57]

Nobile had just made it through the Svalbard–to–North Pole return flight without sleep for almost two days. This was on top of three other exhausting flights in quick succession. He needed a rest, but he was trapped by his culture's (and his) sense of what good leadership was about. Without a second-in-command like Riiser-Larsen, there was no one else who had the courage to tell him to get some rest.[58]

The loud cracks began again—one after another—as ice was hurled from the propeller blades into the skin of the ship. "If this keeps up, the envelope will soon be like cheesecloth!" cried one of the crew.[59]

"Let us get out of this zone quickly," Malmgren urged. "Afterwards, things will go better."[60]

Malmgren was convinced that the bad weather was only local. At his urging, Nobile increased the speed of the engines to escape. Despite increasing the forward speed of the ship by only 7 mph, the resistance was such that fuel consumption actually doubled. For twenty-four hours, they fought the wind like this and gained only nine miles, until 3:00 a.m. on May 25. If Nobile cut the power of the engines, the airship would be close to standing still in the storm, but there was no alternative.[61]

No sooner had he cut speed to save fuel than a clearly anxious Malmgren found him in the cabin. "We aren't going forward. It is dangerous to stop here. The weather might grow still worse."[62]

"Between the two evils, I chose the one which seemed the lesser," wrote Nobile. "Once more I had the engines accelerated."

It was a death sentence, but they couldn't know it. Within the hour, full speed was the only thing that gave the men any control over their ship.

For hours they battled a headwind of forty to fifty knots as well as the fog. The wind and fog, fog and wind, were driving the men deep into themselves. And all the time the crew could hear the gusts biting at the giant vertical fin at the back of the ship every time they tried to use it. The ship bucked up and down in the wind like an unbroken horse, their ability to control it disappearing with every gust.

By 7:30 a.m., they should have been able to see the mountains of Svalbard, but they couldn't. "I was anxiously watching for the northern coast of Svalbard to loom up in front of us," Nobile recalled, "and instead every time I looked out of the portal I saw nothing but the fog and ice."

It was then that Nobile couldn't hide his fears anymore.[63] The crew who knew him could see it in the lines on his face. (The radio operator, Biagi, told the ship at Kings Bay: "If I don't answer, I will have good reason."[64])

There was no sun for a sextant reading: Nobile had to rely on the primitive radio navigational technology of the day. To work out their position, he needed two radio bearings; with the one bearing that he had, he could work out only the direction back to Kings Bay,[65] with no way of knowing how much farther they had to fly before they reached safety. He would later discover that his estimated position of the *Italia* was more than one hundred miles off.

"Passing by my child's photograph . . . ," he noted, "I gave it a rapid glance. Maria's lovely eyes looked back at me. I was struck by the sadness of their expression—they seemed to be misted by tears."

At 9:25 a.m., there was a loud bang, and Nobile heard the cry, "The elevator wheel has jammed!"[66] The controls of the helm were locked, pointing the *Italia* downward, and at an altitude of seven hundred and fifty feet it was hurtling toward the ice—and destruction.

With the engines roaring, the lives of the sixteen men on the airship hung in the balance. Nobile had now been awake for more than seventy-two hours in the noise and cold of the airship, and by now his ability to think straight must have been severely limited.[67]

"All engines, stop!"[68] Nobile cried above the roar of the wind. It was the only thing he could do. With the engines off, the wind should slow the descent of the airship and eventually lift her up again on its currents away from the pack ice.

Then seemingly in a replay of an incident on the 1926 flight, at three hundred feet the ship started to ascend again—and quickly. Then Nobile, his brain starved of sleep, made a questionable decision: he let the airship continue to rise and, as a precaution, vented off some of the precious hydrogen that they might later desperately need for extra lift. He could have chosen to restart the engines instead to slow their ascent.

At three thousand feet, "glorious sunlight"[69] flooded the cabin, lifting the spirits of the crew—but not for long. The sun's rays would quickly start to heat up the hydrogen in the gas cells, and if they stayed too long in the sun, it would become superheated and be automatically vented off to prevent the airship from bursting. There was a real danger that the airship would then plummet to the ground when it descended because as the outside temperature dropped, the gas would condense, leaving it without enough lift.

Uncharacteristically for Nobile, who was keenly aware of the danger, he decided to keep the *Italia* in the direct sunlight for as much as thirty minutes. He could now use the sextant to work out their location and could also finish repairs to the damaged control surfaces, but this was another dangerous move.[70]

With the repairs complete, around 9:55 a.m. Nobile ordered the engines started, but he hesitated for a moment, letting the N-4 sail on without power in the hope that he would see the peaks of Svalbard. But there was no sign of home. All he could see was the freezing fog.

Nobile then had no choice but to let the *Italia* descend again into the cloud. At one thousand feet, the storm had cleared enough for the men to see the ice pack every now and then. The wind dropped, just as Malmgren had predicted. The airship was making a decent 30 mph. Nobile even started to think about his bed at Kings Bay.

But the gods were just toying with them.

It wasn't going to be 1926 all over again. There was no Riiser-Larsen. At 10:30 a.m., the tail of the ship had almost imperceptibly begun to drop. The cry went out: "We are heavy!"[71]

The ship was listing to stern and falling at a rate of about two feet (0.5 m) per second. The earlier release of hydrogen may have condemned the aircraft.

Nobile was shocked. His sleep-starved mind struggled to explain what has happening. The bow was pointing upward, but the ship was falling. It was against the laws of physics.

"The peril was grave and imminent."[72] There was now only one thing he could do. "All engines. Emergency. Ahead at full!" he shouted. But according to his instruments, the increase in speed had no effect.

To try to gain altitude quickly, he screamed, "Up elevators!" But that only made things worse. The bow was tilted so high that if he wasn't careful the ship would stall, making its destruction certain.

"She's still heavy, General!" he was warned, but it was obvious to everyone who was awake. Incredibly, some of the crew had been so exhausted that they were still asleep in the tail.

Nobile must have suddenly realized that what had seemed inexplicable could be explained if one of the valves had frozen open and hydrogen was pouring out. He ordered one of his men to "run aloft and check one of the stern valves." Yet the valves were reported to be in order—and Nobile had himself modified them to protect them from ice before they had left Italy.

There may have been a tear in the envelope, or ice may have covered the ship as it descended,[73] but the problem was they were out of time.

"Look! There is the ice pack!"[74] warned Malmgren, his knuckles white as he fought with the steering wheel to turn the airship away from disaster.

Nobile's eyes were fixed on the variometer. He now knew from the rate of descent that it was inevitable they were going to crash.[75] The engines were on full power. The nose of the airship was up at twenty-one degrees and still the ice was rushing toward them.

"Stop all engines! Close all ignitions!" he shouted, as all they could do now was to try to prevent the spark plugs in the engine from igniting all the hydrogen in the huge envelope above them if they crashed. The danger that the airship would go up like a Roman candle on impact haunted all dirigiblists.

"The elevators have lost all response! The wheel is dead!"[76] shouted Filippo Zappi, one of the navigators and a man with some experience of airships.

Nobile ordered the sky anchor deployed to slow their landing. It had worked at Teller with the *Norge*, and it should work here. But it didn't; the cabin was at such an angle that the men couldn't reach the hatch to deploy it.

There were one hundred feet to go, and they were clearly going to hit the ice too fast—ice that was jagged, not smooth, as it had looked from higher up. There wasn't even a layer of snow to cushion the impact. They were also going to hit the ice tailfirst.

"This is the end," Běhounek said to himself.[77]

"God save us!" were the last words Nobile uttered. The last thing he heard was the snap of his leg bone. His last thought: "It's all over now!"[78]

It was 10:33 a.m. on May 25.

Nine

"We Will Die When God Has Decided"

WHERE THE *ITALIA* HAD hit the ice pack looked like the crash site of any other aircraft, but with one big difference: the airship had survived.

The survivors buried under a tangled mess of metal and canvas must have wondered if they were alive or dead. It was impossible to know who else was beneath the remnants.

The shape of the cabin was evident despite the force of impact. Strips of canvas fluttered noisily in the breeze. The pride of Italy was now a "dreary note of gray against the whiteness of the snow."[1]

It was only the control cabin under the airship and the stern engine that had smashed into the snow and ice. The rest of the airship was still—more or less—intact, and the huge envelope of the airship still filled the sky above the crash site; on its side *ITALIA* was visible in big black capitals.[2]

Free of human control, the airship slowly rose skyward into the bank of fog like the balloon it had now become, its prow pointing up as if it were taking off again, which in a way it was. Two of the three engines were still in place, though useless.

The survivors on the ice could make out the remaining crew staring down at them through the gaping hole where the cabin had once been. Two had been asleep when the crash happened. Now the astonishment on their faces turned to horror as the men realized their fate.

One man on board the airship didn't freeze up but acted quickly. Chief engineer Ettore Arduino started throwing fuel, food, a tent, a pistol, and the portable radio through the gaping hole and, in so doing, saved their lives.

The six men still on the airship were never seen again. The wreckage was never found. No expedition was ever mounted by a government consumed by the desire to destroy their leader, General Nobile. The only clue as to the ultimate fate of the N-4 may have been a column of black smoke that was seen for a while far to the north.

NOBILE WROTE:

I looked up to the sky. Towards my left the dirigible, nose in the air, was drifting away before the wind. . . .

It was only then that I felt my injuries. My right leg and arm were broken and throbbing; I had hurt my face and the top of my head, and my chest seemed all upside down with the violence of the shock. I thought my end was near. . . .

I was calm. My mind was perfectly clear. By now I was feeling . . . a terrible convulsion in my chest. Breathing was a great effort. I thought I had probably sustained some grave internal injury. It seemed that death was very near.

I was glad of this. It meant that I should not have to watch the despair and slow agony of my comrades. What hopes were there for them? With no provisions, no tent, no wireless, no sledges—nothing, but useless wreckage— they were lost, irremediably lost, in this terrible wilderness of ice.[3]

He wasn't alone in thinking this. His men thought that Nobile must be dead when they found him. When he moved and started to speak, he mumbled, and no one could tell that he was saying, "Steady, my lads! Keep your spirits up." They thought he must be praying.

Then—this everyone can agree on—he suddenly cried out, *"Viva l'Italia, viva l'Italia,"* which the other survivors suddenly found they were shouting out as well, almost against their will.

Then there was Finn Malmgren.

The Swede was sitting silently on the ice, his face ash-gray, swollen, and blank, his eyes staring ahead. His only movement was to stroke his left arm.[4] He blamed himself for the forecast that had persuaded Nobile to turn back to Kings Bay rather than try for Canada as he had half planned to.[5] If Nobile had followed his gut instinct, then Malmgren knew that the airship, the crew, and his reputation would have been safe by now.

"Nothing to be done, my dear Malmgren," Nobile told him softly. The young man's angst had jolted Nobile into consciousness again.

The Swede looked directly at Nobile: "Nothing but die. My arm is broken." He got up and turned to Nobile to say one last thing. "General, I thank you for the trip. I go now under the water!" before heading to the water to drown himself. At once, Nobile tried to stop him. "No. No, Malmgren. You do not have the right to do this. We will die when God has decided us to. We must wait." Shocked out of his depression, Malmgren sat down. Perhaps for a moment he remembered he was due to get married when he returned from the flight. Later that day, senior naval officer Mariano reported to Nobile that he had found the Swede again trying to slip away to kill himself, and again he was persuaded not to.[6]

Then suddenly Biagi cried out. "The field station is intact!" The portable radio transmitter protected by its wooden case had been found in one piece, and Nobile began to hope that his men might survive, even if he wasn't sure that he himself would.

In a moment of clarity, Nobile spoke softly to Mariano: "I feel myself dying. I think I have only a few hours to live. I cannot do anything for you. Do all you can . . . to save our men."

"Set your mind at rest," Mariano whispered to Nobile. "There is still hope."

Then Nobile blacked out again.[7]

Nobile's original plan had been to give at least one of the survival sacks to the men who were dropped off at the pole in case the airship was unable to pick them up—a plan that now seemed to belong to a world as far away as that we see depicted in the newsreels. Fortunately, one of the sacks had made it onto the ice with them and the survivors quickly emptied it of its tent, sleeping bag, boxes of pemmican, chocolate, revolver, flare pistol, and matches. Nobile's men then slid him into the sleeping bag for warmth despite the overwhelming pain that every movement caused him. He had refused to wear the heavy wool clothing of the rest of the crew because he wanted to be able to move quickly. He regretted it now.

The one piece of good news was that Nobile's dog had been thrown clear of the crash. "Once inside the sack I thought of Titina and called to her," Nobile wrote. "The dear little thing was scampering gaily on the ice, happy to be free at last and no longer in the air. . . . I was so happy that she was not even surprised at this novel method of landing. I called her to me, but she refused to understand and continued to frisk about, wagging her tail and sniffing the air. I recommended her to the care of one of my officers. Having done this," he added, "I put my head inside the bag and lay motionless, waiting for death to steal over me."[8]

Now Biagi just needed to scavenge among the debris for pieces of metal of the right shape and size to build an antenna. While he was looking through the wreckage of the N-4, he stumbled upon a broken propeller and the shattered parts of an engine. Then he found the mechanic who was in charge of the engine. Vincenzo Pomella looked like he was bending over to retie his shoelace. When he didn't respond, the radio operator shook him slightly. This time he toppled forward and rolled faceup. His face was blackened, crushed by impact. He was dead.

In the end, Biagi took a certain degree of professional pride in the antenna he built with tubing from the airship, guy wires made out of control cables, and the solid stand that had been used for the navigational instruments. At the top of the tall antenna, he tied the Italian flag. After having checked and checked again that the radio was working and on the frequency agreed with the *Città di Milano*, he started to transmit "SOS Italia . . . SOS Italia" five minutes before each hour until he was exhausted.[9]

He just hoped someone was listening.

TODAY DRONNINGEN RESTAURANT CAN be found on the shore of Oslo-fjord, as it has been for a hundred years. The white sails of the yachts are still seen out on the water. The only significant difference in the view is the modernist architecture of the current incarnation of the restaurant.

In 1928, the Dronningen was housed in a more traditional slatted wooden two-story clubhouse with a veranda and look-out perched on its roof. Its diners were a favorite subject for the brushes of local artists.

At the restaurant on May 26 were many of Norway's top explorers, men such as Otto Sverdrup, Oscar Whisting, Gunner Isachsen, and Roald Amundsen.[10] The men had been brought together by the Norwegian newspaper *Aftenposten* for a dinner to celebrate the April flight of George Hubert Wilkins and his copilot, Captain Carl Ben Eielson, from Point Barrow in Alaska to Green Bay, Svalbard, a success that highlighted the struggle of Nobile's airship to make it to Kings Bay.

The men were looking forward to their rich meal of broth with beef marrow, smoked salmon, spinach and scrambled eggs, lamb saddle, cheesecake, and parfait.[11] Barely had they raised their forks to their mouths when a telegram boy rushed in with a message from the paper's correspondent on Svalbard. It was bad news: the *Italia* had not returned from its flight to the North Pole.

The mood of the dinner turned dark. What could possibly have happened to the *Italia*? Could it still be in the air? Where could it have crashed? How would the Italians cope on the ice floe? The celebration of Wilkins and Eielson's triumph was rather forgotten because of Nobile's crash—as it would be across Europe. In the immediate moment, Nobile had his revenge.

A few minutes later, one of the waiters rushed up to tell the editor of the paper that the defense minister wanted to speak to him. He returned with the news that the explorers needed to go straight to the ministry to plan a mission to look for Umberto Nobile and the crew of the *Italia*.[12]

The room went quiet. Everyone looked at Amundsen. "There was no diner there who didn't remember the bitter public quarrel between the two men."[13]

The great explorer's reply was simple: "Tell them at once that I am ready."[14]

THE SURVIVORS OF THE *Italia* now had to find somewhere safe to put their tent, their only shelter from the wind, the intense cold, and the blinding glare of the ice. The pyramidal tent was only eight by eight feet and meant for four people.[15]

Amid the jagged peaks of ice, it was difficult to find an area close enough, flat enough, and safe enough. Certainly no one wanted a huge crack to open under them in the night, plunging everyone and all their supplies into the Arctic Ocean, a distinct possibility should they choose their spot unwisely. The location would also have to be easy for any rescue plane to spot them and for the two badly injured men, Nobile and the chief technician, Natale Cecioni, to reach.

That they found such a spot was a tribute to their determination. Their idea to paint the structure's fabric with red dye from marker bombs that had survived the crash was inspired. Later, this small shelter would become known as the "Red Tent"[16] and come to be seen as a symbol of the men's fight to survive.

None of this meant that the tent was comfortable to sleep in. Far from it: sleep there was hard to come by, with only one large blanket shared by nine men and all of them having to sleep directly on the floor of the tent, which was only a thin fabric covering laid on the unyielding surface of the ice. This must have been particularly excruciating for Nobile and Cecioni.

Those men who could move decided to search the crash site for anything that was of use. They quickly found two sextants, a mercury device used to determine artificial horizon, calculating tables, chronometers, and even navigational charts of the area, which meant they could work out their own location to transmit to the rescuers—if anyone was listening.

The search also led to a greatly improved menu. From the supplies they had found just after the crash, the men estimated that they had enough pemmican and chocolate to last twenty-five days on the basis of 11 ounces per day.[17] Later, some supplies of malted milk, butter, sugar, a chunk of cheese, and Liebig's Extract of Meat that they had found in the wreckage would be added to their haul, and this meant they had enough to last forty-five days[18]—and surely, someone would hear their transmission by then and come to their rescue?

The biggest problem was finding fresh water. It turned out that this was a little more complicated than melting some of the snow or ice that surrounded them, because much of it was made from sea water. They had to find fresh water ice—and it was left to Finn Malmgren, the one man among them who had any relevant experience, to clamber over the ice with his arm in a sling. Luckily, his arm appeared be bruised rather than broken.[19]

There was another reason for the men to have hope. According to the sextants, the pack ice was drifting to the southeast[20] and away from their rescuers, but it was taking them toward Frans Joseph Land, where they might find hunters who would help them. Even if they didn't, at least they would be off the sea ice. The fact they might find themselves marooned on an island was something they didn't want to think about right then.

The bad news for the men was that the small, cramped tent had become in effect a prison for the badly injured Nobile and Cecioni. These two could move only with the help of others, and their tempers quickly began to fray.

When Titina banged against Cecioni's badly injured leg, he swore and lashed out at her. Nobile then demanded that the mechanic be moved away from him. Cecioni asked Nobile, "Do you want me to die, General, putting me over there?" Nobile's reply was short and sharp: "Don't complain. Even that place is too good for you."[21]

Later, the reality of their situation hit Nobile. "Nine men huddled up together in that cramped space," he reflected. "A tangle of human limbs. Outside, the wind was howling, and one could hear the canvas of the tent flapping with a lugubrious rhythm. Cecioni rambled on until weariness overcame him.[22]

"Involuntarily, I reflected that it was better for Pomella to

have died then and there and escaped the lingering death re-
served for us. For my part, I envied him his lot."

Biagi's infectious optimism that they would quickly be rescued began to fade by the end of the day after the crash. Cruelly, although he could hear every transmission of the *Città di
Milano*, they didn't seem to hear him.

Every two hours, Biagi could hear the boat transmit the
same message over and over again: "We have not heard your
radio again. We are listening for you on the 900-m band and
on short wave. . . . Trust in us. We are organizing help."

Then he heard something alarming: "We imagine you are
near the north coast of Spitsbergen, between the fifteenth and
twentieth meridians."[23]

This was a long, long way from their actual position.

The *Italia*'s radio operator became convinced that the crew
of their support ship were not actually listening out for them,
that their messages were just being sent to tick off a box. Indeed, the ship's radio operators seemed more interested in
transmitting messages to reassure those at home that they
were safe. "Do not worry about us" was the gist of the messages they were sending to Rome. "We are safe and in good
health."[24]

"The lack of response to our SOS had profoundly disheart-
ened my comrades," Nobile wrote later. "Their optimism . . .
had now vanished. It had been a bitter blow and they were
beginning to despair."[25]

Cecioni seemed at times to have gone mad. Perhaps this
was the only sane response to the predicament they were in.

"He could not reconcile himself to the idea that he might
die out there," Nobile said. "Wide eyed with terror, he would
throw his arms around my neck and ask me if there was any

hope. I tried to calm and encourage him: 'We must trust in God. . . . Let us resign ourselves to his will.'"[26]

Nobile and Mariano decided to establish routine duties for the men. Their aim was to break up the long, dreary days on the desolate ice pack that were going to be the norm until they were rescued, distract the men from the cold and the hopelessness of their situation. One man would always be on watch for polar bears or the cracking of the ice, another scanning the sky and the horizon for any sign of a plane, airship, ship, or land, another one or two in charge of the housekeeping.[27]

Yet the routines couldn't hide from the men that no one was replying to their radio messages.

"Nothing, Biagi?" Nobile would ask.

The radio operator's reply was just one word: "Nothing."

The general looked at his men in the tent.

"What would become of them?" he worried. "Who would be the first to die of hunger?"[28]

When the crew found a small picture of the Madonna of Loreto, they tied it to the main pole. She was soon joined by pictures of the queen of Italy and Mussolini.[29]

The additions, felt the men, had to help.

THE EXPLORERS GATHERED TOGETHER at the Norwegian Defense Ministry in central Oslo after their dramatic dinner.

Thankfully, all the men at the meeting held similar views as to what had to be done if the crew of the *Italia* were to be brought back alive. The key, they all believed, was rapid, energetic action.[30] The problem for the would-be rescuers was that no one actually knew where the N-4 had come down. This left them a great deal of the Arctic to search.

Most of the explorers, including Riiser-Larsen, recommended a systematic long-range air search of the ice pack northeast of Svalbard toward Franz Josef Land, Novaya Zemlya, and even as far as the Siberian coast. It was just possible the wind had carried the airship that far.

"The area to explore is enormously vast," Riiser-Larsen warned them. "It won't be an easy undertaking."[31]

That just left the question of the best way to carry out the search. By air was the obvious choice. However, it would take time to move planes and airships into position because there were few air bases in the Arctic. And once the aircraft had arrived, there was the fact that only the latest, larger designs had the range and resilience the searchers needed.

Fridtjof Nansen, who wasn't at the meeting, thought that a single large airship that could stay in the air for days would be better than many smaller planes, and wanted to ask the British for one of their dirigibles. The American government had airships large enough for such a rescue mission but these could take days to get there. An airship mast could easily be built in the northeast of Svalbard. Unfortunately, the *Graf Zeppelin* was still under construction.[32] Instead, the German government offered to send state-of-the-art Dornier Wal flying boats whose metal hulls were better able to withstand the rigors of the sea ice.

Professor Hoel of the Norwegian Polar Institute had a different solution. He felt that you needed to use ships to find survivors that far beyond the edge of civilization, and not just any ships, but icebreakers—the most powerful of which were in the hands of the Finns, the Swedes, and the Soviets.

Out of this selection, there was only one of these incredibly powerful ships that was in the right place at the right time, and it was called the *Krassin*.[33] The *Krassin* was well known to the Norwegians as it had saved a Norwegian icebreaker adrift in the Arctic Sea with eighty-seven people on board.

The prime minister of Norway sent a message to Mussolini via the Italian ambassador to say that the consensus was that a large search and rescue would be needed to find Nobile and his men and that Norway was the ideal nation to undertake such a mission given its proximity to the Arctic and its great explorers, like Amundsen, who would be the natural leader of such an undertaking.

Now they just had to wait for the response of Il Duce because the expedition was an Italian mission, and it was Italy that was paying for the rescue attempt.

UNFORTUNATELY, IT DIDN'T LOOK like Mussolini was in any rush to help them.

To start with, the *Città di Milano* took nearly two days to set sail, and even then, it didn't sail very far. Captain Romagna had initially interpreted the last message, sent three and a half hours before the crash, to mean that the *Italia* was simply going to be late. As a result, he subsequently didn't bother to stay in touch with the airship after that or track its anticipated approach to Kings Bay. Later, he would think there was a good chance the men were dead.[34]

The most generous interpretation for Romagna's catastrophic inaction was that no one knew what had happened to the airship—or whether it had even crashed. Richard Byrd, cornered by a journalist, thought that the storm wouldn't be a problem for the dirigible and that there was a good chance that it was in the air.[35] Other aeronauts echoed this opinion.

Equally, Romagna wasn't the only one to think there was a good chance that Nobile and his men must be dead. Maddeningly for the survivors, they could hear news reports from radio stations across Europe declaring that the *Italia* must have crashed into a mountain with the loss of everyone on board.[36] Why chance anyone else's life on a risky and ultimately futile rescue attempt?

When *Città di Milano* eventually did set sail on May 27, the old cable-laying ship headed north but didn't venture much beyond Dane Island and Mossel Bay on the opposite side of Svalbard to the crash site, in part because of the sea ice, which it was ill equipped to deal with. There Romagna landed a search party, including the celebrated hunter Waldemar Kraemer, and predictably found nothing.[37]

If Nobile could think through the pain, cold, exhaustion, and trauma, he must have known in his heart that this was what his enemies had hoped for all along. Balbo had, after all, blocked his request for three seaplanes to accompany them in case of emergency.

And where was Nobile's nemesis? On the day the N-4 disappeared, the newly promoted General Balbo left Italy with a fleet of sixty-one seaplanes on a 1,750-mile circuit around the western Mediterranean,[38] and, Nobile would later claim, ordered the newspapers to downplay the *Italia* crash. In the air, the planes flew in four arrowhead formations, one on each point of a diamond.[39] Spectacularly, at Puerto de los Alfaques all sixty-one planes took off at the same time.[40] Thousands turned out to see their formation flying overhead at Marseille.[41]

Later, it was said that Balbo had offered to fly to the Arctic himself to rescue Nobile if Mussolini thought it would be useful but that Mussolini had vetoed the idea.[42]

THE MESSAGE THE *CITTÀ DI MILANO* repeated over and over again ended with the words "Trust in us. We are organizing help."[43] The men must have had a bitter smile on their faces because it was getting hard for them to trust the *Città* and believe that help was coming. The operators weren't picking up their SOS broadcasts even at the prearranged time.

If he was in a charitable mood, Biagi thought that the *Città* must be in a zone where high-frequency radio transmissions could not be received, known as a skip zone.* Others thought the signal was just too weak. They didn't know what Marconi, the inventor of the radio, thought.

Marconi was conducting further short-wave radio experiments on board his laboratory ship, the *Elettra*, off the west coast of Italy at the time. He listened in to the messages sent by the *Città di Milano* for news of the disaster and was shocked when almost every message turned out to be about a personal matter. "No wonder . . . the SOS of the survivors could not be picked up by the radio operators," he concluded, embarrassingly for Il Duce. "They were simply not paying attention to her signals."[44] When Nobile's brother Amedeo tried to raise this issue back at Kings Bay, he was told by the crew to stop meddling in affairs in which he had no experience.[45]

"THE PACK IS BREAKING UP!" shouted Malmgren. "All outside at once!"

---

* New research suggests that this was the case: that unbeknown to the survivors, the *Italia* had crashed in a skip zone, and that geomagnetic and solar storms in the ionosphere, known as space weather, had made the effect of the skip zone worse (Rachel Fritts, "Space Weather Lessons from a 1928 Dirigible Debacle," *Eos*, 101, July 1, 2020, https://doi.org/10.1029/2020EO146304).

That night, a sudden loud crack like a cannon firing woke them up. Fearing that the ice was breaking up under them, the men scrambled to escape the tent. Nobile and Cecioni were half carried and half dragged outside.

"How serious is the movement?" Nobile asked.

"I don't know," replied Malmgren somberly, "but if a break occurs near the tent we should move immediately to another location on the pack—perhaps 100 yards to the east."[46]

The noises subsided. The danger was over, but for how long?

The survivors were to hear the same loud crack over and over again each night of their prison sentence on the ice. The torturous sleep-wake-sleep-wake pattern was disorienting and depressing.

The next day, May 28, with the sun out, the men could at last use the surviving instruments to try to work out how far they had drifted since the crash.

Nobile couldn't believe the figure when he saw it, but there was no mistake. Their piece of ice had traveled twenty-eight miles to the southeast in just two days, thanks to the powerful ocean currents.[47] It was likely that the land they could now see was the uninhabited Charles XII Island.

Later that day, speaking to Nobile, Mariano first mentioned the Arctic aviators' traditional escape strategy of walking out over the ice. As George Hubert Wilkins had found on his ill-fortuned flight in 1927, it wasn't so much walking over the ice as crawling on hands and knees.

Nobile tried to discourage him, but he could feel what was left of his authority fading. He looked increasingly like a homeless beggar. He was dirty, growing a beard, and wearing what looked like a woolen jumper with a scarf draped over his head.

Nobile must have stunk after so many days in the air and now on the ice. He could sit up only if he was propped against boxes of supplies.[48] If he said no, he feared there was every chance that Mariano and Zappi would simply disobey him.

The general heard Mariano saying rather too loudly to Malmgren that by staying in the camp, they were in effect waiting to die. While the men still had their strength, they should escape over the ice to Svalbard. "With them?" Malmgren queried,[49] indicating Nobile and the badly injured Cecioni. Mariano nodded, but Nobile knew that even with sledges seven weak men couldn't haul them over the ice. The injured would be condemning the healthy to their death.

Nobile still believed in the radio. He wanted everyone to wait longer for a response from the *Città di Milano*. But Mariano and Zappi didn't believe the radio strategy was working. Instead, they told Nobile it was time for the healthy men to attempt to walk over the ice to safety. This would in effect sign his and Cecioni's death warrant.

"They must not be allowed to go!" pleaded the feverish Cecioni. "They ought not to abandon two helpless men just like that! We should all go together."[50]

General Umberto Nobile's sacrificing his life so that the two gallant Italian officers could lead the rest of the survivors to safety was clearly the story that Mussolini and Balbo would want: perfect propaganda, and Balbo would have a rival out of the way. But they hadn't counted on Nobile's stubbornness. He wasn't ready to play that part just yet, not while there was a chance that someone would hear their transmissions.

Nobile insisted at a meeting that night that the decision of splitting the party into two should not be taken lightly. He argued with the men that they should wait for a few more days for a reply to their messages. Just that day, he pointed out, a transmission had been picked up from a journalist to the effect that the supply ship the *Hobby* was moving farther north toward the crash site. What's more, it would no longer be just the *Città di Milano* listening out for them. The *Hobby* would have its own short-wave wireless and radio operator, who might pick up Biagi's messages.[51]

The next morning, the current had again moved them on. Charles II Island was gone. Now they could see two islands just ten miles away. The islands of Broch and Foyn were so close that the sky above their ice floe was full of seagulls and wild geese, but it was terribly frustrating for them to watch. They didn't have a rifle to shoot them with. All the rifles had been carried off with the *Italia*.[52]

Nobile knew that with Broch and Foyn just over the horizon it was going to be impossible for him to stop the men from leaving. He also knew that it was now or never, as the current was taking the ice floe into the wilderness, far away from any hope of rescue.

The only advantage of the change in position of the ice was that Biagi could now hear the powerful new radio station in San Paolo, Rome, which could broadcast across the world,[53] better than he could hear the radio of the *Città di Milano*. He started to transmit additional messages, hoping that San Paolo would pick them up.[54]

By the evening of May 29, the two Italian naval officers, Mariano and Zappi, couldn't wait any longer. They were convinced Biagi's radio didn't work and that staying in the frozen hell would condemn them all to their deaths. The walking party, Malmgren predicted, would cover the 60 miles (160 km) to North Cape in about fifteen or sixteen days.[55]

When Nobile asked, "Who wishes to go?,"[56] the survivors split along lines a proponent of eugenics would have liked: the fit and healthy versus the weak, overweight, or seriously injured. Despite their arguments, Nobile somehow stalled them again—and got them to agree to wait till the morning.

The general knew that he had to let them go. His goal was to keep the departing group as small as possible. He wanted to risk as few lives as possible on a mission that he considered ill conceived and which would condemn him to a truly miserable death.

DESPITE AMUNDSEN'S FAME, IT was the experienced aviator Riiser-Larsen who quickly became the de facto leader of the search operation. While they waited for a response from Rome, he got on with the job of organizing the official search effort with what ships and planes the Italian Embassy had so far agreed to.

Those two elderly ships, a World War I plane, and a dog team weren't much, even if the plane was flown by ace Arctic pilot Lieutenant Finn Lützow-Holm, who had mapped out the rescue plans for Amundsen's aborted attempt to fly from Point Barrow to Svalbard in 1924 and searched for the great man after he crashed in 1926. But it was all that they had. And the deficit wasn't going to stop the giant Norwegian from finding Nobile.

"Give me a machine such as the situation demands," proclaimed Riiser-Larsen, "and I will straight away begin a flight to find the lost men. With me I will take two guns and ammunition; and these will be my only load. If I am compelled to land, the rest can be left to me. The bears and seals will supply me with abundant food and protection against the cold; and next year you can come and fetch me."[57]

Within days of the *Italia* disappearing, Swedish military officials arrived in Oslo to discuss how they could help their former Norwegian subjects, who only gained independence from Sweden in 1904. The Swedes would go on to contribute seven ships and seven planes—some of whose crew had actually escorted the N-4 on its flight over the Swedish capital.[58] The Swedish military also set up a secondary base on Danes Island to give its aircraft that little bit of extra range. (And an effective way to assert Sweden's role in the Arctic.)

The Swedish government told all the mayors in Lapland to look out for the airship and to urge their populations to watch for survivors. The directors of the meteorological stations and the captains of whalers and other ships were similarly instructed by telegraph. Chains of observers and searchers quickly formed along the end of the ice fields from Russia to Svalbard. Indigenous hunters were contacted, too, by local officials.

Soon the whole world, it seemed, wanted to rescue the crew of the *Italia*, even if their own government remained noncommittal at best. The Swedes, Danes, and Finns began to organize missions. The Americans, Germans, French, and Russians all wanted to help, if in a somewhat independent manner that made coordination difficult.

It quickly became clear that the largest-ever international search-and-rescue operation was taking shape in the Arctic. The crews of flying boats, seaplanes, and float planes from across Europe started to make plans to fly to Kings Bay.[59] In all, twenty-three planes and twenty ships from Denmark, Finland, France, Italy, Norway, the Soviet Union, Sweden, and the United States would soon be thrown into the desperate search to find Nobile and his men.[60]

All this meant that Riiser-Larsen didn't have to carry out

his promise to be left in the Arctic for a year. But where was Roald Amundsen?

IT IS HARD TO know for sure why Amundsen so readily agreed to help find General Nobile. Of course, there were the rules of honor that Amundsen fully understood. Then there was the glory. Becoming the leader of the international effort to rescue the crew of the *Italia* would be a worthy end to Amundsen's career. Perhaps Amundsen would be able to forgive Nobile for stealing the credit for the flight of the *Norge* if he could have the delicious final victory of grasping Nobile's hand and pulling him off the ice. Hadn't Nobile written that the age of the explorer was over? Now who needed whom?

Some have wondered if there was something darker lurking in his soul. He had heart problems and had a cancer operation to remove a tumor from his thigh, and this was followed up by further radiation treatment in Los Angeles. These illnesses may have contributed to his unusual behavior. He had even unexpectedly given an old friend and his wife valuable items just before the *Italia* went missing, saying: "Now you should take it. None of us know when the next time could be."[61] When Amundsen was interviewed by Davide Giudici, special correspondent of the Italian newspaper *Corriere della Sera*, in early June 1928, he was first able to lock down these raging emotions behind his words of action and impassive expression. Instead of saying what he felt, he talked to the journalist of the need for the "utmost speed and energy to help Nobile."

He then pointed at a model hanging down from the ceiling of the kind of flying boat he had tried to reach the North Pole in only three years earlier. "If only you knew how splendid it was up there!" he exclaimed. "That's where I want to die, and I wish only that death will come to me chivalrously, will overtake me in the fulfillment of a high mission, quickly and without suffering."[62]

That eternity was on his mind was reinforced by his having sold off his collection of medals and international honors to pay off his debts. He had told his lawyer in Oslo to "make me a free man."[63]

The one thing that he did find difficult to accept was the growing role of Captain Riiser-Larsen in leading the rescue operations. Amundsen must have felt that his former right-hand man was stealing his job. Riiser-Larsen had, of course, accompanied Amundsen on the failed attempt to fly to the North Pole in 1925. One year later, he was the great explorer's chief lieutenant on the flight of the *Norge*. But given Amundsen's ego and insecurities, Riiser-Larsen appeared now more like a traitor.[64]

Furthermore, his former second-in-command hadn't bothered to visit him at all since they had returned from America. Instead, Amundsen had to read about Riiser-Larsen's adventures in the paper and then encounter headlines about how the giant Norwegian was helping Nobile to organize his next expedition.[65]

Amundsen retreated—to the best hotel in Oslo—with instructions to be "informed immediately" if there was news from Mussolini or Nobile.

Mussolini's reply to the proposal from the Norwegian prime minister came late on Tuesday, May 29. Il Duce thanked Riiser-Larsen for making himself available and agreed with the decisions that he had made. However, the rest of his plan for a large-scale rescue operation was just too dangerous.

The next morning, the Norwegian explorer and aviator Major Tryggve Gran stormed into the Norwegian Foreign Ministry. He wanted to know why Amundsen had been sidelined from the rescue mission. He also wanted to know why the army's fleet of modern Fokker planes weren't in the air flying to Svalbard.[66]

"I was even stunned when I realized that the reason for this extraordinary decision [of Mussolini]," wrote Riiser-Larsen, "was namely that no one was prepared to give Roald Amundsen the opportunity following the disagreement over the *Norge* expedition.

"I could not rid myself of the idea that it was preferable for the expedition to suffer a glorious death than a miserable homecoming."[67]

Riiser-Larsen was right. Mussolini had warned Nobile not to defy fate again by returning to the pole. Now that his luck had run out, the only thing Nobile could do after gambling with the glory of Italy was to return to Rome in a coffin as the glorious, heroic victim of science.[68] But there was more to it than that. Amundsen had hoped that the press would forget that he had mocked Nobile and his countrymen, dismissively wondering how they would cope if they ever found themselves trapped on the ice. Luckily for him, the newspapers had forgotten, but unluckily, Mussolini hadn't.

There may have even been some figures in the Norwegian government who were pleased for the excuse to drop Amundsen. He was a man who had become too difficult to deal with owing to his mood swings and his ability to fall out even with his closest allies and then criticize them in print. No one wanted to suffer the fate of the Aero Club of Norway, which enabled the flight of the *Norge* and had then been subject to fierce criticism in *My Life as an Explorer*. Then there were the schemes themselves, which somehow always managed to entangle the government in costly expenditure.

However, the political machinations in Oslo held no sway over the pilots who had volunteered to search for Nobile and his men. It would just take a while for this air armada to assemble. In the meantime, Riiser-Larsen was becoming increasingly uneasy about how safe it was for Lützow-Holm to fly alone in the Arctic. If something happened to his plane, he would be another one who needed rescuing.

He had started lobbying the Italian ambassador and then the Norwegian prime minister for permission to send a second Norwegian plane up to Kings Bay to support the first. Now, at last, he had the green light—and this time he would be the pilot.

Riiser-Larsen had left for Svalbard before Amundsen was told of Mussolini's decision or Riiser-Larsen's own departure. Although it was explained to Amundsen that the decisions were made for entirely military considerations—it was a matter of protocol that a civilian could not be in charge of a military operation—it was a hurt that was hard to get over.[69]

Amundsen wasn't stupid. He could smell a rat. He told his friends that "they had acted behind my back." Riiser-Larsen was no longer merely a traitor. He was an enemy.

And Nobile was now the prize. The great explorer was determined to rescue Nobile before Riiser-Larsen did.

"THERE'S A BEAR!"

On the morning of May 30, panic had broken out on the ice when a polar bear wandered into the men's camp. Displaying none of the depression of the past, Malmgren told Nobile, "Give me the pistol. I am going to hunt it."[70]

Everyone else crawled out of the tent to watch the confrontation, arming themselves with what they had: a knife, an ax, a file, a large nail, and a bit of metal tubing.[71] None of them had ever seen a polar bear outside of a zoo. Titina was the only one who wasn't scared, and Nobile had to hold her muzzle to make sure she didn't bark.

The great beast seemed to view the humans as no threat. It was wrong. Malmgren fired, and his one shot from the Colt pierced the heart of the predator, sending it crashing to the ground. (The queen of Italy, who had hunted on Svalbard, personally recommended the handheld Colt to Nobile as the perfect weapon to bring down game even as big as a polar bear.[72])

"Skin it and cut it up while it is still warm," advised Malmgren, "and it's all edible, except for the liver."[73] The once feared bear soon became a fine skin and around two hundred pounds of fresh meat, enough for three weeks' rations. Weirdly, the stomach of the bear contained a few scraps of paper with English on them, which must have come from one of the navigation books from the *Italia*.[74]

Nobile hoped that this good fortune would keep the group together long enough for someone to reply to their broadcast. It didn't. It only emboldened the officers who wanted to leave. With the sun high in the sky, Zappi came to tell him that the foot party would depart at once. He dismissed everything that Nobile said.

When the mist cleared on the morning of May 30, Zappi shouted, "Land in sight!" It turned out that the ice floe had drifted five miles closer to what must be Foyn Island. It looked almost as though they could run across the seven miles that were left. Cecioni's plea that "it was much better that we all go together"[75] was dismissed out of hand.

Outside the tent, Mariano and Zappi spoke in words meant

for Nobile to hear. "We two should go as we are such good friends."[76] It was clear that they intended to take Malmgren with them.

Nobile asked Malmgren in private what he thought the chance of survival was for the two men. "They don't understand how difficult and dangerous this march will be," the Swede told him. "A few years ago, a perfectly equipped German expedition was lost to a man on such a pack as this."

"And what about us?" asked Nobile.

"You have to face the drift. It will carry you eastward." Then he whispered to Nobile: "Both parties will die."[77]

Nobile prepared notes for his family that the men would take with them. To his wife, he wrote: "If it's God's will that I die out here, you must not imagine it a terrible end. All will take place with serenity and a Christian resignation." To his daughter: "You must keep Mommy from crying, if I don't come back again."

Then there was the dog. "Titina is perfectly happy here, but perhaps she would still rather be at home,"[78] he told Carlotta and Maria.

Mariano then called the other two men together and asked Malmgren who would go first. The Swede answered, "You who have the compass." And those were the last words that Nobile heard Malmgren speak.

For two days, Nobile could follow the progress of the walking party across the ice with his binoculars. In those two days, they covered only three miles (5 km).[79]

Malmgren was right, Nobile must have thought. The men in both parties were going to die.

Ten

"Do You as You Like, but I Am Going Looking for Nobile"

FINN MALMGREN WAS SUPPOSED to be an expert on how to cross the sea ice, recalled Filippo Zappi. It thus came as a shock to him and Adalberto Mariano that the Swede was already starting to struggle by the end of the second day of their attempt to walk to safety. The Malmgren who was a bit of a prankster was long gone. In his place was a glum, miserable young man who struggled to put one foot in front of the other.

It wasn't just his backpack that was burdening Malmgren. Zappi thought the Swede was clearly feeling the weight of the mistakes that had led to the crash of the *Italia* and what looked increasingly like the failure of the plan to walk out over the ice and summon help. [1]

Malmgren had let himself down, his friend Nobile, and his crew members. He had also let his nation down. The Swede was the only representative of a Nordic nation on the N-4, and he had misread the Arctic weather. Yes, the wind had died down as he had predicted but far too late to be of use to the stricken airship. He knew that if he hadn't insisted that his forecast was right, Nobile would have likely flown on to

Canada or back to Kings Bay in a more circuitous route over Severnaya Zemlya.

Now, as they struggled over the ice with their supplies and equipment, it was clear that it was going to take them much longer to reach dry land than they had expected. His dark prediction to Nobile that they would all die looked more likely.[2]

Malmgren, too, was more seriously injured than he realized. The relatively sedate life on the ice floe had hidden a serious trauma to his kidneys, the pain of which became apparent after two days of marching. It wasn't long before every step he took became torture. Furthermore, Mariano turned out not to be as fit as an officer was supposed to be. Overweight and not used to hiking, he was soon struggling to keep up.

On June 2, Malmgren already needed a rest. By the afternoon, they were trapped in a snow and ice storm that reduced visibility to a few hundred painful feet. Their only option was to hack a basic shelter out of a large chunk of ice. Unable to light their stove, they ate their pemmican emergency rations raw.[3]

It was another two days before the storm abated—two days during which the ice had drifted farther away from Foyn Island. They had gone forward only to go backward. Malmgren collapsed in tears on the ice, cursing himself.

"Finn, Finn!" Zappi shouted. "Get off the ice. This is no way to act."

"You two go on. Leave me here," begged Malmgren.[4]

Finally—as Zappi remembered—they were able to light the stove. After some warm food, Malmgren seemed himself again, and they continued the trek. Over the next days, they managed to "march" fifteen hours a day without any problems.

On the tenth day, Malmgren cracked again. On that day, the march had become tougher. They were now trudging through slush and pools of water and over jagged ice fields. The easy walking was gone. He was now falling far behind.

ON THE EVENING OF June 4, Giuseppe Biagi was sitting motionless listening to the radio through his earpiece when he suddenly jumped up and shouted, "Victory!"

Nobile quickly asked: "What is it? Have our signals been heard?"

"No, no, it's not that," said Biagi, now rather embarrassed. "The Italians beat the Spanish team by seven goals to one."[5]

The other men slumped back in silence to the tasks that Nobile had given them to keep them busy. Cecioni was sewing—which he turned out to be surprisingly good at. Běhounek sat working on his scientific notebooks, which had somehow survived the crash. Felice Trojani and Viglieri were reorganizing the steadily disappearing rations in the hope they had miscounted.[6] Felice Trojani was an experienced engineer and dirigiblist who had gone to Japan with Nobile.

Nobile was worried that their routine was now so boring it was just making the men more depressed. After all, good news was in short supply. The wind was blowing the ice away from their rescuers faster than they had expected and into uncharted waters far from dry land.

He had also started to think about a plan to save the four able-bodied men who had remained with him while they still had a chance—Běhounek, Trojani, Biagi, and Viglieri. Ironically, it was similar to the plan of Malmgren, Zappi, and Mariano. Rather than make it to the nearest islands, the four men could march westward across the ice toward Svalbard in the hope they could find land and aid. If they did, they could come back and rescue them.

Again, Nobile knew there would be little hope for him and Cecioni in his own plan. In fact, there was little hope for either of them anyway.

Something had to change—and it already had. Unknown to the survivors, a radio ham more than twelve hundred miles away from the Red Tent in northern Siberia had heard the message for which the world was holding its breath. "Ital . . . Nobile . . . Fran . . . Josef . . . S.O.S. . . . S.O.S. . . . S.O.S. . . . S.O.S. . . ."[7] Nobile and his men were alive.

On June 6, Biagi was listening to the news bulletin when he picked up the broadcast they were desperate to hear. "The Soviet Embassy has informed the Italian Government that an S.O.S. from the *Italia* had been picked up by a young Soviet farmer, Nikolai Schmidt, at Archangel on the evening of June third . . ."[8]

There was an unexpected silence after Biagi told them the good news while their brains slowly processed the news. The men erupted in smiles and cheers. They were going to be rescued. They were going to live. To celebrate, they broke out three grams of malted milk per man, fifteen grams of sugar, and—the best treat of all—a full thimbleful of pure alcohol drained from the mechanism of their compass.[9]

Yet joy turned to dread when they could hear on the news how their message was being misinterpreted. The words *Foyn* and *circa* (to indicate that the coordinates they had given were best guesses rather than exact) had become jumbled together in a new location known as "Francesco," and of course no one knew where this was.[10]

The men had another fear as well. That evening, a radio ham in the United States announced that he had picked up a message from the survivors of the *Italia*. The amateur radio enthusiast claimed to reporters that the airship had crashed into a mountain and they were sheltering in the wreckage. Even worse, he told the newspapers that the survivors were far away from their actual location. The young man later confessed that he had lied to get attention.[11]

The American wasn't the only one. There had been plenty of claims—and there would be more—of messages received from the *Italia*, which Biagi could painfully hear talked about on the news but could not correct.[12]

On the evening of June 8, Biagi suddenly shouted out, "They are calling us! They are calling us!" It was the station in San Paolo, Italy, telling the Red Tent that the *"Città di Milano* heard you clearly, receiving your S.O.S. and your coordinates."

"It can't be! It can't be!" whispered Nobile, hardly daring to believe it.[13]

It quickly became clear that their would-be rescuers thought their SOS might be just another fake message. To confirm that the signal they had picked up was from the real survivors, they had to provide a piece of information no one would else would know. "Give Biagi's registration number [service number]," the message commanded.

"We must send it off at once," Nobile ordered.[14] The next morning, he broadcast: "We only receive on short wave length. We are on the pack without sledges and with two men injured. Dirigible lost in another locality towards the east."

Nobile remembered that he had promised Biagi that he would give him a whole bar of chocolate when they had contacted the base ship—and this message was as good as that.[15]

Outside the Red Tent, the five men had a little prize-giving ceremony. Biagi solemnly accepted the nearly half pound of chocolate and then equally solemnly broke it in two. He handed over the second part to be shared out among the rest of the men.

As the men laughed, cried, and danced, they must have thought there would soon be a plane flying over the horizon to rescue them. It was not to be.

ON JUNE 4, LIEUTENANT LÜTZOW-HOLM of the Royal Norwegian Navy became the pilot of the first rescue plane to reach Kings Bay.[16] He was about to discover how easy it was in the Arctic for the rescuers themselves to end up in need of rescue, no matter how experienced they were. This wasn't exactly surprising given that the searchers were operating right at the limits of their primitive aircraft in an unrelenting climate that would punish any mistake. That said, Lützow-Holm knew his stuff. The pilot had carefully mapped out the rescue plans for Amundsen's attempt to fly from Point Barrow to Svalbard in 1924. He had even accompanied Amundsen back to Kings Bay for his 1925 flight and searched for the great man after he had crashed.

His plane wasn't new, and it wasn't very fast, but it was an excellent design: a German two-seat low-wing seaplane of World War I vintage called the Hansa-Brandenburg W.33, hundreds of which were made after the war. The plane had pedigree. It was designed by Ernst Heinkel, who went on to design the Heinkel bomber of World War II and the world's first jet plane.[17]

Lützow-Holm flew the twelve hundred miles (2,000 km) from Oslo to Tromsø in twenty-three hours.[18] His flight time included a number of stops to refuel, delays that were needed even with the extra fuel tanks that had been fitted the day before.

Like many of the planes that were involved in the search for Nobile, the Hansa didn't have the range to fly to Kings Bay itself. Instead, at Tromsø the seaplane, like the others that would follow, had to suffer the indignity of being strapped on to the deck of the tiny overgrown trawler the *Hobby* to be shipped to Svalbard.[19] The huskies of a dog team sent to join in the search at the request of the Norwegian government had to crowd around the edge of the deck.

The *Hobby* didn't hang around in Kings Bay. It stayed for only a few hours before heading off with the seaplane and dog team toward the northeast of the archipelago, where the crew thought the N-4 might have crashed.

The next day, June 5, the *Hobby* had reached its destination: Broad Bay, southeast of Moffen Island. When the crew found a gap large enough in the ice, the plane would be lowered by a crane onto the water, ready for takeoff. The plane had enough fuel only for four hours' flying time. For safety, Lützow-Holm gave himself three. Landing would be altogether a trickier affair.

Later that day, Lützow-Holm had safely completed the first flight in search of the *Italia*.[20] The next day, he was in trouble after just thirty minutes.[21] The fog bank had gotten lower and lower until the floats of the plane were skimming the top of the waves as he flew along. The lieutenant had taken off at 9:40 p.m. By 1:00 a.m. on June 7 he hadn't returned. Half an hour later they had to report that he was missing.[22] "If at the very start, such a competent pilot as Lützow-Holm should be lost, how many lives would be forfeited before our work was complete?" Rolf Tandberg, leader of the dog team, fearfully pondered.[23]

The *Hobby* was soon joined by a whaler called the *Braganza*. Together they tried to search for the missing plane and airship among the bays and promontories of the islands of North East Land. A storm that raged for three days made the task almost impossible. The two ships had to constantly battle against sea ice blown at them by the wind.

On June 7, Riiser-Larsen arrived in Kings Bay with his plane tied safely to the deck of a ship. The same bad weather that was hampering the *Hobby* stopped Riiser-Larsen from flying to join them.[24]

By June 9, the world discovered that the Soviets had picked up the *Italia*'s SOS radio signals that the men had been broadcasting for twelve days without any response. The news gave the rescuers hope and urgency. Riiser-Larsen thought he was now in the right place at the right time to be the first to reach Nobile.

Three days later, on June 10, there was a break in the weather. Riiser-Larsen was in the air as quickly as possible, and soon he had located the *Hobby*. With the ice closing in on the ship, the veteran pilot had to land quickly and have the plane winched up onto the deck without delay.[25]

Later, the *Hobby* broke into some clear water. Quickly Riiser-Larsen took off again and within forty minutes he had found Lützow-Holm's missing plane—and it looked undamaged. He assumed that it had run out of fuel.[26]

The giant Norwegian was right. Lützow-Holm wasn't dead. He had had a lesson in how dangerous it was going to be for the men searching for Nobile. The lieutenant had been forced down in the fog and then trapped for thirty-six hours by ice that stopped him from taking off again. After thirteen attempts, Lützow-Holm finally succeeded in taking off. By then, he had used up so much fuel that he had only about fifteen minutes of flying time left and no way of finding the *Hobby* in the huge landscape.[27] Without a choice, he had to land again. He headed for a known search point, beached his seaplane, and hoped to be rescued.[28]

The *Hobby* was still fifteen miles from the downed plane when Riiser-Larsen spotted it. This was an easy journey for a dog team. The dogs were landed on the closest beach and the sled loaded with petrol.

It then didn't take long for the dog team, led by the experienced Tandberg, to reach the downed plane. It was not unusual for the explorers to try to "walk out of trouble" rather than wait to see if they would be rescued. Thankfully, the rescuers discovered Lützow-Holm and his mechanic asleep inside a small sailing ship abandoned on the beach by a hunter. Once refueled, it took them only fifteen minutes to fly back to the *Hobby*.[29]

The Norwegian pilot wouldn't be the last of the rescuers to face disaster in the search for Nobile. But he was luckier than some. He was actually found alive.

BENITO MUSSOLINI AND ITALO BALBO may have been content to let Nobile die a martyr to science through their inaction, but other Italians were ashamed of their government and decided to do something about it. These men did so at considerable risk to themselves. Italy was supposed to be a totalitarian society. Their opposition would highlight its contradictions and limitations.

Arturo Mercanti was a well-known businessman in Milan. He had been the head of the air force in the first year of the Fascist regime and was a close friend of Nobile's. He was not going to let his friend die out on the ice.[30] Mercanti had quickly become disillusioned with the lackluster response of the Fascist government,* and he personally requested that the Italian air force dispatch seaplanes or flying boats to help the rescue operations. Each time he did, he was turned down, faced with reams of red tape, passed on to another bureaucrat, or simply told it was impossible. In early June, he threatened Mussolini that he would send planes and pilots paid for out of his own money. He would also make it known to the newspapers that the Italian government would not risk "a few lire" to save their hero's life.[31]

Mercanti's threat worked. Balbo's reply to the Milanese businessman may have declared that the "Royal Air Force is not responsible in any way for this [Nobile's] expedition"; it may have even stated that the expedition was in "false guise of scientific undertaking constituting only Nobile's revenge [on Amundsen]."[32] But Balbo still granted permission for the mission.

Major Umberto Maddalena was a world-renowned long-range pilot in the Italian air force. He would end up a close friend of Italo Balbo's. The flyer would even lead Balbo's 1931 Atlantic flight for him.[33] But back in 1928, it was another story. Like Mercanti, the major had become fed up with the machinations of the Fascist government. He knew what had to be done—and he did it. Luckily, he had at his disposal one of the

---

* Mercanti would later travel to Kings Bay to see the incompetence of the Fascist regime and the chaos of the international rescue effort for himself.

outstanding Italian machines of all time, the same plane that Balbo would fly to the 1933 World's Fair in Chicago. The twin-hulled Savoia flying boat was probably the best aircraft deployed in the search for Nobile.

On June 10, the Italian ace finally took off from a lake near Milan, bound for Kings Bay. Maddalena knew he could find Nobile and his men. Many of the Fascists hoped he wouldn't.[34]

"WE ARE ON THE pack without sledges and with two men injured. Dirigible lost in another locality . . ." Nobile transmitted in reply to the message Biagi had received. "We confirm longitude 280E, latitude 800 301N. Giuseppe Biagi 86891. We only receive on short wave."[35]

The next day, June 9, Biagi could only pick up broken, fragmented messages: "Be ready to make a smoke signal. Airplanes will be . . ." Nobile then repeated his previous message and that evening added one phrase: "We have dyed our tent red." When the journalists heard this, the legend of the Red Tent was born.[36] However, despite the good weather, no search planes appeared then or any other day. The only messages Nobile or Biagi received back was that help was on its way. But help never arrived.[37]

That their supplies were dwindling faster than they expected only added to their sense of panic. Now they only had 220 pounds (100 kg) of food supplies. It was still plenty for three to four weeks, but they were leaving rationality behind. Were they to die of hunger before they saw a plane?

Most of all, they needed medical advice for the two seriously injured men, who had been on the ice in freezing conditions for three weeks. Short of rescue, they also needed a collapsible boat. That may seem like a bizarre aspiration, but the ice had started to melt, and the strong easterly winds meant they were traveling five or six miles a day. They risked being blown out into the open ocean at any time.[38]

Four days later, they knew they had no choice. They were going to have to move the camp. "The ice on all sides of us is broken by large cracks that are growing wider by the hour," warned Viglieri.[39]

It was difficult to work out which direction they should move in. Thick fog had rolled in from the west, making it impossible to see more than a hundred yards, and Viglieri, not far away, nearly lost his way just heading back to the tent. The only other option was to head east to where they had killed the bear.

The four men started to pack for the six of them. The two injured men were still lying on the ground. Suddenly Běhounek cried out: "Listen, I can hear a plane!"[40] Everyone's heart lifted as they all stopped to listen—and the Czech scientist was right. There was a loud humming noise of what sounded like a distant engine. Then Biagi let out a loud groan. It was nothing but the radio antenna vibrating in the wind.

Then Trojani shouted, "The ice! The ice! It's splitting right towards us!"[41] At that moment, there was a series of loud explosions as the surface began to unzip into a canal ten yards wide heading straight for the red tent. The next split of the ice might take the tent, the supplies, and the men.

Nobile hobbled out of the tent with Viglieri's help. It was only the third time he had been outside in more than two weeks and the immense wretchedness of the desolate landscape covered in "the debris of his command"[42] hit him suddenly. His senses reeled in surprise as the healthy crew relocated their tent and belongings. "The ice on which we had been living was churned up and dirty," Nobile noted. "Here and there were puddles of water, and everywhere were wreckages: pieces of twisted tubing, rags, broken instruments . . ."

The tent was moved only a hundred feet or so, but the effort to carry everything over the rough surface, around large puddles of water and across crevasses in the falling snow, was exhausting. Precious supplies would fall off the flimsy bridge they had built over the crevasse into the deep black water and then have to be hauled out by the men before they disappeared forever.

Nobile tried to crawl to the site of the new camp, but he could only manage a few yards until he reached a crevasse that he couldn't pass. He was humiliated. All he could think was that he had now become the dirty, stinking beggar he used to see every day on his walk to school.[43]

"I wished I were dead," Nobile would later write.[44] All he wanted was to collapse and die on the spot. For one moment, he blacked out entirely.

BUT THE RUSSIANS WERE coming—slowly.

In a dock in central St. Petersburg, there is a huge ship with the distinctive rounded reinforced bow of an icebreaker.[45] This is the *Krassin*. Today, after a refit sixty years ago, its superstructure looks like any other modern ship with a single streamlined funnel. In 1928, it looked more like a World War I battleship, with two huge chimneys that pumped out thick black smoke.

The Soviets could see for themselves the chaos of the search operation, and in this chaos, they spied a propaganda opportunity to broadcast the fruits of the Russian Revolution. After all, it was a Soviet amateur radio enthusiast who had picked up the *Italia's* message in the first place.

Under the eyes of Stalin, the Soviets set up their own Nobile relief committee to investigate the feasibility of sending an icebreaker with their own long-range Fokker strapped to its deck to search for the Italian aviators. The Italians possessed the fast, long-range flying boats needed to find Nobile, but these planes were under the command of a certain Italo Balbo, who was rather busy at the time flying around the Mediterranean. The communists knew money would talk, and on June 10 financial arrangements between the Fascists and the Soviets were finally agreed on and the use of the *Krassin* approved. The committee had ordered that the *Krassin* be ready to set sail in just five days. Getting the ship ready this fast was an incredible achievement as it had basically been laid up for the past two years.[46] The crew was scattered to the four winds, and the ship's captain had even declined the new task at first, believing it was impossible.[47]

Five days later, the most powerful icebreaker in Europe left the port of Leningrad with a crew of 110 to sail across the Baltic Sea: destination Bergen and the Arctic Circle. In addition to the crew there were twenty-eight engineers, journalists, pilots, and scientists. Among all these men were two women, the young journalist Mme. Worontzowa, and the cook, Xenia.[48] Wisely, "politics was never mentioned on board the *Krassin* throughout the whole expedition," wrote Davide Giudici,[49] one of the journalists on board.

In charge of the *Krassin* was Nobile's friend, Professor Rudolf Samoylovitch, president of the Institute of Arctic Studies.[50] He had seen Nobile in Berlin earlier in the year to warn him that his plan for five flights was too ambitious. The forty-five-year-old Soviet scientist, himself a veteran of thirteen expeditions, had been proved right.

Strapped to the deck of the ship was a very large German three-engine ski plane called the Junkers G 24. The trimotor was famous for its long range. In 1926, it was the first aircraft to fly from Berlin to Beijing, albeit with stopovers. The pilot of the trimotor on the *Krassin* was the famous Soviet aviator Boris Chukhnovsky. He was thirty, but he had already done his fair share of flying in the Arctic. To Davide Giudici, he looked too slight and feminine to survive in the harsh conditions.[51]

THE ATTEMPT OF THE three men to walk off the ice had, as Malmgren predicted to Nobile, turned into a nightmare that they could not wake up from. The drift of the ice would on some days carry them six or seven miles in the wrong direction when they had struggled to walk three miles in the right direction. As their morale plummeted, the men started to abandon their equipment.

Malmgren still couldn't keep up with the others. He was in too much pain to speak. His feet were too numb to go farther. His only words were pleas to let him die the Nordic way. He knew the code of Arctic survival. "I can't go on," he said to them both on the fourteenth day, according to Zappi. "There is nothing for me but to die, but you must save the others."[52] Malmgren then lay down on the snow, was offered food, and refused to eat. He pulled out his compass. "Give this to my mother in remembrance. And tell them in Sweden why I don't return."[53]

As the Italians later told it, convinced that the Swede was

dying, Zappi dipped his finger in the wet snow and made the sign of the cross on the scientist's forehead while reciting the Latin words of the baptism as best he could because Malmgren had appeared to the crew to be an atheist.[54] Then the two naval officers placed Malmgren in an icy trench, covered him in a soggy blanket, and left him a tin of pemmican. They gave him a yellow icicle to suck on (yellow icicles turned out not to be as salty of the rest of the ice). "I do not think he will recover," Mariano said. "He said he felt no pain any more. This means that the end is near."[55]

The two Italian officers waited there a day to see if Malmgren recovered, according to their account. Then suddenly he raised his head and ordered them to leave him. "Why don't you go on? Get on quickly; don't lose a single moment. The expedition must be saved. . . . Go, in the name of God!"[56]

With that, Zappi and Mariano left Malmgren to his fate around June 16, and he was never seen again. His body was never found. "That dreadful date will remain indelibly impressed on the memories of Mariano and me," Nobile would write.[57]

THE SOLDIERS OF THE elite Sixth Alpine Regiment had been growing restless and none more so than their leader, Captain Gennaro Sora, one of the best ski instructors in the Italian army.[58] Mercanti and Maddalena may have stood up against Mussolini, but Sora was about to go one step further: he would disobey the direct order of his commander and go in search of Nobile at the risk of imprisonment when he returned.

Near the giant airship hangar at Kings Bay, there was a small primitive and rather cold wooden shack that outside had a sign on which was scrawled "Grand Hotel Foyn."[59] Inside, the banners the Alpini had pinned up by their bunks read "Remember You Are an Alpine Soldier," but it was getting easy to forget that was the case.[60] Before the *Italia* left, they had acted more like Sherpas heaving cargo from the ship to the hangar. Once it had set off for the North Pole, there had been little for them to do at all. The men were stuck in the barracks. This inaction didn't seem to change even after the N-4 had disappeared. By May 25, when many people thought that the airship had met with some kind of disaster, there still seemed to be little for them to do, and they were the official rescue team.[61]

Sora had other plans. The captain must have spread out the charts over the wooden table in front of him. He reckoned that the airship must have made it quite a way south before it crashed. With his finger, he traced a route that his crew could take along the north coast of Svalbard as far as North East Land. Then they would venture out onto the ice pack to scout in the vicinity of the islands off the coast to the east—in the direction the survivors actually were.[62]

Rolling up his charts, Sora marched across to the *Città di Milano* to talk to his commander. "I would like to set out at once with my men," he said, "since delay might be fatal to any who still survive."

"You cannot go on a wild goose chase," Romagna replied. "We do not even know for sure that the *Italia* has crashed. And if she has we don't know where."[63]

More to the point, it would be his responsibility if the ski troops died out on the ice.[64] The next two months would show that Romagna had a point. While the Alpine soldiers did manage some exploration, they needed the help of the Norwegians on nearly all of their expeditions.[65]

Sora reluctantly accepted his commander's logic, up to a point. When the message came through from Biagi on June 7, he and his men were convinced that now they would receive their orders to go. But Romagna was still adamant that they couldn't set out. This time, Sora couldn't leave until he had received orders from Rome.[66]

"I cannot authorize you to go," Romagna told him again on June 13. "It is too dangerous for your men and you may accomplish nothing."

"Too dangerous! My men have been trained to face and accept danger," Sora almost shouted at him.

Sora now knew in his gut that the orders from Rome were never coming. He told Romagna that he would set out on his own with or without orders.

"If you go, I will have you court-martialed," warned the commander of the *Città di Milano*.

"Do you as you like," said Sora," but I am going looking for Nobile."[67]

As soon as the captain had left, Romagna warned Rome of the serious insubordination of Sora.

Given the situation, Sora couldn't involve any of his men in his plan. Instead, he made his way to a whaler whose captain had agreed to take him near to Cape North. On board the *Braganza* were a Dutch explorer, Sjef van Dongen, and the Danish engineer and Arctic veteran Ludvig Varming, who would go with him.[68]

On June 18, ten days after the SOS from the *Italia* had been heard, the three men were dropped on Beverly Sound with nine huskies, a sled, and plenty of provisions. Sora's plan was to cross the pack ice that filled the bays along that coast of Svalbard, then swing out onto the frozen sea toward

Foyn Island, which was near where the survivors were reported to be.[69]

Sora would soon discover that mountain warfare hadn't prepared him for Arctic survival.

AMUNDSEN HAD PROBLEMS OF his own. The press may have praised him for wanting to come to the aid of a man he hated, but this praise would soon turn into derision if he didn't do something soon. Unfortunately, Mussolini had blocked his chance to lead the mission to rescue Nobile. His government wasn't going to stand up for him or give him any more funds. There was no help coming from the Aero Club of Norway. And the elderly explorer was broke, as always.

The explorer's big newspaper splash about how he, the explorer Leif Dietrichson (who had flown one of the planes for his 1925 polar flight), and his old friend Lincoln Ellsworth with "German equipment" were going to go to the rescue of Nobile had ended in embarrassment because he hadn't checked with Ellsworth first, and the Norwegian had just spurned his invitation to live with him in his castle in Norway.[70] Without his financial muscle, Amundsen had no hope of paying for the use of a zeppelin or the purchase of either a big Junkers or Dornier aircraft. His reputation wasn't what it was.

Amundsen and Dietrichson tried again, successfully convincing the French government to supply a biplane flying boat. With this arranged, Amundsen sent another telegram to Ellsworth for help. This time, the American came up with the money. Ellsworth blamed his previous "no" decision on a misunderstanding.

The aircraft the two men had secured wasn't without its

problems. It was a prototype Latham 47 seaplane from the
French government. If the Dornier Wal, the Fokker Trimotor, and the Lockheed Vega were state of the art, the Latham
wasn't. It was a large biplane design with a single wood and
steel hull and two engines in tandem in the middle between
the upper and lower wings. There were three open-air cock-
pits, one for the pilots and two for machine gunners. The radio could barely reach sixty miles. Yes, it was a new design
built for transatlantic flights, but its wooden hull belonged
to another era. Its lack of suitability for Arctic exploration
must have been evident even to Amundsen. The wooden hull
meant that the Latham, unlike the Dornier Wal, could not
land on ice or amidst the pack ice. It needed a large stretch of
open water in order to land safely. It had floats at the tips of
each wing, which could be ripped off and cause the flying boat
to sink. If Amundsen found the Red Tent, there was no way
the Latham could land to rescue them. Indeed, with six men
on board for the flight into the Arctic, it would be dangerously
overloaded. The best he would be able to manage was a flyby
and drop supplies. If that wasn't bad enough, the Latham was
only the second of its type constructed (a fire destroyed the
first, which is never a good omen).[71]

That said, the plane was to be flown by Captain René
Guilbaud, one of the best pilots in the French navy. He had
made his name on record-breaking expeditionary flights
over Africa.

As in 1925, Amundsen again didn't bother to flight-test the
aircraft. As in 1926, he wanted plenty of Norwegians on the
plane whom he knew would be loyal to him, even if it meant
overloading it. By valuing Norwegian "old boy" loyalty over
the experience of the French crew, Amundsen didn't seem to

care that he was running the risks of repeating the conflicts that had plagued the *Norge*.[72]

It was now June 16, 1928. Nobile and his men had been stranded on the sea ice for three weeks, and Amundsen was only just now on the train leaving Oslo for the port of Bergen. At Bergen, he would rendezvous with his French plane, and fly up to Tromsø, for the jump to Svalbard.

Twenty-five years previously, almost to the day, he set sail on the expedition to discover the Northwest Passage—which he had done. It was perhaps his greatest achievement, and despite all that had happened since, the greatness of that expedition was forever undeniable.

As if to honor his legacy and his current mission, hundreds of people were on the platform to see him and Dietrichson leave. A little girl ran up to Amundsen on the platform to ask permission to shake his hand. "Pardon my boldness, but I'm only doing what thousands of others would like to do. Please be careful, Norway cannot afford to lose such a son as you." From the steps of his train carriage, he could see Italian and Norwegian dignitaries in the crowd, as well as the usual journalists. It seemed like he was forgiven. He just hoped they would still be there when he got back.

Dietrichson shook his young wife's hand and said "Goodbye" as if he were heading to the office. It was the last time they would ever see each other.

Amundsen's latest lover wasn't at the station. Bess Magids was the young wife of a wealthy American industrialist. She was halfway across the Atlantic on her way to "take up residence in Uranienborg." Initially, Amundsen had appeared to have changed his lifetime habit of being noncommittal with Magids, but now he seemed to be having cold feet. Heading back to the Arctic Circle to rescue Nobile was to embrace the part he knew how to play, that of the hero, and to run away from the part he didn't know.

THE INTERNATIONAL RESCUE EFFORT was building up—as was the "noble competition" between nations that was just below the surface. "Italy, Norway, Sweden, Finland, Russia, and finally France vied with each other in the ambition to arrive at the earliest possible moment at the tent of General Nobile and to snatch him and his party from their deadly peril," observed Davide Giudici.[*][73]

Nowhere was this sense of noble competition more evident than in the harbor of Tromsø. In June 1928, the screeching of seagulls was replaced by the roar of airplane engines, as

* But there was one nation that had refused to join this noble competition: Great Britain (or England, as the English were in the habit of calling the four nations that make up the United Kingdom). The London papers, which had started to criticize the government for its inaction, asked one powerful question: "What has England done?" The simple answer is: "Nothing. Despite the fact that England has better planes than most other countries and has airships which in this case should be very useful. . . . The rescue of the Italia's crew is a task worthy of a joint European effort. The English public has no idea what the Cabinet has discussed and is awaiting an explanation." (Fred Goldberg, Drama in the Arctic: S.O.S. Italia [Lidingö: privately printed by author, 2003], 71.)

Amid all the hyperbole, there was one definite fact. The British did have the manpower, planes, and ships that would have made a tangible difference in the race to save Nobile and his men. The British long-range flying boats would have been ideal for the search-and-rescue operation in the Arctic, especially with the seaplane tenders that could easily and quickly lower float planes onto the water and lift them up out of harm's way.

a stream of flying boats, seaplanes, and ski planes headed for the search flew down the fjord to land on the waters in front of the town.[74]

Once parked, the planes would be repaired and refueled, while the crews rested and readied themselves for the big jump. Some of the smaller, older designs would be tied to the deck of a ship and transported to Kings Bay. Others would attempt the final long and dangerous flight to Svalbard, often with another support aircraft for safety.

The three days from June 16 to June 18 turned out to be particularly busy.

On June 16, one of the first planes to arrive was a large Junkers G 24 trimotor, like the one tied to the *Krassin*. This time the three-engine plane, which looked as if it was made of corrugated metal, had floats rather than skis, and it was in the colors of Sweden, not Russia. (A Junkers trimotor like this would become the first plane to fly across the Arctic Ocean.) The Junkers was so heavy that the crowd watching it take off from the water at Stockholm didn't think it would manage, but it did.

Then, the next day, a Finnish Junker F-13 (from the airline that is now called Finnair) landed. This aircraft, designed by Hugo Junkers himself, was a revolutionary machine: it was the first purpose-built, all-metal airliner with a closed cabin for the passengers. But it would have to be shipped to Kings Bay after it failed to take off.

The star turn for the inhabitants of Tromsø was the arrival early in the morning of June 18 of Amundsen's Latham 47, which had just completed the 758-mile flight from Bergen.

There were also four less glamorous Swedish seaplanes and float planes that looked like they had stepped out of World

War I. Without the use of seaplane tenders, these aircraft took their turn being strapped to a cargo ship for their trip to the Swedish base on Virgo Bay, Danes Island.[75]

The Italian pilot Maddalena instead followed the route that the *Italia* took via Stockholm and Vadsø in his state-of-the-art Italian twin-hull flying boat, capable of flying all the way to Kings Bay.[76] Major Pier Luigi Penzo, a Venetian aviator, would fly a Dornier Wal into Tromsø harbor after Amundsen had left.

Amundsen and Dietrichson went to stay with a friend of Amundsen's, the chemist Fritz G. Zapffe, a few minutes' walk from the harbor. The four French crew members went to stay at the Grand Hotel.

Zapffe had been looking forward to some good conversation with his old friend. Instead, Amundsen was distant. It was as if there was something between them that the explorer could not share. Zapffe would later interpret Amundsen's mood as a premonition of his death. This conviction was reinforced by Amundsen's belief that a Dornier Wal would have been a more suitable aircraft for this mission.[77] As the two men walked to the harbor later that morning, Amundsen gave his friend his lighter to keep. He had taken it on every expedition, but the old man hadn't bothered to fix it for this one, telling Zapffe: "I will have no more use of it." Amundsen was even reluctant to pose for the cameras while getting on the plane. He looked like a man resigned to his fate.[78]

The limitations of the design of the Latham for Arctic exploration that were theoretical in France may have played on his mind in Tromsø. One of the plane's vulnerable floats had already required repair in Bergen. "There were details of the machine that ought to have been improved," Amundsen and Dietrichson admitted to their friends before the flight. It was clear that "neither was entirely satisfied with the type of motor."[79]

Years later, it would be revealed that the French pilot, Captain René Guilbaud, was also worried about the airworthiness of the plane. His sense of duty to France prevented him from speaking up.[80]

Despite his unease about the plane, Amundsen turned down suggestions from the Swedish and Finnish trimotor pilots to wait till the next day so that they could all fly together for safety. He told them that he preferred to fly alone.[81] In truth, his competitive nature meant that he wanted to get to Kings Bay before them.[82] The news that the Italian flying boat had left Vadsø for Kings Bay at 12:15 p.m. further fueled his ambition. The fact that Maddalena had already had to turn back twice owing to thick fog should have been a heeded warning.

At 4:00 p.m., the Latham taxied across the water at Tromsø. She appeared to onlookers to be too heavy, perhaps even overloaded. The underpowered engines of the prototype design roared. As it raced across the still, calm water of the harbor, it was clear it was struggling to take off.* But at last the plane ascended.[83] It was going to be a nerve-racking seven-hour flight to Kings Bay.

The Latham carrying Amundsen was last seen by fishermen out at sea, about forty miles from land. The airplane flew

---

* This may seem counterintuitive, but according to Professor Nicholas Lawson, Chair in Aerodynamics and Airborne Measurement and head of the UK's National Flying Laboratory Centre, it makes sense. If there are waves, there must be wind and the aircraft will take off into the wind and have a shorter takeoff distance because it will quickly start "skipping" over the wave crests, which reduces the drag on the floats, allowing it to get airborne more quickly.

into "a bank of fog that rose up over the horizon," a fisherman told journalists, "and then the machine began to climb presumably to fly over it but then it seemed to me she began to move unevenly but then . . . she ran into the fog and disappeared before our eyes."[84] It is well known that flying in fog caused disorientation and loss of spatial awareness.

Two radio messages were received from the Latham. At 6:00 p.m., when she had been in the air for two hours: "Nothing to report." And then, just after 7:00 p.m., the mysterious: "Do not stop listening. Message forthcoming."

Whatever that message was, the operator didn't have time to send it. A collier (a ship designed to carry large amounts of coal) on its way up to Kings Bay later reported hearing a faint SOS. It is possible that these were the last distress calls ever to be heard from Amundsen and the Latham.[85]

NOBILE MAY HAVE HAD to crawl and be carried to the new site, but he was to find psychological respite there. "All things considered, the pack was less terrible than the spot we had left, chiefly because there were no traces of the catastrophe. Everything was immaculately white, except for a few footprints here and there."[86]

His peace of mind didn't last long. It had now become difficult to send or receive messages. Biagi feared that this blackout was because the batteries were dying. If a search plane did not find them soon, then the radio would fizzle out altogether, and no one would be able to find them. Nobile knew that once the batteries died, his men would give up.[87]

By June 15, the *Città di Milano* didn't seem to be picking up their messages at all. But two days later, they heard the shout they had been longing to hear: "Planes! Planes! Two of them coming in from the south."[88]

Nobile ordered Viglieri to fire the flare pistol and Trojani to light the beacon they had prepared for this occasion. The planes didn't seem to see the first flare, so Viglieri fired two more. The planes still kept up their circular search pattern. "Surely, they should see the signal?" he cried.[89] But the bright Arctic light and the glare from the snow and ice made it hard to spot flares, and their signaling was in vain. When the planes were almost on top of them—or so it seemed—they turned ninety degrees and headed into the west. It would turn out that these were the Norwegian navy's seaplanes, their leader none other than Captain Hjalmar Riiser-Larsen.[90]

Nobile quickly sent a message and hoped that someone would hear it: "Today we sighted two planes heading in our direction. They came within two or three kilometers of us. Weather conditions, especially visibility, are excellent. Take advantage of it to send the things we have requested . . ."[91]

The next morning, Nobile received a message back that the Norwegian planes would return that day. Then an obsession took hold of Nobile, like the tired, shocked, exhausted, and badly injured man that he was. The survivors didn't care in what order they were flown off the ice. They were too busy just staying alive. Rome didn't care. The government would prefer they died. But something had cracked inside Nobile. He was insistent—almost manically—that the order was agreed on by the men and then approved by Rome by radio.

Nobile's list was approved with only a minor change. Cecioni would go first, then Běhounek, Trojani, Biagi, Nobile, and finally Viglieri. At the time, no one paid much attention, but Nobile's list would soon be used to destroy him.[92]

Eleven

"Woman Joins Arctic Search"

"AMUNDSEN OVERDUE IN KINGS BAY Flight; Nobile Again Passed," shouted the front page of the *New York Times*. The newspaper reported that Amundsen and Guilbaud had not arrived in Kings Bay after their seven-hour flight, and that rumors had quickly spread through Oslo that Amundsen had gone straight to search for Nobile and had even rescued him. It was impossible to imagine that anything bad could have happened to a man who seemed immortal.[1]

When the Swedish and Finnish planes landed the next morning in the now rather crowded Kings Bay, the Latham still hadn't arrived. As with the crash of the *Italia*, some of the pilots in the bay were uneasy, others weren't, in the absence of evidence. They saw Amundsen as a man who preferred to operate alone. Indeed, it was perfectly possible that a man like Amundsen may have decided to head straight for the Red Tent, or search for the men who had been trapped on the *Italia*. The Latham had the range for it, even if it would have been difficult for the flying boat with its wooden hull and vulnerable floats to land amid all the sea ice. The French newspapers reported that Amundsen had even planned to land in a bay twenty miles south of where the Red Tent was supposed to be. A story spread that Amundsen had landed on Bear Island.

These rumors were a distraction for the pilots still tasked with searching for the survivors of the *Italia*, as was the news that Amelia Earhart had become the first woman to fly across the Atlantic. In 1928, Earhart was little more than a passenger in a plane flown by men, who never gave her the opportunity to fly the plane that she was promised. Four years later she put that right when she became the first woman to fly solo across the Atlantic.

The ice field stretched from horizon to horizon. Gray-blue lines streaked across it, interrupted every now and then by a larger patch of blue that looked big enough to land a seaplane on, until the unwary pilot tried it. Sometimes these areas of water would stay open for a while. At other times, the ice would crowd back in the moment a plane attempted to land.

Somewhere in this huge landscape was the pathetically small Red Tent. Yet another challenge for the pilots trying to find it was that the ice was not actually flat. There were banks of snow and ice on the floes—some large and some small, but all large enough to break the undercarriage of a plane. The Red Tent would have been invisible to most pilots until they were almost on top of it.[2] Thus it shouldn't have been a surprise that when the survivors next saw a plane—one of the Italians—it circled far away to the northwest. Later that same day, Riiser-Larsen was spotted far to the east.

On June 20, Maddalena's flying boat took off from Kings Bay again after the briefest of rests. This time the plane carried its own radio so that it could be guided to the camp by the men below. At 7:35 a.m., Biagi had made contact with the aircraft, and forty minutes later they heard its engines. "There she is!" Běhounek shouted from his lookout post. He immediately lit the beacon. Biagi guided the pilot in. "Turn ten degrees to the right . . . too much. Come back about three degrees to the left. . . . You are now about 4 km away. . . . On course . . . [n]ow head directly for us."[3] The plane was making a perfect approach. "Closer and closer it came. Now the survivors could see the pilot's head—and then that first hand wave! That was soon followed by the waves of all the crew. Titina ran back and forth, barking at the great shadow that flew over her."

The huge flying boat flew on for a couple of miles while it slowly made the turn back. And it was off course again. Viglieri immediately fired a flare. Biagi try to raise them on the radio again. All the while, they could see the seaplane circling the wrong spot.

It was half an hour before the flying boat returned. This time, it was a resupply run, flying very low. Small parcels "rained down" over the camp. Many of them fell into crevasses or open water. The ones that didn't turned out not to be that useful or so badly damaged to be inoperable. Six pairs of shoes, a few rations, two collapsible boats, smoke signals, a rifle, and batteries were all made worthless by the impact because of careless packing at Kings Bay. The rations, too, had been thrown together with little thought as to what the men needed and what would survive impact—including a jar of marmalade and thirty eggs, which were all smashed.[4]

When Maddalena returned to the crowded waters of Kings Bay, the journalists knew that this time he had found the Red

Tent. The *Città di Milano* blew its siren three times. The crew lined the ship shouting, "Evviva Maddalena!"

"Silenzio," a sailor cried while the Italian pilot conducted a press conference on the deck of the ship. "It was the grandest experience of my life," Maddalena told the Norwegian journalist Arnesen. "But what a pity that I could not slip down and take them back with me. Imagine only being a few meters from safety—I could almost touch their heads."[5]

Maddalena had two concerns to share and one recommendation to make, a suggestion that led to a tragedy. The first concern was that there was so much ice in the surrounding water that it would be impossible for a seaplane or flying boat to land. The only solution to this was a small ski plane that could land on the ice. The second echoed the warning that Samoylovitch had given Nobile in Berlin when he thought about landing a party on the ice: the camp was almost impossible to spot even with the coordinates and a map.

His recommendation? That Nobile should be taken off the ice as quickly as possible to assist with rescuing the men who stayed with the Red Tent, Malmgren's walking party, and the rest of the crew who were trapped in the envelope of the airship as it floated away.[6]

It was a cause for celebration for many Italians that an Italian pilot in an Italian plane powered by an Italian engine had found Nobile and his men. Captain Romagna cringingly telegraphed his "pride and gratitude" to Italo Balbo for dispatching Maddalena and his plane.[7] Balbo would doubtless have preferred a different outcome.

The Italian plane didn't return to the Red Tent as Maddalena had promised over the radio after the supply drop. For an agonizing two days, there was no news despite the great weather. Then, on June 22, the men on the ice heard over the radio that two Italian planes bound for the Red Tent had taken off from Kings Bay.

Meanwhile, the survivors had worked hard to make their camp more conspicuous. They attached red clothes to the radio aerial. They dyed four unwanted charts red and attached them to the tent roof. This time, the planes found the camp without difficulty. The approach to the supply drop was also a great deal more professional. The pilots circled the camp a number of times, calculating the wind speed and direction and the best place to drop the supplies. Then they flew away, turned, and came back very low, and very slowly, almost at their stalling point, to drop the supplies over the camp. This time, parachutes slowed some of the descending packages. Others nearly hit the men. At the back of one of the planes, Nobile noticed one more thing: a cameraman from one of the newsreels was cranking his right arm round and round, recording the rescue mission, and suddenly he felt humiliation in the midst of joy. "We too were used to flying over men's heads. . . . And here we were, reduced to utter wretchedness."[8]

It took the survivors only three hours to collect the eighteen or so packages. The smaller ones had ribbons attached to make them stand out on the ice.[9] Their contents had been given more thought as well: tinned meat, powdered milk, biscuits, and cakes for twenty days. There were also woolen clothes, cigarettes, medicine, another rifle, and a portable stove.

Nobile smiled. They were going to be all right. But while out on the ice, he had forgotten about another danger: Balbo.

Among the dropped packages were letters and newspapers. Nobile was concerned that there was no mention of Mariano, Zappi, and Malmgren. There was no news of Sora's expedition either. Perhaps worst of all was the news that Amundsen's plane had disappeared.

At 7:30 p.m. on the same day, two more planes were spotted, their Swedish pilots evidently rather cocky.

"They seem to have our location down perfectly," said Viglieri admiringly as the pilots carried out aerobatics above the Red Tent. Then they flew in low to drop more supplies. Five parachutes floated slowly to the ground. Their job done, the planes flew off to the south.

The new supplies included five batteries for the radio, another collapsible boat, a rifle, more medicine, oranges, and cigarettes—and a note. "From the Swedish Expedition," it read. "If you can mark a landing area for planes fitted with skis (minimum 250 yards) arrange the red parachutes in T-shape on the leeward side."

"Tonight, we celebrate!" shouted Biagi, holding a bottle of whiskey.[10]

But no one was listening when they tried to transmit their reply. There was only silence.

Now that they had enough food, it seemed almost inevitable that their situation would worsen in other ways. The ice was breaking up at a faster rate right at the moment when the survivors' ability to move camp had diminished. Trojani had been consumed by terrible stomach pains, and Běhounek had hidden a serious injury to his right arm for all these weeks and now he wouldn't be able to help either if they had to move camp in a hurry. This left only Biagi and Viglieri.

Nobile and Viglieri realized that the only solution was to build the boats now, load them with the supplies, and hope they could board without capsizing or smashing them.

And even then, that would be only the beginning. "Once in, we would still be faced with the herculean task of trying to buck the wind and currents to reach land," said Viglieri.[11]

Then they heard another plane approaching.

THE PATHÉ GAZETTE presents exclusively . . . the most dramatic News-pictures taken yet . . . of the search and discovery from the air of the marooned crew of the wrecked Polar Airship Italia.

No book . . . no play . . . no film . . . has such a moment of drama as these pictures of discovery of the tiny encampment of the wrecked Airship Italia on the vast icefields of the Polar Sea.[12]

While office clerks and factory workers sitting comfortably in their local movie theater must have been stunned by the dramatic film, they hadn't seen anything yet. Lieutenant Einar Lundborg was handsome and looked every inch the hero. This wasn't surprising; he had led a rather heroic life. By the time he went looking for Nobile, he had fought in three wars for countries other than his own.

Born in 1895, Lundborg was the son of a Lutheran minister. In 1914, he joined the Swedish army; by all accounts as a cadet he was a bit of a practical joker, but also one of the "finest skiers, horsemen, and athletes" in the Swedish military. Later in World War I, he joined the Kaiser's army, won the Iron Cross, and left a captain. Then Lundborg signed up with the Finns to fight the Russians. His bravery earned him the White Rose of Finland, and he departed a colonel. Lastly, he joined the Latvians and Estonians to fight the might of the Red Army.

At last, Lundborg was now in the service of the air force of his own country. However, he couldn't quite leave behind his soldier of fortune side. In the Swedish air force, he became known as a man with "no sense of personal danger"[13] and, perhaps as a result, an excellent stunt pilot. One journalist described him as "fearless, a quick thinker and a fast actor."[14]

Even though Lundborg had sworn an oath of loyalty to the king of Sweden, he could never quite shake off his attraction to far-flung adventure. Speculation regarding his true motives would only increase as he found himself at the center of one of the greatest aviation mysteries of the 1920s.

Just why was this Swedish pilot desperate to be the first to fly General Nobile off the ice? Speculation swirled that he wanted to bring the general back alive, so he would become famous. A photo of the two of them together was certain to appear on the front page of every newspaper in America and Europe.[15]

Others thought Lundborg was working for an insurance company desperate not to pay out on Nobile's $34,210 life insurance[16] should he perish. Or was he in the pay of the Fascists to make sure that, as Nobile was still alive, he would be caught in their trap? It could have been all three.

In any case, Lundborg was not a man to wait around for the Italians and Russians, and no one ever says no to a hero. His superiors quickly granted him permission for his own expedition to rescue Nobile, along with his choice of equipment and supplies. There was even a backup seaplane that could rescue him and his men if they crashed.[17]

Lundborg was renowned for his snap decisions. The aircraft he selected was a small Fokker CVD two-seat reconnaissance plane with two skis where the wheels would have been. It was very maneuverable, but with its two biplane wings, struts, and wires, it looked antiquated as opposed to advanced.

As a rescue plane, the Fokker was totally inadequate for the task. Even if the plane could safely land, there was hardly room for any passengers other than the two crew, and there was little power to lift them up into the air.

At about 10:00 p.m. on the evening of June 23, Lundborg took off from the Swedes' base camp on Danes Island, near Virgo Bay, and headed northeast toward the Red Tent. Behind him flew the seaplane, ready to help.[18]

Lundborg passed low over the tent and could see Nobile's crew waiting for him outside. The two men so badly injured that they couldn't walk were trying to balance themselves by the entrance to the tent. Two others were racing, falling, and sliding toward the runway they had marked out on the ice.

The runway looked rough and dangerous especially for such a fragile plane; the navigator, Lieutenant Birger Schyberg, had gone white at the thought of trying to land there. But Lundborg didn't feel he had a choice, and he was certainly not one to agonize about a decision like this. He cut his engine back, circled lower and lower, and then the skis hit the snow and ice with a hard thump. The plane clattered across the ice until it came to a stop. One hour after they had taken off, they had landed.[19]

"The long, unutterable torment was at an end," wrote Nobile. "The alternatives of hope and despair, the wearing suspense, the anxiety about the radio . . . At last we were in contact with humanity. Someone had come to rescue us."[20]

Dirty, unkempt, and ill looking, Biagi and Viglieri ran up to the plane to shake the hands of their savior. It was almost a month to the day since they had become inmates in this ice prison. They walked to the tent with him.

"Can the general walk?" was the first question Lundborg asked.[21] The squalor of the camp horrified him. He would later say the scene was "indescribable."

Nobile was in tears when Lundborg embraced him.

"General, I have come to fetch you," Lundborg said. "The field is excellent. I shall be able to take away the lot of you during the night, but you must come first."

"But that is impossible!" Nobile argued. "Take him [Cecioni] first. That is what I have decided."

But Lundborg didn't back down.

"No! I have orders to bring you first because we need your instructions to start looking for the others."[22]

The Swede's argument made sense to Nobile. Only days before, he had been unable to transmit "data and instructions to search for the airship" because radio communication was so poor.[23] If he was back on the *Città di Milano*, he could direct rescue operations more effectively.

Still, Nobile wouldn't give up on his approved order of departure.

"Please take him first," Nobile insisted. "That is my decision."

Now Lundborg started to get annoyed. The engine of his plane had to keep turning to stop it freezing. In the air above them, the seaplane was circling because the ice made it impossible for the plane to land.

"No, General! We will take you to our base not far from here; then I can come back quickly for the others." Then he softened. "I cannot take Cecioni anyway. He is too heavy. It is impossible to take him without leaving Schyberg behind, and

I cannot do that. Later I will come back to fetch Cecioni . . . but we have no time to lose. Please come quickly."[24] Still, Nobile hesitated.

"Come, General," Lundborg barked at his superior officer, ignoring the chain of command, "this is not grand opera."[25]

The danger was real for these early pilots. Lundborg, Maddalena, and De Pinedo would all later die in flying accidents within two years of each other. Lundborg died while test-flying a new Swedish fighter aircraft in 1931, Maddalena when his plane crashed into the sea off the coast of Pisa that same year, and De Pinedo was burned to death after his plane crashed on takeoff in 1933 at start of his own attempt to fly nonstop from New York to Baghdad, independently of Mussolini and Balbo.[26]

Somewhere deep inside, Nobile must have known that the departure of the commanding officer first was at odds with protocol and tradition. However, he was not in any real position to make such a decision or be held accountable for it. He had been in a horrific crash and was very badly injured. He had endured freezing conditions without medical attention for more than a month. Today he would doubtless be diagnosed as suffering from posttraumatic stress disorder and in no fit state to make any decision.

Nobile again consulted his crew, and again they insisted he go. "You had better go first, General," replied Biagi. "It would set our minds at rest."

"You go," urged Cecioni, the survivor most terrified of being left behind. "Then no matter what happens, there will be someone to look after our families."[27]

"Yes! It's better so. You go!" Trojani said, although later he wrote that it was not actually what he was thinking and that, inside, he had been worried about how Nobile's being rescued first would be seen by the world.

He could also hear how persuasive Lundborg was, but was the Swede being honest in his motives? Was it simply the glory that he was after?[28] The pilot had already had a picture taken of him sitting with Nobile on the ground and holding his dog,[29] and he had walked round the camp taking plenty of others too. These pictures would be the only ones of the camp for a good number of weeks.

Nobile persuaded himself that it needed far more courage to go than to stay.[30] He turned back to Lundborg and told him: "I am ready."[31]

It took two or three men to help Nobile to the plane over the rough ice and through slush as deep as their knees. When they got to the aircraft, Nobile heard a bark and looked up. Titina was in the cockpit.

"Titina, come down," said Nobile crossly.

"It's all right," said Schyberg. "She ran up to the plane and I put her on board. She will go too. She weighs nothing."[32]

After the struggle to get Nobile into the cockpit, he gave his last order to Lieutenant Commander Viglieri: "Take command for these last few hours—I will be waiting for you."

Unfortunately for Nobile, he had just given his enemies what they most wanted: himself.

Lundborg may have been a former mercenary, but he had a conscience of sorts. In the end, he kept his promise to Nobile to return for the other men—or rather the general wouldn't let him forget it, even while he was having a brief rest. With a shout of "I'm off," the Swede was back in the air in his Fokker, and six hours later, accompanied by one of the old-fashioned biplanes for safety, he could see the Red Tent again. This time,

he had come alone to maximize the chance of rescuing Cecioni. After that, it should take just a couple of flights and half
a day to bring all the men off the floe.

In the meantime, Cecioni made his way to the landing
strip. His pride hurt by Lundborg's refusal to take him because of his size, the injured man now refused any help. Instead, he dragged himself there on two makeshift crutches,
even falling into pools of freezing water that he had to then
find the strength to crawl out of. For the survivors, the six
hours seemed like an eternity, particularly since they knew all
too well that the good weather could disappear in an instant,
and dangerous cracks could break up the ice runway.

"What could be wrong?" asked Viglieri over and over
again to Biagi while the two of them paced up and down the
landing strip. "The weather holds clear. The Swedes know our
exact compass position and the general would make sure the
rescuers returned to us."

Then suddenly Viglieri shouted out: "I hear it—the plane!"

Lundborg circled the floe a few times before he saw the
camp and landing strip. Unbeknown to the observers, his engine had been spluttering because of water in the petrol. Now
it was doing it again. He had no choice but to start his descent.
Lundborg wasn't going to return without another survivor. He
started his glide in low over the ice but ran into a cross wind
and the plane became difficult to control. It may have been because of tiredness, the brilliant light, overconfidence, or even
inexperience, but it was clear to the men on the ground that
he was going to overshoot the runway. Desperately, Viglieri
and Biagi waved their arms, trying to warn the pilot to go
back around, but he must not have understood them—or he
thought he had no choice—because he kept coming.

The Swede's plane touched down halfway along the short landing strip rather than at the start. He was going too fast and was running out of runway. The plane bumped and bumped. The pilot was fighting to control it, and then suddenly it was all over. One of the skis dug into the slush and flipped the plane over. The nose of the craft (it was known to be nose heavy without a second crew member) was buried in the snow and ice, the tail up in the air. Thick black oil started to leak onto the ice. Lundborg was hanging upside down in the cockpit, safe only because of the seatbelt, blood pouring from his nose, which had smashed against the cockpit.

Viglieri and Biagi rushed over to rescue Lundborg in case the plane caught fire. As they got close, they could hear a stream of Swedish profanities and saw him slip out of the cockpit to safety. At a distance, the plane looked as though it wasn't too badly damaged, but closer inspection revealed that the propeller was crushed and the lower wing had crumpled. These weren't repairs that could be done on the ice.

The Swede was in shock. At one moment, he was the rescuer; the next, he needed rescuing. While Viglieri dried off Cecioni and made the decision to move the camp to the landing strip, Lundborg just sat there. "There are other pilots and planes, you know," he kept saying to himself as he sat amid the wreckage of his plane. "They'll arrive any time now."[33] But they didn't.

When he heard the bad news about Lundborg, Nobile started to wonder in desperation whether he should have his small experimental airship, *Mr*, shipped up from Italy. He figured that he could fly it from the nearest land to lift the men off the ice by himself. "Notwithstanding my physical condition, I felt I was fit to pilot it myself, as I had done in Italy, with both my hands badly hurt."[34]

NOBILE HAD BEEN SAVED, but Amundsen had disappeared. And the Norwegians would never forgive Nobile for his good fortune.

The search for Amundsen began to gain momentum. The difficulty was that no one really knew whether they were looking for him in the right place. It was a case of dropping a pin in the rather large hole in the map.

Norwegian seaplanes that had been searching for the Italians were ordered to search for Amundsen to the south-east of Svalbard. The elderly Norwegian battleship *Torden-skjold* was sent to join the search. The guns of the biggest ship in the Norwegian navy weren't what was needed—it was the vessel's armored hull and powerful engines that could be used to break through the ice. The warship's two World War I seaplanes would be useful as well. The Soviets diverted their icebreaker *Malygin* from the search for the N-4 crew to look for Amundsen instead. The French sent their cruiser *Strasbourg*.

In fact, the rescue effort would be joined by at least ten smaller vessels to search for the hero. From fishing boats to oil tankers, all were on the lookout for anything that would tell them whether Amundsen was alive or dead.

And then came the news that shocked the world: "Woman Joins Arctic Search."[35]

The Italians' lease on the *Hobby* was over, but the ship's role in this disaster wasn't. Amundsen's old supply ship returned to Tromsø to await the arrival of Louise Boyd, the glamorous forty-year-old millionaire. The luggage she took on the expedition had been designed for her by Louis Vuitton himself.

Despite her glamour, Boyd was no stranger to the Arctic. Two years earlier, she had made history when she became the first woman to organize, pay for, and lead an Arctic expedition. To achieve this, Boyd had to face down the veteran captain of the *Hobby* at his initial refusal to let a woman charter his ship. In June 1928, Boyd had been heading back to the Arctic to lead her second polar expedition when she heard the news that Amundsen had gone missing, and she quickly joined an elite group of male explorers in the search for him.[36]

"How could I go on a pleasure trip when those twenty-two lives were at stake?" she said, rather understating her ambitions for her own expedition, which she had now redirected to join in the search for Amundsen.

WHEN THE SEAPLANE CARRYING him dropped out of the clouds, Nobile could see Virgo Bay on Danes Island for the first time. The *Italia* had flown past Danes Island, but this was the first time he was seeing this ill-fated place up close. This was where Swedish engineer and aeronaut Salomon August Andrée had built his hangar for his doomed attempt to fly a hot-air balloon to the North Pole. The remains of the hangar can still be seen today.[37]

Andrée and his men took off in their balloon and were never seen alive again. At least Nobile had made it back alive, even if his men hadn't yet. But he had broken one of the cardinal rules of the sea: the captain of a ship is supposed to be the last person to be rescued. Still, if he had any doubts about the decision—or any awareness of the victory he had handed his enemies—he wasn't letting on.

Nobile had justified his decision to leave his men on the ice floe on the basis that he was the best man to coordinate their rescue. If he didn't play a key role in saving them, his decision to leave would be even harder to defend. His enemies must have realized this as well. To Nobile, Balbo had "declared war" on him for having the temerity to return alive from the crash of the *Italia*.[38] If Nobile had known what was to come, then he might have taken a harder stance against leaving the ice.

Nobile returned to the *Città di Milano* to find the deck crowded with cheering sailors. Tiring quickly, he had to be carried down to his cabin for a rest, only to find journalists, photographers, and cameramen blocking his way. They all wanted their money shot of him; all he wanted was to take a bath.

"Though the world's great papers had not previously been much interested in the 'Italia' expedition, the disaster led to a complete change of attitude . . . ," wrote Odd Arnesen. "All the newspapers that had not had the foresight to send a man to the town of polar flights now send requests of news by the score: 'Send as much as possible—send as quickly as possible—send everything.'"[39]

Francesco Tomaselli, the *Italia* journalist whose turn it had been to stay at Kings Bay, shared Arnesen's view: "For many weeks the foreign press had no alternative but to be happy to publish the Italian press releases. Now the authentic 'ambassadors of truth' arrived on the spot; and the world suddenly opened its ears eagerly, because the revelations were many, and picturesque and astonishing."[40]

Unfortunately for the Italians' attempt to control the flow of information (and their exclusive contract), the radio station at the mine had never agreed to sign any of the contracts the Italians offered to them to buy their services—or their silence. Now the crash had made it worthwhile for the journalists to transmit their stories by the older long-wave technology.

Somehow Nobile managed to push his way through the scrum to his cabin and his needed bath. "I cast a rapid glance of myself into the mirror and saw myself for the first time in thirty-two days—horrible, unrecognizable, with a long, bristly greyish beard smothering my face. . . . All at once I saw the patches of grime on my skin and smelt the stench of my clothes, reeking with the filth accumulated from the thirty days I had been lying stretched out on the ice."[41]

Nobile's critics weren't convinced by his appearance. They thought that he wasn't as badly injured as he was suggesting. "It was obvious that the General was not so badly hurt, as he was able to climb up the side of the *Città di Milano* without aid," wrote Arnesen, who appears not to have witnessed his arrival and instead reported gossip as news.[42]

In the midst of the media scrum, Nobile somehow found the time and space to call a meeting of the leading pilots and Captain Romagna to discuss the plans to rescue all the survivors.[43] When Nobile had washed, changed, and seen a doctor, he met with Captain Egmont Tornberg, commander of the Swedish Air Group. Tornberg immediately agreed to organize extra food drops for the survivors. Nobile also wanted to find a plane bigger than Lundborg's that could take off all the men in just one or two flights. Tornberg thought that one of the Junkers trimotors could do the job if it was equipped with skis and piloted by a very experienced man.

"I think it can be done," said Tornberg.

"It should be done at once," Nobile replied. "I will radio

Rome to have several Moths [the de Havilland Moth was a popular small British two-seat biplane] shipped here immediately if the trimotor cannot land."[44]

Nobile then sent a message to the men he had left behind on the ice about the decisions that had just been made. "Don't be anxious. I am on the *Città*. A Finnish plane is being equipped with skis, but as a precaution we have ordered three small planes from England. You will receive six more batteries from the Swedes, smoke signals, a tent, various medicines, and some solid fuel. I think you have plenty of petrol. But I hope all this will not be needed because I am reckoning on seeing you again very soon."[45]

Nobile had started to think that he had gained the wrong impression of the Italians on board the *Città*. They all seemed keen to help. It was very different from the inactivity that he and his men had experienced at the other end of the radio. He perhaps should have wondered whether they were too keen. One month under the polar sky was bound to dull your intuition.

Then Captain Romagna arrived. "You must help me not only to organize rescue operations for the men on the floe," Nobile insisted, "but to locate Mariano, Zappi and Malmgren, and to search for the *Italia* and the men who drifted north with her."[46]

Romagna clearly had something else on his mind when Nobile was talking. The captain had already radioed Rome with the words that would be used to destroy Nobile's reputation: "It is not yet known what the reasons were for taking Nobile off the ice first."[47] This line was then added to the official communique by his enemies in Rome.[48]

"People might criticize you for coming first, General,"

Romagna told him. "It would be well to give them some explanation."[49]

Nobile was shocked by his attitude. Hadn't Romagna himself given the order for Nobile to be taken first? But the captain denied ever giving such an order; it must have come from the Swedes, Romagna thought.

Nobile was dumbfounded. To begin with, he just couldn't see how anyone could view his actions as those of a coward—and then, perhaps, slowly, he could. He came back fighting. "Well, however that may be," he almost shouted. "The fact is that I did not leave by personal preference. I am here only because I was told it was of great importance to the searchers that I was."[50]

Nobile then made another mistake. Confused, emotional, and injured from a month out in the open in the Arctic, he gave in to Romagna. He quickly wrote a note to be sent to Rome. It didn't help his cause. "The message, a kind of lame apologia in defense of a nonexistent cowardice, served no purpose other than to discredit him further," wrote one author.[51] It would be used by Balbo to prove his cowardice.[52]

Nobile's anger over his treatment only grew. Later that day, he again called Romagna to his cabin to tell him exactly what he thought about the actions of the *Città*. Nobile had left many of the documents and papers that chronicled the expedition for his men to bring, but cannily he had made sure that he had carried two specific notebooks off the ice with him. These notebooks documented all the inefficiency of the rescue effort and the inattention of the *Città* to the calls from the tent.[53]

"You didn't hear us. You didn't attend to our signals as you ought, and so you made us exhaust our batteries for nothing trying to warn you that your deductions and hypotheses were wrong," Nobile told him.[54] "Get it into your head that the three [Malmgren, Mariano, and Zappi] would never have left if they had not been convinced that our SOS would never be heard."[55]

Romagna's defense was convoluted and ridiculous:

If logic is to count for anything then . . . [o]ur last wireless communication with the *Italia* was at 10.30am on 25 May. Then, all of a sudden, there was silence. We put our wits to work. Could this silence be explained by some damage to the transmitting station? No! that was improbable, because there was an emergency set on board. So, it was not a question of damage to the apparatus. Then how was it that you had not even managed to send out an SOS? It was plain as a pikestaff! The wireless operator had been unable to do it. So, we came to the conclusion that Biagi was dead.

And how could that have happened? You see, we thought Biagi had leaned out of the porthole, and at that moment the screw of the wireless had come loose and cut off his head.

The screw was in fact just a small fan used to generate power.[56]

Nobile's speechless rage at Romagna's tortured "logic" didn't do any good. The captain refused to move the ship closer to the crash site, or to establish a base for the two flying boats closer to the Red Tent like the Swedes had done, because, he said, it was too dangerous. When pushed, he would tell Nobile that he hadn't received permission from Rome to order such a deployment. It became clear that the *Città* was just as bad at responding to radio messages from the survivors as it had been when he was out there.

Romagna wasn't the only one to feel Nobile's fury. "When Nobile got on board," Tomaselli declared, the aeronaut told him: "'You should not have sent the miles of nonsense correspondence that you wrote. You should have remembered that you were part of the airship's crew. So, you had to remain silent.'"[57]

Later, the captain of the *Città* came up with a better defense for his actions. "The rescue work," declared Romagna, "[t]ook place through a [radio] traffic that became heavier day after day . . . and that station which had been badly handled, which was designed and built just for the needs of the coal miners, which we were asking to please remain silent . . . when the crowds of journalists arrived it suddenly started to work heavily, and we had to implore the operators to grant us 1–2–3–5–10 times a day those 10 minutes of radio silence in which we wanted to listen to signals from the *Italia* airship."[58]

That said, Nobile would discover that a junior radio operator by the name of Ettore Pedretti had picked up parts of one of Biagi's messages within days of the crash—only to be told by his supervisor to ignore it. The senior officer thought it was an Italian radio station in Mogadishu, the capital of Italian Somaliland, and "in face of skepticism by his superiors, he dared do no more."[59]

Nobile began to notice the prison that the Fascists were trying to build around him on the *Città*. His messages to his crew out on the ice floe were being censored or his radio signature changed to Romagna's to make his men feel as if he had abandoned them.[60] He was barred from planning the search-and-rescue operations or taking up an invitation to join the

Krassin. The foreign airmen were told to have nothing to do with Nobile because he was not in command.

It dawned on Nobile that he was actually under the maritime equivalent of house arrest[61] when Romagna posted armed police ostensibly to protect him from foreign journalists desperate to get an interview with him. It turned out that the guards had another job: to stop Nobile from leaving the ship.[62]

Alone, and under attack, Nobile started to obsess about rejoining his men on the ice. He wanted to "challenge all those spiteful nonentities—show them that I had so little wanted to come away that I was ready to go back and to stay there."[63]

His isolation didn't help the journalists whose job was to cover the disaster. Arnesen's editors expected stories about Nobile. But instead of writing about the Italian and his adventures, Arnesen had to file stories about how Nobile's Titina had frightened off a polar bear or how the dog's coat had turned from black to brown while she was out on the ice.[64] The true story was left untold.

THERE IS A GHOSTLY film of a woman dressed in boots, trousers, and a fisherman's sweater and hat; she is sitting in a lifeboat on the *Hobby* as the ship plows its way through the sea ice. The caption: "Our Only Deck Chairs?"

A few frames later, Louise Boyd is standing with friends in the huge entrance to the empty wooden and canvas airship hangar at Kings Bay. Later, we see her entertaining a succession of aviators with her aristocratic friends—aviators who had risked their lives in the search for Nobile and were now going to risk them again to look for Amundsen.

We see Boyd joking around on the deck of the ship with the glamorous Swedish pilot Lundborg, who had just rescued Nobile. At one moment, he leers directly into the camera. We see Boyd laughing and smiling rather more awkwardly with a Soviet pilot in his ill-fitting utilitarian leather coat.

Later, Riiser-Larsen and Lützow-Holm, who had led the search for Nobile, emerge through the mists of time to sit on the side of the ship, smoking pipes. Out of shot, their seaplanes are strapped to the deck, dwarfing the *Hobby* as she leaves Kings Bay in search of Amundsen.[65]

It wouldn't have been a surprise to anyone who knew Louise Boyd that she had ended up on the hunt for Amundsen. Her family was at the heart of American history. Her mother's side of the family had been minor railroad barons. Her father had made his money in the gold rush. He was a partner in the famous Bodie gold mine in California, now a state historic park. The Boyds survived San Francisco's Great Earthquake of 1906 and saw out the Great Fire that followed. They went to see—and perhaps even met—Roald Amundsen at one of the receptions held for him as he passed through the city in 1906 on his way back from discovering the Northwest Passage. (Later, when her parents grew ill, she would read to them newspaper stories about the Cook-Peary controversy and the further adventures of the man she was searching for now, Amundsen.)[66]

Yet tragedy stalked Louise's life. Her carefree childhood ended abruptly when both her brothers died suddenly of endocarditis one after the other. Her parents were left heartbroken and increasingly dependent on her. As her father's health declined, Boyd learned for the first time to challenge gender expectations and manage her father's multimillion-dollar business. The experience would come in handy later.[67] Her parents died in 1919 and 1920, and at thirty-two years old, Boyd was left a millionaire and alone.

Her inheritance gave her one big advantage over her rival male explorers. It meant that she could finance her own expeditions rather than chase sponsorship from wealthy benefactors and aggressive media organizations.

The American's obsession with the Arctic began in 1924, when on a visit to Svalbard she saw the polar ice cap for the first time. The captain of the passenger steamer she was on asked her what she thought of the ice. She replied, "Captain, I want to be in there someday, looking out; not here looking in."[68]

The following year she was presented to King George V and Queen Mary at Buckingham Palace—not bad for a girl whose father had begun life on a Pennsylvanian farm.[69]

Two years after she had first seen the polar ice cap, she was leading the Louise A. Boyd expedition: the first Arctic expedition organized, led, and financed by a woman. She had chartered Amundsen's sturdy former supply ship the *Hobby* from Tromsø. Her plan was to use it to hunt polar bears, film the Arctic, and become the first woman to reach Franz Josef Land, the *terra nullius* seized by the Soviets to prevent the Norwegians from annexing it.

The *New York Times* reported that the "American girl" shot eleven polar bears herself, killing six in one day. "This, it is considered, is enough to turn envious any arctic hunter," the newspaper reported.[70] The expedition had shot twenty-nine bears in total. Boyd also shot twenty-one thousand feet of motion picture film and seven hundred photographs for scientific research. By the end of the trip, she had earned herself the label "the Girl Who Tamed the Arctic" and even "the Arctic Princess."

In 1928, Boyd was planning a second expedition with the *Hobby* when she learned that Amundsen had disappeared in the search for Umberto Nobile. Boyd immediately offered herself and her ship to the Norwegian government, knowing that it would have little choice but to say yes to both.

By the time the *Hobby* had made it back to Kings Bay, the anchorage was dominated by the warlike *Tordenskjold* and *Strasbourg*. Their captains were busy coordinating the rescue effort. The decision by the Norwegian government to accept Boyd's help placed her right in the wardroom with these powerful men. They had never expected to have a woman in their meetings, and many members of the international rescue team clearly thought women had no place there.

"That to them, I was an object of curiosity and they didn't hide it," she wrote in her diary. "Did they expect me to look different from other women? Was I to have flippers of a seal, tusks of a walrus, or horns of a muskox? Or was I to be some extremely eccentric, awful, hard-boiled old hag, sloppy and dirty-looking in appearance? This latter seemed evident, and my plain, well-made American tweed tailored suit and brown leather low-heeled shoes, well-shampooed and waved hair topped off with felt hat, gloved hands that were useful and had seen all kinds of things, from moving things on the dock to trunks and cases, or wielding the hammer or screw driver, and yet, when not gloved, were seen to be not calloused or the quality of sandpaper, all seemed absolutely incomprehensible to them. Their sphinx-like faces glared still harder on sight of my using face powder and lipstick as the sweat of the Arctic during long work hours rolled down my face and neck."[71]

NOBILE FEARED THAT HIS men were being forgotten in the race to find his old rival—and he had good reason to be worried. Now that he had been saved, the rescue of his men was losing importance.

The general had become first angry, then despondent, and finally depressed by his inability to actually get anything done. With good reason, he feared that his men were about to be abandoned out on the ice—and with them, any hope of saving his reputation.

He wasn't alone in his discontent. The danger of melting ice, the lack of enthusiasm and extreme cautiousness of the Italian authorities, and the limited coordination of the international search effort was sapping the morale of all the pilots. The world's focus on the advance of the *Krassin* had put aircraft out of the minds of even the officers leading the effort.[72] The disappearance of Amundsen's plane and the diversion of ships and planes to look for him and his men meant there were fewer to concentrate on Nobile's crew.

It didn't help Nobile's mood that the press had caught the scent on the wind. Their editorials had started to speculate that Malmgren's group and Captain Sora's party must now be dead—and that the five Italians out on the ice floe would soon have to be abandoned to their fate, unless they could be rescued within a very short time by the *Krassin*.[73]

ZAPPI AND MARIANO WEREN'T dead, not yet. According to Zappi, Mariano had by then been reduced to a zombie-like condition as his tired, numbed, and tortured body kept going. His mind was in a euphoric state, floating somewhere above as death grew closer.

After three weeks on the ice, Mariano was struck blind by the glare of the ice. "I can't see! I can't see!" he screamed. Despite their snow glasses, the intensity of the whiteness seemed able to cut through them like a knife. Zappi rushed over to him to wrap his eyes in a blindfold. "You'll be all right! You must keep your eyes in darkness until the attack passes," he said.[74]

For several days, Zappi, who was in strangely good health, had to lead Mariano by the hand. Together, they stumbled on the dry snow, climbed over large chunks of ice, and jumped channels of water. More often than not, they would end up on their backs on the ice. Zappi could see that Foyn Island never seemed to get any closer despite their struggles.

Mariano's agonies grew worse. Now that he couldn't see where he was going, he would often splash through water, making frostbite inevitable.

"Once," Zappi recalled, "feeling completely exhausted, we scooped out a trench in the dry snow and stayed in it for five or six days, fully prepared to die, but with a feeling of sharp sorrow at being unable to fulfill the mission that the General had entrusted to us."[75]

Around June 20, they saw a black dot in the distance, but the plane had passed overhead before they were able to set fire to anything. The two men began to pray. If they had seen one plane, they were bound to see others as well.

Their prayers were answered. Over the next few days, more and more planes flew over their heads, but they couldn't see them. Zappi realized that they must have found the survivors. He hoped that Nobile, if he was still alive, would tell them the direction the three of them had set off in. He consoled himself that rescue could be only a matter of time.

Just as Mariano's eyesight had started to return, he had an

accident—one that would end his and Zappi's march. Mariano slipped on the ice and twisted his leg, and was never able to walk again while he was on the ice. Like Malmgren, Mariano would have to stay there until he was rescued or died.

Zappi started to think about leaving him. "Save yourself," Mariano said to him. "Save yourself because in so doing you will save our comrades."[76]

By the end of June, Zappi decided that further marching was pointless and that he would stay with Mariano. If they were lucky, the wind and drift of the sea would push them against the coast of a nearby island, such as Broch Island, or even farther on, to Cape Bruun. The warming waters meant that they had to expend their remaining energy on the tricky business of transferring their shelter and belongings from one melting ice floe to another. Unless they resorted to the "custom of the sea," cannibalism, there was no more food, and they put on all their remaining clothing to stay warm. Zappi spelled out in the snow "Help—Food—Mariano and Zappi."[77]

In the weeks that followed, the two men descended into delirium and inactivity. All they had were their feverish dreams of their childhoods or early jobs to keep them company as their lives slowly faded away. "Quietly, we awaited the end," Zappi said.

Still, the drone of aircraft would sometimes pierce Zappi's delirium and bring him back to this world. Some even seemed to come quite close. On July 10—six weeks since the three of them had said goodbye to Nobile and stepped out onto the ice floe—he realized that one of the planes was heading right for them. He managed to lift up the binoculars and realized at once it was a German Junkers with Russian markings on its wings and fuselage. The Russians had come.

"They have seen us!" shouted Zappi. "We are saved!"[78]

The next thing they knew was that the plane had flown a short distance to the north before circling back round to them. Mariano had found what energy he had to get on his feet and wave at the plane. Then they could see it—the hand of the pilot waving back. They had been spotted by one of the search planes of the *Krassin*.

Zappi excitedly told Mariano that they were "bringing supplies now. We shall eat and drink at last."[79]

However, for the next two days nothing happened. They knew they were staring death right in the face. For hope to have been torn away like that . . . It was an awful way to die.

Mariano was critically ill. Zappi would soon follow if he didn't have something to eat and drink soon.

SORA WASN'T DEAD EITHER. "The weak-kneed, yellow-livered little bastard!" Captain Sora had muttered about Romagna as he and his Danish and Dutch companions "coaxed, cursed and badgered" their dog team onward when setting out in search of the crew of the N-4 back in June. "I am ashamed to admit that such an incompetent and timid boob is my countryman."[80]

Despite their making good time to start with, Ludvig Varming started to complain about severe pains in his eyes and then in his stomach. After only two days, he was demanding to be left behind. Sora decided it was best to leave the Dane at a supply depot that had been set up by searchers looking for Malmgren's group; when he felt better, Varming could head back to rejoin the ship.[81]

On the morning of June 20, Sora and Sjef van Dongen

headed east with their dog team, traveling slowly over the melting ice that filled Dove Bay. At times, they had to carry the sledge over the crumbling ice and crevasses. The dogs were able to manage by themselves.

Once across the bay, the two men had to face the greatest challenge of all: they had to head out over the restless pack ice of the Arctic Ocean to Foyn Island, a journey that the Norwegian experts thought impossible at this time of year.[82]

Before they could reach the edge of the sea ice, a storm blew up, trapping them for two days out on the ice in the bay. The men were able to hide in their sleeping bags with the sledge for shelter. The dogs were left to huddle by themselves, and at the end of the storm Sora had to shoot two of the animals that were badly injured or ill.[83]

By June 29, the men had reached Cape Bruun and the starting point for the part of their trip across the open ocean. On that day they were spotted by a plane flown by Lützow-Holm, who dropped a packet with a red marker at them. Wrapped with a wrench to weigh it down was a note that read: "Do not leave the mainland and venture over the sea." [84]

While they realized it was a warning, they didn't know it was from Riiser-Larsen, who had spotted the bad condition of the pack ice the day before. Instead, Sora bit his thumb, then flicked it at the pilot as an insult when he circled back around because Sora thought the message reflected Romagna's wishes for something more than an accurate reading of the state of the ice ahead.[85]

However, the note quickly proved to be correct. It was almost impossible to cross from the coast onto the ice. In some places, the movement of the sea had turned the ice into a jagged barrier that was too difficult to cross with a sledge and dogs. Elsewhere, it was flat but clearly breaking up, threatening to send the two men, their sledge, and seven dogs into the icy sea. He could see why it was known as "the white hell."

After half a day looking for a way onto the ice, Sora lost his temper and declared: "This is where we will try."[86] The sea ice looked like it had formed unsteady, moving stepping-stones just big enough for the men, sledge, and dogs to make it out if they were lucky.

With a great deal of whipping and swearing, Sora and Van Dongen managed to get the sledge and dogs out onto the first large stepping-stone—and then there was a loud crack. The ice split into two beneath them. Sora, the sledge, and two of the dogs were on one side; Van Dongen and the five other dogs on the other.

The ice under Sora was tilting, threatening to send him, the sledge, and the dogs into the freezing water, when the dogs on the other ice floe tried to jump across the chasm. In the pandemonium that followed, the sledge and much of their equipment and provisions slid off and disappeared under the water. The dogs attached to the sledge struggled to free themselves from the harness, but soon they, too, were gone.

"Pull it back!" Sora screamed at Van Dongen.

"I can't get a grip on the ice," the other man gasped.[87]

Somehow Sora and Van Dongen managed to free the sledge and pull it onto the shore, but nearly all their equipment and supplies were gone. All they had left were in the two backpacks they were carrying. Only two half-drowned dogs survived the disaster. They saw the other dogs drown.

On the shore, the two men argued about the next step. Sora was adamant that there was only one way to go and that was across the ice to Foyn Island. Van Dongen told him that they should head back or stay put.

"No way," said Sora. "We must go on."

"That would be suicide," Van Dongen pleaded.

"To go back would be even worse." [88]

Sora won the argument. For the Italian elite officer, turning back would be the equivalent of admitting that Romagna was right.

Before striking out, the men built a cairn and placed a note under the stones at the top: "We are heading NE across the ice to Foyn Island. 1 July 1928 Sora and Van Dongen."[89]

FOR STRANDED MAN-OF-ACTION LUNDBORG, the shock of the inaction of life on the ice floe and the sheer squalor of the camp soon drove him into a depression—and worse. He would later confess to the Czech scientist Běhounek that if he weren't rescued soon he would contemplate suicide.[90]

The Swede's mood soon started to take its toll on the rest of the men. What had been a fairly united group started to break up. Trojani and Cecioni went down the rabbit hole with Lundborg. The others fought depression for as long as they could. Then the camp optimist, Biagi, caught a fever and soon he was depressed like nearly everyone else. Viglieri held out because he was now the leader of the motley crew.

It was the end of June. The ice had started to crack at an alarming rate in the warmth, even crumbling and melting away in places. The men's feet were often in water. The landing strip itself was sinking under the water, making any rescue attempt an even riskier affair.

By now, the increasingly depressed Swede had given up on

the planes. He started to agitate for them all to be allowed to walk out over the ice toward Grosse Island, where the *Krassin* could pick them up. The pilot pushed for this plan even though he must have known that this would spell the end for Cecioni. Planes, he told Nobile in a radio message, could drop them air supplies as they walked along.[91]

When Nobile heard of Lundborg's proposal, he knew it would be suicidal. He urged them all to be calm in one of the few messages he was allowed to send over the radio. Planes were coming, he said; but of course they weren't. The pilots waited too long for perfect conditions. The planes on July 1 didn't come close owing to the fog bank. Then, for five days, hail, snow, and strong winds pinned the aircraft to the ground and made the ice floe shake, while the ice the Red Tent was on crumbled away.[92]

BY JULY 2, SORA AND Van Dongen were making good progress across the sea ice. This was despite the fact that they had fallen into water, waded through freezing cold slush, and were now thoroughly wet.

The next day, they were disturbed by the furious barking of their dogs. Two very large polar bears wandered close by their camp. Sora took his pistol out, but before he had to use it, the bears had passed by. The dogs were too exhausted to follow.[93]

On the evening of July 4, the two men achieved what the experts had said was impossible and what the three-man party from the *Italia* had failed to do: they reached Foyn Island. Van Dongen was running a high fever and there was a forty-foot gap between their piece of sea ice and the shore. In between, there were plenty of ice floes but all were too small for them to walk across.[94]

In the end, Sora decided they were going to have to get wet again if they wanted to set foot on dry land. When the shore seemed closest and the water most shallow, he slipped into the water. With one arm, he supported his companion, while over his head he carried a package of their remaining supplies and equipment, which included his pistol and matches, and the dogs were tied to him.

The two men and two dogs had made it. Unfortunately, the moss and lichen that Sora had planned to use to light fires with was too damp or not enough. The two men thus had no option other than to stay in their sleeping bags and hide from the wind as best as they could. According to Sora, the two dogs abandoned them the moment they made it on to land. (Later, others claimed that the dogs ended up as the men's dinner.)[95]

ON JULY 6, THE MEN Nobile left behind saw a two-person British-built Moth circling overhead. The little biplane, which had been supplied by Sweden rather than Italy, side-slipped in to land on the ice, using barely a third of the runway. (Side-slipping is a way of landing a plane in a strong crosswind by flying slightly sideways.) The spray from its skis made it look as though the plane were waterskiing.[96]

"Schyberg!" When the pilot removed his helmet, Lundborg instantly recognized his old copilot. With tears in Lundborg's eyes, they hugged each other.[97]

When Schyberg asked Lundborg if he had anything he wanted to take back with him, Viglieri knew there would be no rescue for the rest of them. He knew that there would be no discussion of this decision, either, when Lundborg hurriedly clambered on board, leaving behind many of his possessions. It was what Běhounek astutely described as a "panic" flight. No one in the plane knew what the desperate men on the ice might do when they realized they were being left behind.[98]

In the cockpit, Schyberg's pale face and shaking hands told the story. The stress of Arctic flying was starting to take its toll, as was the discouragement from the Italian authorities who seemed uninterested in the fate of their countrymen. The weather, too, had made the task of landing far trickier. The remaining men were doomed to stay on the ice.[99]

Schyberg and Lundborg promised to come back the next day, but it was a promise they didn't keep. The weather changed again.[100]

"We are willing to fly over often and drop supplies," Captain Egmont Tornberg told Nobile when the Italian confronted him, "but quite bluntly, I am reluctant to risk the lives of any men with further landings now that I have a report on the exact conditions of the ice."[101] Instead, the Swedish captain argued that all effort now had to be made to reach the survivors by ship—and this meant the *Krassin*.

But there was one other option. Faced with this situation, Eckener announced to the *New York Times* that he was planning a flight in his new zeppelin to save the *Italia* men in three weeks' time, when the new airship was ready. Unfortunately, the men didn't have three weeks.

ON JULY 8, SORA SAW two planes fly past near the island. One passed just north of them, but apparently the pilot still didn't see them.[102]

Three days later, the good news was outweighed by the bad. Van Dongen seemed to be getting better, but it was Sora's turn to feel ill. They were down to a handful of rations each day and a little water made by melting snow. Their gun still wouldn't fire, and Sora could never find the birds' nests that he knew must be on the island.

The next day brought hope. Sora saw black smoke in the distance. Was it the survivors of the *Italia*? he wondered. Or was it the *Krassin*?

Twelve

"When I Die You Can Eat Me, but Not Before"

"FOR NEARLY SIX WEEKS the whole world had watched in fascinated horror the desperate and seemingly hopeless attempts to find survivors of the dirigible *Italia* somewhere on the floating ice masses off North East Land," wrote Eugene Lyons, an American journalist and Soviet sympathizer, who covered the story from his office in Moscow. The Soviet desire for control and mistrust of Western journalists meant it was through Moscow that the Soviets wanted news of the *Krassin's* progress to reach the world. (Lyons would famously go on to become the first Western journalist to interview Joseph Stalin. Later, and almost as famously, he renounced his faith and became one of the fiercest critics of communism and the Soviet system.) "Meanwhile, Soviet ice-breakers carrying seaplanes and several of the country's ace fliers were slowly nosing their way through the ice floes towards the scene of the tragedy. Their laborious climb northward was scarcely noticed. But as they neared the scene, the civilized world became abruptly aware of the persistent struggle and watched excitedly as the *Krassin* and the *Malygin* elbowed their way through crashing ice masses."[1]

THE *KRASSIN* LEFT BERGEN harbor for the Arctic Circle on June 24 with her bunkers filled with two thousand tons of Welsh coal—the best coal for steam engines. Some of it was even piled high on the deck.[2] As the rusty and battered old ice-breaker left the harbor, it was given three cheers by the men and women who had come to see her go.

Despite her age and rather run-down appearance, the *Krassin* was the most powerful icebreaker in Europe.[3] The 10,500-horsepower three-engine ship was well equipped to confront any formidable challenge the Arctic could throw at her.

Strapped to her deck was a massive wooden crate inside which was a large three-engine Junkers aircraft. On board the ship were 138 people, including four radio operators, the pilots and mechanics for the plane, and a number of journalists— seven Russian, including the "young and charming" Mme. Worontzowa, who would later nurse Captain Mariano, and one Italian, Davide Giudici.[4]

Captain Carl Eggi was in charge. He had a passion for jackboots and a belted jacket. When he gave an order, no one questioned it. In this way, he had gotten the ship ready for sea in less than five days.[5] However, Eggi was not in charge of the expedition. This honor belonged to Umberto Nobile's friend Rudolf Samoylovitch, president of the Institute of Arctic Studies. The veteran of thirteen other Arctic expeditions, it was he whom Nobile had secretly met with in Berlin before the flight of the *Italia*.

Belowdecks, the *Krassin* was never a luxurious ship. In 1928, with 138 people on board, men were sleeping on sofas in the salon and on cushions in the corridor. With the ports and hatches closed because of the rough seas, the air grew heavy and stank from all the bodies.

By June 27, the *Krassin* was still too far away from Svalbard to have any chance of finding the crew of the N-4, but the search party held out hope they might find some clue as to the fate of Amundsen. They were to be disappointed.

At the end of June, just south of Svalbard, the *Krassin* gave the first demonstration of its power when it started to hit the first big chunks of ice.[6] At full speed, the bow would rise high above the ice, and then, just when it seemed the ship was going to be stranded, it would come crashing down like a massive hammer.

"Beneath her enormous weight the expanse of ice gave way with loud reports, and canals opened reminding one of what happens when a big sheet of glass receives a violent blow at its edge," Davide Giudici wrote. "Gigantic blocks were hurled on to the ice which had remained unbroken or plunged with a loud splash into the dark green waters, grating angrily down the sides of the ship. The spectacle of this struggle of man against the forces of Nature was deeply impressive."[7]

When the *Krassin* hit thick ice, water could be pumped from one ballast tank to another to lower or raise the bow or stern, or even make the ship gently roll from side to side. "It's all a matter of patience and coal—if we've got enough of both, we'll win," said Captain Eggi.[8] It was the first time that a ship as large as the *Krassin* had sailed in these Arctic waters.

On June 30, the *Krassin* encountered the first signs of the pack ice and received the latest coordinates for the Red Tent. Two days later, it got wedged in the ice so tightly north of Scoresby Island that even its powerful engines couldn't move it forward. In the distance, the crew could see the masts of the *Braganza*—also blocked by ice at least eight feet thick. Instead, the ship had to head north before turning east again. And now it was starting to run out of coal.

By the evening of July 3, they were out of that ice field, but concerns were growing that the *Krassin* was running out of fuel and—worse still—that there was something wrong with the engines. Four hours of steaming that day had consumed twenty tons of precious coal and had only advanced the ship by a mile.[9] Divers reported that one of the propellers had a blade missing and the steering gear was damaged as well.[10]

Samoylovitch felt he had no option but to radio Moscow on July 5 to explain that they had to turn back. The rescue effort ended there. The next morning, he received his reply: "No return." The government was willing to risk losing the *Krassin* rather than losing face internationally.

"No return. Locate ice smooth enough for airplane take off and descent without serious damage. Airman Chukhnovsky to be allowed to attempt rescue of Viglieri group by air. Continue work of rescue with utmost activity until only 1,000 tons on board for return voyage."[11]

The stokers lost no time shoveling coal into the *Krassin's* boilers to build up the steam, and the mechanics finished testing the engines of the Junkers. By lunchtime, the icebreaker had broken through the ice that had imprisoned them again.

Eleven miles north of Cape Platen, the *Krassin* halted when the seamen found a block of ice big enough to act as a dock and just smooth enough to be a "polar aerodrome." Chukhnovsky was desperate to get into the air. Overnight, the men worked to build a ramp to slide the crate containing the Junkers off the ship and onto the ice thirty feet below. They then dragged it another 150 yards to the point where it could safely be put back together again within the day.[12]

It took Samoylovitch just one look at the bunkers of the ship to know that any hope of rescuing the men of the Red Tent by ship was melting away. There were only seventeen hundred tons of coal left, one thousand tons of which would be needed for navigating to the nearest suitable coaling station. Chukhnovsky's flight had to be a success.[13]

"Too much emphasis," Samoylovitch told Giudici, "cannot be laid on the fact that at this season of the year it is still too early to attempt polar expeditions with ships. . . . If the rescue of the marooned crew of the *Italia* is not possible by means of airplanes, the only vessel that can reach them is the *Krassin*. Only it is necessary to have patience. . . . We have promised to do all that was humanly possible, and we shall keep our promise."[14]

The ship was now so far from help and the ice so thick that "in case of disaster no human effort could save us." Samoylovitch had told the relief community before they set out that "if misfortune overtakes us, do not send help. This would only increase the number of victims without serving any purpose."[15]

On the morning of July 9, the engines of the Junkers roared as it lumbered across the ice runway for its test flight. The runway was wetter than anyone had expected. Snow had turned into pockets of water. The plane nearly overturned, but the pilot saved it, and it was in the air.

The plane was about to land back on the ice when Chukhnovsky was told: "Don't come down!" The men on the ship had spotted that one of the skis was loose. Instead, Chukhnovsky came back around, planed down gradually, and touched down safely. In the evening, the crew drank a ration of vodka.[16]

The next afternoon, the trimotor took off again. This time the plane ran straight into a fog bank. At 5:50 p.m., Chukhnovsky radioed that he had not yet found the survivors and it was time to head back and, at 6:18 p.m., that he was returning. By then, a thick fog had descended, and visibility had declined to two hundred feet. The captain of the *Krassin* ordered the engine room to burn tar to produce a thick black smoke to guide him in. The ship's searchlight was turned on but struggled to make a difference. Out of desperation, a big fire was lit on the polar aerodrome.[17]

But there was nothing. At the time the plane was due to approach, they could hear no sound. Samoylovitch ordered that rockets be fired to help guide the pilot in. Still nothing. Then the *Krassin* received a message. "Cannot find *Krassin* in fog. Have discovered Malmgren trio. Will attempt to land in Seven Islands area."[18]

After that: nothing. The operator of the *Krassin* started to tap out: "Come in CH [Chukhnovsky] . . . Come in CH . . ." But there was silence.

TO MANY ARCTIC VETERANS, the silence meant disaster.

Samoylovitch refused to give up hope—and he was proved right. Around midnight, the radio operator picked up a very faint radio message: "Have . . . landed . . . Cape Wrede or Platen . . . Aircraft damaged, but we are safe . . ."

Samoylovitch was relieved. Then it got even better.

Over the radio came the specific location of the three survivors of the *Italia* who had tried to walk out of trouble. They were on an ice floe surrounded by the warming ocean water. Two of them had been sighted waving handkerchiefs five and a half miles south-southeast of Charles XII Island. A third was lying on the ice.

His report finished: "They seem in poor condition. You must get to them as soon as you can. The *Krassin* is now their only hope."[19]

With this news, the old icebreaker burst into life. They could be with the survivors within three days. Coal was shoveled into the great boilers. The charts were rolled out and the location of the survivors identified. The air base on the ice was dismantled.

Chukhnovsky could wait. He had safely landed on dry land and had two weeks' worth of food.

The boom of the ice hitting the steel of the ship's hull began again, along with the wail of the siren at regular intervals to alert survivors that help was coming.

By the time the *Krassin* was on the move, the news of the sighting of the men had spread around the world. In Sweden, there was national rejoicing. Many Swedes had followed the course of the rescue in the newspapers and radio, and Malmgren had become an unlikely national hero.

At exactly 5:20 p.m. on July 11, Second Officer August Brejnkopf shouted: "There they are!"[20] He pointed at some distant spot on the ice floe. No one else could see anything. Some thought he must have seen a shadow. But then, there they were—the survivors.

"Is it Mariano, Zappi and Malmgren, or the survivors of the Latham?" everyone wanted to know.[21]

As the ship slowed down, the man that the second officer had spotted could clearly be seen through a pair of binoculars. He looked burned black by the sun and reflection from the snow, with a shaggy beard and uncombed hair—"[a] figure of infinite misery"—but he was doing the Roman salute.

When the ship was closer, he had the energy to shout *"Krassin!"* It was Captain Zappi. On the ground, there was a second figure who was too exhausted to raise himself out of the water he was lying in. This was Captain Mariano. His agonized, feverish eyes were unable to meet the gaze of his rescuers. He just said, "Thank you." The third man turned out to be a shadow. Of Malmgren, there was no sign.[22]

Ladders were dropped down the side of the ship, and a rescue party clambered onto the ice. Quickly the sailors got Mariano onto a stretcher and he was lifted onto the ship by crane. It was feared that he wouldn't live for long, so racked by fever, starvation, and frostbite was he. His pulse was weak, he had severe gangrene in one foot, and his speech was rambling and incoherent,[23] and it is alleged that at that moment his greatest fear was that he would be killed and eaten. "When I die you can eat me, but not before," he is reported to have said.[24]

Captain Zappi, on the other hand, was able to refuse a stretcher. Instead, he walked back to the ship and climbed the fifteen-foot ladder back on board without the need of a helping hand, and famously—or infamously—asked for "coffee, very hot coffee,"[25] hardly the usual priority of someone who hadn't eaten for two weeks.

But there was a question that needed answering. Where was the third man? Where was Finn Malmgren?

At this question, Captain Zappi had on the ice initially said something incomprehensible in Italian. On board ship, Samoylovitch asked him again what had happened to the Swede. Zappi became excited, then agitated and aggressive. "He's been dead for a month," he answered.

When he was allowed only one biscuit until the doctor had examined him, Zappi asked, "But why? You have saved us from death by starvation and now you won't let us eat." Despite Zappi's "starvation," he wrote two telegrams with a very steady hand.[26]

The questions didn't end there. Zappi's hands were too sore to take off his own clothes. Instead, one of the crew did. Underneath his sodden garments, the crewman found that Zappi appeared to be wearing Malmgren's boots, socks, trousers, vest, and cap. Malmgren's compass and personal letters were found in Zappi's pocket. Despite a friendship of fifteen years, Mariano had been left to meet his maker with only a handful of clothes compared to Zappi's twelve.[27]

Zappi soon became hysterical, bordering on angry, at the repeated questioning of his account. Why did everyone want to know about Malmgren? Why didn't they want to know what it was like to survive on the pack ice for a month and a half?[28]

The ship's doctor ordered tests on the two survivors to find out how long it was since the two had eaten. The answers weren't the ones that the Italians wanted. Zappi said he hadn't eaten for twelve days, but the tests showed that he had eaten within the past twenty-four hours. A similar test on Mariano showed that he hadn't eaten for eleven days.

Cannibalism might have been taboo in the West, but the so-called custom of the sea did allow for sailors like Filippo Zappi and Adalberto Mariano to draw lots as to who they should eat if they found themselves cast adrift on the open ocean. The man with the shortest straw would be dinner.[29]

Whatever Mariano said, or didn't say, the press quickly picked on the incongruities in their stories. "Mystery about Malgrem's body gives rise to reports of cannibalism," reported one paper.[30] Another: "Nobile Aides Accused of Cannibalism on Icy Trek."[31] *Time* magazine asked: "Was that Swede really eaten by those Italians?"[32]

SAMOYLOVITCH WORRIED THAT ZAPPI'S behavior resembled that of a guilty man and that he had done something unspeakable to the meteorologist.[33] It didn't help that Arctic veterans who heard the story refused to pass judgment on Zappi until there had been a proper investigation.[34] They knew what the snow and ice could drive a man to do. The journalists who interviewed Zappi tended to believe his story.

Nobile didn't believe that Zappi was a cannibal for the simple reason that the three men had left with enough food supplies.[35] Why, Nobile wondered, boast about not eating for twelve days "when his physical appearance revealed no trace of his suffering? It was this idiotic chatter which had given the Press a pretext for its foul slanders."[36]

That said, Nobile did think the officer was selfish, callous, and a stupid braggart. He couldn't forgive Zappi's abandoning him and the rest of the survivors on the ice and afterward telling the world that he had been "chosen by Nobile." Worse, Zappi told the world that the men who were carried away in the *Italia* were now dead—and there was no point searching for them.

Malmgren's mother forgave Zappi and Mariano for the death of her son when Captain Zappi met her to hand over Finn's watch and notebook. She told the *New York Times* that she "believed absolutely" the captain's word.[37] Nonetheless, a few years later, Mussolini's government very quietly gave her a pension, which suggests that there may have been something to the allegations.

Whether she ever forgave General Umberto Nobile is a different matter. A photograph shows a smiling aged Nobile greeting a grim-faced Mrs. Malmgren.[38] Whether Nobile forgave himself is also a matter of speculation. Even in his later years, the general would grow agitated and angry at any discussions of the fate of his Swedish friend that mentioned cannibalism.[39]

AFTER PICKING UP MARIANO and Zappi, the *Krassin* quickly got underway again. This time it headed due east. New information had been received as to the location of the Red Tent. On July 12, as the ship passed Foyn Island, the lookout reported seeing two men on the shore. Captain Eggi guessed from the description of their appearance that the men must be Sora and Van Dongen.

With the two men safely on Foyn Island, the assumption was made—erroneously—that they must be living off game. The decision was made to push on to the Red Tent, which was on the melting sea ice and at the mercy of the ocean currents.

"We will push on, and return for those two later," declared Eggi, without realizing the effect this would have on the men.[40]

Sora had seen the black smoke in the distance and realized it was the *Krassin* and that they were safe. The icebreaker was so close that the two men could hear the ice crashing against the metal hull. [41] Then, abruptly, it turned away.

"Why are they leaving us?" cried the Dutchman. "How many days do they think we can hold out?"

"I don't know. I don't know," replied Sora. He didn't have the heart to tell him that all the food they had left was half a bar of chocolate.[42]

By the end of the afternoon, the *Krassin* reached the location where the Red Tent should have been, but the lookouts couldn't see anything. Thinking that the camp must be hidden behind some lump of snow or ice, the captain ordered an erratic course to be sailed.

At 4:55 p.m., Biagi sent the following message: "We've sighted the *Krassin* about 10 kilometers south-west."[43] But the *Krassin* hadn't seen them.

For once, Nobile was able to persuade the Italians on the *Città di Milano* to take initiative and relay the message directly to the *Krassin*,[44] allowing the Soviets to home in on the survivors' location. A relay station was necessary because the Red Tent survivors only had a short-wave radio, and the *Krassin*, a long-wave radio.

By 9:00 p.m. that night, the *Krassin* had managed what all the high-tech air power had failed to do. It had reached the survivors of the *Italia* despite the damage to the ship. In fact, the *Krassin* achieved the remarkable feat of sailing to within a hundred yards of the Red Tent.[45] Biagi broadcast his last message to the world, thanking the rescuers and ending with the words "Long live the King and Italy."[46]

The huge, dirty icebreaker with thick black smoke billowing out of its two funnels towered over the camp of the survivors of the *Italia*, the brilliant white sea ice, and Lundborg's overturned plane—a stark memorial to their suffering. Viglieri, Trojani, and Běhounek stumbled toward the ship like men released from prison. They were embraced and kissed by Samoylovitch at the bottom of the gangplank.[47] Giudici walked to the camp to greet Cecioni, who had emerged from one of the tents on crutches. Cecioni gave him a salute. Biagi then appeared wearing one of the general's caps, his face hidden behind a beard.

Starved of contact with the outside world, the survivors were suddenly gripped by a wave of energy. For an hour, they seemed keener to show off their camp to the ship's officers and men than have a shower or find a soft, warm bed to sleep in. Proud of what they had achieved, they explained how, for example, they had built their radio antenna and used the upper wings from the Swedish plane as a floor in their camp. "If you had taken any longer to come, we would have all been swimming," Cecioni remarked, laughing. He did not yet know that earlier he had been reported by the newspapers to have had a "pitiful death."[48]

There was one bitter note. It dawned on journalist Davide Giudici that the ice runway near the Red Tent was actually in the same condition as that of the polar aerodrome the crew of the *Krassin* had built for their Junkers.[49] The Swedish or Finnish trimotors could have landed and taken the crew off the ice weeks ago.

THE *KRASSIN* NEVER DID return for Sora and Van Dongen. Mariano needed his leg amputated in the medical bay of the *Città* rather than amid the dirt and grease of the icebreaker. Luckily, Sora and Van Dongen never had to find out how long their sole surviving chocolate bar would last.

With their location now known, three planes were dispatched to drop supplies to the two stranded men. When the pilots flew over the island, they immediately spotted an opportunity: the melting ice had opened a narrow channel just large enough for two seaplanes to land, and each plane could take one man. This thin strip of water wouldn't stay open for long, so the pilots had to act quickly, which they did, displaying a level of initiative unusual that summer.

The only radio-equipped plane stayed circling overhead in case of disaster. The other two seaplanes landed in the channel that Sora and Van Dongen had managed to stumble to, and then the channel started to rapidly close. Out of the two planes, the Heinkel biplane was the first back in the air. The crew of the Junkers went to restart their engines when disaster happened: the third engine refused to start (and, perhaps, demonstrated why the pilots had been reluctant to use their initiative).

The airmen now faced being marooned on the island with Sora and Van Dongen and the pain of watching their state-of-the-art plane crushed by the ice. For half an hour, the men scrambled to fix it in the freezing cold, and then, at the last moment, with the ice closing in, the engine burst into life and the Junkers was back in the air.

Sora looked back at the island that had been his prison and had threatened to be his grave with what must have been mixed emotions. He had proved many of the Norwegian experts wrong. It was possible to cross the sea ice from Svalbard to Foyn Island in the summer.[50] And he had even come close to finding the crew of the N-4.

The Red Tent had floated close to Foyn. One day, Sora thought he had seen smoke and the figures of stick men out on the ice in the distance, but he had dismissed it as a trick of the light. "Just think that one day I was only a few miles from the Red Tent and did not know it!" he later told the Italian journalist Giudici.[51]

Sadly, he had to leave behind on the island two dogs and a historic relic—the oil stove that Wilkins had used on his transpolar flight.[52]

Romagna had been right about one thing. The Italian had come perilously close to disaster.

Sora hoped that the matter of his insubordination would be forgotten. Unfortunately for him, Captain Romagna was not the kind of man to forget. He made sure that everyone remembered that Sora had disobeyed an order. For Sora to have so publicly sided with Nobile was a reckless move by the officer.

A court-martial was convened and Sora was charged with disobeying a direct order. Luckily for the brave man, his commanding officer back in Italy had heard about his heroic exploits and gave him a reprimand instead, which was just a technicality. Van Dongen, his companion, was astounded that the Italians would even contemplate court-martialing such a hero.[53]

IN THE END, BOYD, like the rest of the would-be rescuers, found no trace of the old explorer Amundsen, despite sailing for ten weeks from Tromsø to Spitsbergen, into the Greenland Sea, to Franz Josef Land, and back to Tromsø in search of him, with two planes and pilots accompanying her. Remarkably, her crew managed at the same time to capture twenty thousand feet of motion-picture film.

One of the wing floats of the Latham 47 flying boat was recovered from the sea later in the summer; the struts and wires were still attached to it, indicating it had been torn off the plane. A fuel tank was found near Trondheim, Norway, with a mysterious wooden bung in it. Yet all these pieces of wreckage did was give the explorers false hope of finding the crew alive. Finally, in 1931, in memory of the men, a stone Latham flying boat was carved out of the rocky cliff side near Caudebec-en-Caux in Normandy where the machine was constructed. Nobile was not invited to the ceremony.

The Norwegian government awarded Boyd the Chevalier Cross of the Order of Saint Olav.[54] She was only the third woman and first non-Norwegian to receive the medal.

Yet old attitudes die hard. "Off the train came two entrancing young ladies in the latest Parisian fashions," wrote Riiser-Larsen in his journal, about his experience of meeting Boyd and her companion on her way to receive her Saint Olav. "Lützow-Holm and I looked at each other and thought the same thing. This is what we have sailed with the last three months in the open northern ice???"[55]*

* Boyd would go on to become a "serious scientist." She led four scientific expeditions to the relatively unknown east coast of Greenland in the 1930s and earned herself the rather appropriate nickname of "the Chief." By the outbreak of World War II, she was seen by the American military as a leading expert in her field. During the war, Boyd would be sent on a number of secret missions for the US military in the Arctic. In an echo of Amundsen's vision of the Arctic, these missions included looking for sites for US air bases (Audrey Amidon, "Women of the Polar Archives: The Films and Stories of Marie Peary Stafford and Louise Boyd," *Prologue* 42, no. 2 [Summer 2010], https://www.archives.gov/publications/prologue/2010/summer/polar-women.html).

Louise Boyd died in San Francisco in 1972. News that "the Chief is dead" spread quickly (Geologist Finn Bonner quoted in Anna Kafarowski, *The Polar Adventures of a Rich American Dame: A Life of Louise Arner Boyd* [Toronto: Dundurn, 2017], 298). Obituaries followed in all the major newspapers. But her fortune was gone and the family home sold. Her last wish was for her body to be cremated and her ashes scattered in the Arctic. A close friend agreed to fly her ashes up to Point Barrow in Alaska, where so many flights landed and

Some things aren't forgotten even in death. Amundsen and his family never forgave Riiser-Larsen's betrayal. Lawyers acting for the family prevented the giant Norwegian pilot from attending the funeral. Riven by what must have been guilt, Riiser-Larsen later staged a séance to try to talk to the old man one last time.[56]

Amundsen's body was never found. The suggestion by a Soviet scientist that his frozen body could be brought back to life was fortunately never able to be put to the test.[57] In 2012, DNA tests were used to disprove two Inuit men's claims that their father was Amundsen's son.[58]

The wreckage of the plane remains as elusive as ever. One of the Latham's engines may have been recovered by a trawler in 1933, but it fell back into the sea before they could secure it. In 1964, plywood that might have belonged to the aircraft was found near Svalbard. To this day, expeditions continue to be sent to try to find the wreckage of the Latham. Robots have been deployed to search the seabed for Amundsen's grave.[59]

WROTE EUGENE LYONS OF his time covering the story from Moscow:

> Out of the grudging formal communiqués we fashioned a saga of Soviet daring which will forever embellish the records of Arctic exploration. We did this despite the bureaucratic attitude of a censorship apparatus so rigidly geared for the suppression of facts that it automatically hampered the transmission of a story more favorable to

---

took off from. There is no formal record of where her ashes were scattered (Anna Kafarowski, *The Polar Adventures*, 298–299).

its reputation among the peoples of the globe than any-thing that had happened in years.

The actual events were sufficiently stirring, but the correspondents . . . spread wide the wings of their fancy in blowing up Samoylovitch, Chukhnovsky, and the other heroes to almost mythical dimensions. The icebreaker itself, blunt-nosed, powerful, imperturbable, turned un-der our keys into a symbol of Soviet strength rescuing the world.

That those to whom the Red Samaritans brought suc-cor were Black Fascists enhanced that symbolism. The irony of Soviet Russia bringing life to stranded Italians and putting Mussolini's realm in their debt was not lost on the world.[60]

Thirteen

"Down with Nobile! Death to Nobile!"

ON JULY 26, TWO MONTHS since the crash of the *Italia*, the *Città di Milano* sailed into Narvik to be met by hundreds of Norwegians standing on the quayside in silence. There were no signs of the Italian flag anywhere. A large poster proclaimed: "Reward: 10,000 Kroner for Any Information Leading to the Missing Explorer Roald Amundsen."[1]

It was a case of bad timing by the Italians. That same day, the headline of the newspapers was "The Norwegians Give Up the Hunt for Amundsen," because they were convinced that the explorer and his men were dead.[2] Now the anger of the crowd was all directed at one man, General Umberto Nobile, who had the temerity to have survived and won his last bout with the famous explorer.

The Italians were actually lucky. The local newspapers were saying that Nobile should have hanged himself out of shame for his role in the death of their hero. Others said that he should be met by silence or by shouts of "'Down with the general' or so that the dagos would understand—'Abbasso Nobile! A morte Nobile!' (Down with Nobile! Death to Nobile!)."[3]

Instead, the survivors were met by just hisses from the

mob as they stepped off the ship onto the extraordinarily long gangplank that led not to the dockside but straight into the two railroad cars hired by the Italian government to take the men back to Rome. If Nobile thought that the dockers didn't want him to set foot in Norway again, he would have been right. The workers didn't want him to defile Norway's soil by "setting his dammed feet on it."⁴

The newspapers reported the gossip that the men were being taken back to Italy in "sealed railway carriages," rather like the way Lenin had traveled on his return to Russia from exile in Switzerland in 1917.⁵ It wasn't strictly true, but when Nobile and his men reached the train, they discovered that the curtains of their railroad cars had been closed owing to the delicate international situation. The men were told by the Italian consul not to open them until they had left the city. The consul also warned them not to speak to anyone en route to Italy, particularly members of the press, nor to explore other parts of the train. The men were too exhausted physically to challenge these strictures.

Their reception didn't change after they had left Oslo behind. At each stop, the survivors were given the same silent, angry treatment by the men and women who crowded the platforms. In the safety of the rail car, Nobile was glad for the distraction of a bundle of newspapers to read that he hadn't seen before, but his pleasure was soon tempered. He realized why the crowd was so hostile to him.

Thus concluded one of the worse periods of my life— thirty-two interminable days of indescribable torment. At first, absorbed as I was in organizing the rescue work I

did not even notice what was being plotted in the shadows. Then little by little, I had glimpsed the bitter truth:
a few sentences broken short, vague words, the reticence
of my friends, and more often silence, had finally revealed
the shameful slander campaign that had been unleashed
upon me.

In the train at Narvik, as if to round off the fearful
ordeal, they brought me a bundle of newspapers. There
I read everything that had been printed in the European
press during the last month against the *Italia* expedition.
It was a full, brutal, unexpected revelation.[6]

Everything had served as material for calumny, in-
sinuations, insults. I felt crushed under the avalanche of
abuse hurled at me by mean spirits throughout the world,
which I had been unable to defend myself from.[7]

THE ATMOSPHERE ON BOARD the train lifted when they crossed
the border into Sweden and again into Denmark. Crowds of
people still met the train at the stations they stopped at, but
this time they were friendlier. The Swedes viewed Nobile
more sympathetically than the Norwegians had. The recent
public defense of the general by the Swedish hero Lundborg,
who had rescued him from the ice, could only have helped
his case.

When the train stopped at the Swedish town of Vindeln, a
little girl by the name of Ebba Haggstrom ran up to the general with a bunch of flowers. Nobile made sure he found out
the girl's name because he was determined never to forget her
kind gesture.

"Tell your paper there is much bitterness in my heart," Nobile told a journalist at the station, "but I was deeply affected by this sweet little Swedish girl who handed me the beautiful flowers."[8]

The warm welcomes didn't last for long. In northern Germany, the train was met by jeers as the crowd grew angrier again. "I bought a newspaper," Nobile recorded. "A caricature showed our train with the carriage window barred and the doors padlocked, with horrible allusions to the accusations of cannibalism."[9] When they reached Catholic Bavaria, the crowds on the station grew friendly to the Italians again out of sympathy for their coreligionists victimized by the Protestant Norwegians.

The tension in the railroad cars must have built up as the train approached the Italian border. Just how would the eight men be received by their fellow countrymen? The attitude of their government seemed to be clear. Rumors spread along the train that any kind of public demonstration in support of them had been banned. It was even suggested that mobs had been organized to make sure that any such shows of support were quickly broken up.

Whatever the original intention of the regime, the government announced that it would allow the people to greet the train at the stations it passed through. Despite this, there would be no official representative of the Rome government to greet them, nor would there be a big reception held for them. The only events would be run by regional Fascist organizations and the City of Milan, at which there would be no speeches. When Nobile arrived in Rome, he would head straight back to his home in Via Giovanni Ferrari under what sounded like house arrest.[10]

When the train crossed the border, it was clear that their fellow countrymen were going to treat the men as heroes rather than criminals. The cordons of soldiers placed at each station to control the masses of people were quickly broken up by the crowds,[11] which swarmed into station squares and invaded the platforms themselves in order to show their support of the aviators. Nobile reported that young men repeated one slogan over and over again—"Only command us! We are ready to die for you!"—and that this shout passed from town to town, mouth to mouth along the railroad line to Rome.[12]

Nobile's reception in Rome on July 31 was beyond his wildest dreams. In a direct challenge to the regime, the train was met by a crowd of two hundred thousand people, who saw Nobile in quite a different light than the Norwegians. "A delirious crowd, a crowd which hour by hour had lived through the *Italia* expedition," wrote Nobile, "who had suffered the anguish of silence, the strain of suspense, the uncertainties of the rescue work; a crowd which had lived through all of our tragedy, shared all our suffering, felt all the infamies committed against us."[13]

The Italian newspapers echoed the cheers for Nobile on the street. The report by Professor Běhounek on the scientific accomplishments of all the flights of the N-4 made headlines across the country. Běhounek, whom Nobile had supposedly "abandoned" on the ice, was quoted as saying: "I consider General Nobile a man of exceptional qualities and I feel proud to have had him as my chief."

Pope Pius XI had also remained loyal to Nobile. The pope described the *Italia* expedition as one of those feats "which attain the highest beauty and sublimity that can be encountered in this life."[14]

IT WAS NOW CLEAR to Nobile that Italo Balbo had been waging war on him. Safely home, and with nothing to distract him, Nobile was struggling to contain the two months of anger, *rage*, that was boiling up inside him about Balbo's campaign against him—a war that, if he was honest with himself, dated back to 1924.

"Balbo's hostility towards me had been brewing for a long time," Nobile wrote, "but it had manifested itself openly after the catastrophe. I was told that on the day when the newspapers published the news that the *Italia* had disappeared, Balbo was landing at the aerodrome of Alcazar, in the course of one of his aerial cruises, and he replied in a tone of absolute indifference 'Serves him right.'" It was reported to Nobile by his friends in the air force that Balbo had even toasted the disappearance of the *Italia* at a banquet during the flight.[15]

Nobile believed that Lundborg's crash on the ice had given Balbo the opportunity to "declare open war" against him[16] because the eyewitness to his rescue was trapped on the ice. With Lundborg out of the way, Balbo could then use "every effort . . . to diminish [Nobile's] prestige." Nobile believed that Mussolini allowed the "addition of a poisonous phrase [to the communiqué announcing Nobile's rescue]: 'We do not know the reason why General was taken first.' This was an open invitation to the foreign press to attack me."[17]

What frustrated Nobile the most was that it didn't have to be this way.[18] The Fascist government fiercely defended the reputation of the Italian officers who had abandoned Malmgren on the ice and had been accused of cannibalism in a way that they conspicuously didn't do for Nobile. The propagandists of the Fascist regime billed the fate of the three men as "the untarnished beauty of the episode of the Three.

The sublime, voluntary sacrifice made by Malmgren in order to enable the other two to accomplish an imperative duty towards the *Italia* castaways."[19] It was clearly a choice Mussolini had made and which he kept to even after complaints from the Swedish government over Malmgren's death threatened to turn the incident into a diplomatic crisis. It was a story they were sticking to even when, in 1931, they quietly agreed to pay Mrs. Malmgren a pension.

If Nobile had been less angry, then he may have been able to move his pieces like a chess player. He may have been able to use his widespread popularity to achieve a new accommodation with Mussolini and even Balbo. It was, after all, rather awkward for a populist regime to be as out of touch with the mood of the people as it was over Nobile and the fate of the *Italia* expedition.

Some people would call the general's next step foolish; others, brave. What can be said is simply that his fury made him reckless and even out of control. These weren't qualities that would normally give a man in Nobile's position a long life in Mussolini's Italy. Nonetheless, somehow he survived a stand-up row with the dictator.

Mussolini sent for the general too soon after he had returned for his anger to have cooled down. "How are you, Nobile?" asked Mussolini in a tone that was reminiscent of how they used to talk before Balbo muscled his way into their relationship. "I see that you are still lame."[20] The two of them chatted together about a few of the episodes of the expedition as they used to do only two years previously. At the end of their meeting, Mussolini said, "Very well, my dear Nobile, I think that's enough. If I need anything else I will send for you."

Mussolini then got up to say goodbye, but something

snapped in Nobile. "I had not the least intention of going away quietly," he later wrote.

"*Eccellenza*, now I am going to say something on my own account," he told the shocked dictator. Nobile spread out before him the documents, letters, telegrams, and communiqué that had so enraged him.

"The government's duty was to wait for my explanations before issuing that communiqué," he told Il Duce. "It was not at all necessary to put into this world a statement which would inevitably incite the whole foreign press against me."

Neither of them had moved from their spot in the middle of the room after Nobile's outburst. Mussolini turned pale and went over to his desk. He sat down silently. He took a sip of water. Nobile thought there must be some medicine in it. Then he pressed a bell, and when the usher appeared, he said simply, "Show the General out."

Nobile knew that he had made a big mistake. "I was exasperated," he wrote. "For weeks my soul had been full of bitterness. Now the indignation repressed for so long burst out. Without meaning to, without realizing it, I had raised my voice. I forgot that the man to whom I was speaking had not been accustomed for years to being addressed in that tone; it was years since he had heard himself criticized at all, let alone in this forceful manner."

This was the last time Nobile ever saw Mussolini.[21]

Nobile had also not visited Balbo on his return. He pulled a similar stunt on his return from Japan in 1927—and Nobile knew how Balbo had reacted to that. Now history was about to repeat itself. There was one man you didn't stand up to and that was Italo Balbo. It was said that even Mussolini was scared of him.

"I ought also . . . on my own initiative . . . and according to military etiquette to have called on Balbo," wrote Nobile, "but it seemed quite wrong to me that I have should have paid homage to this man. . . . Of course, I realized the consequences that my attitude might entail and in fact it was not long before they became manifest."[22]

Nobile's foolish actions made certain that the assault on his reputation wouldn't stop. He and Carlotta were ostracized from society. The government reopened investigations into allegations that he held anti-Fascist views and that his factory was a nest of communism. Pressure was also put on the survivors to inform on Nobile. Cecioni was "invited" to visit Balbo. "What Balbo said to him, I do not know, but certainly from that moment onward his conduct toward me radically changed," Nobile wrote.

In one very petty move, Balbo even insisted that Nobile's broken leg be X-rayed again after allegations in the Fascist leader's own paper reported that he had run up to Lundborg's plane. It was lucky that Nobile carried his own X-rays with him, having anticipated precisely such a move.

Then Balbo's killer blow came. In September, Gaetano Arturo Crocco, Nobile's bitter rival, sent for his former protégé. Crocco hadn't been able to stop his ambitious apprentice in the past. Now he had the upstart exactly where he wanted.

In what must have been a humiliating meeting for Nobile, Crocco told his rival that he was being recalled to service after his secondment to the Royal Geographical Society for the duration of the expedition—but not in a way that most people would understand it. Nobile was ordered not to move, speak, write, or above all, go to the theater. He was also ordered to vacate at once his office at the SCA. The door was sealed to make sure he didn't try to reenter it. All his papers were trapped inside, and it was only with the help of a brave lawyer that he was able to retrieve them.

General Nobile quickly realized that he was a prisoner in Rome. He was spied on and followed. A trip to see his sick wife in Naples earned a formal order not to leave Rome again.[23]

"Then the Italian government instituted a formal inquiry into the expedition," wrote Willy Meyer, a pilot in the air force of the Weimar Republic, who had staged his own painstaking investigation into the *Italia* disaster, titled *Der Kampf um Nobile*. "Up until then it could be said that the world had shown some indulgence to badly led, ill equipped expeditions, and sympathy to unlucky explorers. It would seem this was the case no longer.

"What was worse was that the members of the commission were chosen because they fitted three criteria: they were enemies of Nobile, knew little about the Arctic and next to nothing about airships."[24] One of the men had even declared that Nobile should have been put on trial on the *Città di Milano* and executed. Chillingly for the former hero, Gaetano Arturo Crocco was a member of the commission, and his determination to work through the accusations Amundsen had made in the *World's Work* against Nobile made him furious. (Nobile thought that his former mentor should have refused the request—like others had—and complained that as Crocco read the magazine, he must also have seen Nobile's refutation of Amundsen's claims.)

But Meyer was wrong. There was one member of the commission who knew a great deal about the Arctic, exploration, leadership, and what it took to survive: a certain Umberto Cagni, hero of the Pole Star expedition, and exactly the kind of man that Nobile had publicly declared was now redundant in the age of the aeronaut, his skills no longer needed. It turned out that they still were.

Balbo had told the commission that Nobile "was ambitious and politically dangerous." After that coded remark, it was said that it would have required the courage of lions for the commission to have found Nobile innocent.[25]

The beleaguered general was interrogated four times by the commission, and at no time were any allegations put to him.[26] The commission prevented any of the film and photographs he had shot on the expedition from being developed. They were confiscated along with the precious scientific data the N-4 had collected, which was crucial evidence in Nobile's defense of the value of his expedition.[27]

The relentless questioning of Nobile was followed by a bizarre episode that can only be understood as a kind of psychological warfare. Nobile was suddenly allowed back into his office. He could develop his film and write a paper about his research. He was even told in a phone call by the chief of Mussolini's cabinet that the conclusions were entirely favorable to him and that there was nothing to fear.[28]

The chief of the cabinet had lied. On March 4, 1929, Nobile's personal secretary returned from the newsstands with the color drained from his face. The findings of the commission were all over the papers: Nobile was guilty.

"There had been an error of judgment in maneuvering," the papers reported. "His departure with Lundborg could be explained but not excused by mental and physical condition." At that point, Nobile had still never read the accusations against him.

"All the intrigue woven against me over the last seven

months and culminating in this impudent lie . . . had now come to light," he wrote. He now realized that the recent courtesy paid to him was little more than a trick so that he would "suspect nothing and would not be able to defend [him-] self in time." The judgment of the commission was now a fait accompli.[29]

Nobile received a message from Mussolini advising him to ask to be put on the retired list, which would mean that he would maintain his rank and have a pension. He was so out-raged that he replied to Mussolini that he had no intention of doing any such thing. Instead, Nobile resigned, and the royal decree accepting his resignation was published two days later. He thought he would now be able to defend himself, but it wasn't to be the case.[30]

Nobile's book *L'Italia al Polo Nord* was published but cen-sored. Its distribution was impeded, and it soon disappeared from shops. Libraries were warned not to stock it. Any mag-azine that gave it a good review was hauled over the coals by the government. Balbo wrote to the minister of education drawing his attention to an academic magazine that had dared to publish a positive review of Nobile's book. "I consider that the presence of the book in students' libraries is harmful."[31]

Balbo didn't have it all his own way. News of the way the Fascist regime was persecuting Nobile spread across Europe. Voices began to be raised in Germany, Czechoslovakia, Swe-den, and the Soviet Union that challenged the findings of the Italian government's commission. Many of these men from other countries had seen for themselves how the Italian gov-ernment had left their men to die on the ice.

"It is beyond doubt that Nobile's airship, well piloted, was of a perfect type, and it demonstrated this splendidly during hurricanes and tempests, in rain, snow and fog, admirably resisting the assaults of the bad weather," Běhounek wrote in *Seven Weeks on the Pack*. "That it would have been impossible not to admire the general, who, as a perfect leader, took care of the whole expedition down to the smallest details, and in the most exhausting flights, by his tirelessness, he set us a magnificent example."[32]

Quickly, it became a rather unequal propaganda war between the power of the Fascist state and Nobile's band of supporters. It wasn't a surprise when Běhounek's book was banned in Italy and when copies found in the luggage of visitors were confiscated—though it was startling when suddenly the Italian authorities allowed the book to be published in Italy.[33] This change in the behavior of the Fascist regime toward Nobile should have been a warning sign that worse was to come.

Despite the Fascists' onslaught, Nobile's reputation and the reputation of the *Italia* expedition had started to improve. On February 16, 1930, Nobile was in Sweden to receive the Andrée Plaque for Polar Studies from the Swedish Geographical Society when the Fascist government made a perfectly timed move to push news of his award out of the headlines: the government unexpectedly published the report in full,[34] in order, it claimed, to correct the account given in a number of books on the subject, including the general's own account, which was "inaccurate but audacious."[35]

The *New York Times* headline that day was damning for Nobile: "Nobile Is Censured in Official Report; Commission Blames Him for Loss of Dirigible Italia on Polar Flight . . . Board Points Out His Lack of Experience as Pilot and His Conduct in Being Rescued First From Ice. Envelope Torn at Start. 'Lacked Experienced Pilot.' His Return First Censured."

The commission's report appeared simultaneously in all the Italian newspapers. Tens of thousands of copies were printed in two editions—cheap and deluxe. Thousands more were distributed for free throughout Italy.[36] It would seem that the Fascist regime had buried Nobile for good, but then the general began receiving thousands of letters and telegrams from unknown supporters from "every country in Europe" and even as far away as North America, Egypt, and Argentina. Celebrities rallied to his banner, even from Amundsen's own country. "The verdict against Nobile shows the horrifying signs of dictatorship," wrote Norwegian author Sven Elvestad. "When we compare all that has been written about the expedition and the catastrophe, including the accounts of other people besides Nobile's, we gain a clear impression that the enterprise was well prepared and led. The truth is gaining."[37]

Captain Willy Meyer published his own verdict: "The judgment on Nobile makes me rebel: it is unjust. In this case Italy has availed herself of the scapegoat system and has created a new kind of Dreyfus case."[38]

Fourteen

"This Is Real Exploring despite the Luxury"

THE MASSIVE SILVER MONSTER floated mere feet above the waters off Hooker Island. Its gondola was just touching the freezing-cold sea that was perfectly still on a windless day and dotted here and there with chunks of ice. Above the goliath towered the gray mountains of the Franz Josef Land archipelago, streaked by white dashes of snow. In the valleys between their peaks, huge thick glaciers stretched down to the water's edge.

In the bay was the Soviet icebreaker *Malygin* that the giant airship had come to rendezvous with—a ship that seemed to resemble a pleasure cruiser more than a real workhorse of the sea. In between them, a wooden boat ferried sacks of mail for the airship and dignitaries.

The year was 1931. The date was July 27, and Umberto Nobile's dream of giant airships that would explore the Arctic was being realized. Unfortunately, the airship wasn't Italian. On its side was stamped *GRAF ZEPPELIN*, and at the helm was Hugo Eckener.

Eckener was asked before he left, "Aren't you afraid that something will go wrong with you, too, over the Arctic

Ocean?" His reply was brutal: "No, because he [Nobile] is a 'skittish colt,' as we put it. Such people should stay away from aviation!"[1]

First flown three years before, by the time of its Arctic flight, the giant airship had already completed the first commercial passenger flight across the Atlantic and back. The airship had also completed a 21,500-mile round-the-world luxury passenger flight in five legs, paid for by media mogul William Randolph Hearst. Hearst had paid $100,000 for the media rights to the flight outside Europe. He had wanted to buy worldwide rights, but Eckener couldn't afford to offend the German newspapers.[2] Tens of thousands of Germans had turned out to see it take off from Berlin.

Now stripped off all her luxury trappings—other than a good kitchen and chef—the craft was in the Arctic to finally make good Eckener's promise to explore the Arctic in an airship. Eckener had even succeeded in landing on the Arctic Ocean, something that Nobile hadn't achieved.

But there was one place the giant airship wouldn't go: the North Pole. The insurance company would not allow it.

The eighty-three-hundred-mile (13,310 km) five-stage flight would rewrite the map of the Arctic. The huge airship would prove to be an ideal stable platform for scientific research and the accurate collection of scientific data in a way that the planes of the time weren't.

On board the airship was also Lincoln Ellsworth, the American millionaire and friend of Roald Amundsen. "This is real exploring despite the luxury," Lincoln Ellsworth tried to convince himself. And in the icebreaker, bobbing about in the shadow of the beast, was Umberto Nobile.

Eckener had declined Nobile's offer to accompany him on

the flight as a "polar expert" (Eckener's words). "I declined with thanks, for we did not intend to accumulate the experiences on a cake of ice," wrote Eckener later.[3] Nobile thought the Italian Embassy in Berlin had put pressure on Eckener not to invite him.[4]

Professor Samoylovitch had invited Nobile to join him on the *Malygin*, and the invitation came as a blessed relief to Nobile, desperate to escape his persecution in Italy. He would soon discover that there was a price to be paid for Soviet hospitality.

When the boat carrying Nobile pulled alongside the *Graf Zeppelin*, Ellsworth stretched his hand out through one of the portals to shake the hand of Nobile, who was standing in the stern. "I had to look twice to recognize him," wrote Ellsworth. "It was Umberto Nobile, whom I had not seen since the *Norge* flight of 1926. He had aged visibly since then. The *Italia* disaster had made a different man of him. . . . [T]he scene had an element of pathos that I can never forget."[5]

Then a sudden wind blew up that risked the safety of the airship. Eckener ordered his men to take off, leaving behind the shocked and bemused crew of the icebreaker—and a disappointed Nobile, who had hoped to step on board.

The *Graf Zeppelin* rose majestically into the air, turned north, and disappeared into the distance, never to return.

Epilogue

The Kremlin, Moscow, 1933

"NOBILE UNDER THE KNIFE in Moscow," reported the *New York Times*.[1] Before Nobile's first airship for Joseph Stalin could take to the sky he had become very seriously ill. The doctor who came to visit him in his flat near Red Square had promptly called a surgeon, who took one look at the stricken airship designer and declared: "I will operate at once." Nobile barely had time to write to his wife before he was rushed into the hospital of the Kremlin.[2] The next day the *New York Times* reported that "Nobile is in serious condition."[3] The surgeons hadn't expected the operation to drain his abdomen of pus to be successful, and following the procedure, Nobile hovered between life and death.

It is easy to believe at this moment of utmost peril for Nobile that his mind would replay the mistakes he had made. He had said no to the speculators who wanted to buy his factory in 1919. He could easily have put up a few more posters of Mussolini on his factory walls after the March on Rome rather than being accused of having socialist sympathies. Nobile had helped to design Italy's first all-metal plane in 1922. Why did he then become obsessed with airships? Nobile had paid a high price for his arrogance. He could have just slowed down when he was driving Amundsen to the Roman coast back in 1925—the elderly explorer was clearly terrified—but instead he'd felt compelled to drive aggressively fast, giving his enemies added ammunition against him for years. Then there were his decisions to travel to Japan in 1926 and his refusal to visit Balbo first on his return to Italy in 1927 and again when he returned from the North Pole in 1928. Worst of all, of course, was Nobile's blazing row with Mussolini, never a good move in a totalitarian state, when a cannier man would have used his popularity to achieve an accommodation with the regime. And then there was the almost split-second decision that changed everything, could never be forgotten or reversed, and haunted him for the rest of his life. Why did he allow himself to be flown off the ice first, abandoning his men on the ice? The captain is always the last one to leave the ship.

Then perhaps he saw the ghosts of all the men who had died on his watch. The thirty-four men of the *Roma* who died when the airship exploded. The six men of the N-4 who were trapped in the envelope when it floated off and Vincenzo Pomella who died in the crash. Roald Amundsen, Leif Dietrichson, René Guilbaud, and the rest of the crew of the Latham. And worst of all, Finn Malmgren, whose fate was best not to contemplate. The graves of many of these men were never discovered, and the crashes of the *Roma* and *Italia* only helped discredit airships in the eyes of politicians and the public.*

---

* There were many others. In October 1930, the R-101 British airship dived into the ground during a storm, killing forty-eight and becoming the deadliest civilian airship crash in history. The bodies of the dead men were transported back to London with a military escort and laid in state in Westminster Hall, the oldest part of Parliament, where thousands queued

Nobile's condition didn't appear to be improving. The medical staff in the Kremlin became so convinced that he was about to die that when Nobile recovered consciousness, he found a French Catholic bishop performing the last rites at his bedside.[4] One overeager American journalist reported that Nobile had actually died—Nobile then had the pleasure of reading in his hospital bed the headline: "Gen. Nobile Dead, Says Rome Report . . . Had Brilliant Career as Airman and Had Charge of Italy's Plane Building in the War."[5] He simply noted that the "obituaries were kind."

THE HAPPIEST YEARS OF Nobile's life had begun the year before, in 1932, with him standing in a muddy field at the end of a rough track just outside Moscow. Before him extended the land where Aeroflot wanted to build its new airship factory. The fields would be cemented over to build the workshops, laboratories, hangars, and housing for a population the size of a small town[6] that would be necessary if Stalin's ambitious plans for a fleet of more than four hundred airships like the *Italia*

---

to pay tribute to the aeronauts. After this, they were taken in a military procession through the streets of London, lined by silent crowds, to Euston station and then by train to Cardington. The forty-eight were buried in a mass grave (as many of the bodies were unrecognizable) with full military honors. A memorial service for the men was held in St. Paul's Cathedral, "the Empire's Valhalla" ("The Nation Bows Its Head," British Pathé, 1930, uploaded April 13, 2014, https://www.youtube.com/watch?v=30_jgv5e3I0), that morning. The flag flown by the R-101 when it crashed hangs in the parish church. The crash led to the cancellation of the Imperial Airship Service, the breaking up of the successful R-100 design, and the end of British interest in the development of airships for a good number of decades. Drivers today largely ignore the white marble memorial by the side of the road in Cardington.

were to be realized—and Stalin was not a man you wanted to disappoint. The Soviet plan called for a network of scheduled commercial airship services that would stretch across the Soviet Union. The first would be a service between Moscow and Murmansk.[7] Western journalists such as Eugene Lyons were already hopping on planes to fly to Baltic cities like Riga when they needed a break from Moscow.

If he wanted to carry on building airships, his contract with the Soviets was Nobile's only choice. Balbo had scrapped all his complete airships. When the Soviets wanted to buy the completed but not inflated N-6, a sister ship of the N-4 *Italia*, Balbo had all its metal components melted down—or so he thought. Nobile was able to smuggle some of the key structural parts out of his old factory before Balbo could get to them. Nobile would use them in the construction of his record-breaking V-6, which was about to begin.[8]

The show trial of six British Vickers engineers in 1933 by the Soviets for espionage and sabotage did not dissuade him. He could tell himself that this was just the kind of political interference that he was used to. The commute to and from the airship factory was tiring, but he could feel the idealism of his youth returning. "It was as though I had become young again; the ideals of my adolescence had blossomed once more in my mind," Nobile wrote of his time in the Soviet Union—that one sentence proving all the suspicions about his true political affiliations to be correct.

Then everything changed for many of Nobile's friends. Communist leader Sergei Kirov was assassinated in 1934—probably on Stalin's orders—and a number of the heroes of the *Krassin* started to disappear. The destruction of one of Nobile's airships in a suspicious hangar fire led to Nobile being followed and his engineers questioned by the dreaded GPU secret police. Nobile himself, though, seemed to live a charmed life. One of his interpreters confessed that he, Nobile, was under surveillance but that the GPU weren't interested in him, just his Italian engineers.

The V-6 *Klim Voroshilov* was ready to fly at the end of October. It was a superior version of the N-4. It was faster than the Italian airship and could carry more passengers and a greater payload. "The Soviet engineers were very proud of it, and I myself even prouder, seeing the success that had crowned two years of work in the midst of so many difficulties," wrote Nobile.[9]

Tragically, at this moment of vindication for Nobile's design, his wife, Carlotta, was taken ill in Rome, and she died while he was flying home to be with her.

The V-6 went on to complete a number of short flights in 1935, piloted by Nobile himself. Two years later, now under the control of the Red Army, the airship flew successfully from Moscow to Murmansk with twenty passengers, testing the feasibility of regular passenger flights on that route.

Fortuitously, Nobile returned home to Rome late in 1936. Two years later, his personal secretary was "disappeared" by the secret police, and his old friend Professor Samoylovitch was declared an enemy of the people and shot in March 1939.

On September 29, 1937, the V-6 took off for a flight that would represent Nobile's greatest triumph and the final vindication of his design. The V-6 went for a circular flight over the European regions of the Soviet Union to try to break the record Nobile had set in the *Norge* years before. In command was an experienced Soviet air force officer called Ivan Pankow who was determined to break every record he could.

Pankow kept the *Klim Voroshilov* in the air for nearly five and a half days. The record set by the *Norge* was shattered first, and then that of Hugo Eckener's *Graf Zeppelin*. The men on board had grown beards by the time it headed to Moscow for its victory flight.

"I am writing my last notes in the log, and now and again looking out of the window," wrote the airship's commander, Pankow. "The people in the streets and squares of Moscow are stopping to look up and wave to us. Another airship has appeared in the sky, trailing a long red banner on which we can read words of greeting. Airplanes, too, are coming to meet us. The moment of landing approaches."[10]

At 5:15 p.m. on October 4, 1937, the V-6 *Klim Voroshilov* landed back at its base after having remained in the air for 130 hours and 27 minutes. "All the non-stop records for dirigibles of every type and class had been broken," Nobile wrote.

Yet, hidden as it was behind a wall of Soviet secrecy, the world never heard of the success of the V-6.

ON HIS RETURN FROM Moscow, Umberto Nobile didn't last long in Italy. Although Mussolini allowed him to work, Italo Balbo made sure it was not in any role of importance in the aeronautical industry. This was despite the best efforts of the aircraft designer Gianni Caproni.[11] Nobile's designs even had to be patented in the names of others. When he tried lecturing, he found that he was not allowed to take his students around any industrial facilities, thanks to Balbo and—perhaps—because of an underlying suspicion cast on him after his long stay in the Soviet Union.

Nobile quickly realized that there were no doors open to

him in his country. His only hope was that the Fascist regime would be overthrown—but there seemed to be little hope of that. Or, like so many other Italians, he would have to emigrate.

Pope Pius XI had remained a supporter of Nobile. Now he came to Nobile's rescue with the offer of a job in a little-known school just outside Chicago. An advertisement in *Aviation* made Nobile's new status as a salesman clear: "Umberto Nobile, Former General of Italian Royal Air Force, Joins . . . Faculty of Lewis Holy Name School of Aeronautics" above a large picture of Nobile in his military uniform.[12]

The former general was to lecture at the engineering facility at the Lewis Holy Name School of Aeronautics in Lockport, Illinois. Yet even in the United States, he couldn't escape the Fascist regime. He had to take care in speaking to journalists because his daughter and other members of his family were still in Italy.

When war broke out between the United States and Fascist Italy, Nobile was offered a choice. He could become an American citizen, be interned, or leave the country. As a patriot, he decided to return to Italy—where his services were again not wanted. He left for Spain, where he stayed until Italy surrendered. After the war, Nobile was pardoned and his rank restored, and he became a wealthy man. His back pay was paid in full, and he began a second, albeit brief, career as a Communist Party politician (an insight into what Italo Balbo saw in Nobile that made him such a threat), before settling down to a life as an academic and marrying Gertrude Stolp, who was thirty years younger than him. Then in 1959, Nobile had the satisfaction of suing Knut Eckener, Hugo's son, and his publisher, over his claims that the *Italia* crashed due to his moral failure or professional incompetence, and won.[13]

General Nobile was never allowed to disappear. Every time a new book, film, or TV program about the *Italia* was released, he was back in the spotlight. Nobile disliked a commercially successful Italian-Soviet feature film that was made about the crash of the *Italia* called *The Red Tent*, with Peter Finch playing Nobile and Sean Connery in the role of Amundsen, because it played fast and loose with the facts. He objected to it even though it helped restore his reputation. In the film, Nobile and Amundsen are cast as friends, and each night Nobile is tormented by his decisions out on the ice—a torment that usually ends with him being put on trial in his dreams by his fellow explorers.

However, Nobile did discover the sweet irony of fame. He was famous because the expedition had been a disaster. If it had been a success, the flight of the *Italia* would have been forgotten just like that of the *Norge*.

In the end, Nobile outlived all his enemies, which must have given him a grim sense of satisfaction. Balbo would eventually die, shot down by his own men. Unlike Mussolini, Balbo was not seduced by Hitler's charms or by the chance to invade France in 1940. He knew that war would be a disaster for Italy, and he opposed the rounding up of the Jews. To him, the Jews were Italians.

Although he opposed the alliance with Hitler, Mussolini must have known that Balbo would be one of his most effective and ambitious war leaders. At the same time, Mussolini's instinct must have warned him not to let Balbo anywhere near the central leadership of the war. Instead, he was sent to be governor of the Italian colony of Libya—at which, by all accounts, he proved to be very successful. Perhaps too successful. His plane was shot down over the front lines in Libya, allegedly by his own men.

Bitterly for Nobile, Balbo's losses on his great flights were worse than his own, and yet Balbo was the hero. It is an interesting, if uncomfortable, calculation that Balbo's loss of five big Italian flying boats and the lives of seven airmen on his four flights across the Atlantic was seen as less than Nobile's, who had carried out four Arctic flights at the cost of one airship and eight men.[14]

Unsurprisingly, Nobile could never forgive Crocco for what he saw as his betrayal. Nobile spent a whole chapter of his first book published after the fall of fascism in 1945, *Posso dire la verità*, attacking Crocco.

On July 30, 1978, Nobile died in Rome fifty years after the crash of the *Italia* and the rescue of the survivors.

Neither Umberto Nobile nor war nor age could dampen rival Gaetano Arturo Crocco's spirit of invention. Crocco would continue to invent, patent, and publish his research until he was in his eighties. His students liked to say, "Everything I use or see, Oh my Crocco is made by thee."[15] In the late 1920s, while Nobile was fighting for his life, his reputation, and his airships, Crocco's ever-restless spirit had moved on from airships and was focused on the new science of rocketry. In 1929, he built the first liquid-propellant rocket motor in Italy—the kind that would power the V-2 rocket and pave the way for space exploration.

Crocco's real legacy was in the stars. The scientific breakthrough of Wernher von Braun's V-2 rocket opened the door for Crocco to explore space flight. In 1951, he founded the Italian Rocket Association and would regularly lecture on the challenges of manned space flight a decade before Yuri Gagarin orbited the planet. His research would lay the foundation for the Italian space program and ultimately for the European Space Agency.

When he was eighty years old, he published a paper outlining what has been dubbed the "Crocco Grand Tour." At the Seventh Congress of the International Astronautical Federation, Rome, in 1956, he suggested exploiting the Mars and Venus gravitational fields as propelling forces to dramatically cut the traveling time of a space capsule. NASA didn't use his "gravitational slingshot," but it did influence NASA's research.[16] Mathematician Gary Flandro called his own gravitational slingshot approach "the Grand Tour" after Crocco's. Flandro's mathematics would be used on the Mariner and Voyager missions to the outer planets and beyond.[17]

Hugo Eckener's name may have been forgotten, but his airships haven't. Every high school student has heard of the crash of the *Hindenburg*. What is little remembered is that Eckener's *Graf Zeppelin* was the mainstay of a commercial airship service between Germany and Brazil, which for six years competed successfully with the great ocean liners.

With the horrific fire caught live by the newsreel cameramen, the crash of the larger *Hindenburg* would end the golden age of the airship in the popular imagination. Despite the fact that the giant airship had completed eleven trips to the United States and seven to Brazil, the crash is widely perceived to have led to the cancellation of the entire program three years later. The accident was a shock because the aviation industry had assumed that the Germans had mastered the safe use of flammable hydrogen in airships. In fact, the story was more complicated than that. The US government was not willing to sell the nonflammable replacement gas, helium, to the Nazi regime, which would have made the zeppelins safer. Eckener had also made an enemy of a number of the Nazi leaders, including Joseph Goebbels and Hermann Göring.

The *Graf Zeppelin II*, a sister ship to the *Hindenburg*, had already been built. It would go on to make thirty flights over eleven months in 1938–39, but without a supply of helium, it was not allowed to carry passengers. In what feels like an episode of an alternative history drama, the last flights of the great ship around the coast of Great Britain were used to probe Britain's radar defenses. It is not known whether a Spitfire ever intercepted the giant airship.

In the end, Eckener and Nobile had more in common than the German would have liked to think. It was his own uncomfortable relationship with the Nazis that would doom his ships. Like Nobile, he had relied on populism to build his ships, and now he would be destroyed by the new masters. Eckener made enemies in the regime when he refused to let his ships be used for propaganda flights. He found his own Balbo in Hermann Göring, who wanted to wipe airships from history. The Reichsmarschall would sign the order scrapping the *Graf Zeppelin*, the *Graf Zeppelin II*, and the frame of a new airship that was under construction, despite pleas by the company to preserve one for use after the war. The great zeppelin hangars at Frankfurt were demolished.

Amundsen's ghost still stalks the world. In 1976, Nobile's name and the Italian flag were omitted from memorials in Alaska and Svalbard to the flight of the *Norge*, leading to a diplomatic incident. The Italian newspaper *Corriere della Sera* demanded to know whether this was "by coincidence or on purpose?"[18] Books are published today that talk about the Amundsen-Ellsworth expedition. The Last Viking would have liked that.

The story isn't finished. The Arctic ice holds many secrets. Global warming may soon reveal the last resting place of Amundsen and the Latham—and of the *Italia* and the six men. Their spirits may still roam the land, but perhaps not for much longer.

Acknowledgments

I could not have started or completed *N-4 Down* without the love and support of my wife, Rebecca, and our two boys, Finn and Mylo. The project wouldn't have happened without the hard work of my agent, Erin Cox, and the team at Rob Weisbach Creative Management. It is great to have had Erin on my side to navigate the world of publishing. My deepest thanks are also due to my editors at Custom House: Geoff Shandler, for spotting the story of the Arctic airship briefly mentioned in another proposal and for working with me to develop it to the point that he could commission it, as well as for his line edit of the manuscript, and Peter Hubbard, who took over the project two weeks before the pandemic hit New York, for navigating it through those dark times and over the finishing line, as well as his great editing of my manuscript and his vision for the book. I knew the manuscript was in safe hands when Peter told me he had Roald Amundsen and Lincoln Ellsworth's book *The First Crossing of the Polar Sea* on his bookshelf. I would also like to thank Molly Gendell at HarperCollins for answering my questions and ensuring that I met every deadline. Thanks also have to go to the indefatigable Kirsty Seymour-Ure for reading my manuscript and being my researcher and translator on the ground in Italy, and Kathryn Pearson for her translation of Lise Lindbæk's *Brennende Jord*. Finally, I have to thank Michael Bhaskar, writer and cofounder of the publisher Canelo, for persuading me that the world needed a book about airships and that I should start the journey that ended here.

I would also like to thank Dr. Tim O'Neill, who took some time out from his business to travel with me to Oslo and Svalbard in search of the Arctic airship's secrets, and Renate Krelle for her support. The trip to Svalbard changed my whole approach to the book. A huge thank you is also due to Ivar Stokkeland, the main librarian at the Norwegian Polar Institute, for helping me navigate the Institute's archives, his hospitality while I was in Tromsø, and the introduction to Ove Hermansen (1933–2019). I will never forget the two days I spent interviewing Hermansen in Copenhagen, particularly his commentary while we watched the film *The Red Tent* together. I also want to thank Martina Aronne from the North Pole Expedition Museum for her help.

Thanks also go to Steinar Ass, Gregg A. Bendrick, Roald Berg, Giles Camplin, Scott Danneker, Maurizio Fantato, Ron Hochstetler, Nick Lawson, Shane McCorristine, Arnold Nayler, @CardingtonSheds, and everyone else who helped me on this journey.

Notes

Introduction: **Once upon a Time in the North**

1. Philip Pullman, *Northern Lights*, bk. 1, His Dark Materials (London: Penguin Random House, 2015), chap. 8, Kindle.
2. Pullman, chap. 8.
3. Roald Berg, "Gender in Polar Air: Roald Amundsen and His Aeronautics," *Acta Borealia* 23, no. 2 (2006): 130–44, http://dx.doi.org/10.1080/08003830601026818.

Prologue: **The Arctic Ocean, May 25, 1928**

1. Umberto Nobile, *With the Italia to the North Pole*, trans. Frank Fleetwood (London: Allen & Unwin, 1930), 153.
2. Steinar Aas, "New Perspectives on the *Italia* Tragedy and Umberto Nobile," *Polar Research* 24, nos. 1–2 (2005): 5–15, 6, https://doi.org/10.3402/polar.v24i1.6249.
3. Gregg A. Bendrick, Scott A. Beckett, and Elizabeth B. Klerman, "Human Fatigue and the Crash of the Airship *Italia*," *Polar Research* 35, no. 1 (2016): 27–105, https://www.tandfonline.com/doi/full/10.3402/polar.v35.27105.
4. Nobile, *With the Italia*, 141.
5. Nobile, 141.
6. Nobile, 84.
7. Nobile, 143.
8. Nobile, 23.
9. Nobile, 148.
10. Nobile, 54.

One: **"You Are Supposed to Be Dead"**

1. Stephen R. Brown, *The Last Viking: The Life of Roald Amundsen* (Boston: De Capo Press, 2012), 283.

2. Tor Bomann-Larsen, *Roald Amundsen*, trans. Ingrid Christophersen (Stroud, UK: History Press, 2011), chap. 12, Kindle.

3. Bomann-Larsen, chap. 12.

4. Bomann-Larsen, chap. 12.

5. Roald Amundsen, *My Life as an Explorer* (London: Forgotten Books, 2018), 70.

6. Brown, *Last Viking*, 122.

7. Roland Huntford, *The Last Place on Earth: Scott and Amundsen's Race to the South Pole* (London: Hachette Digital, 1999), chap. 30, Kindle.

8. Shane McCorristine, *The Spectral Arctic: A History of Ghosts & Dreams in Polar Exploration* (London: UCL Press, 2018), 12.

9. Huntford, *Last Place on Earth*, chap. 30.

10. Brown, *Last Viking*, xxi.

11. Roald Berg, "Gender in Polar Air: Roald Amundsen and His Aeronautics," *Acta Borealia* 23, no. 2 (2006): 130–44, 139, http://dx.doi.org/10.1080/08003830601026818.

12. Bomann-Larsen, *Roald Amundsen*, chap. 28.

13. Garth James Cameron, *From Pole to Pole: Roald Amundsen's Journey by Flight* (Stroud, UK: Pen & Sword Discover, 2013), 22.

14. Cameron, 24.

15. Steinar Aas, "The Amundsen-Ellsworth-Nobile Transpolar Flight and Its Aftermath in Norway," Nord University, Bodø, Norway, lecture notes, Rome, May 2018.

16. Cameron, *From Pole to Pole*, 28.

17. Tony Reichhardt, "The First Arctic Flight—in 1914," *Air & Space*, September 12, 2014, https://www.airspacemag.com/daily-planet/first-arctic-flight-1914-180952688/.

18. Cameron, *From Pole to Pole*, 35.

19. Berg, "Gender in Polar Air," 138.

20. "The *Maud* Expedition (1918–1925)," Fram—The Polar Exploration Museum, accessed March 21, 2021, https://frammuseum.no/polar-history/expeditions/the-maud-expedition-1918-1925/.

21. Brown, *Last Viking*, xviii.

22. Bomann-Larsen, *Roald Amundsen*, chap. 1.

23. Cameron, *From Pole to Pole*, 47.

24. Cameron, 48.

25. Cameron, 50.

26. "Son of the Vikings Navigates the Northwest Passage," *New York Times*, December 10, 1905.

27. *New York Times*, September 6, 1924.

28. Amundsen, *My Life*, 116.

29. Brown, *Last Viking*, 246.

30. Brown, 108.

31. Alexander McKee, *Ice Crash: Disaster in the Arctic, 1928* (London: Souvenir Press, 1979), 21.

32. McKee, 22.

33. Berg, "Gender in Polar Air," 139.

34. Beekman H. Pool, *Polar Extremes: The World of Lincoln Ellsworth* (Fairbanks: University of Alaska Press, 2002), 29.

35. Brown, *Last Viking*, 252.

36. Brown, 249.

37. Brown, 250.

38. Interview with Professor Steinar Aas, June 26, 2018; Steinar Aas, "New Perspectives on the *Italia* Tragedy and Umberto Nobile," *Polar Research* 24, nos. 1–2 (2005): 5–15, 6, https://doi.org/10.3402/polar.v24i1.6249.

39. Aas, 6.

40. Dag Avango, "Svalbard Archaeology," Michigan Technological University, May 10, 2018, http://www.svalbardarchaeology.org/history.html.

41. Avango.

42. Avango.

43. Avango.

44. "The History of the Norwegian Polar Institute," last updated February 20, 2018, https://www.npolar.no/en/history/.

45. Avango, "Svalbard Archaeology."

46. "The History of the Norwegian Polar Institute."

47. "'Swedish Activism' in WWI," Radio Sweden, August 6, 2014, https://sverigesradio.se/sida/artikel.aspx?programid=2054&artikel=5931605.

48. "The History of the Norwegian Polar Institute."

49. Frank Jacobs, "The Cold War That Wasn't: Norway Annexes Greenland," Big Think, March 4, 2016, https://bigthink.com/strange-maps/the-cold-war-that-wasnt-norway-annexes-greenland.

50. Steinar Aas, "New Perspectives on the *Italia* Tragedy and Umberto Nobile," *Polar Research* 24, nos. 1–2 (2005): 5–15, 5, https://doi.org/10.3402/polar.v24i1.6249.

51. McCorristine, *Spectral Arctic*, 2.

52. McCorristine, 14.

53. McCorristine, 26.

54. McCorristine, 24.

55. McCorristine, 181.

56. McCorristine, 206.

57. McCorristine, 176–179.

58. Andrew C. Revkin, *The North Pole Was Here: Puzzles and Perils at the Top of the World* (Boston: Kingfisher, 2006), 27.

59. Revkin, 29–30.

60. Revkin, 30.

61. Revkin, 27.

62. Quoted in Constance Martin, "Arctic Profile Elisha Kent Kane (1820–1857)," Arctic Institute of North America, Calgary, AB, http://pubs.aina.ucalgary.ca/arctic/Arctic37-2-178.pdf.

63. Martin, 178.

64. David Chapin, "'Science Weeps, Humanity Weeps, the World Weeps': America Mourns Elisha Kent Kane," *Pennsylvania Magazine of History and Biography* 123, no. 4 (1999): 282, 278, http://www.jstor.org/stable/20093316.

65. Revkin, *North Pole Was Here*, 35.

66. Lyle Zapato, "Here's What They Expect to Find at the North Pole," ZPi, January 11, 2015, https://zapatopi.net/blog/?post=201501116510.the_reed_hollow_earth_exploring_club.

67. *Brisbane Telegraph*, October 1909, https://trove.nla.gov.au/newspaper/article/177856617.

68. Stanley A. Freed, "Fate of the Crocker Land Expedition," *Natural History*, June 2012. http://www.naturalhistorymag.com/features/092248/fate-of-the-crocker-land-expedition.

69. Simon Worrall, "The Mysterious Discovery of a Continent That Wasn't There," *National Geographic*, December 18, 2016, https://news.nationalgeographic.com/2016/12/crocker-land-peary-arctic-continent/.

70. Worrall.

71. Worrall.

72. Worrall.

73. Worrall.

74. "Norway Not U.S. to Get Arctic Lands," *New York Times*, March 4, 1924, https://timesmachine.nytimes.com/timesmachine/1924/03/04/119035792.html?pageNumber=2.

75. Brown, *Last Viking*, 250.

76. "'Wal' (Whale) Flying Boat by Dornier," Russian Aviation Museum, accessed May 10, 2018, http://ram-home.com/ram-old/wal.html.

77. "Wal."

78. Brown, *Last Viking*, 257.

79. Brown, 238.

80. Cameron, *From Pole to Pole*, 64.

81. Cameron, 63–64.

82. Berg, "Gender in Polar Air," 138.

83. Cameron, *From Pole to Pole*, 67.

84. Jeff Maynard, *Antarctica's Lost Aviator: The Epic Adventure to Explore the Last Frontier on Earth* (New York: Pegasus Books, 2019), 16.

85. Maynard, 16.

86. "Expeditions: The N24/N25 Flight Towards the North Pole (1925)," Fram—The Polar Exploration Museum, accessed March 20, 2021, https://frammuseum.no/polar-history/expeditions/the-n24-n25 -flight-towards-the-north-pole-1925/.

87. Brown, *Last Viking*, 258.

88. Maynard, *Antarctica's Lost Aviator*, 17.

89. Brown, *Last Viking*, 258.

90. Brown, 258.

91. Maynard, *Antarctica's Lost Aviator*, 18.

92. Cameron, *From Pole to Pole*, 71.

93. Cameron, 72.

94. Cameron, 73.

95. Cameron, 74.

96. "Amundsen Missing 112 Hours in Arctic," *New York Times*, May 26, 1925, https://www.nytimes.com/1925/05/26/archives/amundsen-missing-112 -hours-in-arctic-our-navy-may-act-threatened.html.

97. "Coolidge Favors Amundsen Relief Should He Need It," *New York Times*, May 27, 1925, https://www.nytimes.com/1925/05/27/archives /coolidge-favors-amundsen-relief-should-he-need-it-president-would .html.

98. "Coolidge."

99. "Coolidge."

100. Maynard, *Antarctica's Lost Aviator*, 18.

101. Cameron, *From Pole to Pole*, 75.

102. Lincoln Ellsworth, "Arctic Flying Experiences by Airplane and Airship," in *Problems of Polar Research*, American Geographical Society Special Publication No. 7, ed. W. L. G. Joerg (New York: American Geographical Society, 1928), 412.

103. Maynard, *Antarctica's Lost Aviator*, 18.

104. Ellsworth, "Arctic Flying Experiences," 412.

105. Cameron, *From Pole to Pole*, 75.

106. Cameron, 76.

107. Brown, *Last Viking*, 264.

108. Aas, "The Amundsen-Ellsworth-Nobile Transpolar Flight."

Two: "There Is No Room for Prima Donnas in the Italian Air Force"

1. *The Amundsen Polar Flight* (British Pathé, 1925), YouTube, uploaded April 7, 2012, https://www.youtube.com/watch?v=aLeLohOIsD4.

2. Roald Berg, "Gender in Polar Air: Roald Amundsen and his Aeronautics," *Acta Borealia* 23, no. 2 (2006): 130–144, 138, http://dx.doi.org/10.1080/08003830601026818.

3. Jonathan Jones, "The 1926 Painting That Foresaw How London Would Look Today," *Guardian*, January 15, 2015, https://www.theguardian.com/cities/2015/jan/15/1926-painting-foresaw-london-look-today-artistic-vision-montague-black.

4. Christopher Gray, "Not Just a Perch for King Kong," *New York Times*, September 26, 2010.

5. Gray.

6. Gray.

7. Alexander McKee, *Ice Crash: Disaster in the Arctic, 1928* (London: Souvenir Press, 1979), 26.

8. Leonardo Bizzaro, "I dirigibili, il tricolore e la tenda rossa: Il Polo Nord di Umberto Nobile, pilota aristocratico," trans. Mark Piesing and Maurizio Fantato, *La Repubblica*, May 13, 2016, https://www.repubblica.it/ambiente/2016/05/13/news/nobile_spedizione-139724411/.

9. "Eboli ricorda il 130° anniversario della nascita di Umberto Nobile," trans. Mark Piesing and Maurizio Fantato, *Politica de Mente*, January 22, 2015, http://www.massimo.delmese.net/81145/eboli-ricorda-il-130-anniversario-della-nascita-di-umberto-nobile/.

10. Bizzaro, "I dirigibili, il tricolore e la tenda rossa."

11. McKee, *Ice Crash*, 27.

12. Garth James Cameron, *Umberto Nobile and the Arctic Search for the Airship* Italia (Stroud, UK: Pen & Sword Discover, 2017), 30.

13. "Gaetano Crocco—Italian Aerospace Pioneer," SciHi Blog, October 26, 2015, http://scihi.org/gaetano-crocco-italian-aerospace-pioneer/.

14. "Gaetano Crocco."

15. "Gaetano Crocco."

16. "The Experience of Air Power in Libya," *Pathfinder: Air Power Development Centre Bulletin*, no. 152 (March 2011), http://airpower.airforce.gov.au/APDC/media/PDF-Files/Pathfinder/PF152-The-Experience-of-Air-Power-in-Libya.pdf.

17. Sven Lindqvist, *A History of Bombing*, trans. Linda Haverty Rugg (London: Granta, 2012), 82.

18. Lindqvist, 78.

19. "The Experience of Air Power."

20. Wilbur Cross, *Disaster at the Pole: The Crash of the Airship Italia—a Harrowing True Tale of Arctic Endurance and Survival* (New York: The Lyons Press, 2000), 10.

21. Umberto D'Aquino, "Crocco, Gaetano Arturo," *Dizionario biografico degli Italiani*, vol. 31 (1985), Treccani, http://www.treccani.it/enciclopedia/gaetano-arturo-crocco_%28Dizionario-Biografico%29/.

22. Cross, *Disaster at the Pole*, 11.

23. McKee, *Ice Crash*, 27.

24. McKee, 309.

25. Umberto Nobile, "Semirigid versus Rigid Airship," *Aviation Week*, December 12, 1921, 683.

26. Nancy E. Sheppard, *The Airship* Roma *Disaster in Hampton Roads* (Charleston, SC: History Press, 2016), chap. 1, Kindle.

27. Nobile, "Semirigid versus Rigid Airship."

28. Sheppard, chap. 1.

29. Sheppard, chap. 1.

30. Sheppard, chap. 1.

31. Sheppard, chap. 1.

32. *The Wrecked* Roma (British Pathé, 1922), YouTube, uploaded April 13, 2014, https://www.youtube.com/watch?v=Lt0kxp8IxIg.

33. Sheppard, *Airship* Roma, epilogue.

34. Sheppard, appendix.

35. Ovidio Ferrante, *Umberto Nobile* (Rome: Claudio Tatangelo Editore, 1985), 162, translated by Kirsty Seymour-Ure.

36. Ferrante, 122.

37. "The Goodyear Semirigid Airship," *Aviation Week*, October 16, 1922, 517.

38. Casualties of World War I chart, Facing History and Ourselves, accessed October 5, 2019, https://www.facinghistory.org/weimar-republic-fragility

-democracy/politics/casualties-world-war-i-country-politics-world
-war-i.

39. Luca Gorgolini, "Prisoners of War (Italy)," International Encyclope-
     dia of the First World War, 1914-1918 online, accessed October 5, 2019,
     https://encyclopedia.1914-1918-online.net/article/prisoners_of_war
     _italy.

40. "Italian Delegates Return to Paris Peace Conference," History, ac-
     cessed October 5, 2019, https://www.history.com/this-day-in-history
     /italian-delegates-return-to-paris-peace-conference.

41. Nicholas Farrell, *Mussolini: A New Life* (London: Sharpe Books, 2018),
     chap. 7, Kindle.

42. Farrell, chap. 7.

43. Farrell, chap. 8.

44. Farrell, chap. 10.

45. Umberto Nobile, *Posso Dire La Verita*, trans. Mark Piesing and Maur-
     izio Fantato (Rome: Arnoldo Mondadori, 1945), 23.

46. Nobile, 24.

47. Nobile, "Semirigid versus Rigid Airship."

48. Nobile, 25.

49. Cross, *Disaster at the Pole*, 13.

50. Cross, 15.

51. Cross, 16.

52. Cross, 17.

53. Interview with Ove Hermansen, Copenhagen, June 2018. Herman-
     sen (1933–2019) was a retired air traffic controller, historian/author,
     compiler of a unique Umberto Nobile archive now kept at the Nor-
     wegian Polar Institute, friend of Nobile (1966 onwards), and his repre-
     sentative in Scandinavia on air historical matters.

54. Cross, *Disaster at the Pole*, 18.

55. Claudio G. Segrè, *Italo Balbo: A Fascist Life* (Berkeley and Los Angeles:
     University of California Press, 1987), 5.

56. Cross, *Disaster at the Pole*, 18.

57. Cross, 18.

58. Cross, 19.

59. Introduction and notes by Rhoda R. Gilman, "Zeppelin in Minneso-
     ta: The Count's Own Story," translated by Maria Bach Dunn, *Min-
     nesota History Magazine*, Summer 1967, http://collections.mnhs.org
     /MNHistoryMagazine/articles/40/v40i06p265–278.pdf.

60. Sarah Hopkins, "America's Champion Aeronaut in the Civil War: Daredevil Balloonist John H. Steiner," *Military Images*, Autumn 2015, https://militaryimages.atavist.com/americas-champion-aeronaut-in -the-civil-war-autumn-2015.

61. Curt Brown, "Balloon Ride over St. Paul Fueled Count Zeppelin's Dream," *Star Tribune* (Minneapolis), February 10, 2019, http://www .startribune.com/balloon-ride-over-st-paul-fueled-count-zeppelin-s -dream/505616692/?refresh=true.

62. Hugo Eckener, *My Zeppelins*, trans. Douglas Robinson (London; Putnam, 1958), 15.

63. "Alte PostKarte Polar Expedition Polaires Cook Peary," OldThing, accessed December 10, 2019, https://oldthing.de/ALTE-POSTKARTE -POLAR-EXPEDITION-POLAIRES-COOK-PEARY-Zeppelin-cpa -postcard-Ansichtskarte-AK-0029867744.

64. John McCannon, "Sharing the Northern Skies: German-Soviet Scientific Cooperation and the 1931 Flight of the *Graf Zeppelin* to the Soviet Arctic," *Russian History* 30, no. 4 (Winter 2003): 407, https://www .jstor.org/stable/24660765.

65. "The Race to the Pole 3: Ny-Ålesund," Spitsbergen-Svalbard.com, accessed December 10, 2019, https://www.spitsbergen-svalbard.com /spitsbergen-information/history/amundsen.html.

66. McCannon, "Sharing the Northern Skies," 403–31.

67. Aviation historian Ian Castle quoted in "World War One: How the German Zeppelin Wrought Terror," BBC News, August 4, 2014, https:// www.bbc.co.uk/news/uk-england-27517166.

68. Hugo Eckener, *My Zeppelins* (London; Putnam, 1958), translated by Douglas Robinson, 18.

69. "DELAG: The World's First Airline," Airships.net, accessed August 7, 2018, https://www.airships.net/delag-passenger-zeppelins/.

70. Eckener, *My Zeppelins*, 201.

71. John Duggan and Henry Cord Meyer, "Airships in International Political Competition, 1924–28," in *Airships in International Affairs, 1890–1940* (London: Palgrave Macmillan UK, 2001), 107.

72. Duggan and Meyer, 108.

73. "Zeppelin Bid for Amundsen," *New York Times*, June 23, 1925, https:// timesmachine.nytimes.com/timesmachine/1925/06/23/99345853.pdf.

74. Lieut.-Col. W. Lockwood Marsh, "Twenty-One Years of Airship Progress," *Flight*, January 3, 1930, 85.

75. Long Branch Mike, "Empire of the Air: The Imperial Airship Service," London Reconnections, August 18, 2016, https://www.londonreconnections.com/2016/empire-of-the-air-the-imperial-airship-service/.

76. Long Branch Mike.

77. Long Branch Mike.

78. Long Branch Mike.

79. Airship Sheds, United Kingdom—Howden, Airship Heritage Trust, accessed August 20, 2018, https://airshipsonline.com/sheds/Howden.html.

80. Duggan and Meyer, "Airships," 111.

81. Imperial Airship Scheme 1930–1935 map, Airship Heritage Trust, accessed August 20, 2018, https://www.airshipsonline.com/airships/imperial/images/Imperial%20Map.gif.

82. "Imperial Airship Scheme," Airship Heritage Trust, accessed August 20, 2018, https://www.airshipsonline.com/airships/imperial/index.html.

83. Cardington Sheds (@CardingtonSheds), "R101, Cotton end. THE Bell Public House," Twitter, April 10, 2021, 10:46 a.m., https://twitter.com/CardingtonSheds/status/1380819366384656384.

84. Cardington Sheds (@CardingtonSheds), "R101," Twitter, December 31, 2020, 10:02 p.m., https://twitter.com/CardingtonSheds/status/1344765995651641344.

85. Cardington Sheds (@CardingtonSheds), "Another Cardington sheds that look about as good as the balloon shed. The Cardington mooring mast winch sheds where R101 left on Oct the 4th 1930. Slowly rotting into obscurity. This should also be saved.....," Twitter, April 26, 2021, 9:38 a.m., https://twitter.com/CardingtonSheds/status/1386600465115267075.

86. "Spectators Didn't Realise Danger They Were In," *Oxford Mail*, February 28, 2012, https://www.oxfordmail.co.uk/news/8879493.spectators-didnt-realise-danger/.

87. Marsh, "Twenty-One Years," 85.

88. Marsh, 85–86.

89. "*Graf Zeppelin* History," Airships.net, accessed August 20, 2018, https://www.airships.net/lz127-graf-zeppelin/history/.

90. Owen Edwards, "Holiday Delivery from the *Graf Zeppelin*," *Smithsonian Magazine*, December 2009, https://www.smithsonianmag.com/arts-culture/holiday-delivery-from-the-graf-zeppelin-147375125/.

91. "Hindenburg's Transatlantic Service to North America, LZ-129 Hindenburg: A Detailed History," Airships.net, accessed March 20, 2021, https://www.airships.net/hindenburg/lz129-hindenburg-detailed -history/.

92. "The Hindenburg's Interior: Passenger Decks," Airships.net, accessed April 20, 2021, https://www.airships.net/hindenburg/interiors/.

93. "Interiors R 101," Airship Heritage Trust, accessed March 20, 2021, https://www.airshipsonline.com/airships/interior/R101Interior .htm.

94. "The Hindenburg's Interior."

95. Natasha Frost, "The Brief, Wondrous, High-Flying Era of Zeppelin Dining," Atlas Obscura, October 18, 2017, https://www.atlasobscura .com/articles/zeppelin-hindenburg-dining-food-aviation-blimp.

96. Frost.

97. John Toland, *The Great Dirigibles: Their Triumphs and Disasters*, quoted in Natasha Frost, "The Brief, Wondrous, High-Flying Era of Zeppelin Dining," Atlas Obscura, October 18, 2017, https://www.atlasobscura .com/articles/zeppelin-hindenburg-dining-food-aviation-blimp.

98. Dan Grossman, airship historian and author of *Zeppelin Hindenburg: An Illustrated History*, quoted in Natasha Frost, "The Brief, Wondrous, High-Flying Era of Zeppelin Dining," Atlas Obscura, October 18, 2017, https://www.atlasobscura.com/articles/zeppelin-hindenburg-dining -food-aviation-blimp.

99. Grossman.

100. Umberto Nobile, *My Polar Flights: An Account of the Voyages of the Airships* Italia *and* Norge, trans. Francis Fleetwood (London: Frederick Muller, 1961), 15.

101. Alex Graham, "Fascism, Futurism & Aviation," review of *Fascism, Aviation and Mythical Modernity*, by Fernando Esposito, Counter-Currents, February 6, 2018, https://www.counter-currents.com/2018 /02/fascism-futurism-and-aviation/.

102. McKee, *Ice Crash*, 27

103. McKee, 25.

104. "Amundsen Sees Mussolini," *New York Times*, April 8, 1924, https:// timesmachine.nytimes.com/timesmachine/1924/04/08/104247211 .html?pageNumber=3.

105. Roald Amundsen, *My Life as an Explorer* (London: Forgotten Books, 1927), 122.

106. Brown, *Last Viking*, 122.

107. Brown, 122.

108. "Massed Attack on Polar Region Begins Soon," *New York Times*, March 7, 1926, https://timesmachine.nytimes.com/timesmachine/1926/03/07/100055799.html?pageNumber=203.

109. Olga A. Krasnikova, "To the Arctic in a Balloon," *Science First Hand* 3, no. 45 (2016), https://scfh.ru/en/papers/to-the-arctic-in-a-balloon/.

110. McKee, *Ice Crash*, 50.

Three: "Do You Know Where Amundsen Is?"

1. "Amundsen Arrives Tells Plan to Fly to Pole in Dirigible," *New York Times*, https://timesmachine.nytimes.com/timesmachine/1925/10/10/issue.html.

2. Roald Amundsen's House, 1908–1928, Museene I Akerhus, accessed July 20, 2019, https://mia.no/follomuseum/story.

3. Tor Bomann-Larsen, *Roald Amundsen*, trans. Ingrid Christophersen (Stroud, UK: History Press, 2011), chap. 4, Kindle.

4. Bomann-Larsen, chap. 21.

5. Malcolm Fife, *British Airship Bases of the Twentieth Century* (Stroud: Fronthill Media, 2015), 231.

6. Garth James Cameron, *Umberto Nobile and the Arctic Search for the Airship* Italia (Stroud, UK: Fronthill Media, 2017), 55.

7. Bomann-Larsen, *Roald Amundsen*, chap. 40 and 41.

8. Gregg A. Bendrick and Sergio Alessandrini, "No Second-in-Command: Human Fatigue and the Crash of the Airship *Italia* Revisited," *Polar Research* 38 (2019): 13, https://doi.org/10.33265/polar.v38.3467.

9. Bomann-Larsen, *Roald Amundsen*, chap. 6.

10. Bomann-Larsen, chap. 41.

11. Bomann-Larsen, chap. 41.

12. Bomann-Larsen, chap. 41.

13. Alexander McKee, *Ice Crash: Disaster in the Arctic, 1928* (London: Souvenir Press, 1979), 30.

14. Nicholas Farrell, *Mussolini: A New Life* (London: Sharpe Books, 2018), chap. 7, Kindle.

15. Amundsen, *My Life as an Explorer* (London: Forgotten Books, 1927), 133.

16. McKee, *Ice Crash*, 32–33.

17. Amundsen, *My Life*, 133.

18. Amundsen, 154.

19. McKee, *Ice Crash*, 35.

20. Garth James Cameron, *From Pole to Pole: Roald Amundsen's Journey by Flight* (Stroud, UK: Pen & Sword Discover, 2013), 89.

21. McKee, *Ice Crash*, 38.

22. McKee, 34.

23. Bomann-Larsen, *Roald Amundsen*, chap. 42.

24. Lise Lindbæk, *Brennende Jord*, trans. Kathryn Pearson (Oslo: Tiden, 1958), 51.

25. Lindbæk, 52.

26. Lindbæk, 52.

27. Lindbæk, 52.

28. Lindbæk, 53.

29. Lindbæk, 53.

30. Lindbæk, 52.

31. Lindbæk, 52.

32. Lindbæk, 52.

33. McKee, *Ice Crash*, 37.

34. Interview with Ove Hermansen, curator, friend of Nobile and his representative, June 2018.

35. Amundsen, *My Life*, 138.

36. Amundsen, 139.

37. Amundsen, 140.

38. Amundsen, 140.

39. Amundsen, 140.

40. Stephen R. Bown, *The Last Viking: The Life of Roald Amundsen* (Boston: De Capo Press, 2012), 271.

41. Brown, 269–270

42. Brown, 271.

43. Umberto Nobile, *With the Italia to the North Pole*, trans. Frank Fleetwood (London: Allen & Unwin, 1930), 343.

44. Wilbur Cross, *Disaster at the Pole: The Crash of the Airship Italia—a Harrowing True Tale of Arctic Endurance and Survival* (New York; The Lyons Press, 2000), 27.

45. Umberto Nobile, *My Polar Flights: An Account of the Voyages of the Airships Italia and Norge*, trans. Francis Fleetwood (London: Frederick Muller, 1961), 17.

46. McKee, *Ice Crash*, 50.

47. McKee, 41.

48. Cameron, *From Pole to Pole*, 94.

49. Amundsen, *My Life*, 150.

50. Amundsen, 156.

51. McKee, *Ice Crash*, 45.

Four: **"She Would Be There to Inform on Us"**

1. Lise Lindbæk, *Brennende Jord*, trans. Kathryn Pearson (Oslo: Tiden,1958), 54.

2. Lindbæk, 55.

3. Lindbæk, 56.

4. *Flight International*, September 4, 1924, 550.

5. Lindbæk, *Brennende Jord*, 56.

6. Lindbæk, 56.

7. Lindbæk, 56.

8. Tor Bomann-Larsen, *Roald Amundsen*, trans. Ingrid Christophersen (Stroud, UK: History Press, 2011), chap. 42, Kindle.

9. "2,000 Mile Range for Norge's Radio," *New York Times*, May 12, 1926, https://timesmachine.nytimes.com/timesmachine/1926/05/12 /98376975.pdf.

10. "2,000 Mile Range for Norge's Radio."

11. Garth James Cameron, *From Pole to Pole: Roald Amundsen's Journey by Flight* (Stroud, UK: Pen & Sword Discover, 2013), 91.

12. "Map of the Imperial Airship Scheme," Imperial Airship Scheme, accessed March 26, 2021, https://www.airshipsonline.com/airships /imperial/images/Imperial%20Map.gif.

13. Lindbæk, *Brennende Jord*, 57.

14. Lindbæk, 57.

15. Roald Amundsen and Lincoln Ellsworth, *The First Flight Across the Polar Sea* (London: Hutchinson & Co, 1929), photo, Some of the members of the expedition after their audience with the pope, 60.

16. Bomann-Larsen, *Roald Amundsen*, chap. 41.

17. Bomann-Larsen, chap. 41.

18. Lindbæk, *Brennende Jord*, 57.

19. Bomann-Larsen, *Roald Amundsen*, chap. 41.

20. Umberto Nobile, *With the* Italia *to the North Pole*, trans. Frank Fleetwood (London: Allen & Unwin, 1930), 50.

21. Mark Piesing, "The Giant Hangar Built for an Arctic Airship," BBC Future, September 12, 2018, http://www.bbc.com/future/story/20180911 -the-giant-hangar-built-for-an-arctic-airship.

22. Piesing.

23. Piesing.

24. Amundsen and Ellsworth, *The First Flight Across the Polar Sea*, 50.

25. Alexander McKee, *Ice Crash: Disaster in the Arctic, 1928* (London: Souvenir Press, 1979), 45.

26. McKee, 45.

27. Roald Amundsen, *My Life as an Explorer* (London: Forgotten Books, 1927), 162.

28. Lindbæk, *Brennende Jord*, 58.

29. McKee, *Ice Crash*, 46.

30. Umberto Nobile, *My Polar Flights: An Account of the Voyages of the Airships* Italia *and* Norge, trans. Francis Fleetwood (London: Frederick Muller, 1961), 31.

31. Nobile, 31–32.

32. Amundsen, *My Life*, 163.

33. Amundsen, 164.

34. McKee, *Ice Crash*, 47.

35. Lindbæk, *Brennende Jord*, 58.

36. "Norfolk Village Celebrates First Transatlantic Flight, 100 Years On," BBC News, July 13, 2019, https://www.bbc.co.uk/news/uk-england-norfolk-48954974.

37. The scale of RNAS Pulham can be sensed in this Pathé film of the arrival of the R-34. *R-34 Airship (1919)*, YouTube, uploaded April 13, 2914, https://youtu.be/lvp8XqNmHps.

38. Nobile, *My Polar Flight*, 35.

39. Nobile, 38.

40. Nobile, 38.

41. Nobile, 39.

42. "2,000 Mile Range for Norge's Radio."

43. Nobile, *My Polar Flight*, 40.

44. Nobile, 42.

45. Nobile, 43–44.

46. Nobile, 48.

Five: "The Most Sensational Sporting Event in Human History"

1. Stephen R. Bown, *The Last Viking: The Life of Roald Amundsen* (Boston: De Capo Press, 2012), 286.

2. Bown, 289.

3. Bown, 285.

4. Hanne E. F. Nielsen, "Hoofprints in Antarctica: Byrd, Media, and the Golden Guernseys," *The Polar Journal* 6, no. 2 (2016): 342, https://doi.org/10.1080/2154896X.2016.1253825.

5. Andrea Thompson, "Did Admiral Byrd Fly over the North Pole or Not?" Live Science, April 15, 2013, https://www.livescience.com/28727-byrd-didn-t-fly-over-north-pole.html.

6. Raimund E. Goerler, ed., *To the Pole: The Diary and Notebook of Richard E. Byrd, 1925–27* (Columbus: Ohio State University Press, 1998), 44.

7. Goerler, 41.

8. "1925 Fokker F. VII Tri-motor Airplane, 'Josephine Ford,' Flown over the North Pole by Richard Byrd," The Henry Ford, accessed April 28, 2018, https://www.thehenryford.org/collections-and-research/digital-collections/artifact/54447#slide=gs-376858.

9. Goerler, *To the Pole*, 43.

10. Goerler, 43.

11. Goerler, 43.

12. Goerler, 51.

13. Goerler, 54.

14. Roald Amundsen, "The Rows about the *Norge*," *World's Work*, no. 397, August 1927, 397.

15. Goerler, *To the Pole*, 58.

16. Goerler, 75.

17. Goerler, 54.

18. Amundsen, "Rows," 397.

19. Amundsen, 397.

20. Goerler, *To the Pole*, 54.

21. Amundsen, "Rows," 398.

22. Amundsen, 398.

23. Goerler, *To the Pole*, 78.

24. Goerler, 50.

25. Thompson, "Did Admiral Byrd Fly?"

26. Goerler, *To the Pole*, 55.

27. Lisle A. Rose, *Explorer: The Life of Richard E. Byrd* (Columbia, Missouri: University of Missouri Press, 2008), 123.

28. Edwin P. Hoyt, *The Adventures of Admiral Byrd: The Last Explorer* (New York: John Day, 1968), 126.

29. Goerler, *To the Pole*, 50–51.

30. Goerler, 115.

31. Garth James Cameron, *From Pole to Pole: Roald Amundsen's Journey by Flight* (Stroud, UK: Pen & Sword Discover, 2013), 129.

32. Tor Bomann-Larsen, *Roald Amundsen*, trans. Ingrid Christophersen (Stroud, UK: History Press, 2011), chap. 41, Kindle.

33. Alexander McKee, *Ice Crash: Disaster in the Arctic, 1928* (London: Souvenir Press, 1979), 61.

34. Amundsen, "Rows," 399.

35. McKee, *Ice Crash*, 62.

36. Amundsen, "Rows," 399.

37. McKee, *Ice Crash*, 62.

38. Wilbur Cross, *Disaster at the Pole: The Crash of the Airship Italia—a Harrowing True Tale of Arctic Endurance and Survival* (New York: The Lyons Press, 2000), 29.

39. McKee, *Ice Crash*, 65.

40. Umberto Nobile, *My Polar Flights: An Account of the Voyages of the Airships* Italia *and* Norge, trans. Francis Fleetwood (London: Frederick Muller, 1961), 60.

41. Roald Amundsen and Lincoln Ellsworth, *The First Flight Across the Polar Sea* (London: Hutchinson & Co, 1929), 117.

42. Nobile, *My Polar Flights*, 61.

43. Amundsen, "Rows," 401.

44. McKee, *Ice Crash*, 65.

45. Cross, *Disaster at the Pole*, 30.

46. Cross, 30.

47. McKee, *Ice Crash*, 67.

48. Amundsen, "Rows," 401–2.

49. Nobile, *My Polar Flights*, 67.

50. Nobile, 65.

51. Nobile, 67.

52. Nobile, 69.

53. Nobile, 69.

54. Nobile, 69.

55. Nobile, 70.

56. Nobile, 72.

57. Nobile, 72.

58. Nobile, 73.

59. Nobile, 73.

60. Nobile, 74–75.
61. Nobile, 75.
62. Nobile, 76.
63. Amundsen, "Rows," 401.
64. Nobile, *My Polar Flights*, 79.
65. Umberto Nobile, *With the* Italia *to the North Pole*, trans. Frank Fleetwood (London: Allen & Unwin, 1930), 346.
66. Nobile, 346.
67. Nobile, *My Polar Flights*, 95.
68. Nobile, 89.
69. W. T. Whitlock, "Cleveland Airport Ohio," *Aviation Week*, August 10, 1926. http://archive.aviationweek.com/issue/19260816/#!&pid=300.
70. McKee, *Ice Crash*, 82.
71. "Nobile Acclaimed on Arrival Here," *New York Times*, July 15, 1926, https://timesmachine.nytimes.com/timesmachine/1926/07/15/98491563.pdf.

Six: "Let Him Go, for He Cannot Possibly Come Back to Bother Us Anymore"

1. "Nobile Sails Home with Five of Crew," *New York Times*, July 25, 1926, https://timesmachine.nytimes.com/timesmachine/1926/07/25/issue.html.
2. Umberto Nobile, *With the* Italia *to the North Pole*, trans. Frank Fleetwood (London: Allen & Unwin, 1930), 347.
3. Benito Mussolini introducing Umberto Nobile, photo by Mondadori via Getty Images, accessed March 20, 2021, https://www.gettyimages.co.uk/detail/news-photo/the-president-of-the-council-of-ministers-of-the-kingdom-of-news-photo/186168141.
4. Alexander McKee, *Ice Crash: Disaster in the Arctic, 1928* (London: Souvenir Press, 1979), 87.
5. Nobile, *With the* Italia, 347.
6. Nobile, 22.
7. Umberto Nobile, "The Dirigible and Polar Exploration," *Journal of the American Geographic Society*, The Problems of Polar Research, 1928, 419.
8. Nobile, 425.
9. Editorial, *Aviation* 22, no. 14 (April 4, 1927), https://archive.aviationweek.com/issue/19270404#!&pid=660.
10. Nobile, "The Dirigible," 425.

11. Joe Jackson, *Atlantic Fever: Lindbergh, His Competitors, and the Race to Cross the Atlantic* (London: Picador; Reprint edition, 2013), Transatlantic Timeline, Kindle.

12. Louis Pizzitola, *Hearst over Hollywood: Power, Passion, and Propaganda in the Movies* (New York: Columbia University Press, 2003), chap. 14, Kindle.

13. Pizzitola, chap. 41.

14. Stewart B. Nelson, "Airships in the Arctic," *Arctic* 46, no. 3 (September 1993): 276–83, 282, http://pubs.aina.ucalgary.ca/arctic/Arctic46-3-278 .pdf.

15. John Duggan and Henry Cord Meyer, "Airships in International Political Competition, 1924–28," in *Airships in International Affairs, 1890–1940* (London: Palgrave Macmillan UK, 2001), 107.

16. "Amundsen through with Polar Flights," *New York Times*, June 28, 1926, https://timesmachine.nytimes.com/timesmachine/1926/06/28 /104208997.pdf?pdf_redirect=true&ip=0.

17. Nobile, *With the* Italia, 24.

18. Master Carpenter Ferdinand Arild, "Vil Nobile kjope hangaren I Kings Bay?" ("Will Nobile Buy the Hangar at Kings Bay?"), Oslo Aftenavis, 1926, the personal collection of Ove Hermansen, curator, friend of Nobile and his representative.

19. "Nobile Acclaimed on Arrival," *New York Times*, July 15, 1926, https:// timesmachine.nytimes.com/timesmachine/1926/07/15/98491563.pdf.

20. Christopher Borrelli, "Future of Balbo Monument, a Gift from Mussolini, Uncertain," *Chicago Tribune*, August 18, 2017, http://www.chicagotribune.com/entertainment/ct-ent-balbo-monument-20170817-story.html.

21. Stefano Esposito, "Italo Balbo, a Complex and Controversial Figure, from Italy to Grant Park," *Chicago Sun-Times*, June 26, 2018, https:// chicago.suntimes.com/news/italo-balbo-history-italy-grant-park -drive-ida-wells-congress-parkway/.

22. Garth James Cameron, *Umberto Nobile and the Arctic Search for the Airship Italia* (Stroud, UK: Fronthill Media, 2017), 67–68.

23. N-3, Japan, photo, Bain News Service, May 24, 1927, https://www.flickr .com/photos/library_of_congress/26775146275/in/photostream/.

24. Cameron, *Umberto Nobile*, 68,

25. Cameron, 68.

26. McKee, *Ice Crash*, 89.

27. Robbin Laird, "The History of the Italian Air Ministry Building," SLDinfo.com, November 7, 2013, https://sldinfo.com/2013/11/the-history -of-the-italian-air-ministry-building/.

28. Claudio G. Segrè, *Italo Balbo: A Fascist Life* (Berkeley and Los Angeles: University of California Press, 1987), 192–93.

29. "Savoia-MarchettiS.55×FlyingBoatUpdate," *WarbirdDigest*,March1,2018, http://warbirdsnews.com/aviation-museum-news/savoia-marchetti -s-55-x-flying-boat-update.html.

30. Derek O'Connor, "Italy's Consummate Showman: Italo Balbo," HistoryNet, accessed October 17, 2018, https://www.historynet.com /italys-consummate-showman-italo-balbo.htm.

31. McKee, *Ice Crash*, 95.

32. Umberto Nobile, *My Polar Flights: An Account of the Voyages of the Airships Italia and Norge*, trans. Francis Fleetwood (London: Frederick Muller, 1961), 101.

33. Nobile, 101–2.

34. McKee, *Ice Crash*, 90.

35. Nobile, *With the* Italia, 29.

36. Nobile, 29.

37. Nobile, 29.

38. Nobile, 29.

39. Nobile, 80.

40. Nobile, 29.

41. Claudio Sicolo, Historiographical Contributions, Italia 90th Anniversary Memorial Conference, Società Geografica Italiana, May 24, 2018, Rome, transcript, 34.

42. Sicolo, 33.

43. Sicolo, 33.

44. Sicolo, 33.

45. Nobile, *With the* Italia, 31.

46. McKee, *Ice Crash*, 100.

47. Nobile, *With the* Italia, 75.

48. Umberto Nobile, Chapter VI: Five Years in Russia, manuscript in the archives of the Norwegian Polar Institute, Tromsø, 319.

49. McKee, *Ice Crash*, 100.

50. Sicolo, Historiographical Contributions.

51. Sicolo.

52. Sicolo.

53. Nobile, *With the* Italia, 48.

54. Nobile, 44.

55. McKee, *Ice Crash*, 50.

56. Nobile, *With the* Italia, 50.

57. Gregg A. Bendrick and Sergio Alessandrini, "No Second-in-Command: Human Fatigue and the Crash of the Airship *Italia* Revisited," *Polar Research* 38 (2019): 16–17, https://doi.org/10.33265/polar.v38.3467.

58. Nobile, *With the* Italia, 64.

59. Nobile, 65.

60. Nobile, 77.

61. Nobile, 77.

62. Nobile, 77.

63. Nobile, 78.

64. "Seddin," Abandoned, Forgotten and Little-Known Airfields in Europe, accessed March 20, 2021, https://www.forgottenairfields.com /airfield-seddin-633.html.

65. Nobile, *With the* Italia, 78.

66. Nobile, 78.

67. Tor Bomann-Larsen, *Roald Amundsen*, trans. Ingrid Christophersen (Stroud, UK: History Press, 2011), chap. 44, Kindle.

68. *World's Work*, no. 397, August 1927, contents page.

69. Roald Amundsen, "The Rows about the *Norge*," *World's Work*, no. 397, August 1927, 389.

70. Amundsen, 391.

71. McKee, *Ice Crash*, 93.

72. Von Uwe Klußmann, "Conquering the Capital: The Ruthless Rise of the Nazis in Berlin," Spiegel International, November 29, 2012, https:// www.spiegel.de/international/germany/how-the-nazis-succeeded-in -taking-power-in-red-berlin-a-866793.html.

73. McKee, *Ice Crash*, 98.

74. McKee, 99.

75. McKee, 97.

76. McKee, 98.

77. McKee, 98.

78. Nobile, *With the* Italia, 83.

79. Nobile, 84.

Seven: **"We Are Quite Aware that Our Venture Is Difficult and Dangerous . . . but It Is This Very Difficulty and Danger which Attracts Us"**

1. Umberto Nobile, *With the* Italia *to the North Pole*, trans. Frank Fleetwood (London: Allen & Unwin, 1930), 82.

2. "The Italian Polar Expedition," *New York Times*, April 27, 1928, https://timesmachine.nytimes.com/timesmachine/1928/04/27/91506055.html?pageNumber=24.

3. Nobile, *With the* Italia, 82.

4. Steinar Aas, "New Perspectives on the *Italia* Tragedy and Umberto Nobile," *Polar Research* 24, nos. 1–2 (2005): 5–15, 6, https://doi.org/10.3402/polar.v24i1.6249

5. Aas, 6.

6. Nobile, *With the* Italia, 89.

7. Alexander McKee, *Ice Crash: Disaster in the Arctic, 1928* (London: Souvenir Press, 1979), 110.

8. Nobile, *With the* Italia, 90

9. "Rivals in the Arctic," *New York Times*, February 14, 1928, https://timesmachine.nytimes.com/timesmachine/1928/02/14/91473804.html?pageNumber=22.

10. "Rivals in the Arctic."

11. Hubert Wilkins, "The Flight from Alaska to Spitsbergen, 1928, and the Preliminary Flights of 1926 and 1927," *Geographical Review* 18, no. 4 (1928): 527–55, https://doi.org/doi:10.2307/207946.

12. Wilkins, 537.

13. Wilkins, 538.

14. *North Pole Flight, 1928* (Hollywood Daily Citizen), The Newsreel Archive, YouTube, uploaded January 18, 2009, https://www.youtube.com/watch?v=1RoO2NBVxE0.

15. Bryan R. Swopes, "15–21 April 1928," This Day in Aviation, April 21, 2020, https://www.thisdayinaviation.com/15-16-april-1928/.

16. Wilbur Cross, *Disaster at the Pole: The Crash of the Airship* Italia—*a Harrowing True Tale of Arctic Endurance and Survival* (New York: The Lyons Press, 2000), 53.

17. Jane Dunford, "The Wind Makes Karst People Stay in, and Gives Them Character" (interview with Nick Hunt), *Guardian*, January 12, 2018, https://www.theguardian.com/travel/2018/jan/12/karst-plateau-bora-wind-slovenia-italy-nick-hunt.

18. Cross, *Disaster at the Pole*, 53.

19. Cross, 53.

20. Nobile, *With the* Italia, 91.

21. McKee, *Ice Crash*, 112.

22. Nobile, *With the* Italia, 92.

23. Nobile, 92.

24. "Nobile Ship Fights Fury of the Elements," *New York Times*, April 16, 1928, https://timesmachine.nytimes.com/timesmachine/1928/04/16/91499308.pdf.

25. "The Italian Polar Expedition." *New York Times*, April 27, 1928, https://timesmachine.nytimes.com/timesmachine/1928/04/27/91506055.pdf?pdf_redirect=true&ip=0.

26. "The Italian Polar Expedition."

27. "Would Make *Italia* Proof Against Hail," *New York Times*, April 18, 1928, https://timesmachine.nytimes.com/timesmachine/1928/04/18/91500846.pdf.

28. Cross, *Disaster at the Pole*, 56.

29. *Captain Wilkins and Lt. Eielson Stand Near an Aircraft in Spitsbergen, Svalbard after Completing a Trans-Arctic Flight*, Paramount News, Critical Past, accessed September 23, 2019, http://www.criticalpast.com/video/65675070313_George-Hubert-Wilkins_Carl-Benjamin-Eielson_civilian-garb_Lockheed-Vega-aircraft.

30. Amundsen quoted in Richard A. Hindle, "The Impossible Flight," Wilkins Foundation, accessed March 21, 2021, https://wilkinsfoundation.org.au/research/The-Impossible-Flight.pdf.

31. "Nobile Thinks Wilkins May Have Missed Land," *New York Times*, April 25, 1928, https://timesmachine.nytimes.com/timesmachine/1928/04/25/91504170.html?pageNumber=2.

32. "The Italian Polar Expedition."

33. "The Italian Polar Expedition."

34. Cross, *Disaster at the Pole*, 56.

35. Cross, 57.

36. Lise Lindbæk, *Brennende Jord*, trans. Kathryn Pearson (Oslo: Tiden, 1958), 62.

37. Cross, *Disaster at the Pole*, 57.

38. Garth James Cameron, *Umberto Nobile and the Arctic Search for the Airship* Italia (Stroud, UK: Pen & Sword Discover, 2017), 474.

39. McKee, *Ice Crash*, 114.

40. Fred Goldberg, *Drama in the Arctic: S.O.S.* Italia *The Search for Nobile and Amundsen A Diary and Postal History* (Lidingö: privately printed by author, 2003), 5–6.

41. Cross, *Disaster at the Pole*, 59.

42. Goldberg, *Drama in the Arctic*, 6.

43. Cameron, *Umberto Nobile*, 75.

44. McKee, *Ice Crash*, 114.

45. Cross, *Disaster at the Pole*, 61.

46. Nobile, *With the* Italia, 102.

47. McKee, *Ice Crash*, 115.

48. Cameron, *Umberto Nobile*, 77.

49. Goldberg, *Drama in the Arctic*, 7.

50. Cross, *Disaster at the Pole*, 63.

51. Cross, 64.

52. Nobile, *With the* Italia, 103.

Eight: **"God Save Us!"**

1. Wilbur Cross, *Disaster at the Pole: The Crash of the Airship* Italia—*a Harrowing True Tale of Arctic Endurance and Survival* (New York: The Lyons Press, 2000), 64.

2. Cross, *Disaster at the Pole*, 65.

3. Umberto Nobile, *With the* Italia *to the North Pole*, trans. Frank Fleetwood (London: Allen & Unwin, 1930), 104.

4. Nobile, 104.

5. Nobile, 104.

6. Nobile, 105.

7. Cross, *Disaster at the Pole*, 65.

8. Alexander McKee, *Ice Crash: Disaster in the Arctic, 1928* (London: Souvenir Books, 1979), 140.

9. McKee, 129.

10. McKee, 142.

11. McKee, 139.

12. McKee, 129.

13. McKee, 129.

14. McKee, 127.

15. McKee, 127.

16. McKee, 129.

17. Nobile, *With the* Italia, 108.

18. Cross, *Disaster at the Pole*, 66.

19. Nobile, *With the* Italia, 107.

20. McKee, *Ice Crash*, 129.

21. Nobile, *With the* Italia, 109.

22. Nobile, 109.
23. Nobile, 110.
24. McKee, *Ice Crash*, 130.
25. McKee, 132.
26. Nobile, *With the* Italia, 117.
27. Nobile, 116.
28. Nobile, 117.
29. McKee, *Ice Crash*, 135.
30. Nobile, *With the* Italia, 118–9.
31. McKee, *Ice Crash*, 136.
32. McKee, 137.
33. McKee, 138.
34. McKee, 139.
35. McKee, 139.
36. McKee, 140.
37. Cross, *Disaster at the Pole*, 67.
38. Cross, 68.
39. Cross, 69.
40. Cross, 69.
41. McKee, *Ice Crash*, 144.
42. McKee, 145.
43. McKee, 147.
44. McKee, 147.
45. Cross, *Disaster at the Pole*, 69.
46. McKee, *Ice Crash*, 151.
47. McKee, 151.
48. McKee, 151.
49. Nobile, *With the* Italia, 140.
50. Nobile, 140.
51. Nobile, 140.
52. Nobile, 141.
53. McKee, *Ice Crash*, 141.
54. McKee, 156.
55. Nobile, *With the* Italia, 144.
56. Cross, *Disaster at the Pole*, 75.
57. McKee, *Ice Crash*, 159–60.
58. Gregg A. Bendrick and Sergio Alessandrini, "No Second-in-Command: Human Fatigue and the Crash of the Airship *Italia*

Revisited," *Polar Research* 38 (2019): 22, https://doi.org/10.33265/polar.v38.3467.

59. Cross, *Disaster at the Pole*, 74.

60. Nobile, *With the* Italia, 145.

61. Cross, *Disaster at the Pole*, 75.

62. Nobile, *With the* Italia, 146.

63. Nobile, 147.

64. Cross, *Disaster at the Pole*, 76.

65. McKee, *Ice Crash*, 161.

66. Nobile, *With the* Italia, 149.

67. Gregg A. Bendrick, Scott A. Beckett, and Elizabeth B. Klerman, "Human Fatigue and the Crash of the Airship *Italia*," *Polar Research* 35, no. 1 (2016): 1, https://www.tandfonline.com/doi/full/10.3402/polar.v35.27105.

68. Inspired by Nobile, *With the* Italia, 150: "There was nothing to be done but to stop the engines—which I did without an instant's hesitation."

69. Nobile, *With the* Italia, 151.

70. Bendrick, Beckett, and Klerman, "Human Fatigue," 12.

71. Nobile, *With the* Italia, 153.

72. Nobile, 155.

73. Garth James Cameron, *Umberto Nobile and the Arctic Search for the Airship* Italia (Stroud, UK: Pen & Sword Discover, 2017), 166–167.

74. Cross, *Disaster at the Pole*, 83.

75. Nobile, *With the* Italia, 153.

76. McKee, *Ice Crash*, 83.

77. McKee, 166.

78. McKee, 168.

Nine: **"We Will Die When God Has Decided"**

1. Umberto Nobile, *With the* Italia *to the North Pole*, trans. Frank Fleetwood (London: Allen & Unwin, 1930), 155.

2. Nobile, 155.

3. Nobile, 155.

4. Nobile, 156.

5. Wilbur Cross, *Disaster at the Pole: The Crash of the Airship Italia—a Harrowing True Tale of Arctic Endurance and Survival* (New York: The Lyons Press, 2000), 90.

6. Nobile, *With the* Italia, 157.

7. Nobile, 157.

8. Nobile, 159.

9. Cross, *Disaster at the Pole*, 91–92.

10. Alexander McKee, *Ice Crash: Disaster in the Arctic, 1928* (London: Souvenir Press, 1979), 187.

11. Fred Goldberg, *Drama in the Arctic: S.O.S.* Italia *The Search for Nobile and Amundsen A Diary and Postal History* (Lidingö: privately printed by author, 2003), 12–13.

12. Goldberg, 12–13.

13. Cross, *Disaster at the Pole*, 127.

14. Cross, 127.

15. Nobile, *With the* Italia, 165.

16. Cross, *Disaster at the Pole*, 102–3.

17. Nobile, *With the* Italia, 160.

18. Cross, *Disaster at the Pole*, 107.

19. Cross, 107.

20. Nobile, *With the* Italia, 173.

21. Cross, *Disaster at the Pole*, 104.

22. Nobile, *With the* Italia, 161.

23. Cross, *Disaster at the Pole*, 104.

24. Cross, 104.

25. Nobile, *With the* Italia, 167.

26. Nobile, 167.

27. Cross, *Disaster at the Pole*, 105.

28. Nobile, *With the* Italia, 168.

29. McKee, *Ice Crash*, 182.

30. McKee, 188.

31. Giudici, *The Tragedy*, 16.

32. Goldberg, *Drama in the Arctic*, 25.

33. McKee, *Ice Crash*, 189.

34. Cross, *Disaster at the Pole*, 125.

35. "Byrd Allows *Italia* 100 Hours to Cruise," *New York Times*, May 27, 1928, https://timesmachine.nytimes.com/timesmachine/1928/05/27/95580163.pdf.

36. McKee, *Ice Crash*, 183.

37. McKee, 183-184.

38. Derek O'Connor, "Italy's Consummate Showman: Italo Balbo," HistoryNet, accessed March 20, 2021, https://www.historynet.com/italys-consummate-showman-italo-balbo.htm.

39. Claudio G. Segrè, *Italo Balbo: A Fascist Life* (Berkeley and Los Angeles: University of California Press, 1987), 196.

40. Segrè, 198.

41. O'Connor, "Italy's Consumate Showman."

42. Segrè, *Italo Balbo*, 199.

43. Nobile, *With the* Italia, 172.

44. Cross, *Disaster at the Pole*, 125.

45. Cross, 126.

46. Cross, 109.

47. McKee, *Ice Crash*, 192.

48. Italian solider and explorer Umberto Nobile (1885–1978), photo, Getty Images, accessed January 15, 2020, https://www.gettyimages.co.uk /detail/news-photo/italian-solider-and-explorer-umberto-nobile-lies -amid-news-photo/56767222.

49. Nobile, *With the* Italia, 174.

50. Nobile, 175.

51. McKee, *Ice Crash*, 195.

52. McKee, 195

53. Claudio Sicolo, "Airship *Italia*: New Discoveries in Umberto Nobile's Polar Expedition of 1928," Historical Museum of the Military Air Force in Vigna di Valle, Italy, 2018, https://www.academia.edu/36236534 /Airship_Italia_new_discoveries_about_the_radio_on_board.

54. McKee, *Ice Crash*, 196.

55. McKee, 197.

56. McKee, 197.

57. Davide Giudici, *The Tragedy of the* Italia (New York: Appleton and Company, 1929), 15.

58. Fred Goldberg, *Drama in the Arctic: S.O.S.* Italia *The Search for Nobile and Amundsen A Diary and Postal History* (Lidingö: privately printed by author, 2003), 5.

59. McKee, *Ice Crash*, 189.

60. Unpublished research by Ove Hermansen, curator, friend of Nobile and his representative.

61. Karen May and George Lewis, "The Deaths of Roald Amundsen and the Crew of the Latham 47," *Polar Record* 51, no. 1 (January 2015): 1–15, 2, https://www.cambridge.org/core/services/aop-cambridge -core/content/view/4BCCFDBCC7B30A4BC9F666CD27436139 /S0032247413000375a.pdf/deaths_of_roald_amundsen_and_the _crew_of_the_latham_47.pdf.

62. Giudici, *Tragedy of the* Italia, 29–30.

63. May and Lewis, "Deaths of Roald Amundsen," 3.

64. Tor Bomann-Larsen, *Roald Amundsen*, trans. Ingrid Christophersen (Stroud, UK: History Press, 2011), chap. 46, Kindle.

65. Bomann-Larsen, chap. 46.

66. Bomann-Larsen, chap. 46.

67. Bomann-Larsen, chap. 46.

68. Bomann-Larsen, chap. 46.

69. Bomann-Larsen, chap. 46.

70. Nobile, *With the* Italia, 191.

71. Nobile, 191.

72. Nobile, 193.

73. McKee, *Ice Crash*, 198.

74. McKee, 199.

75. Nobile, *With the* Italia, 196.

76. McKee, *Ice Crash*, 200.

77. Nobile, *With the* Italia, 198–99.

78. McKee, *Ice Crash*, 202–4.

79. McKee, 205.

Ten: "Do You as You Like, but I Am Going Looking for Nobile"

1. Alexander McKee, *Ice Crash: Disaster in the Arctic, 1928* (London: Souvenir Press, 1979), 278.

2. Wilbur Cross, *Disaster at the Pole: The Crash of the Airship* Italia—*a Harrowing True Tale of Arctic Endurance and Survival* (New York: The Lyons Press, 2000), 226.

3. Cross, 226.

4. Cross, 228.

5. Cross, 147.

6. Cross, 148.

7. McKee, *Ice Crash*, 207.

8. McKee, 207.

9. McKee, 208.

10. Umberto Nobile, *With the* Italia *to the North Pole*, trans. Frank Fleetwood (London: Allen & Unwin, 1930), 229.

11. McKee, *Ice Crash*, 208.

12. McKee, 209.

13. McKee, 211.

14. Nobile, *With the* Italia, 233.
15. Nobile, 233.
16. McKee, *Ice Crash*, 214.
17. Fred Goldberg, *Drama in the Arctic: S.O.S.* Italia *The Search for Nobile and Amundsen A Diary and Postal History* (Lidingö: privately printed by author, 2003), 20.
18. Goldberg, 17.
19. Davide Giudici, *The Tragedy of the* Italia (New York: Appleton and Company, 1929), 13.
20. McKee, *Ice Crash*, 215.
21. McKee, 215.
22. McKee, 216.
23. McKee, 216
24. McKee, 216.
25. McKee, 217.
26. McKee, 217.
27. McKee, 218.
28. McKee, 217.
29. McKee, 218.
30. Cross, *Disaster at the Pole*, 132.
31. Cross, 132.
32. McKee, *Ice Crash*, 300.
33. Claudio G. Segrè, *Italo Balbo: A Fascist Life* (Berkeley and Los Angeles: University of California Press, 1987), 218.
34. Cross, *Disaster at the Pole*, 131.
35. Cross, 168–169.
36. McKee, *Ice Crash*, 213.
37. Cross, *Disaster at the Pole*, 171.
38. Cross, 171.
39. Cross, 172.
40. Cross, 172.
41. Cross, 172.
42. McKee, *Ice Crash*, 219.
43. Nobile, *With the* Italia, 247.
44. Nobile, 247.
45. Icebreaker *Krassin*, Saint-Petersburg.com, accessed March 20, 2021, http://www.saint-petersburg.com/museums/icebreaker-krasin/.
46. Giudici, *Tragedy of the* Italia, 25.
47. Giudici, 36.

48. Giudici, 38.

49. Giudici, 42.

50. Giudici, 38.

51. Giudici, 40.

52. Giudici, 100.

53. Cross, *Disaster at the Pole*, 230.

54. Cross, 230.

55. Cross, 231.

56. Giudici, *Tragedy of the Italia*, 101.

57. Giudici, 102.

58. Cross, *Disaster at the Pole*, 160.

59. Cross, 159.

60. Cross, 160.

61. Cross, 161.

62. Cross, 161.

63. Cross, 161.

64. Cross, 161.

65. Piero Bosco and Ian R. Stone, "Black Feathers in Svalbard: The Alpini Expeditions, 1928," *Polar Record* 40 (no. 4): 303–8, 304 https://doi.org /10.1017/S0032247404003651.

66. Cross, *Disaster at the Pole*, 162.

67. Cross, 162

68. Cross, 163.

69. Cross, 163.

70. Tor Bomann-Larsen, *Roald Amundsen*, trans. Ingrid Christophersen (Stroud, UK: History Press, 2011), chap. 47

71. Karen May and George Lewis, "The Deaths of Roald Amundsen and the Crew of the Latham 47," *Polar Record* 51, no. 1 (January 2015): 1–15, 5–6, https://www.cambridge.org/core/services/aop-cambridge-core/content /view/4BCCFDBCC7B30A4BC9F666CD27436139/S0032247413000375a .pdf/deaths_of_roald_amundsen_and_the_crew_of_the_latham _47.pdf.

72. Bomann-Larsen, *Roald Amundsen*, chap. 47.

73. Giudici, *Tragedy of the Italia*, 25.

74. McKee, *Ice Crash*, 225.

75. McKee, 221–227.

76. McKee, 225.

77. Bomann-Larsen, *Roald Amundsen*, chap. 47.

78. Bomann-Larsen, chap. 47.

79. Bomann-Larsen, chap. 47.

80. May and Lewis, "The Deaths of Roald Amundsen," 8.

81. Bomann-Larsen, *Roald Amundsen*, chap. 47.

82. Bomann-Larsen, chap. 47.

83. Garth James Cameron, *From Pole to Pole: Roald Amundsen's Journey by Flight* (Stroud, UK: Pen & Sword Discover, 2013), 166.

84. Stephen R. Bown, *The Last Viking: The Life of Roald Amundsen* (Boston: De Capo Press, 2012), 322.

85. May and Lewis, "Deaths of Roald Amundsen," 5.

86. Nobile, *With the* Italia, 248.

87. Cross, *Disaster at the Pole*, 174.

88. Cross, 175.

89. Cross, 175.

90. Cross, 176.

91. Cross, 176.

92. Cross, 177.

Eleven: **"Woman Joins Search for Amundsen"**

1.   *New York Times*, June 20, 1920, https://timesmachine.nytimes.com/times machine/1928/06/20/issue.html.

2.   *Polar Airship "Italia" Lost?* (British Pathé, 1928), YouTube, uploaded August 27, 2014, https://www.youtube.com/watch?v=YnnA7K2utoI.

3.   Wilbur Cross, *Disaster at the Pole: The Crash of the Airship* Italia—*a Harrowing True Tale of Arctic Endurance and Survival* (New York: The Lyons Press, 2000), 180.

4.   Cross, 184.

5.   Alexander McKee, *Ice Crash: Disaster in the Arctic, 1928* (London: Souvenir Books, 1979), 234.

6.   Cross, *Disaster at the Pole*, 182.

7.   Fred Goldberg, *Drama in the Arctic: S.O.S.* Italia (Lidingö: privately printed by author, 2003), 77.

8.   Umberto Nobile, *With the* Italia *to the North Pole*, trans. Frank Fleetwood (London: Allen & Unwin, 1930), 266–267.

9.   Cross, *Disaster at the Pole*, 187.

10. Cross, 188.

11. Cross, 190.

12. *Polar Airship "Italia" Lost?*

13. Cross, *Disaster at the Pole*, 192.

14. Cross, 191.
15. Arctic explorers' personalities, 1928, photo, Getty Images, accessed March 20, 2021, https://www.gettyimages.ca/detail/news-photo/arctic -explorers-personalities-pic-1928-north-pole-news-photo/80748969.
16. "Nobile Insured for $34,210 for Dirigible Polar Trip," *New York Times*, April 8, 1928, https://nyti.ms/2psTZCp.
17. Cross, *Disaster at the Pole*, 192.
18. Cross, 193.
19. Cross, 193.
20. Umberto Nobile, *With the* Italia *to the North Pole*, trans. Frank Fleet-wood (London: Allen & Unwin, 1930), 281.
21. Cross, *Disaster at the Pole*, 194.
22. Nobile, *With the* Italia, 282.
23. Nobile, 282.
24. Nobile, 282–83.
25. Nobile, 195.
26. McKee, *Ice Crash*, 244.
27. Nobile, *With the* Italia, 283.
28. McKee, *Ice Crash*, 244.
29. Arctic explorers' personalities.
30. Nobile, *With the* Italia, 283.
31. Cross, *Disaster at the Pole*, 196.
32. Cross, 197.
33. Cross, 203.
34. Nobile, *With the* Italia, 313.
35. "Woman Joins Arctic Search," *Night Journal*, Lincoln, Nebraska, July 3, 1928, quoted in Joanna Kafarowski, *The Polar Adventures of a Rich American Dame: A Life of Louise Arner Boyd* (Toronto: Dundurn, 2017), 101.
36. Kafarowski, 102.
37. Transcript, Louise Arner Boyd: First Woman to Lead Arctic Expeditions, Unladylike2020: Unsung Women Who Changed America, PBS, https://www.pbs.org/wnet/americanmasters/louise-arner-boyd -first-woman-lead-arctic-expeditions-wetprz/14106/.
38. Nobile, *With the* Italia, 291.
39. Claudio Sicolo, Historiographical Contributions, Italia 90th Anniversary Memorial Conference, Società Geografica Italiana, May 24, 2018, Rome, transcript, 38.
40. Sicolo, 38.

41. Nobile, *With the* Italia, 290.
42. McKee, *Ice Crash*, 250.
43. Nobile, *With the* Italia, 290.
44. Cross, *Disaster at the Pole*, 208.
45. Nobile, *With the* Italia, 290.
46. Cross, *Disaster at the Pole*, 209.
47. McKee, *Ice Crash*, 250.
48. Cross, *Disaster at the Pole*, 211.
49. McKee, *Ice Crash*, 251.
50. Cross, *Disaster at the Pole*, 210.
51. Cross, 210.
52. Nobile, *With the* Italia, 291.
53. Nobile, 296.
54. Nobile, 297.
55. Nobile, 298.
56. McKee, *Ice Crash*, 253.
57. Sicolo, Historiographical Contributions, 40.
58. Sicolo, 41.
59. McKee, *Ice Crash*, 254.
60. Cross, *Disaster at the Pole*, 213.
61. Cross, 216.
62. Cross, 212.
63. Nobile, *With the* Italia, 292.
64. McKee, *Ice Crash*, 252.
65. *Louise Boyd 1928 Expedition*, US National Archive, YouTube, uploaded July 12, 2010, https://www.youtube.com/watch?v=sSgnfd9l3C4.
66. Kafarowski, *Polar Adventures*, 50.
67. Kafarowski, 55.
68. Kafarowski, 64.
69. Kafarowski, 67.
70. "American Girl Shot 11 Bears in Arctic," *New York Times*, September 26, 1926, https://timesmachine.nytimes.com/timesmachine/1926/09/26/issue.html.
71. Kafarowski, *Polar Adventures*, 105.
72. Nobile, *With the* Italia, 312.
73. McKee, *Ice Crash*, 291.
74. Cross, *Disaster at the Pole*, 232.
75. Davide Giudici, *The Tragedy of the* Italia (New York: Appleton and Company, 1929), 103.

76. Giudici, 105.
77. Cross, *Disaster at the Pole*, 236.
78. Cross, 237.
79. Cross, 238.
80. Cross, 239.
81. Cross, 240.
82. Cross, 240.
83. Cross, 243.
84. Cross, 243.
85. Cross, 244.
86. Cross, 244.
87. Cross, 245.
88. Cross, 247.
89. Cross, 248.
90. McKee, *Ice Crash*, 265.
91. Nobile, *With the* Italia, 309.
92. Cross, *Disaster at the Pole*, 221.
93. Cross, 249.
94. Cross, 249.
95. Cross, 250.
96. Cross, 222.
97. Cross, 223.
98. McKee, *Ice Crash*, 265.
99. Cross, *Disaster at the Pole*, 223.
100. McKee, *Ice Crash*, 265.
101. Cross, *Disaster at the Pole*, 224.
102. Cross, 251.

Twelve: **"When I Die You Can Eat Me, but Not Before"**

1. Eugene Lyons, *Assignment in Utopia* (New York: Harcourt, Brace and Company, 1937), 152.
2. Davide Giudici, *The Tragedy of the* Italia (New York: Appleton and Company, 1929), 37.
3. Wilbur Cross, *Disaster at the Pole: The Crash of the Airship Italia—a Harrowing True Tale of Arctic Endurance and Survival* (New York: The Lyons Press, 2000), 255.
4. Giudici, *Tragedy of the* Italia, 38.
5. Giudici, 40.

6. Giudici, 47.

7. Giudici, 60.

8. Alexander McKee, *Ice Crash: Disaster in the Arctic, 1928* (London: Souvenir Press, 1979), 262.

9. Giudici, *Tragedy of the* Italia, 66.

10. Giudici, 69.

11. Cross, *Disaster at the Pole*, 259–60.

12. Guidici, *Tragedy of the* Italia, 72.

13. Guidici, 74.

14. Guidici, 75.

15. Guidici, 77.

16. Guidici, 78.

17. Giudici, 83.

18. Giudici, 84.

19. Giudici, 85.

20. Giudici, 91.

21. Giudici, 92.

22. Giudici, 94.

23. Cross, *Disaster at the Pole*, 269.

24. An extract from Maurice Parijanine, *The Krassin*, quoted in "An Arctic Tragedy," *The Age* (Australia), March 9, 1929, 4, https://www.news papers.com/image/119624470/?terms=Zappi&match=1.

25. Giudici, 95.

26. McKee, *Ice Crash*, 273.

27. McKee, 274.

28. McKee, 275.

29. Bill Schutt, *Eat Me: A Natural and Unnatural History of Cannibalism* (London: Wellcome Collection, Main edition, Jan. 2017), 116–17.

30. "Rumors Cause High Feeling," *The Huntington Herald*, July 28, 1928, 1, https://www.newspapers.com/image/40261302/?terms= Cannibalism&match=1.

31. "Nobile Aides Accused of Cannibalism on Icy Trek," *Oakland Tribune*, July 23, 1928, 1, https://www.newspapers.com/image/95894513/?terms =Cannibalism&match=1.

32. Garth James Cameron, *Umberto Nobile and the Arctic Search for the Airship* Italia (Stroud, UK: Pen & Sword Discover, 2017), 140.

33. McKee, *Ice Crash*, 276.

34. Umberto Nobile, *With the* Italia *to the North Pole*, trans. Frank Fleetwood (London: Allen & Unwin, 1930), 334.

35. McKee, *Ice Crash*, 276.

36. Nobile, *With the* Italia, 334.

37. "Malmgren's Mother Accepts Zeppi Story," *New York Times*, July 30, 1928, https://timesmachine.nytimes.com/timesmachine/1928/07/30 /95590770.pdf.

38. Umberto Nobile and Finn Malmgren's mother, photo, North Pole Expedition Museum, Longyearbyen, Svalbard, Norway.

39. Interview with Ove Hermansen, curator, friend of Nobile and his representative, June 2018.

40. McKee, *Ice Crash*, 272.

41. Cross, *Disaster at the Pole*, 252.

42. Cross, 252.

43. McKee, *Ice Crash*, 281.

44. McKee, 281.

45. McKee, 282.

46. Guidici, *Tragedy of the* Italia, 118.

47. Guidici, 116.

48. McKee, *Ice Crash*, 290.

49. Guidici, *Tragedy of the* Italia, 118.

50. McKee, *Ice Crash*, 284.

51. Guidici, *Tragedy of the* Italia, 180.

52. Guidici, 181.

53. Cross, *Disaster at the Pole*, 277.

54. Audrey Amidon, "Women of the Polar Archives: The Films and Stories of Marie Peary Stafford and Louise Boyd," *Prologue* 42, no. 2 (Summer 2010), https://www.archives.gov/publications/prologue/2010/summer /polar-women.html.

55. Joanna Kafarowski, *The Polar Adventures of a Rich American Dame: A Life of Louise Arner Boyd* (Toronto: Dundurn, 2017), 120.

56. Shane McCorristine, *The Spectral Arctic: A History of Dreams and Ghosts in Polar Exploration* (London: UCL Press, 2018), 50.

57. "Soviet Expert Proposes Reviving of Amundsen," *New York Times*, September 29, 1935, https://timesmachine.nytimes.com/timesmachine /1935/09/29/issue.html.

58. Anita Li, "Norwegian Explorer Roald Amundsen Didn't Father Son in Nunavut, Tests Reveal," *Toronto Star*, January 30, 2012, https://www .thestar.com/news/canada/2012/01/30/norwegian_explorer_roald _amundsen_didnt_father_son_in_nunavut_tests_reveal.html.

59. Christoph Seidler, "The Search for Amundsen: Dive Robot to Aid

in Search for Legendary Polar Explorer," *Spiegel International*, February 2, 2009, 16.39, http://www.spiegel.de/international/zeitgeist /the-search-for-amundsen-dive-robot-to-aid-in-search-for-legendary -polar-explorer-a-609863.html.

60. Lyons, *Assignment in Utopia*, 137.

Thirteen: **"Down with Nobile! Death to Nobile!"**

1. Steinar Aas, "New Perspectives on the *Italia* Tragedy and Umberto Nobile," *Polar Research* 24, nos. 1–2 (2005): 5–15, 7, https://www.tan dfonline.com/doi/pdf/10.3402/polar.v24i1.6249.

2. "The Norwegians Give up Hunt for Amundsen," *New York Times*, July 29, 1928, https://timesmachine.nytimes.com/timesmachine/1928/07 /29/121605355.pdf.

3. Aas, "New Perspectives," 7.

4. Aas, 7.

5. Umberto Nobile, *With the* Italia *to the North Pole*, trans. Frank Fleetwood (London: Allen & Unwin, 1930), 338.

6. Umberto Nobile, Epilogue to the story of the "Italia" expedition, manuscript, archives of the Norwegian Polar Institute, Tromsø, i.

7. Nobile, ii.

8. "The Norwegians Give Up."

9. Nobile, *With the* Italia, 341.

10. "The Norwegians Give Up ."

11. Nobile, Epilogue, 1.

12. Nobile, *With the* Italia, 341.

13. Nobile, 342.

14. "The Norwegians Give Up."

15. Nobile, Epilogue, 1.

16. Nobile, 3.

17. Nobile, 4.

18. Nobile, 5.

19. Nobile, 5.

20. Nobile, 6.

21. Nobile, 7.

22. Nobile, 8.

23. Nobile, 8.

24. Nobile, 9.

25. Nobile, 10.

26. Nobile, 11.
27. Nobile, 12.
28. Nobile, 13.
29. Nobile, 14.
30. Nobile, 15.
31. Nobile, 16.
32. Nobile, 17.
33. Nobile, 18.
34. Nobile, 18.
35. Nobile, 18.
36. Nobile, 19.
37. Nobile, 19.
38. Nobile, 20.

Fourteen: **"This Is Real Exploring despite the Luxury"**

1. Hugo Eckener, *My Zeppelins* (London: Putnam & Co. Ltd., 1958), 124.
2. Eckener, 76.
3. Eckener, 129.
4. Alexander McKee, *Ice Crash: Disaster in the Arctic, 1928* (London: Souvenir Press, 1979), 307.
5. Umberto Nobile, Chapter VI: Five Years in Russia, manuscript in the archives of the Norwegian Polar Institute, Tromsø, 266.

Epilogue: **The Kremlin, Moscow, 1933**

1. "Nobile under Knife in Russia," *New York Times*, March 2, 1933.
2. Umberto Nobile, Chapter VI: Five Years in Russia, manuscript in the archives of the Norwegian Polar Institute, Tromsø, 286.
3. "Nobile in Serious Condition," *New York Times*, March 3, 1933, https://timesmachine.nytimes.com/timesmachine/1933/03/03/99213635.html?pageNumber=16.
4. Nobile, Five Years, 287.
5. "Gen. Nobile Dead, Says Rome Report," *New York Times*, April 23, 1933, https://timesmachine.nytimes.com/timesmachine/1933/04/22/105388181.html?pageNumber=13.
6. Nobile, Five Years, 268.
7. Nobile, 272.
8. Nobile, 269.

9. Nobile, 309.

10. Nobile, 319.

11. Alexander McKee, *Ice Crash: Disaster in the Arctic, 1928* (London: Souvenir Press, 1979), 309.

12. "Umberto Nobile Joins Faculty of Lewis Holy Name School of Aeronautics," advert, *Aviation*, July 1939, 119, https://archive.aviationweek.com/search?QueryTerm=Umberto+Nobile&DocType=All&sort=.

13. Gregg A. Bendrick, Scott A. Beckett, and Elizabeth B. Klerman, "Human Fatigue and the Crash of the Airship *Italia*," *Polar Research 35*, no. 1 (2016): 27–105, 8, https://www.tandfonline.com/doi/full/10.3402/polar.v35.27105.

14. McKee, *Ice Crash*, 312.

15. "Gaetano Crocco—Italian Aerospace Pioneer," SciHi Blog, October 26, 2015, http://scihi.org/gaetano-crocco-italian-aerospace-pioneer/.

16. Ben Evans and David M. Harland, *NASA's Voyager Missions: Exploring the Outer Solar System and Beyond* (London: Springer, 2004), 283.

17. Evans and Harland, 42.

18. Steinar Aas, "New Perspectives on the *Italia* Tragedy and Umberto Nobile," *Polar Research* 24, nos. 1–2 (2005): 8–9, https://doi.org/10.3402/polar.v24i1.6249.

Index